About Panel Publishers, Inc.

Panel Publishers derives its name from a panel of business professionals who organized in 1964 to publish authoritative, timely books, information services, and journals written by specialists to assist accountants, tax practitioners, attorneys, and other business professionals; human resources, compensation and benefits, and pension and profit-sharing professionals; and owners of small to medium-sized businesses. Our mission is to provide practical, solution-based "how-to" information to business professionals.

Also available in the Panel Answer Book series:

Health Insurance Answer Book
The Pension Answer Book
Nonqualified Deferred Compensation Answer Book
Employee Assistance Law Answer Book
Employee Benefits Answer Book

All Panel publications are supplemented periodically to ensure that the information presented is accurate and up-to-date. If you would like to receive updates for this volume, please contact our Customer Service Department at 1-800-457-9222.

PANEL PUBLISHERS, INC.
Practical Solutions for Business Professionals

Personnel Law Answer Book

Special Supplement

Forms & Checklists

James O. Castagnera, Esq.
Kristine Grady Derewicz, Esq.

THE PANEL ANSWER BOOK SERIES

by
PANEL PUBLISHERS, INC.
A Wolters Kluwer Company
36 West 44th Street
New York, NY 10036
(212) 790-2090

ISBN 1-878375-66-0

Printed in the United States of America

Introduction

Over the years, a significant number of subscribers to *The Personnel Law Answer Book* have asked for a product that provided them with the practical tools that are necessary to implement the solutions that are found in *The Personnel Law Answer Book*, Panel's bestselling personnel law guide in question-and-answer format. Requests have ranged from examples of the various types of employment agreements that are available to formalize the employer-employee relationship and sample language that can be used as the basis for a newly developed or revised employee handbook to comprehensive, technical checklists to ensure that employers comply with the latest Department of Labor (DOL) and Equal Employment Opportunity Commission (EEOC) guidelines when recruiting, evaluating, promoting, disciplining, and/or terminating employees and summaries to outline the advantages and disadvantages of the various types of executive compensation programs that are available to employers today.

This *Special Supplement, Forms & Checklists* is specifically designed to meet these requests. The principal value of this newly developed, stand-alone forms book is that it provides you with over 300 pages of checklists, worksheets, sample forms, sample plan language and/or sample documents that allow you to easily understand and implement successful strategies for even the most complex aspects of your personnel needs. An added value for subscribers of *The Personnel Law Answer Book* is that this *Special Supplement, Forms & Checklists* organizes its material in the same manner as the chapters of topical reference information found in that question-and-answer book so that you can easily move from locating a specific answer to the corresponding material necessary to successfully implement your solution.

How To Use This Book: This *Special Supplement, Forms & Checklists* directly complements *The Personnel Law Answer Book* and contains numerous aids to help you move easily within the supplement as well as from the supplement to the main volume. These aids include an alphabetical, key-word index at the back of the book that quickly illustrates where specific information in both the supplement and the main volume is located. In addition, the text of the supplement contains numerous cross references to specific questions and answers found in the main volume and cumulative supplement. To distinguish whether the question referred to appears in the main volume or the cumulative supplement, all entries that refer to the cumulative supplement are followed by a bold-faced "S." For example, where are cross reference states "see Q. Q. 28–Q. 32 and Q. 18.2S–Q. 23.9S," questions 28 through 32 appear in the main volume while questions 18.2 through 23.9 appear in the cumulative supplement. Therefore, whenever you would like more information on how to implement an answer found in *The Personnel Law Answer Book*, simply refer either to the specific cross reference or to the Index at the back of the book. Finally, one other aspect of this *Special Supplement* is designed to increase its ease of use. The larger 8½″ x 11″ size and "superbind" binding will allow you to photocopy the forms easily and for an extended period of time so that you can customize each form and directly insert it into your working files.

About the Author

JAMES O. CASTAGNERA is a labor lawyer with Saul, Ewing, Remick & Saul, a Philadelphia firm of nearly 200 lawyers with offices in Washington, D.C., Wilmington, Delaware and elsewhere. He has authored several books, including the *Personnel Law Answer Book* and *How to Prepare an Employee Handbook* for Panel Publishers. Mr. Castagnera holds his J.D. and Ph.D. from Case Western Reserve University and has taught law at the University of Texas in Austin.

KRISTINE GRADY DEREWICZ is an associate in the Labor and Employee Benefits Department at Saul, Ewing, Remick & Saul in Philadelphia. Her practice focuses on employee-related issues in both union and non-union settings. Ms. Derewicz received her J.D. from the University of Pennsylvania Law School in 1990. She is admitted to the state bars of Pennsylvania and New Jersey.

Summary Table Of Contents

Table Of Contents

Chapter 2

Hiring and Evaluating Employees

Chapter 7

Employee Fringe Benefits

Chapter 1

The Employer-Employee Relationship

The employer-employee relationship is one of mutual responsibility and although the parameters of each party's duties can be specified orally, more and more employers are insisting on formal employment documents that concretely outline the responsibilities and rights of both the employer and the employee during the employment term. Another advantage of written employment documents is that they can also define the responsibilities and rights, if any, that remain between the employer and employee after the employment relationship has been terminated. This chapter focuses on four situations in which formal employment documents are most often used.

1:1 Employment Contracts

As is more fully discussed in Chapter 1 (see Q. 1–31 and Q. 1**S**–Q. 33.1**S**) of the *Personnel Law Answer Book,* employment relationships can take many forms. At its simplest, employment-at-will requires no written employment contract. (But see Q. 32.1**S**.) In fact, the vast majority of working people, many of whom have been employed by the same organization for many, many years, report to work every working day of their lives without the benefit or the bother of a written employment contract. However, the more responsible the position and the higher the compensation the more likely it is that the employment relationship will be embodied in the four corners of an employment contract.

Employment contracts can take many forms, ranging from a simple letter agreement acknowledged at the bottom by the employee, to long, complex and formal contracts, such as those that might be signed by CEO's and highly educated professionals. (See Q. 18–Q. 23, Q. 28–Q. 32, and Q. 18.2**S**–Q. 23.9**S**.) This section presents five examples of employment contracts ranging from a sample letter agreement, through sample contracts for several mid-level positions, and ending with an example of what a chief executive officer's contract might look like. How might you make use of these sample contracts? Certainly none of these examples—nor any other forms in this book—should be duplicated for wholesale use. Rather, in preparing to draft an employment contract or in reviewing an existing employment contract, these examples should be used to:

1. Identify the provisions that can and should be incorporated into a contract covering the situation at hand;
2. Compare actual contract provisions against the sample provisions presented here; and

3. Establish the structure, form and flow of a package of actual employment contracts that reflects and conforms with a particular employer's company philosophy.

1:1.1 Sample Letter Agreement

AGREEMENT, made this _________ day of _________, 19____, by and between [EMPLOYER] (hereinafter "Employer"), a [STATE OF INCORPORATION] corporation with its principal place of business at [ADDRESS] and [NAME OF EMPLOYEE] (hereinafter "Employee"), an individual residing at [ADDRESS].

In consideration of the mutual covenants and agreements herein contained, and intending to be legally bound, the parties hereto agree as follows:

1. *Employment.* The Employer hereby employs the Employee as [POSITION TITLE]. During her term of employment, the Employee shall perform such duties as reasonably shall be required of her by the Employer, reasonable duties being defined for this purpose as duties substantially similar to those she has performed for the Employer as its [POSITION DESCRIPTION] in the past.
2. *Performance.* The Employee agrees to devote her full time, energy and attention to the performance of her duties hereunder.
3. *Term.* The effective date of this Agreement shall be [ ] year(s).

Notwithstanding the foregoing, this Agreement may be terminated by the Employer upon the occurrence of any of the following:

(a) the death of the Employee;

(b) the physical or mental disability or incapacity of the Employee rendering her incapable of performing her duties under this Agreement for a period of time exceeding 180 consecutive days; or,

(c) the commission by the Employee of any felony, or any misdemeanor carrying a possible term of incarceration, or any deliberate and premeditated act against the interests of the Employer.

Additionally, this Agreement can be terminated without cause by the Employer at any time, provided the Employer continues the Employee's salary and benefits, as provided hereafter, for the remainder of this Agreement's term.

4. *Compensation.* As compensation for all of the services rendered by the Employee during the first year of this Agreement, the Employer shall pay the Employee $_________ per year, payable in equal monthly installments on or about the last day of each month.

   At the meeting of the Board of Directors of the Employer most proximate to the start of each succeeding year of this Agreement, the Board shall decide the salary of the Employee for that succeeding year, which salary shall at least be the same as that specified above for the first year of this Agreement.

In addition to the foregoing salary, the Employee shall receive the following benefits:

(a) *Vacation.*

(b) *Insurance.*

(c) *Other.*

5. *Entire Agreement.* This Agreement constitutes the entire understanding of the parties concerning the subject matter hereof, and supersedes all prior agreements, both oral and written. No modification of this Agreement shall be binding upon either party unless reduced to a writing signed by both parties. This Agreement may not be assigned by either party except with prior written consent of the other party, provided however that the sale of all or a part of the stock of the Employer shall not affect the validity and enforceability of this Agreement in any way.
6. *Choice of Law.* This Agreement shall be construed and enforced, both as to interpretation and performance, according to the laws of the State of ________________.
7. *Void Provisions.* If any provision of this Agreement conflicts with any statute or rule of law or rule or regulation of any person or entity having jurisdiction over any portion of the subject matter herein then such provision shall be deemed null and void to the extent that it may conflict therewith but the remaining provisions hereof shall remain in full force and effect.
8. *Captions.* The captions in this Agreement are inserted only as a matter of convenience and for references and in no way define, limit or describe the scope of this Agreement nor the intent of any provision thereof.

IN WITNESS WHEREOF, the parties hereto, intending to be legally bound, have executed this Agreement on the day and year first above written.

[EMPLOYER]

______________________________ BY: ______________________________
[EMPLOYEE]

______________________________ ______________________________
Witness Witness

1:1.2 Middle Level Manager Employment Contract

AGREEMENT, made this ________ day of ________, ________, by and between [NAME OF EMPLOYER] (hereinafter "Employer"), a [STATE OF INCORPORATION] corporation with its principal place of business at [ADDRESS] and [NAME OF EMPLOYEE] (hereinafter "Employee"), an individual residing at [ADDRESS].

In consideration of the mutual covenants and agreements herein contained, and intending to be legally bound, the parties hereto agree as follows:

1. *Employment.* The Employer hereby employs the Employee as [POSITION TITLE] (which shall include without limitation, management of [describe range of responsibilities]). During his term of employment, the Employee shall perform such duties as reasonably shall be required of him by the Employer, reasonable duties being defined for this purpose as duties substantially similar to those he has performed for the Employer as a Manager in the past.
2. *Performance.* The Employee agrees to devote his full time, energy and attention to the performance of his duties hereunder.
3. *Term.* The effective date of this Agreement shall be [ ] year(s).

Notwithstanding the foregoing, this Agreement may be terminated by the Employer upon the occurrence of any of the following:

(a) the death of the Employee;

(b) the physical or mental disability or incapacity of the Employee rendering him incapable of performing his duties under this Agreement for a period of time exceeding 180 consecutive days; or,

(c) the commission by the Employee of any felony, or any misdemeanor carrying a possible term of incarceration, or any deliberate and premeditated act against the interests of the Employer.

Additionally, this Agreement can be terminated without cause by the Employer at any time, provided the Employer continues the Employee's salary and benefits, as provided hereafter, for the remainder of this Agreement's term.

Exercise of the Employer's right to terminate this Agreement according to the aforesaid provisions of this Section 3 shall not affect the Employer's rights or the Employee's obligations under Section 5, 6, and 7 hereafter.

4. *Compensation.* As compensation for all of the services rendered by the Employee during the first year of this Agreement, the Employer shall pay the Employee $________, payable in equal monthly installments on or about the last day of each month.

   At the meeting of the Board of Directors of the Employer most proximate to the start of each succeeding year of this Agreement, the Board shall decide the salary of the Employee for that succeeding year, which salary shall at least be the same as that specified above for the first year of this Agreement.

In addition to the foregoing salary, the Employee shall receive the following benefits:

(a) *Vacation.*

(b) *Insurance.*

(c) *Other.*

5. *Confidential Information.* The Employee acknowledges that the services which he will perform for the Employer and the knowledge which he will obtain of the Employer's business practices and plans, financial data, know-how, etc. through his close relationship with the Employer, are of a confidential and valuable nature. The Employer agrees that he will not divulge to others or use for his own benefit, or the benefit of anyone other than the Employer, at any time during or subsequent to this employment, any information obtained in the course of his employment, concerning such business practices and plans, financial data, know-how, etc. without first obtaining the Employer's written permission, unless such information has become public knowledge by a means other than a breach of the provisions of this section. The Employee agrees that the remedy of the Employer for his breach of his section shall be as set forth in section 7 below.

6. *Agreement Not to Compete.* The Employee agrees that during the term of his employment by the Employer and for a period of two years thereafter, he will not directly or indirectly own, manage, operate, control, participate in, work for, have a financial interest in, or be connected in any manner with any company, corporation, partnership, syndication or other enterprise engaged in the same or approximately similar business as the Employer within 50 miles of the Employer's principal place of business.

   The Employee expressly acknowledges that he has received special compensation and consideration from the Employer for his execution of this provision of the Agreement, and that the existence of any claim or cause of action of the Employee against the Employer shall not constitute a defense to the enforcement of the covenant by the Employer.

   The Employee agrees that the remedy of the Employer for his breach of this section shall be as set forth in section 7 below.

7. *Injunctive Relief.* The Employee agrees that, because any breach of the terms of this Agreement, especially section 5 and 6 above, will result in irreparable harm to the Employer, the Employer will be fully entitled to obtain injunctive relief to the maximum extent provided by the law in the event of a breach or threatened breach of this Agreement, and this remedy shall be available without showing or proving actual damage sustained by the Employer.

   However, nothing stated herein shall be construed as prohibiting the Employer from pursuing any other remedies available to the Employer for such breach or threatened breach, including recovery of damages from the Employee.

8. *Entire Agreement.* This Agreement constitutes the entire understanding of the parties concerning the subject matter hereof, and supersedes all prior agreements, both oral and written. No modification of this Agreement shall be binding upon either party unless reduced to a writing signed by both parties. This Agreement may not be assigned by either party except with prior written consent of the other party, provided however that the sale of all or a

part of the stock of the Employer shall not affect the validity and enforceability of this Agreement in any way.

9. *Choice of Law.* This Agreement shall be construed and enforced, both as to interpretation and performance, according to the laws of the State of ________________.

10. *Void Provisions.* If any provision of this Agreement conflicts with any statute or rule of law or rule or regulation of any person or entity having jurisdiction over any portion of the subject matter herein then such provision shall be deemed null and void to the extent that it may conflict therewith but the remaining provisions hereof shall remain in full force and effect.

11. *Captions.* The captions in this Agreement are inserted only as a matter of convenience and for references and in no way define, limit or describe the scope of this Agreement nor the intent of any provision thereof.

IN WITNESS WHEREOF, the parties hereto, intending to be legally bound, have executed this Agreement on the day and year first above written.

[EMPLOYER]

________________________ BY: ________________________

[EMPLOYEE]

________________________ ________________________

Witness Witness

1:1.3 Commissioned Employee Employment Contract

AGREEMENT made as of this ________ day of ________, 19___ between ________________ a ________________ corporation with offices at ________________ (the "Company"), and ________________, an individual residing at ________________ (the "Employee").

1. *Employment.* The Company hereby employs the Employee as [TITLE] of the Company and the Employee accepts such employment. During the term of employment the Employee shall perform subject to the direction of the [BOARD OF DIRECTORS] or [PRESIDENT] of the Company such duties as shall reasonably be required of a [TITLE] of the Company.
2. *Performance.* The Employee agrees to devote his entire business efforts to the performance of his duties hereunder.
3. *Term.*
   3.1. The initial term of the employment of the Employee shall be for a period of ________ years commencing on the date of this Agreement and thereafter shall continue for successive terms of ________ years[s] unless otherwise terminated in accordance with this Agreement.

   3.2. The employment may be terminated by either party hereto at the end of the initial term of ________ year(s) if the party desiring to terminate shall give written notice of its desire to terminate at least [period of days or months] prior to the termination of that ________ year period.

   3.3. The employment may be terminated at any time after the initial term of ________ years by the Company giving the Employee notice of the Company's desire to terminate at least [period of days or months] prior to the end of the then current ________ year term.

   3.4. The employment may be terminated at any time after the initial term of ________ years by the Employee giving the Company notice of the Employee's desire to terminate at least [period of days or months] prior to the end of the then current ________ year term. [3.3. *and* 3.4. *may be consolidated if termination notice is the same.*]

   3.5. The employment created hereunder may also be terminated by the Company upon the occurrence of any of the following:

   (a) the death of the Employee; or

   (b) the commission by the Employee of any deliberate and premeditated act against the interests of the Company; or

   (c) the conviction by the Employee of a felony; or

   (d) the breach by the Employee of any terms of this Agreement not cured within ________ days subsequent to notice from the Company to the Employee of the breach.

   3.6. The employment created hereunder may also be terminated by the Employee if the Company breaches any of the terms of this Agreement not cured within ________ days subsequent to notice from the Employee to the Company of the breach.
4. *Compensation.* The basic annual compensation of the Employee for his employment services hereunder shall be $________. The Company and the Employee agree that the Employee's basic annual compensation will be adjusted on [FIRST ANNIVERSARY OF AGREEMENT OR SUCH OTHER

DATE AS DESIRED] and at regular twelve-month [MORE OR LESS AS DESIRED] intervals thereafter if the United States Department of Labor Bureau of Labor Statistics (B.L.S.) Consumer Price Index for Urban Wage Earners and Clerical Workers — Revised all-city average for [CITY, STATE OF PLACE OF BUSINESS], (the "Index") indicates that the cost of living has increased or decreased during the period preceding each computation date. On [SAME DATES AS ABOVE], the Company shall compute the percentage of change which has occurred in the Index since the date of this Agreement by comparing the latest available Index with the Index as of the date of this Agreement. On all computations subsequent to [same date as above], the percentage of change shall be computed by comparing the latest available Index on the computation date with the Index used for the immediately preceding computation. The Employee's basic annual compensation shall then be increased or decreased, as the case may be, by an amount equal to the percentage of change multiplied by the Employee's then existing salary. The Employee's basic annual compensation shall be payable to him in equal [DESCRIBE PERIOD OF PAYMENTS].

In addition to the Employee's basic annual compensation, the Employee shall receive an annual bonus equal to:

____

____

____.

The bonus shall be payable within [PERIOD OF MONTHS] following the publication of the Company's annual financial statements for the relevant fiscal year.

[CHOOSE ONE OF THE FOLLOWING TWO PARAGRAPHS]

Upon the death of the Employee the Company shall pay to his estate the Employee's salary earned to the date of death plus [ ] weeks of additional salary and nothing else. For purposes of this paragraph the Employee's salary shall be determined only in relation to the Employee's basic annual compensation.

OR

If the Employee shall die while employed by the Company, the Company shall continue to pay on a weekly basis to his widow or his estate as he shall designate in writing or his estate if he shall not have so designated _________% of the Employee's basic annual, adjusted as provided herein, for a period of _________ years from the date of death of the Employee. [*Note: to be an effective salary continuation plan, the Employee should have no right in the funding apparatus*].

In addition to the other compensation payable pursuant to this Section 4, the Employee shall participate in such fringe benefits to which executives of the Company shall be entitled in accordance with employment policies of the Company. Notwithstanding any policy that may be adopted, the Company shall purchase and maintain an insurance policy on the life of the Employee in the face amount of not less than $_________ and the Employee shall have the right to designate the beneficiary of that policy and the Company shall provide and maintain an automobile for use by the Employee in connection with the performance of his duties hereunder.

5. *Agreement Not to Compete.* Employee agrees that during the term of his employment and for a period of [TWO] years thereafter he will not in any capacity engage or have financial interest in any business competing with the

Company or any affiliate of the Company in the jurisdictions of [must be reasonable] except that he may own less than 1% of the outstanding stock of such competing business. The Employee expressly agrees that upon breach of this provision the Company in addition to all other remedies shall be entitled as a matter of right to injunctive relief in any court of competent jurisdiction. [*Note: This is probably only enforceable in connection with a "new" employment. If not "new" employment, you may consider making the employee a consultant during the period of non-competition as some nominal compensation.*]

6. *Secret Processes and Confidential Information.* The Employee will not divulge so long as this Agreement is in effect and thereafter other than in the regular and proper course of business of the Company any knowledge or information with respect to the operation or finances of the Company or any of its affiliates or with respect to confidential or secret processes, techniques, machinery, plans, devices or products licensed to or by, manufactured or sold by the Company or any other company affiliated with the Company, provided, however, that the Employee has no obligation, express or implied, to refrain from using or disclosing to others any such knowledge or information which is or hereafter shall become available to the public without breaching this Agreement. All new processes, techniques, know-how, inventions, plans, products, patents and devices developed, made or invented by the Employee, alone or with others, while an employee of the Company shall become and be the sole property of the Company unless released in writing by the Company.
7. *Removal of the Employee.* The Company shall have the right to remove the Employee from the position in which he is employed hereunder. Under such circumstances the Employee's compensation described in Section 4 hereunder will continue for the term of his employment unless the employment is terminated in accordance herewith.
8. *General.* The terms of this Agreement shall be governed by the laws of the State of ________________.

The Employee may not assign his interest in this Agreement.

This Agreement shall be binding upon and inure to the benefit of the Company, its successors and assigns.

IN WITNESS WHEREOF, the parties hereto, intending to be legally bound, have hereunto duly executed this Agreement the day and year first written above.

(Corporate Seal)

[EMPLOYER]

______________________________ BY: ______________________________

[EMPLOYEE] President

______________________________ ATTEST: ______________________________

Witness Secretary

1:1.4 Executive Officer's Employment Agreement

AGREEMENT made this ________ day of ________, ________, and effective as of this date, by and between [NAME OF EMPLOYER] (hereinafter "Employer"), a [STATE OF INCORPORATION] corporation with its principal place of business at [ADDRESS] and [NAME OF EMPLOYEE] (hereinafter "Employee"), an individual residing at [ADDRESS].

In consideration of the mutual covenants and agreements herein contained, and intending to be legally bound, the parties hereto agree as follows:

1. *Employment.* The Employer hereby employs the Employee as Vice President-[AREA OF RESPONSIBILITY] for all current and future projects of the Employer throughout the initial term and all extensions, if any, of this Agreement. During his term of employment, the Employee shall perform such duties as shall reasonably be required of him by the Employer.
2. *Performance.* The Employee agrees to devote his full time, energy and attention to the performance of his duties hereunder.
3. *Term.* The effective date of this Agreement shall be the day it is executed, and it shall continue for one year thereafter. This Agreement shall automatically be renewed thereafter for successive one-year terms unless terminated as provided herein.

Notwithstanding the foregoing, this Agreement may be terminated at any time, during the first or any successive year, by either party upon ninety (90) days prior written notice to the other party. In the event of notice of termination by the Employer to the Employee, the Employer at its sole discretion may terminate the employment relationship prior to the running of the 90-day notice period by tendering to the Employee adequate compensation in lieu of all or part of the required 90-day notice. For purposes of this provision only, adequate compensation is defined as the dollar equivalent of the salary and benefits the Employee would have earned were he permitted by the Employer to continue performing for the entire 90-day notice period.

Additionally, this Agreement shall automatically terminate if the Employee dies. Furthermore, this Agreement may be terminated by either party upon ten (10) days' written notice to the other party, or that other party's successor in interest, upon the occurrence of any of the following:

(a) the Employee is unable to perform his duties hereunder by reason of illness, or physical or mental disability, for a period in excess of one hundred eighty (180) consecutive days;

(b) a breach of any term or terms of this Agreement by the other party is not cured by the breaching party within ten (10) days of written notice of the breach from the injured party;

(c) voluntary or involuntary proceedings are instituted in bankruptcy or insolvency against the other party, or there is appointed, with or without the other party's consent, an assignee or receiver for the benefit of creditors; or

(d) the other party is arrested or indicted for any felony or for any misdemeanor carrying a possible term of incarceration.

4. *Compensation.* As compensation for all of the services rendered by the Employee pursuant to this Agreement, the Employer shall pay the Employee $________ during the initial one-year term of this Agreement. During successive one-year terms of this Agreement, if any, the Employer shall pay the employee such salary as may be fixed for each such successive one-year term by the Employer's Board of Directors. Failing such action by the Board of Directors prior to the renewal of this Agreement for a successive one-year term, the Employee's salary for that successive term shall be the same as his salary at the end of the immediately preceding term until such time during the successive term that the Board may act to increase it.

In addition to the foregoing salary, the Employee shall receive the following benefits:

(a) Medical insurance, which will be approximately equivalent to such insurance provided by the Employer to its other officers, fully paid by the Employer;

(b) Use of a company car, which will be approximately equivalent to such cars provided by the Employer to its other officers, and use of which will be the exclusive and unrestricted privilege of the Employee while this Agreement remains in effect, with the purchase price and finance charges, if any, to be paid by the Employer;

(c) Reasonable business expenses as approved in advance by the Employer's President;

(d) Annual paid vacation approximately equivalent to vacations provided by the Employer to its other officers.

5. *Confidential Information.* The Employee acknowledges that the services which he will perform for the Employer and the knowledge which he will obtain of the Employer's business practices and plans, financial data, know-how, etc. through his close relationship with the Employer, are of a confidential and valuable nature. The Employee agrees that he will not divulge to others or use for his own benefit, or the benefit of anyone other than the Employer, at any time during or subsequent to this employment, any information obtained in the course of his employment, concerning such business practices and plans, financial data, know-how, etc, without first obtaining the Employer's written permission, unless such information has become public knowledge by a means other than a breach of the provisions of this section. The Employee agrees that the remedy of the Employer for his breach of this section shall be as set forth in section 7 below.

6. *Agreement Not to Compete.* The Employee agrees that during the term of his employment by the Employer and for a period of two years thereafter, he will not directly or indirectly own, manage, operate, control, participate in, work for, have a financial interest in, or be connected in any manner with any company, corporation, partnership, syndication or other enterprise engaged in the same or approximately similar business as the Employer within 50 miles of any project of the Employer which project has not been entirely completed and marketed by the Employer.

The Employee expressly acknowledges that he has received special compensation and consideration from the Employer for his execution of this provision of the Agreement, and that the existence of any claim or cause of action of the Employee against the Employer shall not constitute a defense to the enforcement of the covenant by the Employer.

The Employee agrees that the remedy of the Employer for his breach of this section shall be as set forth in section 7 below.

7. *Injunctive Relief.* The Employee agrees that, because any breach of the terms of this Agreement, especially sections 5 and 6 above, will result in irreparable harm to the Employer, the Employer will be fully entitled to obtain injunctive relief to the maximum extent provided by the law in the event of a breach or threatened breach of this Agreement, and this remedy shall be available without showing or proving actual damage sustained by the Employer.

However, nothing stated herein shall be construed as prohibiting the Employer from pursuing any other remedies available to the Employer for such breach or threatened breach, including recovery of damages from the Employee.

8. *Arbitration.* Any claim or controversy arising out of or relating to this Agreement may be settled, if the Employer so chooses, by arbitration before an arbitrator in [CITY], [STATE] chosen in accordance with the rules of the American Arbitration Association, and judgment upon the award rendered by said arbitrator may be entered and enforced by either party in any court having jurisdiction thereof.
9. *Notices.* Written notices given according to the provisions of this Agreement shall be sent by registered or certified mail, return receipt requested, to the addresses set forth below:
   (a) If to the Employer:
      [NAME]
      [ADDRESS]
   (b) If to the Employee:
      [NAME]
      [ADDRESS]
10. *Entire Agreement.* This Agreement constitutes the entire understanding of the parties concerning the subject matter hereof, and supersedes all prior agreements, both oral and written. No modification of this Agreement shall be binding upon either party unless reduced to a writing signed by both parties. This Agreement may not be assigned by either party except with prior written consent of the other party, provided however that the sale of all or part of the stock of the Employer shall not affect the validity and enforceability of this Agreement in any way.
11. *Choice of Law.* This Agreement shall be construed and enforced, both as to interpretation and performance, according to the laws of the State of ________________.

12. *Void Provisions.* If any provision of this Agreement conflicts with any statute or rule of law or rule or regulation of any person or entity having jurisdiction over any portion of the subject matter herein then such provision shall be deemed null and void to the extent that it may conflict therewith but the remaining provisions hereof shall remain in full force and effect.
13. *Captions.* The captions in this Agreement are inserted only as a matter of convenience and for references and in no way define, limit or describe the scope of this Agreement nor the intent of any provision thereof.

IN WITNESS WHEREOF, the parties hereto, intending to be legally bound, have executed this Agreement on the day and year first above written.

[EMPLOYER]

______________________________	BY: ______________________________
[EMPLOYEE]	[OFFICER OF EMPLOYER]
______________________________	ATTEST: ______________________________
Witness	

1:1.5 Chief Executive Employment Contract

EMPLOYMENT AGREEMENT dated as of ________, 19___, between [NAME OF EMPLOYER], a [STATE OF INCORPORATION] corporation (the "Company"), and [NAME OF EMPLOYEE] (the "Executive").

The Executive possesses considerable knowledge and expertise relating to the management of technology-oriented businesses. The Company desires to avail itself of such knowledge and expertise by employing the Executive, and the Executive desires to accept such employment, on the terms and conditions hereinafter set forth.

NOW, THEREFORE, in consideration of the premises and the mutual covenants and obligations hereinafter set forth, the parties agree as follows:

1. *Employment.* The Company hereby employs the Executive, and the Executive hereby accepts employment by the Company, on the terms and conditions hereinafter set forth.
2. *Term.* The employment of the Executive hereunder shall be for the period (the "Employment Period") commencing on ________, 19___ (the "Commencement Date"), and ending on (i) the fourth anniversary of the Commencement Date (such fourth anniversary being referred to herein as the "Scheduled Termination Date") or (ii) such earlier date (the "Termination Date") on which the employment of the Executive shall terminate in accordance with the provisions hereof.
3. *Duties.* The Company shall initially employ the Executive as its Chairman of the Board and Chief Executive Officer reporting to its Board of Directors (the "Board"). During the Employment Period, the Executive shall perform well and faithfully such duties for, and render such services to, the Company and its affiliates and subsidiaries in the conduct of their businesses as are from time to time assigned to him by the Board and are consistent with such positions.
4. *Time to be Devoted to Employment.* Except for reasonable vacations and, subject to Section 8(a), absences due to temporary illness or incapacity, during the Employment Period the Executive shall devote substantially all of his working time, attention and energies to the business of the Company and its affiliates and subsidiaries; *provided, however,* that the Executive may engage in any of the following activities (the "Stipulated Activities"): (i) with the approval of the Board, serving as a director or member of any committee of any organization and (ii) delivering lectures, fulfilling speaking engagements and engaging in charitable and community activities to the extent and in the manner consistent with the Executive's engagement in such activities prior to the Commencement Date, so long as such activities are not, in the reasonable judgment of the Board, inconsistent with any provision of this Agreement. During the Employment Period, the Executive shall not be engaged in any business activity (other than the Stipulated Activities) which, in the reasonable judgment of the Board, conflicts with the Executive's duties hereunder, whether or not such activity is pursued for gain, profit or other pecuniary advantage.

5. *Compensation.*

(a) The Company shall pay to the Executive an annual base salary (the "Base Salary") during the Employment Period at a rate of $_________ per annum, payable in such installments (but not less often than monthly) as is generally the policy of the Company with respect to its executive officers.

(b) In addition to the Base Salary, the Executive shall be entitled to receive a bonus payment (the "Bonus") in cash equal to $_________ subject to the provisions of Section 12 hereof. Unless the Executive shall otherwise elect in accordance with Section 5(c), the Bonus shall be payable on _________, 19____. The date on which the Bonus is payable pursuant to this Section 5(b) is referred to herein as the "Initial Bonus Payment Date."

(c) At any time up to 90 days prior to the Initial Bonus Payment Date, the Executive may elect to defer receipt of the Bonus otherwise payable on the Initial Bonus Payment Date pursuant to Section 5(b) to the earliest to occur of (i) the date on which the Executive's employment with the Company shall terminate for any reason, (ii) the Executive's death or total and permanent disability (within the meaning of Section 22 (e) (3) of the Internal Revenue Code of 1986, as amended) and (iii) such other date designated by the Executive in the Deferral Notice (as hereinafter defined); *provided, however,* that in no event shall the Bonus be payable prior to the Initial Bonus Payment Date. The Executive may exercise such election to defer receipt of the Bonus by delivering to the Company written notice of such election in substantially the form of Exhibit A (the "Deferral Notice"). In addition, the Executive may elect in the Deferral Notice to receive the Bonus in a lump sum or in more than one installment over a period of time to be specified by the Executive therein. The date on which the Bonus shall become payable pursuant to this Section 5(c) is referred to herein as the "Final Bonus Payment Date." In the event the Executive shall elect to defer receipt of the Bonus in accordance with this Section 5(c), the Company shall, not later than the Initial Bonus Payment Date, irrevocably deposit the Bonus into a trust (the "Trust") established pursuant to an agreement to be entered into by the Company and the trustee thereunder for the purpose of establishing a fund from which to pay the Bonus. The Executive may recommend to the Company the manner in which the Bonus shall be invested consistent with the terms of the Trust; *provided, however,* that the Company shall retain the sole and exclusive right to veto any such recommendation and to direct the trustee of the Trust as to investment policy. Any interest earned on or proceeds derived from investment of the Bonus by the trustee of the Trust shall inure to the benefit of the Executive. An election by the Executive to defer receipt of the Bonus in accordance with this Section 5(c) shall be irrevocable; *provided, however,* that, in the event of the Executive's severe financial hardship or emergency due to circumstances beyond the Executive's control, the Company may, in its sole discretion, allow such election to be partially or wholly revoked and cause to be paid to the Executive such amounts from the Trust as shall be necessary in the Company's judgment to alleviate such hardship or emergency.

(d) The Company may, at its sole option and expense, maintain life and disability insurance policies (collectively, the "Insurance Policies") covering the Executive in such amounts as the Company shall determine to meet its payment obligations under Section 12(b) in the event of the death or disability of the Executive (which policies may be in addition to any other life or other insurance policies covering the Executive which are maintained by the Company). The Executive will cooperate with the Company and provide such information or other assistance as the Company may reasonably request in connection with the Company's obtaining and maintaining of the Insurance Policies.

(e) On the Commencement Date, the Company shall grant the Executive an option to purchase [ ] shares of Common Stock, $_________ par value, of the Company pursuant to the Stock Option Plan of the Company and in accordance with the terms and subject to the conditions thereof and of a stock option agreement dated the date hereof between the Company and the Executive (the "Option Agreement").

(f) On the Commencement Date, the Company shall grant the Executive certain rights to receive future payments of cash or shares of Series B Convertible Preferred Stock, $_________ par value, and Series C Preferred Stock, $_________ par value, of the Company in accordance with the terms and subject to the conditions of a phantom stock agreement dated the date hereof between the Company and the Executive (the "Phantom Stock Agreement").

6. *Expenses.* The Company shall reimburse the Executive, in accordance with the practice from time to time for other senior executives of the Company, for all reasonable and necessary travel expenses and other disbursements incurred by the Executive for or on behalf of the Company in the performance of his duties hereunder. In addition, (i) the Company will pay directly or reimburse the Executive for up to $10,000 for professional fees incurred by the Executive in connection with the review and negotiation on behalf of the Executive of this Agreement and the transactions contemplated hereby and (ii) subject to approval by the Board as to reasonableness, the Company will pay directly or reimburse the Executive for all reasonable and necessary costs and expenses incurred or paid by the Executive in relocating his principal residence to the geographic area of the Company's principal executive offices, including, but not limited to, real estate brokers' fees, shipping and storage fees, interim housing costs (if any), mortgage "points" or other reasonable and equitable adjustments to compensate for any residential mortgage interest rate differential, and any costs in connection with obtaining a third party guarantee of a minimum sale price on the sale of the Executive's home located in [CITY, STATE]. The Company will, at the Executive's request, provide the Executive with an interest-free bridge loan in the principal amount not to exceed $600,000 to facilitate the Executive's purchase of a home in the geographic area of the Company's principal executive offices. Proceeds received by the Executive upon the sale of his home located in [CITY, STATE] (including any payments received under the aforementioned third party guarantee) shall be used to repay the principal of such loan.

7. *Benefits.* During the Employment Period, the Executive shall be entitled to all benefits as are made generally available from time to time to senior executives of the Company. In particular, the Company shall (i) provide the Executive with such life insurance, health insurance and disability insurance benefits as are provided to its senior executives generally and (ii) cause the Executive to be covered by any directors' and officers' liability insurance policies which the Company maintains for its directors and officers generally. In addition, during the Employment Period, the Executive shall be entitled to the use of an automobile owned or leased by the Company. The responsibility for the payment of expenses associated with the Executive's use of such automobile (including, without limitation, maintenance expenses and insurance costs) shall be borne by the Company.
8. *Involuntary Termination.*
   (a) If the Executive is incapacitated or disabled by accident, sickness or otherwise so as to render him mentally or physically incapable of performing the services required to be performed by him under this Agreement for a period of 180 consecutive days or longer or for an aggregate of 180 days during any twelve-month period (such condition being hereinafter referred to as a "Disability"), the Company may, at that time or within any reasonable time (not to exceed 30 days) thereafter, at its option, terminate the employment of the Executive under this Agreement immediately upon giving him written notice to that effect (such termination, as well as a termination under Section 8(b), being referred to herein as an "Involuntary Termination"). The Executive shall be entitled to receive his compensation pursuant to Section 5(a) notwithstanding any such Disability.
   (b) If the Executive dies during the Employment Period, the Employment Period shall be deemed to have terminated as of the date of his death.
9. *Termination For Cause.* The Company may terminate the employment of the Executive hereunder at any time for Cause (as hereinafter defined) (such termination being referred to herein as a "Termination For Cause") by giving the Executive written notice of such termination, such termination to take effect immediately upon the giving of such notice to the Executive; *provided, however,* that prior to the giving of the aforementioned notice, (i) the Company shall have given the Executive prior written notice of the meeting of the Board at which such termination is to be considered, specifying in detail the nature of the alleged cause, and (ii) the Executive shall have been given an opportunity to be heard at such meeting. As used herein, the term "cause" shall mean (A) the Executive's knowing and willful misconduct with respect to the business and affairs of the Company or any subsidiary or affiliate thereof, including a material violation by the Executive of any policy of the Company relating to ethical business conduct or practices or fiduciary duties of a senior executive of the Company, (B) the Executive's knowing and willful neglect of duties or knowing failure to act (where action would reasonably be required and where such failure to act is not the result of the reasonable and prudent exercise of business judgment by the Executive) which materially adversely affects the business and affairs of the Company or any subsidiary or affiliate thereof, (C) the material breach by the Executive of any of the provisions of this Agreement or the Option Agreement, which breach (if it is, in the reasonable judgment of the Board, remediable) has not been remedied by the Executive within a reasonable time specified by the Board in a notice to the Executive or (D) the conviction of the Executive of

a felony or the commission by the Executive of an act involving moral turpitude or fraud.

10. *Termination Without Cause.* The Company may terminate the employment of the Executive hereunder at any time without cause (such termination being referred to herein as a "Termination Without Cause") by giving the Executive notice of such termination, such termination to take effect on the date specified in such notice, which date shall not be earlier than the date of the notice.

11. *Voluntary Termination.* Any termination of the employment of the Executive hereunder other than as a result of an Involuntary Termination, a Termination For Cause or a Termination Without Cause shall be deemed to be a "Voluntary Termination."

12. *Effect of Termination.*

(a) Upon the termination of the Executive's employment hereunder for any reason whatsoever, neither the Executive nor his beneficiaries or estate shall have any further rights or claims against the Company under this Agreement except to receive (i) the unpaid portion, if any, of the Base Salary pursuant to Section 5(a) computed on a *rata* basis to the Termination Date (based on the actual number of days elapsed over a year of 365 or 366 days, as applicable), (ii) reimbursement for any expenses for which the Executive shall not have been reimbursed as provided in Section 6 and (iii) any unpaid accrued benefits of the Executive pursuant to Section 7.

(b) Anything to the contrary contained herein notwithstanding, in the event of the termination of the Executive's employment hereunder for any reason other than a Termination for Cause or a Voluntary Termination, the Executive (and his beneficiaries or estate) shall have the further right (i) to continue to receive the Base Salary pursuant to Section 5(a), payable in such installments as paid to the Executive prior to such termination of employment, through the Scheduled Termination Date, reduced by any amounts received by the Executive as salary or other cash compensation from subsequent employment as such amounts are paid to the Executive (or his beneficiaries or estate), and (ii) to receive the Bonus pursuant to Section 5(b) or (c), as the case may be. In order to carry out the intent of clause (i), the Executive agrees, for himself and his beneficiaries or estate, to provide the Company with such information as the Company may reasonably request regarding the Executive's receipt of salary and other cash compensation from subsequent employment.

(c) With respect to the Option granted to the Executive in accordance with the Option Agreement and the rights regarding the Phantom Stock Units granted to the Executive pursuant to the Phantom Stock Agreement, in the event of a conflict between the terms of the Option Agreement or the Phantom Stock Agreement and this Agreement in connection with the termination of the Executive's employment with the Company, the terms of the Option Agreement or the Phantom Stock Agreement, as the case may be, shall control.

13. *Disclosure of Information.*

(a) The Executive recognizes and acknowledges that the trade secrets and proprietary information and processes of the Company, as they may exist from time to time, are valuable, special and unique assets of the Company, the access to and knowledge of which are essential to the Executive's performance of his duties under this Agreement. The Executive will not, at any time prior to or after the expiration of the Stipulated Period (as defined in Section 15(a)), in whole or in part, disclose such secrets, information or processes to any person, firm, corporation, association or other entity for any reason or purpose whatsoever (whether or not for profit and whether or not in connection with any business, educational, lecturing, publishing or other activities undertaken by the Executive), nor shall the Executive make use of any such secrets, information or processes for his own purposes or for the benefit of any person, firm, corporation, association or other entity (except the Company or any of its subsidiaries or affiliates) under any circumstances, at any time prior to or after the expiration of the Stipulated Period, except as required by law, authorized in writing by order of the Board or necessary in the ordinary course of the Executive's performance of his duties under this Agreement.

(b) Upon the termination of the Employment Period for any reason, or upon the demand by the Company at any time, the Executive shall deliver to the Company all memoranda, books, papers, letters, formulae and other data, and all copies thereof and therefrom, which (i) in any way relate to the business of the Company or any of its subsidiaries or affiliates as conducted or as planned to be conducted on the date of such termination (the "Business") and were made by the Executive or otherwise came into his possession or under his control at any time prior to the expiration of the Stipulated Period or (ii) relate to any work, inventions, ideas, disclosures and improvements subject to Section 14(a).

(c) Nothing in this Section 13 shall abrogate or reduce any other restrictions on the Executive under applicable law.

14. *Transfer and Assignment of Work.*

(a) Subject to the last sentence of this Section 14(a), the Executive hereby transfers and assigns to the Company, or to any other person or entity designated by the Board, the entire right, title and interest of the Executive in and to all work, inventions, ideas, disclosures and improvements, whether patented or unpatented, and copyrightable material, made, conceived, reduced to practice or learned by the Executive, solely or jointly, or in whole or in part, at any time on or prior to the date of termination of the Employment Period, which in any way relate or pertain to the Business. The Executive shall promptly communicate and disclose to the Company, and shall maintain corporate notebooks containing all information, details and data pertaining to the aforementioned work, inventions, ideas, disclosures and improvements. The Executive shall, at any time (including any time after the termination of the Employment Period), execute and deliver to the Company such formal transfers and assignments and such other papers and documents as may be required of the Executive to perfect the Company's rights hereunder and to permit the Company or any person or entity so designated by the Board to file and prosecute patent applications and, as to copyrightable material, to obtain copyrights thereon. The Executive shall deliver the aforementioned corporate notebooks to the Company promptly upon the termination of the Employment Period for any reason (and promptly upon any creation of or supplement to such corporate notebooks thereafter) or upon the demand by the Company at any time. Any work, invention, idea, disclosure or improvement by the Executive relating to the Business within one year following the termination of the Employment Period shall be deemed to fall within the provisions of this Section 14(a) unless proved by the Executive to have been first conceived and made following such termination.

(b) Nothing in this Section 14 shall abrogate or reduce any other restrictions on the Executive under applicable law.

15. *Noncompetition Covenant with Respect to the Business.*

(a) The Executive shall not, at any time prior to the termination of the Employment Period or during the two-year period ending on the second anniversary of the Termination Date or Scheduled Termination Date (as the case may be) (such two-year period being referred to herein as the "Stipulated Period"), (i) engage in any business or activity, whether or not for profit, which in any way involves or relates to any aspect of the Business or (ii) interfere with, disrupt or attempt to disrupt the relationship, contractual or otherwise, between the Company and any third party, including, but not limited to, any customer, supplier or employee of the Company. The Executive shall be deemed to have violated the provisions of the foregoing sentence if he shall (A) hire or otherwise retain the services of any person who shall have been an employee of the Company within the immediately preceding 12-month period or (B) be an employee, officer or director of, consultant to or owner of an equity interest in any person or entity engaged or intending to engage in any activity which would violate the provisions of the foregoing sentence if engaged in by the Executive; *provided, however,* that the Executive may own up to, but not more than, a passive 1% equity interest in any public company.

(b) During the Employment Period and the Stipulated Period, the Executive shall inform all Designated Persons (as defined below) of the existence of this Agreement and the relevant terms hereof (including, without limitation, Sections 13, 14 and 15). As used herein, the term "Designated Person" shall mean any person or entity proposing to hire or retain the Executive as an employee, director, consultant or advisor.

16. *Acknowledgments by the Executive.* The Executive understands that the restrictions contained in Sections 13, 14 and 15 may limit his ability to earn a livelihood in a competing business, but the Executive nevertheless believes that he has received and will receive sufficient consideration and other benefits as an employee of the Company and as otherwise provided hereunder to clearly justify such restrictions which, in any event (given his education, skills and ability), the Executive does not believe would prevent him from earning a living.

17. *Enforcement; Severability; Etc.* It is the desire and intent of the parties that the provisions of this Agreement shall be enforced to the fullest extent permissible under the laws and public policies applied in each jurisdiction in which enforcement is sought. Accordingly, if any particular provision of this Agreement shall be adjudicated to be invalid or unenforceable, such provision shall be deemed amended to delete therefrom the portion thus adjudicated to be invalid or unenforceable, such deletion to apply only with respect to the operation of such provision in the particular jurisdiction in which such adjudication is made.

18. *Remedies.* The Executive acknowledges and understands that the provisions of Sections 14, 15 and 33 of this Agreement are of a special and unique nature, the loss of which cannot be adequately compensated for in damages by an action at law, and that the breach or threatened breach of the provisions of this Agreement would cause the Company irreparable harm. In the event of a breach or threatened breach by the Executive of the provisions of this Agreement, the Company shall be entitled to an injunction restraining him from such breach. Nothing contained herein shall be construed as prohibiting the Company from or limiting the Company in pursuing any other remedies available for any breach or threatened breach of this Agreement.

19. *Notices.* All notices, claims, certificates, requests, demands and other communications hereunder shall be in writing and shall be deemed to have been duly given, delivered and received if personally delivered or if sent by nationally-recognized overnight courier, by telecopy, or by registered or certified mail, return receipt requested and postage prepaid, addressed as follows:

    (a) If to the Executive, at his last address appearing in the records of the Company; and

    (b) If to the Company, to:

    [NAME OF EMPLOYER]

    [ADDRESS]

    or to such other address as the party to whom notice is to be given may have furnished to the other parties in writing in accordance herewith. Any such notice or communication shall be deemed to have been delivered and received (i) in the case of personal delivery, on the date of such delivery, (ii) in the case of nationally-recognized overnight courier, on the next business day after the date when sent, (iii) in the case of telecopy transmission, when received, and (iv) in the case of mailing, on the fifth business day following the day on which such communication is posted.

20. *Governing Law.* This Agreement will be governed by, and construed and enforced in accordance with, the laws of the State of ________________ applicable to agreements made and to be performed wholly therein.

21. *Waiver of Breach.* The waiver by any party of a breach of any provision of this Agreement by any other party must be in writing and shall not operate or be construed as a waiver of any other or subsequent breach by such other party.

22. *Entire Agreement; Amendments.* This Agreement (together with the other writings referred to herein) contains the entire agreement between the parties with respect to the subject matter hereof and supersedes all prior agreements or understandings between the parties with respect thereto. This Agreement may be amended only by an agreement in writing signed by the parties.

23. *Headings.* The section headings contained in this Agreement are for reference purposes only and shall not affect in any way the meaning or interpretation of this Agreement.

24. *Assignment*. This Agreement is personal in its nature and no party shall, without the consent of the other party hereto, assign or transfer this Agreement or any rights or obligations hereunder; *provided, however,* that the provisions hereof shall inure to the benefit of, and be binding upon, the respective heirs, legal representatives and successors of the parties including, with respect to the Company, successors by merger, consolidation, transfer of all or substantially all of the assets of the Company or otherwise.

IN WITNESS WHEREOF, the parties have duly executed this Employment Agreement as of the date first above written.

[NAME OF EMPLOYER]

BY: ______________________________

NAME:

TITLE:

____

[NAME OF EMPLOYEE]

____

Witness

1:1.5A Supporting Documentation

As is the case with the recruitment of most chief executives, the executive compensation package outlined in the Chief Executive Officer Employment Agreement presented at 1:1.5 is extensive and complicated. Included in the agreement are bonus payments and two types of nonqualified deferred compensation arrangements: incentive stock options and phantom stock. This executive compensation package requires the following supporting documentation:

1. An Incentive Stock Option Agreement;
2. A Phantom Stock Agreement;
3. An Employment Letter of Intent;
4. A Base Salary and Bonus Payment Guarantee;
5. A Bonus Deferral Notice; and
6. A Trust Agreement.

All of the supporting documentation required by this particular employment agreement has been drafted to accompany it and is found in the chapter of executive compensation at 8:1.1–8:1.5.

1:2 Non-Competition, Confidentiality And Patent/Copyright Protection Agreements

It is a characteristic of our information age that a company's most important assets often are not large machines that can be bolted to the floor or sprawling manufacturing and production facilities. Rather, intellectual property and proprietary information (such as customer lists, software programs, manufacturing processes, etc.) frequently are a company's most valuable possessions. While a departing employee might find it difficult to carry off a punch press, a rolodex or a computer diskette fits easily into a briefcase that can be carried out the front door. Consequently, a growing number of employers are demanding that newly hired employees at all levels execute non-competition and confidentiality agreements, usually when they first walk in the front door. (See Q. 24**S**.)

There is a widely held misconception among both lawyers and lay persons alike that non-competition agreements (alternatively referred to as non-solicitation agreements) are against public policy and unenforceable. This simply is not true. The common (court made) law of most of the fifty states recognizes the validity of non-competition agreements when they are (1) reasonable as to the time and geographic coverage of their restraints, and (2) supported by appropriate consideration such as initial employment. (See Q. 25.1**S**, Q. 26, and Q. 27.)

Similarly, U.S. common law, by and large, recognizes a company's proprietary interest in its closely-guarded trade secrets. Therefore, a confidentiality agreement requiring an employee, both during and after employment, to respect and not misappropriate such trade secrets will generally be enforced in a court of law. (See Q. 25.–Q. 27 and Q. 25.1**S**.)

The employer's right to protect patents and copyrights is granted even greater legal recognition. The key here, however, is to commit employees, who are likely to develop inventions at the company's expense, to turn over these creative inventions to the company as company property.

With respect to some key employees, a company may want to require a sort of omnibus agreement containing non-competition, confidentiality, patents/copyright agreements. All of these may be incorporated into an even broader employment contract, such as the examples presented in Section 1.1.

Once again, the sample agreements that follow must be carefully adapted—preferably with appropriate legal counsel—to the specific needs of your organization and with an eye toward any particular requirements of the statutory and common law of the state(s) in which business is conducted.

1:2.1 Non-Competition (Non-Solicitation) Agreement: Time Of Hire

THIS AGREEMENT made this ________ day of ________, 19___, between [NAME OF EMPLOYER] (hereinafter referred to as "Company") and [NAME OF EMPLOYEE] (hereinafter referred to as "Employee"):

WITNESSETH

That the parties hereto agree as follows:

In consideration of your employment with Company, and/or any of its affiliates or subsidiaries of the covenants set forth herein, and for other good and valuable consideration, it is agreed that if your employment with Company should terminate for any reason, you will not, directly or indirectly, for a period of two (2) years after the date of such termination of your employment, in any capacity whatsoever (either as an employee, officer, director, stockholder, proprietor, partner, joint venturer, consultant or otherwise), solicit, sell to, divert, serve, accept or receive insurance agency, brokerage or consulting business or actuarial, employee benefits, or employee benefit reporting (Benefacts) business, from any customer or active prospect of Company which you personally, alone or in combination with others, handled, serviced or solicited at any time during the two (2) year period immediately proceeding termination of your employment.

It is further understood and Employee acknowledges that in the course of his/her employment hereunder, he/she will become acquainted with confidential client information of Company, relating to persons, firms and corporations which are customers or active prospects of Company during the period of employment, and sources with which insurance is placed, which confidential client information includes, but is not limited to policy expiration dates, policy terms, conditions and rates, familiarity with customer's risk characteristics, and information concerning the insurance markets for large and complex commercial risks. Employee agrees that he/she will not without the express, written consent of Company during the term of employment and for two (2) years after termination thereof, disclose, copy or make any use of such confidential information except as may be required in the course of his/her employment hereunder.

In the event of a breach or threatened breach of the provisions of this Agreement, Company shall be entitled to any injunction restraining such breach; but nothing herein shall be construed as prohibiting Company from pursuing any other remedy available for such breach or threatened breach. The covenants herein contained are intended to be separate and divisible and if, for any reason, any one or more of such covenants should be held to be invalid and unenforceable in whole or in part, it is agreed that the same shall not be held to affect the validity or enforceability of any other covenant of this Agreement.

In the event of your termination (except for death, permanent or total disability or retirement), Company agrees that it will pay you a sum equivalent to one (1) month's salary computed as of the date of such termination.

Employee agrees that adherence to this agreement does not preclude Employee from earning a livelihood. Rather, Employee recognizes that this agreement is reasonably necessary to protect Company's legitimate interest in the customers and accounts Employee develops as a salaried employee of Company.

Dated at ______________________ [NAME OF EMPLOYER]

______________________, 19__ BY: ______________________

______________________ ______________________

Witness [NAME OF EMPLOYEE]

1:2.2 Non-Competition (Non-Solicitation) Agreement: Post Employment Settlement And Release

THIS AGREEMENT, made this ________ day of ________, 19___, by and between [EMPLOYER] and [NAME OF EMPLOYEE] is intended by the parties to be a settlement and release whereby [EMPLOYER] and [NAME OF EMPLOYEE] extinguish their respective rights and claims against one another as hereinafter enumerated.

FOR VALUABLE CONSIDERATION, receipt of which is hereby acknowledged, [NAME OF EMPLOYEE] agrees as follows:

1. [NAME OF EMPLOYEE] agrees that upon the execution of this Agreement (s)he will surrender to legal counsel client lists in whatever form they are possessed by [NAME OF EMPLOYEE] including but not limited to, computer printout(s), index cards, mailing labels, floppy disk(s) or other methods of computer storage, photostatic, typewritten and handwritten copies of the same.
2. [NAME OF EMPLOYEE] further agrees that (s)he will not, singly or jointly, or through any agent, employee, officer, director or affiliate, solicit any additional business which is currently [EMPLOYER'S] business nor any client of [EMPLOYER] for a period of twelve (12) months from the date of this Agreement. For purposes of this provision of this Agreement, the term "solicit" includes, but is not limited to, communication with [EMPLOYER'S] clients by means of letter, telephone and personal contact, both direct and indirect, and expressly includes response by [NAME OF EMPLOYEE] to inquiries from [EMPLOYER'S] clients when said inquiries were stimulated by letters or other solicitation by [NAME OF EMPLOYEE] prior to the date of this Agreement.

For purposes of this provision of this Agreement, the term "business" includes, but is not limited to, all forms and types of insurance, insurance policies, insurance coverage, brokerage and agent services, consulting services, annuities, riders, claims, inquiries, leads, bids, estimates, and contracts of whatever nature.

For purposes of this provision of this Agreement, the term "client" includes, but is not limited to, individuals, corporations, partnerships, institutions, sole proprietorships, government agencies, and any and all other entities currently doing any "business" with [EMPLOYER] as "business" is defined above.

3. [NAME OF EMPLOYEE] releases and discharges [EMPLOYER], its successors and assigns, directors, officers, shareholders and employees, from all rights, claims and causes of action which [NAME OF EMPLOYEE] had, now has, or may hereafter have, which arose, arise or may arise out of any action, contract, conduct or course of conduct whatsoever at any time prior to the date of the signing of this Agreement, specifically, but not limited to, any and all claims and causes of action arising out of or pertaining to [NAME OF EMPLOYEE] employment by [EMPLOYER] and its termination.
4. In consideration of the foregoing promises of [NAME OF EMPLOYEE] and notwithstanding any other provision of the Agreement, [EMPLOYER] agrees that [NAME OF EMPLOYEE] may retain the clients listed on the pages attached hereto and collectively designated Exhibit [________] and incorporated herein by reference. However, during the twelve (12) months follow-

ing the date of the Agreement, [NAME OF EMPLOYEE] will not solicit this list of clients to sell them additional "business," as that term is defined above.

5. By way of further consideration for the aforesaid promises of [NAME OF EMPLOYEE], [EMPLOYER] hereby releases and discharges [NAME OF EMPLOYEE], his/her successors, assigns, directors, officers, shareholders, partners and employees from all rights, claims and actions which [EMPLOYER] had, now has, or may hereafter have which arose, arise or may arise out of any action, conduct or course of conduct whatsoever at any time prior to the date of this Agreement.
6. Notwithstanding any other provision of this Agreement, it is agreed among the parties hereto that [EMPLOYER] expressly retains the right to seek equitable and legal relief in any appropriate court or forum with respect to the acquisition prior to the date of this Agreement by [NAME OF EMPLOYEE], or his/her agent or affiliate, of any business or client of [EMPLOYER] not listed in Exhibit [_________] hereto.
7. The parties, in executing this Agreement, do not rely on any inducements, promises or representations made by any other party, or a party's agents or attorneys, other than those expressed herein. The parties have read this Agreement, consisting of _________ pages and have had the consequences explained by their respective attorneys. In executing this Agreement the parties intend to be legally bound.

____
[EMPLOYEE]

____
[EMPLOYER]

BY: ___________________________

DATE: _________________________

1:2.3 Employee Agreement Not To Invest In Competitive Enterprises

THIS AGREEMENT NOT TO INVEST IN COMPETITIVE ENTERPRISES dated as of this _________ day of _________ 19___ (the "Competitive Investment Agreement"), by and between [NAME OF EMPLOYER], a [STATE OF INCORPORATION] company (the "Company") and [NAME OF EMPLOYEE], an individual residing at [ADDRESS] ("Covenantor").

WITNESSETH

WHEREAS, the Company intends to enter into the business of [BRIEF DESCRIPTION OF BUSINESS];

WHEREAS, Covenantor is [an employee, officer, etc. of] the Company.

NOW, THEREFORE, in consideration of the foregoing, and of the promises and mutual covenants contained herein and for other good and valuable consideration, the receipt and sufficiency of which is hereby acknowledged, the parties hereto, intending to be legally bound, hereby agree as follows:

1. Covenantor hereby agrees that, during the term hereof, he will not, directly or indirectly, invest in or become an owner in or a shareholder of any partnership, corporation, joint venture, proprietorship, firm or other business enterprise or association (all such partnerships, corporations, joint ventures, proprietorships, firms or associations being hereinafter referred to as "Company competitors"), which competes with the intended activities of the Company as set forth in this section, from time to time, or which, within the territory described in paragraph 5 hereof, engages in any business of the kind intended to be engaged in by the Company, as follows:

   [DETAILED DESCRIPTION OF ALL ASPECTS OF COMPANY'S BUSINESS]
2. Covenantor hereby warrants and represents that he does not presently, directly or indirectly, have an investment or ownership interest in, nor is he a shareholder of, any Company Competitor which is in the business described in Section 1 above, within the geographic area described in Section 5 hereof.
3. Covenantor hereby further agrees that, during the term hereof, he will not, directly or indirectly, lend his credit or money for the purpose of assisting another to establish or operate any Company Competitor; or operate, manage or control any Company Competitor.
4. Anything to the contrary in this Competitive Investment Agreement notwithstanding, neither (i) the ownership of less than five percent (5%) of the stock of any corporation listed on the New York Stock Exchange or the American Stock Exchange, nor (ii) the continued ownership and operation of the Covenantor's private practice, shall constitute a violation of this

Competitive Investment Agreement. Furthermore, to the extent that the Covenantor is participating in any group or entity but does not receive any share of the profits or losses of such group or entity, such participation shall not be deemed to be an investment or ownership interest subject to the terms and conditions of this Agreement; provided, however, that if at any time subsequent hereto the Covenantor commences to receive any share of the profits or losses of such group or entity, such participation shall constitute an investment or ownership interest and shall no longer be exempt from this Agreement.

5. The territory covered by this Agreement is a circle having a [ ] mile radius with its center located at [ ].
6. The term of this Competitive Investment Agreement shall commence on the date hereof and shall continue for a period of [ ] years.
7. The Company hereby agrees, as consideration for the Covenantor's agreement hereunder, to pay to the Covenantor the sum of $_________, payable [PAYMENT SCHEDULE], as follows:

   [PARTICULAR DATES OF PAYMENT OF INSTALLMENTS]
8. Acceptance of this Competitive Investment Agreement by the Covenantor shall be accomplished by the Covenantor executing this Competitive Investment Agreement and delivering it to the Company on or before the Closing Date.
9. In the event the Company breaches this Competitive Investment Agreement by failing to make any payment in accordance with Section 7 hereof, the obligations of the Covenantor hereunder shall cease as of the date such payment was due; however, the Company shall have six (6) months from the date of such payment in which to cure said breach by making the required payment in full, at which time the Covenantor's obligations hereunder shall be restored, prospectively, to full force and effect.
10. The parties acknowledge that the restrictions contained herein are reasonable and that any violation would result in irreparable injury to the Company. If the geographic area or period of time specified in Section 5 or 6 hereof should be adjudged unreasonable in any proceeding, then the geographic area or period of time shall be reduced by the elimination of that portion thereof adjudged unreasonable so that such restriction may be enforced for such geographic area or time as is adjudged to be reasonable. Covenantor agrees that the remedy at law for any breach by him of this Competitive Investment Agreement will be inadequate, and that, in the event of such breach, the Company shall be entitled to preliminary and permanent injunctive relief as well as an equitable accounting of all earnings, profits and other benefits arising from such violation, which rights shall be cumulative and in addition to any other rights or remedies to which the Company may be entitled. In the event of such violation, the period referred to in Section 6 hereof shall be extended to a period of time equal to that period beginning when such violation commenced and ending when the activities constituting such violation shall have been fully terminated in good faith.
11. This Competitive Investment Agreement may be enforced by the Company or its successors and assigns.

12. Neither the failure nor any delay on the part of any party to exercise any right, remedy, power or privilege under this Competitive Investment Agreement shall operate as a waiver thereof, nor shall any single or partial exercise of any right, remedy, power or privilege preclude any other or further exercise of the same or of any other right, remedy, power or privilege, nor shall any waiver of any right, remedy, power or privilege with respect to any occurrence be construed as a waiver of such right, remedy, power or privilege with respect to any other occurrence. No waiver shall be effective unless it is in writing and is signed by the party asserted to have granted such waiver.
13. This Competitive Investment Agreement and all questions relating to its validity, interpretation, performance and enforcement, shall be governed by and construed in accordance with the laws of the State of [ ], notwithstanding any conflict of laws provisions to the contrary.
14. All notices, requests, demands and other communications required or permitted under this Competitive Investment Agreement shall be in writing and shall be deemed to have been duly given, made and received when personally delivered or upon actual receipt of registered or certified mail, postage prepaid, return receipt requested, addressed as set forth below:
    (a) If to the Company:
        [NAME]
        [ADDRESS]
    (b) If to the Covenantor:
        [NAME]
        [ADDRESS]

In addition, notice by mail should be by air mail if posted outside of the continental United States.

Any party may alter the address to which communications or copies are to be sent by giving notice of such change of address in conformity with the provisions of this paragraph for the giving of notice.

15. This Competitive Investment Agreement shall be binding upon and inure to the benefit of the parties hereto and their respective heirs, personal representatives, successors and assigns, except that no party may assign or transfer its rights or obligations under this Competitive Investment Agreement without the prior written consent of the other parties hereto excepting that the Company may assign its rights and obligations hereunder (without the consent of the Covenantor) to any party who purchases substantially all of the assets of any business of the Company.
16. The provisions of this Competitive Investment Agreement are independent of and separable from each other, and no provision shall be affected or rendered invalid or unenforceable by virtue of the fact that for any reason any other or others of them may be invalid or unenforceable in whole or in part.

17. This Competitive Investment Agreement contains the entire understanding among the parties hereto and with respect to the subject matter hereof, and supersedes all prior and contemporaneous agreements and understandings, inducements or conditions, express or implied, oral or written, except as herein contained. This Competitive Investment Agreement may not be modified or amended other than by an agreement in writing.

IN WITNESS WHEREOF, the parties have executed this Agreement as of the month, day and year first above written.

[NAME OF EMPLOYER]

BY: ______________________________

NAME OF SIGNER:
TITLE:

____
[NAME OF COVENANTOR]

____
Witness

1:2.3A Acknowledgment Form For Individuals

STATE OF :

: SS

COUNTY OF :

On this _________ day of _________, 199__, before me personally appeared _________, being by me duly sworn, known to me to be the person(s) whose name(s) is (are) subscribed to the foregoing Signature Page who acknowledged that he [SHE] [THEY] executed the same.

____

Notary Public

(Seal)

My Commission Expires: __________

1:2.4 Employment And Confidentiality Agreement Including Patent/Copyright Protection

AGREEMENT made and entered into as of ________ day of ________, 19___, by and between [EMPLOYER], including companies owned, controlled, operated or otherwise affiliated with said corporation (collectively referred to hereafter as the "Company") and [NAME OF EMPLOYEE] ("Employee").

RECITALS

The Company is in the business of [BRIEF DESCRIPTION OF THE BUSINESS] and desires to employ Employee in connection with such business activity, and Employee desires to engage in such employment.

In connection with such employment, Employee may be given access to, generate, or otherwise come into contact with certain proprietary and confidential information of the Company and its clients.

The Company and Employee desire to prevent the dissemination or misuse of such information for the protection of the goodwill of the Company.

NOW, THEREFORE, for and in consideration of the mutual covenants and agreements contained herein, the parties hereto, each intending to be legally bound hereby, agree as follows:

1. *Employment of Employee*. Company hereby employs or continues to employ Employee and Employee hereby accepts such employment, upon the following terms:
2. *Work Product*. The Company shall have sole proprietary interest in the work product of Employee during the term of his or her employment ("Work Product") [*Note: inclusion of the following paragraph text is optional.*]

   and Employee expressly assigns to the Company or its designee, all rights to, title and interest in, any and all copyrights, patents, trade secrets, improvements, inventions, sketches, models and all documents thereto, manufacturing processes and innovations, and any other Work Product developed by Employee, either solely or jointly with others, where said Work Product relates to any business activity in which the Company is involved at the time or prior to Employee's creation of such Work Product, or where such Work Product is developed with the use of Corporation's time, material or facilities; and Employee further agrees to disclose any and all such Work Product to the Company without delay. [*Note: inclusion of the following paragraph text is optional.*]

   Employee shall, from time to time as requested by the Company, take all appropriate steps to establish or document Corporation's ownership in and place Company in possession of such Work Product, including but not limited to, the execution of appropriate copyright applications or assignments, and Employee agrees not to disclose any knowledge of the existence and contents of such Work Product herein unless and until released in writing by the Company from such obligations.
3. *Other Confidential Information*. The Company shall also have sole proprietary interest in any and all other confidential information developed by the Company, its employees or clients including but not limited to any and all invention improvements, other drawings, blueprints, other reproductions, models, patterns, samples, devices or parts thereof, data, data sheets, data books, reports, business methods, client lists, prospective client lists, any

information provided by a client or prospective client, or any other object or document developed for the Company's business. All such information, in addition to Employee's Work Product, shall be confidential.

4. *Non-Disclosure.* Employee shall not, without the express written consent of an executive officer of the Company during the term of his or her employment and for a period of [REASONABLE NUMBER] years thereafter, disclose to any unauthorized third party or use any confidential information of the type set forth in Sections 2 and 3 hereof. The Employee agrees he or she shall not reproduce or photocopy any such documents or objects which contain, or are derived from, any such confidential information hereof, nor take with them any such information upon the termination of this Agreement.
5. *Non-Competition.* Employee agrees that during the term of this Agreement and for a period of [REASONABLE NUMBER] years following termination of this Agreement, he or she shall not engage, directly or indirectly, alone or as an officer, director, employee, agent, shareholder, partner, or fiduciary of any person or entity, in any activity similar or in connection with the activities of Company within a radius of [REASONABLE NUMBER] miles of the Company.
6. *Remedies.* The parties agree to the reasonableness of the restrictions in the covenants set forth above and acknowledge that they have been fairly negotiated, and they agree that such restrictions shall be legally enforceable and shall not be challenged by the Employee in any court proceeding. In the event of breach of this Agreement, Employee agrees that the Company shall be entitled, in addition to any other available remedies, to temporary and permanent injunctive relief without the necessity of proving actual damage or immediate or irreparable harm or for posting a bond. [*Note: the following language may be included as an optional part of this paragraph.*]

   Notwithstanding the foregoing, if any court shall determine such restrictions to be unreasonable, the parties agree to the reformation of such restrictions by the court to limits which it finds to be reasonable and that the employee will not assert that such restrictions should be eliminated in their entirety by such court.

IN WITNESS WHEREOF, the said parties have hereunto set their hands and seals this ________ day of ________, 19___.

(CORPORATE SEAL) [NAME OF EMPLOYER]

ATTEST: ______________________ BY: ______________________
Secretary Name of Executive Officer:
Title:

ATTEST: ______________________ BY: ______________________
Secretary [NAME OF EMPLOYEE]

1:3 Model Employee Handbook

Employee handbooks, once considered a frill that only large companies could afford, are now commonplace in most companies. They are effective tools for providing employees with information on policies, wages, employee benefits, and a host of other subjects.

Ongoing personal contact between management and employees is an important component of a successful business. However, many managers find that the demands of a growing business curtail the amount of time that they can spend getting to know their employees and personally resolving employee problems on a case-by-case basis. Although an employee handbook cannot (and should not) replace personal contacts, it can be used to establish policies and improve communication. This helps the company run more efficiently because employees who are better informed tend to be more secure, and therefore more loyal and productive.

A comprehensive employee handbook plays a major role in orienting and informing new employees. For experienced employees, it should also serve as a reference for clarification on company policies, benefits, and other issues.

Employee handbooks can cover many subjects. At the bare minimum, however, employees using an employee handbook should be able to understand:

- What the employer expects of them and what they can expect of the employer;
- The employer's policies on wages, working conditions, and benefits;
- How much time, thought, and money go into making their jobs secure;
- How the company provides service to its customers;
- The company's place in the community and in the industry; and
- Why a job in the company is good and permanent employment.

An employee handbook is not a "silver bullet." That is, it cannot ensure that a company will have no problems. It cannot replace—only reinforce and complement—an effective program of employee relations and communications carried out by competent and concerned managers. But a handbook, thoughtfully and effectively written, *and* faithfully implemented, can minimize a company's exposure to the mushrooming phenomenon of lawsuits for wrongful discharge, discrimination, and other employment-related allegations. Moreover, providing employees with a clear picture of your company's commitment to them robs unions of one of their major attractions for unhappy, insecure workers. (For a discussion of how to cope with labor unions, see Chapter 3 and Q. 113–Q. 169 and Q. 117**S**–Q. 169.1**S**)

It is obvious that no two employees handbooks are exactly alike—nor should they be. Each company has its unique needs and circumstances, which must be reflected in its instructions to its employees. Some handbooks are comprehensive sources of information, down to detailed descriptions of group insurance plans. Others are simple "code of ethics" that outline the basic principles of the employer-employee relationship, but make no attempt to describe such things as fringe benefits or payment plans. Regardless of the type of employee handbook desired, it cannot be stressed enough that careful drafting of this document is imperative. Why? Because an employer can create implied contractual terms of employment with an employee handbook, often without knowing it! (See Q. 33**S** and Q. 33.1**S**.) Therefore, when adapting—again, preferably with review by the appropriate legal counsel—the sample employee handbook that appears at 1.3:1, employers should keep the following four general guidelines in mind:

1. Avoid making promises about career opportunities, future compensation, or expected job duties.
2. Use disclaimers, such as "unless our plans change" or "if we continue to do as well as we have done in the past," if promises are made.
3. Describe benefits using words such as "currently," "at present," or "now," and note that plans are "subject to change."
4. Include the statement that employment is "at will" and that "the employee or employer may terminate the employment at any time, and no oral or written promises regarding any term or conditions of employment can be made, or should be relied upon, except for those made in writing by a designated officer of the company."

1:3.1 Model Employee Handbook

The following pages present one example of an employee handbook. As noted at 1:3, this handbook should not be adopted wholesale but should only serve as a blueprint for an employee handbook that reflects your company's unique needs and circumstances. For those employers that wish only a simple "code of ethics," this model may provide too much information. Conversely, for those employers that wish for a comprehensive source of employment information, this model may very well meet their needs. Regardless of the type of employee handbook a company desires, employers should consult with appropriate legal counsel before implementing their employee handbook.

Employee Handbook

Introduction

This handbook is intended to inform you about your job and about the Company. We are proud of our Company and the many employees who have contributed to our excellent reputation. We hope that you will share in our pride and be an active and positive participant in our operation.

It is the intent of the Company to employ people who will contribute to the overall growth and success of the Company and to have an atmosphere in which all employees derive the maximum satisfaction from their work. While new employees are selected with care, selection is done without regard for the applicant's race, religion, age, sex, national origin or non-job related handicap or disability. All of the employment and job related policies of the Company are governed by our commitment to equal opportunity for everyone. In a very real sense, your progress within the Company depends solely upon our ability, willingness and effort.

All new employees must work through a 60 day probationary period to enable the Company to evaluate their performance and ability. After this probationary period has been successfully completed, the employee will be considered a regular employee and entitled to the benefits described later in this handbook. An employee's probationary period may be extended to enable the employee to have every possible opportunity to establish his ability to do the work to which he is assigned.

The Company wants you to enjoy your work here and to fully realize your potential. Shortly after your employment, you will meet with your immediate supervisor who will explain your specific job duties and responsibilities and review the operating policies of the Company. The highlights of the benefits given to regular employees will also be explained at that time.

The Company encourages you to ask questions and consult with your supervisor whenever you wish information about your benefits and conditions of employment. Unless your supervisor knows what may concern you, he cannot help. From time to time, you may have a problem about which you do not wish to speak to your supervisor. In those cases, you are invited to talk directly to any other management person you feel may be of help.

About Your Job

The following is a description of the various benefits available to you as an employee of the Company as well as the procedures that govern your period of employment.

Employment Classifications

The Company has established the following employment classifications in order that it may relate to you our fringe benefit program.

Probationary employee: Employees newly hired or rehired shall be considered probationary until they have successfully completed sixty (60) working days (days the employee has worked) from the start date of employment.

During the probationary period, an employee may be discharged without prior notice if his performance is not satisfactory. His performance shall be documented in a written evaluation. During the probationary period, employees will not be eligible for the benefits and privileges given to regular employees, except as noted in the "Summary of Fringe Benefits."

Regular full-time employees: A regular full-time employee is one who has satisfactorily completed the probationary period and works at least forty (40) hours per week, on a regularly scheduled basis. This employee is entitled to fringe benefits as listed in the "Summary of Fringe Benefits."

Regular part-time employees: Part-time employees are those who have successfully completed the probationary period and are regularly scheduled to work less than 40 hours per week. Part-time employees are entitled to fringe benefits on a pro-rated basis as listed in the "Summary of Fringe Benefits."

Employment Record

The official Employee Personnel Record is maintained in the Company's Main Office.

Your personnel record will consist of pre-employment data, your letter of employment and all subsequent information relevant to your employment at the Company. This information includes changes in job positions, wages, education, evaluation reports. It is essential that you notify the payroll section about any change in your name, address, telephone number, marital status, additional education or other accomplishments, in order to keep your record up to date. Upon request, employees may inspect the contents of their personnel file, except for pre-employment data. If you wish to make such an inspection, request it in writing to your supervisor.

Promotions and Transfer

The Company has a long-standing policy of promotion from within. Jobs are filled by promotion from a lower position within the immediate department involved, if a qualified employee is available. Qualification for promotion includes:

1. Ability to meet the mental and physical demands of the job;
2. Promptness and regularity in reporting to work;
3. Cooperation with supervisors and other employees; and
4. Aptitude and willingness to provide good service to the Company and our customers.

If you are interested in a particular position, notify your supervisor. He will assist you in completing the necessary application. Appropriate instructions as well as qualifications for each job will be furnished on request.

If qualified candidates are not available within the Company, the supervisor filling the vacancy will recruit from outside.

Absenteeism and Tardiness

When you are absent or late, you create a hardship for your fellow employees who are responsible for work in process and deadlines and cost the Company additional wages and other expenses. Repeated incidences of unexcused absences or tardiness will result in discipline and may lead ultimately to the termination of your employment.

Abandonment of Position

Absence from work for a period of three consecutive scheduled work days without proper notification or satisfactory excuse given to your immediate supervisor will be construed to be an abandonment of your employment and a voluntary quit.

Resignation or Layoff

An employee who voluntarily leaves the employment of the Company is expected to furnish notice of 10 working days. In the event an employee does not give the required notice, the accrued vacation pay and other similar compensation will be reduced in the last pay check by an amount equal to the wages which would have been paid over the balance of the notice period.

An employee who is laid off due to elimination of his position or lack of work will be given as much notice as possible.

Among employees with equal ability and work record, a layoff will be determined on the basis of seniority. If laid off, the employee will receive pay for all vacation to which he may be entitled and for holidays earned but not taken at the time of layoff.

Responsibility and Obligations

No employee will be discharged or disciplined except for just cause. Except in extreme cases warranting immediate discharge, employees will be given corrective discipline. The discipline procedure is as follows:

1. *First Offense*—the supervisor will discuss the infraction with the employee and make note of the discussion in the employee's file. The employee will receive a copy of the note.
2. *Second Offense*—the department head will issue a written notice to the employee and refer to the prior discussion of the infraction. A copy of the written notice will be placed in the employee's file.
3. *Third Offense*—after the third infraction, an employee will be subject to disciplinary action, such as suspension or discharge.

It is our intention with this policy to avoid misunderstanding and to give fair and reasonable notice to our employees of their responsibilities and obligations and an opportunity to correct deficiencies. Occasionally, infractions of company rules may require an immediate disciplinary suspension or discharge. Some examples of such serious violations are falsification of company records (application forms, punching someone else's time card, etc.), theft, being under the influence of or bringing intoxicating beverages or behavior affecting drugs onto the premises, insubordination, intentional damaging or misuse of company property, willful disregard of safety rules.

Reemployment

An employee who has been terminated will not be considered for reemployment if the termination was due to:

1. A discharge for cause;
2. Leaving without giving proper notice; or

3. Failing to meet satisfactory standards during the probationary period.

Hours Of Work

The following is a description of the policies governing the period of time you are at work.

Working Hours

The regular work week consists of at least 40 hours within a seven day period. This is generally established as five working days, eight hours per day. However, the nature of the Company's business often makes it impossible to operate on a completely regular schedule. Consequently, you may be required as part of your job to have different starting times or, different total working hours from week to week or day to day. Your supervisor will inform you of any schedule change as far in advance of that change as possible.

Recording of Time Worked

In order to comply with Workers' Compensation Insurance laws, Wage and Hour laws, as well as for other payroll purposes, employees are required to record accurately the time that they start work and the time they end their work. In order to accomplish this, the Company has established a number of ways for employees to record their time worked. You will be required to record your working time every day by one of these means as described by your supervisor.

Regardless of the system that you use, no employee may record the time worked of another. Any employee violating this rule will be subject to immediate discharge.

An employee is expected to be ready for work before recording his start time. No employee is permitted to record his starting time more than 5 minutes before his scheduled start time or more than 5 minutes after his scheduled quitting time unless he receives prior permission to do so from his supervisor.

Meal Period

Your supervisor will specify the length of your meal period and schedule your meal break.

It is important that you adhere to the schedule in order that no interruption in the work flow will occur. If you intend to leave the premises during your meal time, you must notify your supervisor before leaving and upon your return.

Wage Policies

The following is a description of the Company's policies governing employee compensation.

Pay Period

For purposes of computing pay, the period begins on Monday at 12:01 a.m. and continues through the next Sunday ending at 12:00 Midnight.

You will be paid by check every week on the second Monday following the close of the pay period. If a payday falls on a holiday, employees will be given their paycheck the day after the regular payday.

Your paycheck is your personal business. If you have questions in regard to your pay, please speak with your immediate supervisor.

Personnel who will be off on payday may receive their paycheck the day after the regular payday.

With each regular paycheck will be your personal "statement of earnings and deductions." This information indicates all deductions for the particular pay period such as Federal Income Tax, other required taxes and voluntary deductions.

Please note that the following payroll deductions are required by law:

1. Federal Income Tax;
2. Social Security Tax;
3. [ ] State Income Tax;
4. Local Wage Tax, if applicable.

Garnishment

An employee whose payroll account with the Company is served with a summons as garnishee will be advised of the summons in order that he may pay the creditor immediately and arrange to have the garnishment withdrawn. Any attachment of wages will be carried out pursuant to the laws of the [STATE] and only to the extent permitted by those laws.

Overtime

Overtime is permitted only as authorized by your supervisor. The Company will pay overtime in accordance with the Federal Wage and Hour Law.

Salary Increases

For every position in the Company there is an established pay range. Rates of pay are reviewed quarterly and adjustments may be made based upon a number of criteria, including the quality of your work performance, attendance record, financial condition of the company, etc. You are invited to discuss any pay increase with your supervisor if you have any question regarding its fairness or appropriateness.

Fringe Benefit Program

The following outlines the fringe benefits that employees are entitled to.

Holidays

The Company observes the following holidays for full time employees:

New Year's Day	January 1
Easter Sunday	Variable
Memorial Day	Last Monday in May
Independence Day	July 4
Labor Day	First Monday in September
Thanksgiving Day	Fourth Thursday in November
Christmas Day	December 25

Eligibility for the holiday: Employees are entitled to holidays as enumerated in the "Summary of Fringe Benefits."

In weeks in which holidays occur, eligible employees are assured that their weekly wage will not be less than in weeks when no holiday occurs. That is, if an eligible employee is not scheduled to work on a day because that day is a holiday, he will either be scheduled for make up hours on other days to insure the maintenance of his regular week's wage or will be paid for the hours missed, not to exceed 8 hours, at the option of the company. If an eligible employee is required to work on a holiday, he will be paid twice his regular rate for all hours worked. Holiday work will be equalized among all eligible employees.

In order to be eligible for holiday benefits, an employee must have worked his entire last scheduled work day before and entire first scheduled work day after the holiday, except in the case of illness or accident preventing the employee from working as evidenced by written certification of a physician or other proof if requested by the Company.

Personal Days

The Company provides a maximum of one paid personal day a year to each eligible full time employee as set forth in the "Summary of Fringe Benefits."

Eligibility for personal days:

1. Permanent full time employees are eligible for personal days.
2. During the first year of employment, the personal day is advanced to the employee at the satisfactory completion of the probationary period.
3. Each subsequent year, employees will be advanced their personal day at the beginning of the calendar year.
4. The personal day is advanced on the assumption that the employee will be employed the full year. In the event the employee resigns or is terminated, he shall be entitled to his personal day based on one half day for each six months worked during the calendar year. Any unused portion of the personal day at time of termination will be cashed out; any excessive use of the personal day at time of termination will be deducted from the employee's last paycheck.

Limitations on use of personal days: Personal days may be used for any reason and taken at any mutually acceptable time as determined and scheduled by you and your supervisor; however,

1. No personal day may be taken in conjunction with a legal holiday.
2. No personal day may be taken in conjunction with vacation days.
3. The personal day may not be accumulated from one calendar year to the next.
4. If the personal day is not used within the year that it is earned, it is forfeited.
5. No personal day may be taken between November 15 and December 31 of any year.
6. Each employee will be obligated to keep track of his own personal day to insure that it will not be forfeited.

7. The Company may refuse your request to take a personal day due to its need to have you work.

Vacation

Full time employees are entitled to a paid vacation based on their length of service. With the exception of bonus days during the first year of employment, vacations are earned and not advanced. Vacations are earned according to the following schedule:

1. Employees with one complete year of service but less than two complete years of service by June 1 of any year will receive one week's vacation with pay.
2. Employees with two complete years of service but less than five complete years of service by June 1 of any year will receive two week's vacation with pay.
3. Employees with five or more complete years of service by June 1 of any year will receive three weeks' vacation with pay.
4. Employees who are hired less than twelve months but more than three months before June 1 of any year shall be given the following bonus vacation days to be taken after that June 1:

Date of Hire	*Vacation Bonus*
June 1 - August 31	4 days
September 1 - November 30	3 days
December 1 - February 28	2 days

Use of vacation: Employees must take their vacation in periods of one week. The scheduling of vacation shall be arranged through your supervisor in accordance with the work requirements of your department and the needs of the Company. Vacation benefits may not be accumulated from one year to the next.

Vacation days not used before June 1 of the next year will not be redeemed for pay. Each employee is responsible to keep track of their own vacation days to be sure that they will not be forfeited at the end of the year.

Vacation days may not be taken in conjunction with personal days.

Whenever possible, priority for vacation periods will be granted according to length of service within your department.

Vacation pay: An employee will receive vacation pay before commencing his vacation, provided such a request is made at least two weeks in advance of the last payday before the beginning of the vacation.

Vacation entitlement at termination of employment: An employee who has been at the Company for one full year and who resigns or is terminated shall be paid for the number of days of accrued vacation that have not been taken, if the employee gives notice of his resignation at least two weeks before the anticipated last day of work.

Because vacation is not earned until an employee has worked one full year, employees who are terminated or resign during the first year of service are not entitled to any vacation pay at time of termination.

Paid Leaves of Absence

Sick leave: The purpose of sick leave is to protect the employee from loss of pay due to illness. Regular full time employees are entitled to three days per year sick leave. Probationary and part time employees are not entitled to any sick leave. Upon completion of the probation period, an employee will be credited with the number of sick days to which he is entitled prorated to the end of the calendar year. The full allotment will be available at the start of the new year. An employee will not be paid for unused sick leave on termination of employment. Sick leave may be taken in units of one day only.

To be eligible for a sick leave day, the employee must notify his supervisor of his illness at least one hour before the start of his regularly scheduled work day. For each additional sick day, the employee must notify his supervisor and keep him informed of his progress. The Company may require written certification by a physician as proof of illness or injury. Employees who have been on sick leave three consecutive days may also be required to be examined by the Company's doctor before being permitted to return to work.

Funeral leave: Funeral leave with pay shall be granted for all employees in the case of a death in the employee's immediate family according to the following schedule:

1. *Death of a Spouse, Child or Parent*—All scheduled work days beginning with the day of death and ending with the day of the funeral, inclusive, to a maximum of five days.
2. *Death of a Grandparent, Brother, Sister or Relative Residing with the Employee*—All scheduled work days beginning with the day of death and ending with the day of the funeral, inclusive, to a maximum of three days.
3. *Death of a Parent-in-Law*—day of the funeral only.

Employees who work on any day for which they may be entitled to a leave with pay under this section shall not be entitled to funeral leave pay in addition to their regular wages.

Jury duty: It is the policy of the Company that an Employee will not lose pay because he may be required to serve up to three days on a petite jury. Jury duty shall apply to employees in accordance with the "Summary of Fringe Benefits." Eligible employees shall be compensated at the difference between their base rate of pay for regularly scheduled work days lost and Jury Duty pay for the same period. The receipt of a notice for Jury Duty must be reported immediately to your supervisor. No Jury Duty pay will be given an employee until they present to the Company a receipt for the Jury Duty pay paid by the government or court. The Company may request the employee be excused or exempt from Jury Duty, if in the opinion of the Company, the employee's services are considered essential at the time of proposed Jury service.

Unpaid Leaves of Absence

Employees may have unpaid leaves of absence for any reason which may appear reasonable to the company and is in accordance with the "Summary of Fringe Benefits."

An employee may be granted a leave of absence without pay, upon the written approval of the Employer. The leave of absence is permitted for purposes such as: military service, extended illness, education, and other personal reasons. A leave of absence will not be given to allow the employee to take another job and employment during a leave of absence will automatically result in the termination of the employee with no rights to reinstatement of reemployment. The granting of a leave of absence is wholly the prerogative of the Company. A leave of absence is for a stated period of time and should not exceed six months. The only exception shall apply in the case of military service which shall be granted in accordance with applicable law.

An employee who is on a leave of absence shall have his personnel file remain active; however, no vacation, sick leave or holiday time will be accumulated.

Reinstatement from an unpaid leave of absence: Employees who return from an unpaid leave of absence will be reinstated to active employment in their former position or one of like status only if such a position is available. If no such position is available, the individual will be given preference in filling any vacancy for which he is qualified.

Employee Insurance Benefits

The following list of health and life insurance benefits are available to employees according to the "Summary of Fringe Benefits."

Blue Cross/Blue Shield and major medical: If you are a full time regular employee the Company covers the full cost for you of Hospitalization and Major Medical insurance. If you desire to have your spouse or other dependent covered, you may arrange to have them included by paying the additional premium. A complete copy of the health benefit program for hospitalization and medical coverage will be given to you by your supervisor.

Group life, accidental death and dismemberment insurance: The Company pays the full cost for life insurance as well as for accidental death and dismemberment insurance for all full time regular employees. A copy of the policy description is available to you upon request.

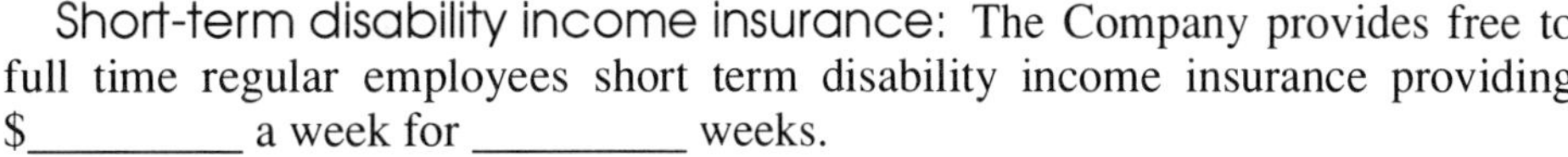

Short-term disability income insurance: The Company provides free to full time regular employees short term disability income insurance providing $________ a week for ________ weeks.

Workers' compensation insurance: Your employment at the Company is covered by Workers' Compensation Insurance. If you should have an accident while at work, no matter how small, it is essential that it be reported to your supervisor of your department head immediately. This will insure your protection under the Workers' Compensation Program.

Summary of Fringe Benefits Program

Fringe Benefits	Available	FTE	PTE
Vacation			
Bonus Vacation Days			
Holidays (7)			
Personal Day			
Sick Leave (3)			
Health and Hospitalization Insurance			
Major Medical			
Short-Term Disability			
Life Insurance			
Paid Leave (a) Jury Duty (b) Funeral Leave			
Unpaid Leave (a) Sick (b) Personal			
Pension			
Workers' Compensation			
Unemployment Compensation			

General Provisions

The following outlines the remaining areas governed by this Handbook that were not covered in the previous sections.

Confidential Information

Any information to which you have access or of which you become aware regarding records, personnel information, financial information, etc. is to be held in the strictest confidence. Such information is not to be discussed with other employees or persons not employed by the Company.

Safety

It is your responsibility to help in the prevention of accidents, as well as to report conditions which may cause accidents to other employees. Safety is everyone's job.

Use of Premises

Employees will not be permitted on the Company's premises except during assigned duty hours.

Lockers

If your job requires the use of a locker, one will be assigned to you by your supervisor. A locker is on loan to you for storage of your personal belongings. The Company retains ownership of the locker and reserves the right to examine it for defects and/or contents.

Package Inspection

The Company reserves the right to inspect any packages being carried into or out of its buildings by employees. A permission slip to carry out packages containing company property is to be obtained through your supervisor.

Soliciting

No person not employed by this Company will be permitted to solicit on behalf of any cause or organization at any time on Company property.

No person employed by this Company will be permitted to solicit on behalf of any cause or organization during working time or in work areas during work time. Working time is defined as all hours of work exclusive of authorized meal periods and other authorized non-working periods, e.g., breaks.

Any non-employee found violating this rule will be ejected from company property.

Any employee found violating this rule will be subject to discipline, up to and including discharge.

Revisions

All personnel policies and procedures that are changed after publication of this Employee Handbook will be published and furnished to all supervisors who will, in turn, make you fully aware of these changes and/or additions. If you have any questions as to policies and procedures, we encourage you to speak to your supervisor.

1:4 Independent Contractor Agreements

One of the most widely litigated issues of personnel law is the distinction between who is considered an employee and who is considered an independent contractor. (See Q. 39.) The advantages of treating a worker as an independent contractor, rather than as a company's employee, are fairly obvious: independent contractors:

1. Are generally not protected by employment discrimination laws;
2. Need not be paid minimum wage or overtime premiums;
3. Trigger no unemployment tax or social security tax deductions; and
4. May have very little recourse against the company if injured while performing their duties (especially if those duties are performed with their own equipment off the company's premises).

Recognizing the temptation that exists for companies to classify a worker as an independent contractor when possible, the law has, for a long time, looked beyond the formal characterization of the relationship to the underlying realities of the relationship. The so-called "right-to-control" test places substance over form, holding that a company that has the right to control the manner and means that the job is performed is the employer of the worker performing that job, regardless of whether the parties have entered into an independent contractor agreement. (See Q. 37 and Q. 38.)

Nonetheless, there are many circumstances in which an independent contractual relationship is not only desirable but perfectly legal, if appropriately structured. The following forms are samples of independent contractor agreements for salespeople, truck drivers, and professional people, but that can be adapted to cover a wide range of positions. When attempting to adopt these examples to particular situations, as many indicia of real independence as possible should be incorporated into the independent contractor agreement. In a recent court case, concerning whether the plaintiff was an employee (and thus covered by Title 7 of the 1964 Civil Rights Act for discrimination) or an independent contractor, one U.S. Court of Appeals identified the following twelve factors to be considered in making such a determination:

1. The extent of the employer's right to control the "means and manner" of the worker's job performance;
2. The kind of occupation, with reference to whether the work usually is done under the direction of a supervisor or by a specialist without supervision;
3. The skill required;
4. The person responsible for furnishing the equipment and the workplace;
5. The length of time the individual has worked;
6. The method of payment (by time or by the job);
7. The manner in which the work relationship can be terminated;
8. Whether annual leave is given;
9. Whether the individual's work is an integral part of the employer's business;
10. Whether the individual accumulates retirement benefits;
11. Whether the company pays social security taxes on the individual; and
12. The intent of the parties.

(EEOC v Zippo Mfg Co, 713 F2d 32, 37 (3rd Cir 1983))

1:4.1 General Independent Contractor Agreement

THIS AGREEMENT made this ________ day of ________, 19___, by and between [NAME OF EMPLOYER] of [CITY, STATE] (hereinafter "the Corporation") and [NAME OF EMPLOYEE] (hereinafter "the Contractor").

WITNESSETH THAT

WHEREAS, the Corporation requires the services of [DESCRIPTION OF JOB];

WHEREAS, the Contractor is a trained, experienced and fully-qualified [DESCRIPTION OF JOB], and desires to provide services to the Corporation; and

WHEREAS, the Corporation and the Contractor desire to enter into an Agreement to carry out the foregoing.

NOW, THEREFORE, in consideration of the mutual covenants and agreements contained herein, the parties mutually agree as follows:

1. The Contractor agrees to perform the following services to the Corporation, as an independent contractor:
   (a) The Contractor agrees to perform, or have performed by qualified persons of his choosing: ________, such performance to commence on or about ________, 19___, and to be completed on or about ________, 19___.
   (b) The Contractor will procure such equipment as in his professional judgment is required to perform said services as described in paragraph 1(a) above, and retain such other assistants or others as he may deem necessary to his timely and professional performance of these services.
   (c) The Contractor hereby warrants that he is a fully-qualified professional ______________; that he acknowledges that the Corporation has no in-house expertise in ______________ and that the Corporation is relying upon him for the safe, efficient and professional performance of the services outlined in paragraphs 1(a) and (b). The Contractor will exercise all diligent efforts to retain only professional and experienced people to assist him, and to procure, maintain and operate all necessary equipment in safe and serviceable condition, and in a safe manner.
   (d) The Contractor hereby expressly waives his right and the rights of his heirs, administrators, executors, beneficiaries and assigns to sue or otherwise make claim against the Corporation, its officers, directors, agents and employees for all loss, liability, or damage which he may incur in performance of his obligations under this Agreement or at any time thereafter related to this Agreement. The Contractor further agrees to save and hold harmless the Corporation, its officers, directors, agents and employees from all loss, damage, or claims by others retained by the Contractor in his performance of this agreement, or by any federal, state or local governmental agency, whether on account of withholding of employment taxes or any other claim or cause arising out of the Contractor's relationship with his employees, suppliers, subcontractors or any others. The Contractor further agrees to obtain a Waiver and Release form executed in favor of the Corporation from all assistants or others retained by him in the performance of this agreement.
2. In consideration of the performance of the Contractor's obligation in full under this Agreement, the Corporation agrees to pay the Contractor the sum

of $_____________ This sum is payable upon the following schedule ________________.

All prepayments are repayable to the Corporation upon the Contractor's material breach of this Agreement.

3. The Corporation further agrees that in consideration of Waiver and Release forms executed in its favor by the Contractor and any and all others he retains to assist him in the performance of this Agreement, the Corporation will provide at its sole expense accidental death and dismemberment life insurance coverage in the amount of $________ for the benefit of the Contractor and others whom he retains and whom he designates to the Corporation in writing, prior to the time they are retained by him. (No other individuals shall be entitled to insurance as described herein. Said insurance shall remain in full force and effect from ________, 19___, through ________, 19___; thereafter such insurance will be null and void.)
4. In the event either party commits a material breach of any term of this Agreement, the other party shall have the right to terminate this Agreement immediately.
5. The Agreement constitutes the entire Agreement and understanding between the parties and shall not be modified, altered, changed or amended in any respect unless in writing and signed by both parties.
6. This Agreement shall be governed by the laws of the State of ________________, both as to interpretation and performance.

IN WITNESS WHEREOF, the parties hereto have executed this Agreement the ________ day of ________ 19___, and same shall be considered binding upon both parties and shall remain in full force and effect unless and until cancelled according to the terms of this Agreement.

CONTRACTOR: [NAME OF EMPLOYER]

______________________________ BY: ___________________________

Title: _________________________

1:4.2 Independent Contractor-Carrier Operating Agreement

THIS AGREEMENT made between ______________________________ of ________________ (the "CARRIER"), and __________________________, (the "CONTRACTOR").

WITNESSETH THAT

WHEREAS, the CARRIER, an Interstate For Hire Common Motor Carrier, operating under a Certificate of Public Convenience and Necessity Issued by the Interstate Commerce Commission ("ICC") and pursuant to exemptions from economic regulation specified by the Interstate Commerce Act, wishes to obtain transportation through an agreement with CONTRACTOR; and

WHEREAS, the CARRIER is engaged in the business of transporting freight by motor vehicle, and

WHEREAS, the CARRIER and CONTRACTOR desire to enter into an agreement to carry out the foregoing.

NOW, THEREFORE, in consideration of the mutual covenants and agreements contained herein, the parties mutually agree as follows:

1. The CONTRACTOR agrees to use the Equipment more specifically described in Exhibit "A", and by reference made a part hereof (the "Equipment"), together with drivers and all other labor CONTRACTOR deems appropriate to transport, load and unload on behalf of CARRIER, or on behalf of such other certificated carriers as CARRIER may designate through authorized "Trip Lease" or interchange agreements, such commodities, as the CARRIER may make available to the CONTRACTOR. The CARRIER agrees to make commodities available from time to time for transportation by the CONTRACTOR, however, this shall not be construed as an agreement by the CARRIER to furnish, nor the CONTRACTOR to accept any specific number of loads or pounds of freight for transportation at any particular time or any particular place.
2. It is understood and agreed that the performance of this Agreement, and the relationship of the parties hereunder shall be in accordance with the requirements of the Interstate Commerce Act, and the rules and regulations of the ICC, and the U.S. Department of Transportation, as modified and amended from time to time.
3. The CONTRACTOR is not obligated to purchase or rent any products, equipment, or services from the CARRIER, as a condition to entering into this Agreement.
4. For each trip made by the CONTRACTOR under the terms of this Agreement, the CARRIER agrees, with such exceptions as agreed to between CARRIER and CONTRACTOR, and specifically provided for on CARRIER's prenumbered trip record issued to CONTRACTOR or its driver for each trip, to pay CONTRACTOR according to the terms of the Schedule set forth in the addendum to this Agreement, which addendum may be modified from time to time notwithstanding Paragraph 20.

   This amount shall constitute full payment to CONTRACTOR, including all payments for pickup, delivery and transportation between points of origin and destination and all loading and unloading. Any amounts overpaid by CARRIER for pickup, delivery, overcharge claims on previous loads, and similar items shall be deducted from this amount. The CARRIER will make available to CONTRACTOR for its examination, upon reasonable request, copies of its tariffs.

5. The CARRIER shall settle with CONTRACTOR within 15 days after the CONTRACTOR submits, by mail or in person, the necessary delivery documents and other paperwork concerning a trip in the service of the CARRIER. The required documents shall include all signed delivery receipts, and related shipping documents, including bills of lading, driver's daily logs, mileage reports, vehicle inspection reports and such other evidence of proper delivery as may be required by the Rules and Regulations of the ICC or the U.S. Department of Transportation. It is understood and agreed that all of the aforementioned documents and/or related documents may contain information relating exclusively to CARRIER's business and must not be released to any parties other than duly authorized CARRIER personnel. In any case where the CONTRACTOR has secured an advance of any kind from the CARRIER, or if there shall be any other amounts due to the CARRIER, or to affiliates of the CARRIER from the CONTRACTOR or CONTRACTOR's authorized agents or employees, the CARRIER shall be authorized to deduct the amount of such advance or other amounts due to the CARRIER from the CONTRACTOR in settling with the CONTRACTOR under the terms of this Agreement. In addition, the CARRIER shall have a period of thirty (30) days after termination of this Agreement to verify the account of the CONTRACTOR as to money owed the CONTRACTOR and to make appropriate deductions before final settlement.

6. The CONTRACTOR recognizes that CARRIER's business of providing motor carrier transportation services to the public is subject to regulation by the Federal Government acting through the ICC and the U.S. Department of Transportation, and by various state and local governments. The CONTRACTOR shall have the responsibility of:

   (a) Maintaining or causing the Equipment to be maintained in the state of repair required by all applicable regulations;

   (b) Operating the Equipment in accord with all applicable regulations;

   (c) Hiring only those drivers to operate the Equipment who are qualified under all applicable regulations;

   (d) Doing all other things necessary to conduct the transportation services provided in this Agreement in accord with all applicable regulations.

7. The CONTRACTOR shall determine the means and methods of the performance of all transportation services undertaken by the CONTRACTOR under this Agreement. The CONTRACTOR shall retain all responsibility for:

   (a) Hiring, setting the wages, hours and working conditions and adjusting the grievances of, supervising, training, disciplining and firing all drivers, drivers' helpers and other workers deemed necessary by CONTRACTOR for the performance of its obligations under the terms of this Agreement, which drivers, drivers' helpers, and other workers are and shall remain the employees of the CONTRACTOR;

   (b) Selecting, purchasing or leasing, financing, and maintaining or causing the Equipment to be maintained;

   (c) Paying all operating expenses including, but not limited to, all expenses of fuel for Equipment, road taxes, fuel or mileage taxes, fines for parking, moving or weight violations (except that CARRIER shall be responsible for fines for overweight and oversized trailers when trailers are preloaded or the load is containerized) and for improperly permitted overdimension loads unless the violation results from the act or omission of the CONTRACTOR, empty mileage, permits of all types, tolls, ferries, detention and accessorial services, or any other levies or assessments resulting from the performance of this Agreement.

(d) Purchasing fuel in the amount necessary to balance fuel taxes due in each state. CARRIER will arrange for an independent accounting firm to provide state motor carrier fuel-tax reporting services for CONTRACTOR. CONTRACTOR agrees to keep and make available fuel tickets, drivers records and other documents necessary for reporting purposes, and authorizes CARRIER to deduct from CONTRACTOR's settlements such amounts as are necessary to pay for the cost of the reporting service. CONTRACTOR further authorizes CARRIER to deduct from each settlement the total amount necessary to compensate CARRIER for the amount it must pay for CONTRACTOR's failure to balance such fuel purchases.

8. The CONTRACTOR has and shall maintain sole financial responsibility for all federal highway use taxes, withholding and employment taxes due to Federal, state or local governments on account of drivers, drivers' helpers and other workers deemed necessary by CONTRACTOR for the performance of its obligations under the terms of this Agreement. The CONTRACTOR agrees to save and hold harmless the CARRIER from any claim by drivers, drivers' helpers and other workers used by the CONTRACTOR, or by any Federal, state or local governmental agency, on account of withholding and employment taxes, or any other actions arising from the CONTRACTOR's relationship with its employees.

9. Responsibility for obtaining insurance coverage shall be as follows:

(a) The CARRIER shall obtain and maintain in effect insurance coverage for the protection of the public pursuant to ICC regulations.

(b) The CONTRACTOR shall obtain and continue in force and effect Workers' Compensation insurance covering itself, its drivers, drivers' helpers and laborers employed by it in the performance of this Agreement, and shall furnish CARRIER with a copy of policy evidencing such coverage or a Certificate of Insurance in lieu thereof. CONTRACTOR agrees to protect, defend, indemnify, and hold CARRIER harmless from and against any claim, loss or damage brought or alleged by CONTRACTOR or its employees against CARRIER for any injury, including death, to CONTRACTOR or its employees resulting from the performance of this Agreement.

(c) The CONTRACTOR agrees to carry Insurance Coverage of $________ for physical loss or damage to CARRIER's equipment; Bobtail and Deadhead Insurance Coverage with respect to public liability and property damage in the limits of $________ for any person, $________ for any accident and $________ property damage in any accident concerning the Equipment and/or CARRIER's equipment when used not in performance of a duty under this Agreement; and agrees to furnish evidence of such coverage to CARRIER and arrange for CARRIER to be named as additional insured under such policy.

10. The CONTRACTOR shall be responsible and liable to CARRIER and agrees to pay for shortage of, loss of, or damage to cargo transported by CONTRACTOR in the event that such shortage, loss or damage is caused directly or indirectly by the operations of CONTRACTOR or its employees or agents. Such monies shall be deducted from any monies due CONTRACTOR under this Agreement. CARRIER will make available to CONTRACTOR a written explanation and itemization of any deductions for cargo or property damage prior to or at the time such deductions are made. If any losses, shortages or damages to cargo are brought to the attention of CONTRACTOR on delivery, CONTRACTOR shall first notify CARRIER, and obtain authorization prior to signing any delivery receipts or similar documents acknowledging the losses, shortages or damages to cargo. Failure to do so on CONTRACTOR's part shall make CONTRACTOR liable for the losses, shortages, or damages to cargo.

11. The CONTRACTOR shall indemnify, reimburse, and save harmless the CARRIER for any loss and/or damage to the person or property of third parties; and CONTRACTOR shall defend, indemnify, reimburse, and save harmless CARRIER from any and all claims, costs and expenses arising out of or in any way connected with the loss and/or damage to the person or property of third parties by reason of the performance of this Agreement. When moving shipments loaded on CARRIER's trailers, CONTRACTOR shall be responsible to CARRIER for damage, loss and/or theft of the CARRIER's equipment and/or component parts caused by carelessness, negligence, improper usage and/or abuse of said equipment, and further agrees:

    (a) Not to make any alterations, changes or modifications in CARRIER's equipment, except as may be necessary to comply with applicable regulations, without written consent of CARRIER.

    (b) To immediately remove flat tires to prevent irreparable damage and loss of said tires.

    (c) To return CARRIER's equipment with same tires that were mounted on said equipment at time CONTRACTOR or its agents took possession of same. In the event foreign tires are found on CARRIER's equipment, CONTRACTOR will be held liable.

    (d) To use CARRIER's equipment only in the ordinary course of CARRIER's business as a Motor Common Carrier.

    In the event of such loss to the CARRIER, the loss will be deducted from CONTRACTOR's settlement. CARRIER will make available to CONTRACTOR a written explanation and itemization of any deductions for damage to CARRIER's equipment prior to or at the time such deductions are made.

12. The CARRIER may require CONTRACTOR to deposit with the CARRIER $________ to be placed in an escrow fund. The fund shall be established by depositing $________ per week from payments due CONTRACTOR under this Agreement until such time as a total of $________ has been accumulated. Additional deposits shall be made from payments due CONTRACTOR as necessary to maintain a balance of $________. Upon cancellation of this Agreement, the escrow fund will be used to clear CONTRACTOR's account. Any charges to or purchases made by the CONTRACTOR from CARRIER will be deducted from the escrow fund and the balance will be paid to CONTRACTOR within forty-five (45) days of

cancellation of this Agreement. In the event CARRIER temporarily advances funds to CONTRACTOR so as to enable CONTRACTOR to fulfill its obligations under Paragraph 5 of this Agreement, such advances shall be considered as reductions in the escrow account until repaid. CARRIER shall provide to CONTRACTOR an accounting of any transaction involving the escrow fund. This accounting will be provided upon CONTRACTOR's request at any time and shall include all deductions or additions made to the escrow fund. Interest derived from the escrow fund shall be paid to CONTRACTOR on a quarterly basis. This payment will be made on the first settlement after the end of each quarter. Interest will be paid on the average daily balance in the account during each quarter. The interest rate will be established on the first day of the quarter and shall be the average yield on 91-day, 13-week U.S. Treasury Bills as established in the most recent weekly auction prior to the first day of the quarter by the Department of Treasury.

13. The CONTRACTOR agrees and it is mutually understood that if CONTRACTOR, or its employees and/or agents used in the performance of this Agreement, shall collect any sums of money from customers on account of bills rendered to customers by CARRIER, during the course of CONTRACTOR's operations, it will hold such money as a trustee for CARRIER and will hold it apart from its own funds and will deliver such money to CARRIER forthwith.

14. In the event either party commits a material breach of any term of this Agreement, the other party shall have the right to terminate this Agreement immediately and hold the party committing the breach liable for damages.

15. The CONTRACTOR shall exercise all diligent efforts to conduct its operation under this Agreement to assure continued satisfaction of CARRIER's customers.

16. As required by the ICC Lease and Interchange Regulations, this Agreement shall continue in effect for a period of thirty (30) days from the day and date first above-written, said term to be automatically renewed for successive thirty (30) day periods unless either party hereto shall give to the other written notice of cancellation thirty (30) days prior to the expiration of the initial term or any renewal thereof.

17. If for any reason, CONTRACTOR shall fail to complete transportation of commodities in transit, or abandons a shipment or otherwise subjects CARRIER to liabilities to shippers or governmental agencies on account of the acts or omissions of CONTRACTOR enroute, CONTRACTOR expressly agrees that CARRIER shall have the right to complete performance using the same or other equipment, and hold CONTRACTOR liable for the cost thereof and for any other damages. CONTRACTOR hereby waives any recourse against CARRIER for such action and agrees to reimburse CARRIER for any costs and expenses arising out of such completion of such trip, and to pay to CARRIER any damages for which CARRIER may be liable to shipper arising out of such breach of contract by CONTRACTOR.

18. This Agreement constitutes the entire Agreement and understanding between the parties and shall not be modified, altered, changed or amended in any respect unless in writing and signed by both parties.

19. The parties intend to create by this Agreement the relationship of CARRIER and INDEPENDENT CONTRACTOR and not an EMPLOYER-EMPLOYEE relationship. Neither the CONTRACTOR nor its employees are to be considered employees of the CARRIER at any time under any circumstances

for any purpose. Neither party is the agent of the other and neither party shall have the right to bind the other by contract or otherwise except as herein specifically provided.

20. A waiver by either party at any time of any of the terms, conditions, or covenants of this Agreement, or of any default or breach shall not be deemed or taken as a waiver at any time thereafter of the same or any other term, condition or covenant herein contained, nor of the strict and prompt performance thereof. Any term, condition or covenant herein contained that is held to be invalid by any court of competent jurisdiction shall be considered deleted from this Agreement, but such deletion shall in no way affect any other term, condition or covenant herein contained or the parties' obligations with respect thereto.
21. It is agreed that each and all of the rights or remedies under this Agreement are cumulative, and no one of them shall be exclusive of the other or exclusive of any remedies provided by law, and that exercise of one right, option or remedy by either party shall not impair that party's rights to any other right, option or remedy.

IN WITNESS WHEREOF, the parties hereto have executed this Agreement this ________ day of ________, 19____, and same shall be considered binding upon both parties and shall remain in full force and effect unless and until cancelled according to the terms of this Agreement.

______________________________	______________________________
CONTRACTOR	CARRIER
______________________________	______________________________
Witness	Witness

1:4.3 Independent Contractor Agreement: Professional Employee

THIS AGREEMENT made and entered into this ________ day of ________ 19___, by and between [EMPLOYER], a [STATE] Corporation having its principal place of business at [ADDRESS], (hereinafter called "the Company") and [EMPLOYEE], an individual having his/her principal place of business at [ADDRESS], (hereinafter called "Contractor").

WHEREAS, the Company is engaged in the business of counseling and assisting individuals with respect to admission to boarding schools, professional programs and institutions of higher learning; and

WHEREAS, Contractor is a licensed psychologist, having special knowledge, skill and competency in his/her field, relative to the needs of Company's clients; and

WHEREAS, the Company and Contractor desire to enter into an association whereby Contractor will provide services to Company's clients.

NOW THEREFORE, the Company and Contractor agree as follows:

1. *Contractor's Duties.* Contractor will provide counseling and/or psychological assessment services of the type normally provided by members of his/her profession, and as appropriate to the needs of Company's clients, to clients of the Company.

For purposes of this Agreement, the Company clients are defined as clients seeking and/or receiving psychological assessment and counseling services (possibly including related therapy) with respect to admission to boarding schools, professional programs or institutions of higher learning, during the term of the Agreement. Clients receiving therapy or other services from the Contractor, unrelated to admission to boarding schools, professional programs or institutions of higher learning, are clients of the Contractor.

2. *Compensation.* In consideration of the counseling and/or psychological assessment services provided by Contractor to Company's clients as outlined in section (1) above, the Company shall pay to Contractor a share of net fees (as defined hereinafter) collected from clients by the Company for said counseling services of the Contractor.

Net fees for purposes of this provision of this Agreement shall be determined as follows:

(a) The Company shall charge clients for counseling services provided to them by the Contractor at an appropriate rate from the schedule of rates prepared by the Company and approved by the Contractor.

(b) The Contractor shall assist the Company in billing clients for his/her services by promptly providing the Company with a written report on a biweekly basis, listing in said report the name of each client counseled by the Contractor during that period, the time such counseling session(s) occurred and the length of time of each counseling session.

(c) The Company shall bill clients for services rendered by Contractor along with, but on a separate invoice from, the Company's usual and regular bills to said clients. Fees collected from such billings are defined herein as gross fees.

(d) Net fees payable to the Contractor shall consist of gross fees recovered from clients, less 20% of all such gross fees for the Company corporate overhead.

(e) The Contractor's share of net fees shall be due and owing to the Contractor within 14 days of receipt of payment by the Company from any such client. The Company shall have no liability to Contractor for fees not collected, provided Company has properly billed for such fees.

3. *Overhead.* In consideration of the retention by the Company of 20% of Contractor's gross fees as defined in section (2) above, the Company shall provide to the Contractor at no additional cost:

(a) telephone, secretarial, and other appropriate office support as reasonably required by Contractor in performing his/her duties herein;

(b) listing of Contractor as associated with the Company on Company's stationery and any advertising or promotional material published and/or distributed by the Company;

(c) a special announcement to the Company's clients, announcing the Contractor's association with the Company;

(d) billing services as outlined in section 2(c), above, all of the foregoing at the Company's sole expense.

4. *Insurance.*

(a) Contractor shall be responsible for ensuring that (s)he maintains, at his/her own cost, professional malpractice liability insurance ("Malpractice Insurance") from a commercial carrier covering him/her (and naming the Company as an additional insured) against claims arising out of the performance of professional services hereunder in the minimum amounts required by law, or in the absence of such legally required amounts, in the minimum amount of $_________ per claim and a minimum aggregate annual amount of $_________; shall file all necessary reports and otherwise take all action necessary to maintain such Malpractice Insurance; and if such Malpractice Insurance is maintained on a "claims made" basis, shall maintain, at his/her own cost, tail or prior acts coverage to cover claims made after the termination of such Malpractice Insurance or of this Agreement for occurrences prior to any such termination. Contractor shall provide the Company with certificates evidencing such Malpractice Insurance and agree to notify the Company at least thirty (30) days in advance of any cancellation or modification of such Malpractice Insurance coverage.

(b) Company shall have the right to terminate this Agreement immediately upon verification that the insurance coverage required by Section 4(a) hereof is not maintained by Contractor.

5. *Relationship Between Parties.*

(a) It is the intent of the parties hereto that Contractor shall be considered to be an Independent Contractor with respect to the Company under this Agreement. The parties acknowledge that, except as expressly set forth herein, Contractor shall not be under the apparent or actual direction or control of the Company.

(b) Company shall have no duty hereunder to withhold income taxes or pay Social Security or unemployment taxes for Contractor. Contractor shall not be entitled to any salary or other compensation from the Company or to any employee benefits provided by the Company, including, but not limited to, disability, life insurance, pension and annuity benefits, educational allowances, professional membership dues, and sick, holiday and vacation pay. Contractor agrees to indemnify the Company for, and hold it harmless from, any liability related to any requirement for withholding income taxes or paying Social Security or unemployment taxes for Contractor unless a final decision by a court of law, with no appeals pending, determines that Contractor was, in fact, an employee of the Company and that the Company is liable for such taxes.

6. *Confidentiality and Non-Solicitation.*

 (a) During the term of this Agreement and any extensions thereof, Contractor agrees that (s)he will perform psychological assessment and counseling services of the type performed under this Agreement exclusively for and in association with the Company. The Company expressly recognizes that Contractor will maintain his/her own office and practice, and acknowledges that Contractor is free to provide any other professional services in conjunction with his/her own practice, provided such services create no conflict of interest.

 (b) During the term of this Agreement and any extensions thereof, the Company agrees to recommend the Contractor to all the Company clients who require psychological assessment and counseling services of the type performed by Contractor under this Agreement. However, the parties hereto expressly recognize that applicable professional rules require that clients of the Company be apprised that they are free to retain alternative psychological assessment and counseling services at their discretion.

 (c) During the term of this Agreement, any extension thereof, and for two (2) years following termination of this Agreement or any extension thereof, Contractor agrees to maintain in strictest confidence all information concerning the identity of any then-current Company client, and any client served by Contractor in association with the Company during the previous one (1) year; Company's methods and techniques for working with clients; and, any and all other trade secrets and confidential information of the Company.

 (d) Following termination of this Agreement and any extension thereof, Contractor agrees not to solicit or accept any then-current Company client, or any Company client serviced by Contractor during the previous one (1) year, on behalf of him/herself, or any other person, corporation, agency, or other entity performing the same or similar services as the Company, *provided, however,* that if such client was receiving therapy from Contractor prior to termination, Contractor may continue to provide such therapy at said client's option.

 (e) Contractor expressly acknowledges that money damages will be insufficient to rectify a breach of Subsection 6(a) through (d) above, and that it will be appropriate for the Company to seek equitable remedies in addition to money damages in the event of any such breach by Contractor.

7. *Termination.* This Agreement may be terminated by 30-day written notice of one party to the other. Termination by either party shall not affect Contractor's right to fees for services performed prior to termination, provided Contractor abides by the provisions of Section 6 above, nor shall termination by either party for any reason affect the Company's rights under Section 6, above.

8. *Entire Agreement.* This Agreement contains the entire agreement between the parties hereto, and there are no agreements or covenants between them not set

forth herein. All prior negotiations, agreements and understandings are superseded hereby. This agreement may not be amended or revised except by a writing signed by both parties hereto.

9. *Choice of Law/Choice of Forum.* This Agreement shall be construed in accordance with the laws of the State of _______________. All disputes arising hereunder shall be resolved by arbitration in accordance with the commercial arbitration rules of the American Arbitration Association.

Intending to be legally bound, the parties have entered this Agreement on the date first written above.

[EMPLOYER]

BY: ___________________________ ___________________________
[CONTRACTOR] [EMPLOYEE/ INDEPENDENT CONTRACTOR]

Title: ___________________________

Dated: ___________________________

1:4.4 Consulting Agreement

This Agreement is made as of this ________ day of ________, 19___ by and between [COMPANY'S NAME], a [STATE OF INCORPORATION] corporation, having its principal address at [ADDRESS] (the "Company") and [CONSULTANT'S NAME] (the "Consultant").

RECITALS

The Consultant has served the Company as a [PREVIOUS POSITION] continuously since [DATE].

Presently, the Company desires to obtain the benefit of the unique experience, ability and services of the Consultant upon the terms and conditions hereinafter set forth.

The Consultant is willing to render such consulting services and to devote his/her best efforts to the Company upon such terms and conditions.

WITNESSETH

NOW, THEREFORE, in consideration of the foregoing and of the mutual covenants contained herein, the parties hereto, each intending to be legally bound hereby, agree as follows:

1. *Nature of Consulting Services.* The Consultant agrees to act in a consulting capacity with respect to the business of the Company and the Company agrees to retain the Consultant in his/her capacity. The Consultant will perform such consulting services by rendering general advice and assistance to the Company regarding matters previously handled by the Consultant in his/her capacity as [PREVIOUS POSITION], including but not limited to [RECITATION OF AREAS OF EXPECTED ADVICE AND ASSISTANCE].
2. *Term.* The term of this Agreement shall extend for a [ ] year period commencing on the date hereof (the "Consulting Term").
3. *Compensation.* For all consulting services performed by the Consultant during the Consulting Term, the Company shall pay to the Consultant a consulting fee of $________ which shall be payable in [SCHEDULE OF PAYMENTS] during the Consulting Term. [IDENTIFY ANY ADDITIONAL COMPENSATION OR BENEFITS.]
4. *Title and Duties.* Notwithstanding any of the provisions set forth in Section 5 of this Agreement, the Consultant is retained and employed by the Company solely for the purposes set forth in this Agreement and his/her relation to the Company during the Consulting Term shall be that of an independent contractor solely responsible for the manner and means by which he/she carries out his/her duties hereunder. (S)He shall not have the power to bind the Company and he/she shall not be construed for any purpose to be an employee subject to the control and direction of the Company. In the performance of his/her duties hereunder, the Consultant shall not represent him/herself as an officer of, or use the title of an executive officer of the Company, but shall represent him/herself an independent "financial management consultant" to the Company. In the performance of his/her duties hereunder, the Consultant shall report to and shall take instructions from the Company's President and from the Board of Directors of the Company. The Consultant agrees to perform the services hereunder with good faith and in

the best interests of the Company with a view toward maintaining and enhancing the reputation and good standing of the Company.

5. *Time Requirements.* During the Consulting Term, the Consultant shall devote such time and attention to his/her duties hereunder as is reasonably required to provide satisfactory consulting services to the Company pursuant to this Agreement. Notwithstanding the foregoing, the time during which, and the locations at which, the Consultant shall perform his/her services hereunder shall be subject to the mutual agreement of the Consultant and the Company.

6. *Expenses.* The Consultant will be reimbursed by the Company for all reasonable expenses incurred by him/her in connection with the performance of his/her duties on behalf of the Company hereunder provided that the Consultant provides the Company with a reasonable accounting for such expenses. The reasonableness of such expenses shall be subject to the determination of the Company's Board of Directors.

7. *Agreement Not to Compete.* The Consultant agrees that during the Consulting Term and for a period of three years thereafter, he/she will not, directly or indirectly, in any capacity, render his/her services, engage or have a financial interest in any business which is competitive with any of those business activities in which the Company was engaged during his/her association with the Company, including, without limitation, the purchase and sale, distribution, marketing, brokering of or dealing in [ ]. If a court determines that the foregoing restrictions are too broad or otherwise unreasonable under applicable law, including with respect to time or space, the court is hereby requested and authorized by the parties hereto to revise the foregoing restriction to include the maximum restrictions allowable under the applicable law. For the purposes of Sections 7, 8, 9, 13 and 14 of this Agreement, the term "Company" refers to the Company and any incorporated or unincorporated subsidiaries or affiliates of the Company.

8. *Confidential Information.*

   (a) The Consultant has had and will have possession of or access to confidential information relating to the business of the Company, including but not limited to writings, equipment, processes, drawings, reports, manuals, invention records, financial information, business plans, customer lists, the identity of or other facts relating to prospective customers, inventory lists, arrangements with suppliers and customers, computer programs, or other material embodying trade secrets, customer or product information or technical or business information of the Company. All such information, other than any information which is in the public domain through no act or omission of the Consultant or which he is authorized to disclose, is referred to collectively as the "Company Information". The Consultant agrees that during the Consulting Term and for an indefinite period thereafter, he shall not (i) use or exploit in any manner the Company Information for him/herself or any other person, partnership, association, corporation or other entity other than the Company (ii) remove any Company Information, or any reproduction thereof, from the possession or control of the Company and (iii) treat Company Information otherwise than in a confidential manner.

   (b) All Company Information developed, created or maintained by the Consultant, alone or with others during the Consulting Term or thereafter shall remain at all times the exclusive property of the Company. The Consultant agrees to return to the Company all Company Information, and reproductions thereof, whether prepared by him/her or others, which are in his/her possession immediately upon request and in any event upon completion of the Consulting Term.

9. *Remedies*. The Consultant expressly agrees that the remedy at law for any breach of the foregoing will be inadequate and that upon breach of this provision, the Company shall be entitled as a matter of right to injunctive relief in any court of competent jurisdiction, in equity or otherwise, to enforce the specific performance of the Consultant's obligations under this provision without the necessity of proving the actual damage to the Company or the inadequacy of a legal remedy. The rights conferred upon the Company by the preceding sentence shall not be exclusive of any other rights or remedies which the Company may have at law, in equity or otherwise.

10. *Termination by the Company*. The Company shall have the right to terminate this Agreement upon 30 days' written notice to the Consultant as a result of (i) a material breach by the Consultant of any provision of this Agreement; (ii) the gross negligence, or willful malfeasance or misfeasance of the Consultant in the performance of his/her duties hereunder; or (iii) the Consultant's incapacity for a continuous period of 90 days during the Consulting Term which renders him/her unable to perform his/her duties hereunder. Upon the expiration of such 30-day period, the Company shall be relieved of any further obligations hereunder.

11. *Termination by the Consultant*. The Consultant shall have the right to terminate this Agreement upon 30 days' written notice to the Company at any time as a result of a material breach of this Agreement by the Company. Upon the expiration of such 30-day period, the Consultant shall be relieved of any further obligations hereunder with the exception of the obligations contained in Sections 7, 8 and 9 of this Agreement.

12. *Life Insurance*. The Company shall assign to the Consultant, for no consideration, whatever rights it has in a $________ life insurance policy on the Consultant's life at the time when such policy is subject to renewal; provided, however, that the Company's obligations hereunder are subject to the conditions of the policy regarding assignments thereof.

13. *Prior Agreements*. Any and all prior agreements or arrangements entered into between the Company and the Consultant are hereby terminated and each of the parties hereto releases and discharges the other from any and all obligations and liabilities existing under or by reason of any such agreements. It is the intention of the Company and the Consultant that this Agreement shall supersede and shall be in lieu of any and all prior agreements or understandings between them.

14. *General*.

    (a) *Binding effect*. The rights and obligations of the Company under this Agreement shall inure to the benefit of and shall be binding upon the Company's successors, transferees and assigns. This Agreement may not be assigned by the Consultant.

    (b) *Entire agreement; modification*. This instrument sets forth the entire understanding of the parties with respect to the consulting services to be provided by the Consultant and no other modifications, additions or undertakings shall be enforceable unless contained in a subsequent written agreement signed by the parties hereto.

(c) *Enforceability.* In the event any portion or portions of this Agreement are declared to be void for illegality, then the remaining portions of the Agreement shall remain and shall be valid and binding, unless the purpose and intent of this Agreement is substantially distorted by the deletion of the void portion or portions, in which event this entire Agreement shall be void.

(d) *Notices.* Any and all notices referred to herein shall be in writing and shall be deemed to have been given when personally delivered or when mailed, registered or certified mail, postage prepaid, to the following addresses:

To consultant:

[NAME]

[ADDRESS]

To the company:

[NAME]

[ADDRESS]

(e) *Governing law.* This Agreement shall be construed under and shall be governed by the laws of the State of _________.

(f) *Duration.* Notwithstanding the termination of the Consulting Term, this Agreement shall continue to bind the parties for so long as any obligations remain under this Agreement, and in particular, the Consultant shall continue to be bound by the terms of Sections 7, 8 and 9.

(g) *Waiver.* No waiver by the Company of any breach by the Consultant of this Agreement shall be construed to be a waiver as to succeeding breaches.

IN WITNESS WHEREOF, the parties have executed this Agreement as of the day and year first written above.

[COMPANY'S NAME]

BY: ____________________________

CONSULTANT

BY: ____________________________
[CONSULTANT'S NAME]

Chapter 2

Hiring and Evaluating Employees

Ask any Human Resources professional what their major objective is and they will respond by stating, "selecting and retaining qualified employees." As the workplace and the workforce change and diversify and government regulations continue to guide corporate life, having the best staff is an organization's most important asset.

This chapter provides sample employment applications and performance evaluations. It also examines approaches to employee discipline in both traditional and non-traditional progressive manners. Sample employee handbook business rules of conduct and proactive, participatory discipline and grievance procedures for both union and non-union environments are included in step-by-step format. Retention of employees often includes counseling and guidelines for affirmative discipline. Both employer and employee responsibilities are presented with samples of policy statements and peer review procedures. To assist organizations in assessing their workplace, a sample employee survey is incuded that provides for essential confidentiality.

2:1 Job Applications

It is not an unfair observation that many companies give little or no consideration to the content of their job application forms. Many either develop a form with very little forethought, or even worse, borrow a form from somewhere else, white-out that company's name and type in their own. There are important negative and positive reasons why you should not do that.

On the negative side, the variety of anti-discrimination laws impact upon information that companies used to require routinely from job applicants. For example, not only can you not inquire about such protected information as race, color, religion, age and disability, but even inquiries concerning an applicant's arrest record or national guard status may be viewed as illegal.

On the positive side, a thoughtful and well constructed application can elicit much useful information, without running afoul of any anti-discrimination or other statute.

2:1.1 Sample Employment Application

Once candidates are identified and invited for an interview or a series of tests, the most important document becomes the employment application form. Regardless of job level or whether a résumé is supplied, employers should have each job candidate complete an employee application in order to:

- *Provide uniformity.* By having applicants fill out a standard application, uniformity is imposed on the employment process. Interviewers will have solid background information and can tailor the interview accordingly.
- *Avoid legal problems.* The law requires all applicants to be treated the same (i.e., in a fair and respectful manner). In many organizations, the senior staff tends to be white males. Thus, an organization runs a higher risk of being accused of a Civil Rights Act violation if, for example, it exempts only senior managers from filling out employment applications.
- *Seek the truth.* Résumés can be structured to fit applicants' needs and to hide any objectionable background or weaknesses. The interviewer may miss gaps in work history, for instance, because the résumé is functional in approach or provides only years of employment. The employee application, on the other hand, asks applicants to list in reverse chronological order all past work experience and to provide months of employment as well as years. Additionally, information on an application is more likely to be true than on a résumé because the application says that falsification of information may lead to termination.
- *Obtain information.* The application is a good way for personnel to obtain information before ever meeting with applicants (unless the decision is made to meet with applicants before the form is completed). School information, personal and professional references, and salary information are all important bits of data that can be obtained before meeting an applicant.

Occasionally, an applicant may submit salary history with a résumé, but more often than not, it is not included. Additionally, it is recommended that applicants are requested to state a desired salary on the application. Therefore, early in the recruitment process it may be determined whether the applicant has realistic salary expectations. Even if the applicant writes in "open" or leaves the space blank, there is still a written reminder for personnel to discuss salary during the screening interview.

The employment application, such as the one that follows, is an important document that can be used effectively in several ways. First, the employment application, through its graphics and the information it asks for, immediately gives applicants a sense of the company's values. As candidates address each question on the application, they will gain an understanding of the organization. For example, some applicants object when an application requests a Social Security number. They believe that the potential employer is too curious and may go to great lengths to delve into their background (and will use the Social Security number to do so).

How can personnel address this issue ahead of time? The answer is simple. Applicants' Social Security numbers must not be requested before they become members of the organization. Therefore, the employee application form should not ask for the Social Security number.

Second, the employment application is a systematic way to obtain relevant information and to quickly process new employees. Page four of the employee application that is provided is an employment form checklist. It lists the items that personnel must obtain to start a file on each new employee and to get him or her on the payroll (otherwise known as "in-processing"). Of course, this information will be obtained only after the applicant is hired.

Third, the employee application asks the potential staff member to become a member of the team. To protect the company, the application can state that the employee will be hired under the at-will employment doctrine, unless the employer has bargained that right away under a union contract. The form can also warn applicants that their references will be checked, their fingerprints and photographs will be taken, and, once employed, they will be required to keep all information about the organization's customers confidential.

Fourth, the employee application is a legal written reference in itself. The written statements that were attested to on a particular date by the applicant become a permanent record that may prove useful some time in the *future*. It is extremely important that it is treated as such; therefore, all information should be reviewed at the time the form is filled out for correctness, completeness, and accuracy. Additionally, the application must meet all current legal requirements. The application should be periodically scrutinized to ensure total compliance with the law.

The sample employment application provided does not ask for school attendance dates. Although there is no law that prohibits this question, there are laws that protect applicants from discrimination based on age. Calculating an individual's age from school attendance dates is obviously fairly easy.

Last, the employee applicant form provides another way in which to gain insight into the applicant. How is the penmanship? Is there evidence of sloppiness? Are the answers written carefully and are they well thought out? In order to obtain accurate answers to these questions, all applicants must complete the form in front of reception area personnel. Otherwise, it is possible that someone else may actually complete it. Perhaps the applicant cannot read or write. The selection process is too important to take anything for granted.

The employee application under no circumstances replaces the résumé. The purpose of the recruitment and selection process is to learn as much about the candidates as possible. If the applicant provides a résumé or letters (even those that start "To Whom It May Concern"), accept them and make these items part of the applicant's file.

APPLICATION FOR EMPLOYMENT

APPLICATION FOR EMPLOYMENT

Federal and state laws prohibit discrimination in employment practices on account of race, creed, color, national origin, ancestry, sex, age, marital status, veteran status or handicap.

Last Name, First Name, MI	Date

Is any additional information relative to change of name, use of an assumed name or nickname necessary to enable a check on your work record? Explain.

Present Address (Include Street, City, State and Zipcode)	Phone #

Last Previous Address (if at present address less than two years)

Are you over 17 years of age?	If under 18, do you have working papers?
Are you legally employable within the United States at the present time?	Have you ever been convicted of a crime? Give details.
Have you ever applied to this organization for a job before? If yes, when? Were you ever employed by this organization?	What brought you to this organization? ☐ newspaper ad ☐ friend/employee ☐ employment agency ☐ on my own ☐ school ☐ other source ☐ state employ. service
Position Desired:	Salary Desired: $
Status (circle one): full/parttime/summer	Earliest start date:

Work Experience—account for all employment since high school or last ten years, whichever is less, with most recent experience first.

From Mo./Yr.	To Mo./Yr.	Employer Name, Address	Principal Duties	Salary Beg.	Salary End	Supervisor's Name, Title, #	Reason for lvg.

Account for all unemployment since leaving school and between positions for the last ten years.

From Mo./Yr.	To Mo./Yr.	State what you were doing	Persons other than relatives who can confirm unemployment (give tel #)

APPLICATION FOR EMPLOYMENT **page 2**

Education Background

Name	Address	Course of Study	Graduate? If Yes, state degree
High School:			
College/Tech/Bus Scl:		Major: Minor:	
Graduate School:		Major: Minor:	

Are you still in school? If yes, where?

How many courses are you currently taking? Number of credits:

What is the course of study?

Special Skills (fill in only if job related):

Do you speak any foreign languages? Read? Write?

If there are any positions or types of positions for which you should not be considered or job duties you cannot perform in a reasonable manner because of a physical, mental or medical disability, please describe.

Personal Reference: Give the name, address and telephone number of a personal reference other than a relative or employer.

Name	Address	Telephone #

Employee Responsibility to the organization. (Please read before signing.)

As a condition of my employment, I accept the principle that the welfare of the organization depends upon the conduct and honesty of the members of the staff and upon the trust and confidence of the public. Our customers rightly expect honesty, security and confidentiality in their affairs. I therefore agree to the following:

1. I agree to give no unauthorized information relative to the accounts of the organization or its relation with others, and to discuss no matters of a confidential nature relating to the organization's affairs unless such discussion is in the necessary course of the organization's business and is in accordance with the organization's policy.

2. I also agree to inform the management of the organization, without delay, of any fraud, false entry, substantial error, embezzlement or employee misconduct, which I discover or know to have taken place in any records, property or funds of the organization, and to report any transaction or matter that seems damaging to the organization.

I acknowledge and understand that any violation of this Agreement may result in the termination of my employment.

Name Signature Date

APPLICATION FOR EMPLOYMENT **page 3**

Please also read before signing. If you have any questions regarding this statement, please ask them of any interviewer before signing.

In the event of my employment with this organization, I will comply with all the rules and regulations as set forth in the organization's policy manual or other communications distributed to all staff members. I understand that such employment is conditioned upon a favorable health evaluation which may include a physical examination by a doctor selected by the organization and to which I hereby assent. I further agree to complete all necessary forms in that regard. Additionally I authorize the organization to supply my employment record, in whole or in part, and in confidence, to any prospective employer, government agency, or other party, with a legal and proper interest.

I certify that all statements made by me on this application are true and complete to the best of my knowledge and that I have withheld nothing that would, if disclosed, affect this application unfavorably. I understand this falsification could result in termination of my employment. In consideration of my employment, I agree to conform to the rules and regulations of the organization. I agree that my employment and compensation can be terminated, with or without cause, and with or without notice, at any time, at the option of either the organization or myself. This is not a contract of employment. Any individual who is hired may voluntarily leave employment upon proper notice and may be terminated by the employer at any time. Any oral or written statements to the contrary are hereby expressly disavowed and should not be relied upon by any prospective or existing employee. I further understand and agree that any employment will be at the sole discretion of the organization. If accepted for employment, I agree to have my fingerprints and photograph taken for the purposes of identification and the maintenance of internal security. I understand that past employers/educational institutions and/or the military will be contacted for references. For reference purposes,

you may ☐ you may not ☐ contact my present employer.

I hereby acknowledge that I have read the above statement and understand the same.

____
Applicant's Signature

____
Date

APPLICATION FOR EMPLOYMENT **page 4**

For Personnel Use Only: Employment Form Check List For Employment Processing

Employee No.	Date of Hire	Department Name	Dept. No.	Job Code
Pay Grade	Title	Base Annual Sal	Hourly Sal	Wkly Sal
Review Date	Replace ☐	Req. No.	EEO Job Code	Monthly Sal
Status	New Pos. ☐	Referral Source	Ethnic Code	Handicap Code
Full Time ☐ Part Time ☐ Per Diem ☐ Summer ☐	Hours:	Social Security Number: Date of Birth: (mo, day, year) / /	Marital Status Single ☐ Married ☐	Sex Male ☐ Fem ☐ Veteran Code

Identification Card Number: Date issued:

	yes	no		yes	no
I-9 Form			Employment Benefits Package		
Social Security Card			Hospitalization Card		
Proof of Birth Date			Surgical/Major Medical Card		
Working Papers			Life Insurance Card		
Diploma/Degree			Supplemental Life Insurance Card		
Transcript			Long Term Disability Card		
NYState/City Tax Form			W4 Tax Form		

Emergency Notification Data:

Name(s)

Address

Relationship | Telephone Number with Area Code:

References Received (type, date and by whom):

Processed by:

Date:

2:1.2 Sample Position Screening Applications

Screening applications are often used for positions that require volume screening and an initial testing process. The form that follows is an abbreviated version of a screening application that can be used for several positions. Such forms provide a brief, effective way to screen candidates. Applicants who fail to meet basic requirements for a position during screening frequently do not move on in the selection process.

This form is a short application form that might also be used to prescreen a large number of applicants without going through a lengthier process. This form may also be used as a stand-alone document for part-time employees because it contains information that relates to specific job requirements. The form asks about work availability in terms of hours and days, as well as location and transportation arrangements, so that these items will be discussed and sorted out early in the interview process. The interviewer may not wish to go through the process of requesting (or confirming) other information about the applicant's (for example) education that he or she might want for full-time employees; thus these areas are left off the application.

2:1.2A Secretarial Screening Application Form

SCREENING APPLICATION (ABBREVIATED VERSION)

SCREENING APPLICATION FOR SECRETARIAL CANDIDATES

Salary Desired: $__________

Name: ____

Address: ____

____

Telephone Number Home (   ) ____________________

Job (   ) ____________________

Skills:

Typing: ______ WPM

Steno: ______ WPM

Word Processing Equipment Used:

☐ IBM PC (software) __________

☐ Wang (type) ______________

☐ Linear

☐ Multimate

☐ Dec Mate

☐ Other ____________________

Years of secretarial experience: __________

1 2 3 4 5

2:1.2B Large Applicant Pool Prescreening Form

SHORT APPLICATION FORM (PRESCREENING FOR LARGE APPLICANT POOL)

APPLICANT DATA SHEET		Date of Completion:
Last Name:	First Name:	Middle Initial:

Address:	Apt. #:	City:	State:	Zip:

Are you 18 years of age or older? Yes _____ No _____	If no, please state your age:

Have you ever worked for this organization before? Yes _____ No _____ If yes, please give dates, department, location, title, and dates of employment here. Then list your three most recent positions on the lines provided below.

From/to Dates	Position/Department	Location	Title/Description of Duties

Position(s) desired:	Location(s) desired:

	When are you available? Day	Hours
How did you come to us?	Monday	
How will you get to work? How long will it take you each way?	Tuesday	
	Wednesday	
Comments (for Personnel Dept. only):	Thursday	
	Friday	
	Saturday	
	Sunday	

2:1.3 The Interview and Interview Report

The interview report form that follows is an example of a form that trains staff members to become effective interviewers in a painless and effortless way. Illegal questions, such as "Do you have any children," "Are you married," or "What does your husband do," are usually asked without malicious intent. Most of the time they are asked because the interviewer has run out of questions.

If an interviewer can follow a well-structured form, he or she will never be at a loss for words during the interview, and, more importantly, will avoid the traps that frequently lead to the asking of illegal questions.

With structured interview report forms, the interviewer will be more at ease with the entire interviewing process. The interview report form provides categories—for example, work experience, education, interests—to help interviewers formulate questions. The interviewer will become a better listener while using this form, since he or she will concentrate more on the interviewee's answers instead of worrying about the next questions to ask. The report form will also reduce the interviewer's fear of omitting important questions. Once the categories or questions listed in a form are covered, there is no reason to search for more questions.

However, the interview report form should never be used during the interview, but only to help prepare for the interview. Taking notes during an interview encourages applicants to learn how to read sideways or upside down. It creates the wrong environment, since note taking encourages people to be more guarded about answering the questions they are asked. Questions can be written down on a separate piece of paper that link the form categories to relevant questions that pertain to the specific position applied for. The report form should be completed immediately after the interview.

2:1.3A Interview Report

INTERVIEW REPORT		Rating Code: Favorable—Unfavorable 1 2 3 4 5
Applicant Name ______		For Position ______
Interviewer Name ______		Date: ______
Category	**Rating**	**Comments**
Appearance Greeting Self-expression Responsiveness		
Work Experience Relevance Skill Level Process/Result Orient. Motivation Interpersonal Skills Initiative Leadership Growth and Development Teamwork		
Education Sufficiency Relevance Intellectual development		
Background Basic Values and Goals Attitudes toward Achievement Self-image		
Present Activities and Interests Management of time Energy level Maturity and Judgment Intellectual Growth Diversity of Interests Social Skills Leadership Basic Values and Goals		
Strengths:		Weaknesses:
Summary and Recommendations:		
Final Rating ☐		

2:1.3B Interview Report and Assessment Form
Job Applicant Report and Assessment

Interviewer:	Date:
Applicant's Name:	Position:

Interviewer's Name:	First Impression (Check One): Excel-lent	Very Good	Good	Border-line	Unsatis-factory

If we offer you a position, do you have a dependable way to get to work? Please describe. ______

______

Have you ever worked extra hours or off hours? Did you mind that kind of schedule? ______

______

What is it about our organization that makes you want to join us? ______

______

______

What makes you interested in leaving your current (or most recent) employer? ______

______

______

Describe a typical day on your current (or most recent) job. ______

______

______

______

What do (did) you like about this employer? ______

______

______

What do (did) you dislike? ______

______

On your application you list your reason for leaving (name of organization) as ______.

Please explain. ______

______

______

How many days have you missed from work or school during the past 12 months? Explain. ______

______

______

JOB APPLICANT REPORT AND ASSESSMENT page 2

If you had not taken your last job, what would you be doing at this time? ______

______

______

______

What do you like best about your current (most recent) job? ______

______

______

______

What do you like least? ______

______

______

______

What has been your greatest accomplishment in your current (most recent) job? ______

______

______

______

What were you doing between ______ (date) and ______ (date) ? (To be asked if there are any gaps in employment of a month or more duration.) ______

______

______

What was your last performance review rating? ______ Date? ______

What comments did your supervisor make at that time? ______

______

Describe your relationship with that supervisor. ______

______

Are you planning any trips in the foreseeable future? If yes, please describe. ______

______

______

Overall Rating (Check one):	Excellent	Very Good	Good	Borderline	Unsatisfactory

2:1.4 Reference Checks and Job Offers

There is more concern about references today than ever before. The worry is twofold: (1) employers are concerned that bad references may lead to legal action, and (2) applicants are now aware of the legal issues involved in reference checks and think that references are not treated seriously. The result is a greater willingness among applicants to risk résumé and/or application "embellishments."

The potential employer, therefore, must get to know the applicants, and can do so with reference checks. Three sample reference forms are provided:

1. Education verification (2:1.4A);
2. Employment verification (2:1.4B);
3. Telephone reference check guide (2:1.4C); and
4. Job Offer Letter (2:1.4D).

The telephone reference check continues to be a good source for verifying the candidate's reputation. Even though employers are not legally required to discuss a current or former employee with prospective employers (because of the risks involved), more often than not it is possible to obtain colorful, accurate information about the applicant. Note that the form provided for a telephone reference check includes a statement, to be signed by the applicant, that gives permission to the prospective employer to obtain information and to hold the former employer harmless. This form should be signed by the applicant before the reference is obtained. For best results, the candidate's immediate supervisor should be contacted.

Because of their explicit instructions, reference check forms themselves can train staff who are responsible for obtaining reference checks. They also serve as good follow-up documents, if questions are raised during the recruitment and selection process.

An example of a job offer letter that should be generated by an effective personnel department is found at 2:1.4D. The name and address of each applicant who is to be offered a position would be inserted in the appropriate spaces.

The name of the department, job title, starting date, and salary can be individually inserted as well. In fact, if the appropriate database software is used, all the data can be inserted at once, thus ensuring that transcription errors are not made while the new employee's file is set up.

The job offer is an organization's most important means of communication. The job offer letter conveys to the applicant that the offer is in "good faith" and that he or she is highly regarded by the organization. The job offer letter has other purposes as well.

Without a job offer letter, how would it be determined whether or not the applicant understood the terms and conditions of the job offer? With lower-level positions, there is a greater risk that the offer will be misunderstood. Nothing is worse than having to deal with a new employee who questions the first paycheck, recalling that he or she was promised more money. With a good job offer letter, risk of misunderstanding can be reduced or eliminated altogether.

The job offer letter also makes applicants feel like their arrival is important to the organization. It allows applicants to share this feeling and the news about the new job with family and friends. Adding to the job offer letter's significance is that so few organizations give an offer in writing, especially at the lower levels. Therefore, those organizations that do so will truly shine.

2:1.4A Education Verification

Employer's Request for Information

The EMPLOYER will fill in the appropriate areas and send this form to the college, together with a stamped, self-addressed return envelope.

Date ______________________

TO BE RETURNED BY THE SCHOOL TO

NAME AND ADDRESS OF SCHOOL

EMPLOYER ______________________

EMPLOYER REPRESENTATIVE ______________________

ADDRESS ______________________

____

ATTN: OFFICE OF THE DEAN

REQUEST TO SCHOOL: The individual named below is being considered for employment as ______________________ (type of position)

Applicant indicates attendance at above school. Your cooperation in furnishing the following information will expedite consideration of the applicant.

APPLICANT'S NAME AND ADDRESS Last (Fill in) First (Fill in) Class Number (1)				ON REGISTER OF THIS SCHOOL FROM MONTH YEAR TO MONTH YEAR
APPLICANT INDICATES ATTENDANCE AT THIS COLLEGE FROM TO				DATE OF BIRTH AS GIVEN BY APPLICANT (FOR SCHOOL RECORD IDENTIFICATION AND VERIFICATION) MONTH DAY YEAR
GRADUATION DATE		TYPE OF DIPLOMA		ATTENDANCE DURING LAST TWO SEMESTERS (if available) NUMBER OF DAYS ABSENT _____ TERM ENDING _____ NUMBER OF DAYS ABSENT _____ TERM ENDING _____
TOTAL NUMBER IN GRADUATING CLASS	CUMULATIVE AVERAGE	NUMERICAL STANDING	QUARTILE	

IF THIS APPLICANT IS NO LONGER IN ATTENDANCE, GIVE APPROXIMATE DATE AND REASON FOR LEAVING SCHOOL

HAS APPLICATION BEEN MADE FOR ADMISSION TO GRADUATE SCHOOL OR OTHER SPECIAL SCHOOL? NO ☐ YES ☐ If yes: [DAY ☐ EVE ☐]	GIVE NAME OF EACH SCHOOL TO WHICH APPLICATION HAS BEEN MADE

This information supplied below will be treated as confidential by the employer.

REMARKS: (AWARDS, HONORS, CLASS OFFICES HELD, ACTIVITIES, GENERAL ATTITUDE, OUTSTANDING QUALIFICATIONS OR TRAITS SUCH AS DEPENDABILITY, COOPERATION AND COURTESY.)

____

____

____

____

(ADDITIONAL SPACE ON REVERSE SIDE)

IS APPLICANT RECOMMENDED FOR FAVORABLE CONSIDERATION? ______________________

SIGNED ______________________ TITLE ______________________ DATE ______________

2:1.4B Sample Employment Verification Letter

EMPLOYMENT VERIFICATION

(Date)

Personnel Manager
(Name of Company)

New York, New York 10017

To Whom It May Concern:

The applicant named below has applied to us for employment. He/she claims to have been employed by you as indicated and has authorized release of all information requested.

The information you furnish will be considered in strict confidence, and we will be pleased to reciprocate at any time.

Sincerely yours,

Manager, Personnel

Applicant's Name ______________________ SS# ____________
Claims Employment as ______________________ From __________ To __________
Employed as ______________________ From __________ To __________
Salary: $ ____________ per ____________
Job Performance ______________________
Reason for Termination of Employment ______________________
____
Remarks (Attendance, Attitude, etc.) ______________________
____
____
Signed ______________________ Title ______________ Date __________

2:1.4C Telephone Reference Check Guide

TELEPHONE REFERENCE CHECK GUIDE

Applicant: ______ Date: ______

Reference From: ______ Position: ______

Company: ______ City/State: ______ Tel: ______

I would like to verify some of the information given to us by ______ who is applying for employment with our company.

What are the dates of his/her employment with you? From/To ______

Please describe his/her job function: ______

Please describe his/her performance: ______

How would you describe his/her:

Dependability on completing assignments: ______

Supervision requirements: ______

Attendance: ______

Ability to take responsibility: ______

Work attitude: ______

Working relationship with co-workers: ______

Advancement potential: ______

What are his/her strengths? ______

What are his/her limitations? ______

Describe any personal difficulties that adversely affected his/her work: ______

What were his/her earnings? ______

TELEPHONE REFERENCE CHECK GUIDE **page 2**

Why did he/she leave your company? ______________________________

____

Would you reemploy? Yes? _____ No: _____ (Why not?) ______________________________

____

Is there anything else that we should know about? ______________________________

____

Completed by (Applicant): ______________________________

I give permission to ______________________________ to obtain employment references necessary to make a hiring decision and hold persons giving reference harmless and free of any and all liability that could result from this process.

Applicant: ______________________________

Date: ______________________________

2:1.4D Sample Job Offer Letter

(Name)
(Address)

Dear (First Name):

As you and I have discussed, it is with great pleasure that I provide you with additional details regarding our offer of employment to join (name of department) of (name of company).

To summarize our understanding, discussed below are the details of our arrangements.

You will be joining the (name of department) as a (title). You will receive (amount) on a biweekly basis.

In addition, after completing one year of service with our company, you will be eligible to participate in the bonus program. Although the company does not guarantee that a bonus will be paid, and reserves the right to cancel the bonus payment at any time, the company has customarily paid a bonus in December. The bonus is based on individual performance.

On the first business day following the completion of three full months of service, you will become eligible for medical and insurance benefits.

It is important to note that employment at our company is at will, and subject to termination at any time, by the company or yourself, with or without cause.

I understand that you will begin work on (date). This offer is, of course, contingent upon satisfactory proof of permission to work in this country, and the receipt of satisfactory references.

If you begin work on (date), you will receive your first salary payment on (date).

We are looking forward to having you join us.

Sincerely,

2:1.5 Employment Agency Agreements

If an organization seeks the assistance of employment agencies (often called recruiting firms or, more correctly, contingency agencies), a letter should be sent to them that states the terms and conditions under which the agreement will work and the basis for fee payment. An organization should not assume that if such a letter were not sent to or received from an agency that a "contract" does not exist. The courts have consistently ruled that at the moment an organization asks (or allows) an agency to help it find a candidate, an agreement has been struck. Instead of relying on recall about the terms and conditions and the payment schedule, an organization should use a fee agreement such as the one at 2:1.5A.

The fee agreement should include an equal employment organization compliance statement (see 2:1.5B) as well as a copy of a telephone reference form (see 2:1.4C). The compliance statement helps monitor employment agencies' and executive recruiters' EEO compliance.

Once in a while, agencies will resist personnel's requests to seek references, even if the request is included in the fee agreement (see item one of the fee agreement at 2:1.5A) that they have signed and returned. Personnel should ask the agency to explain the steps they take in recruiting candidates. Whatever agencies seek an organization's business, they often give assurances that their candidate will be thoroughly checked out before they are interviewed. Once agencies gain an organization's confidence, however, the reference checking part of the agreement is sometimes forgotten. Occasionally, even when six-figure positions are involved, candidates are never seen (much less checked out) by the agency providing the introduction.

An executive recruiter working on a retainer basis does not require a fee agreement, since a recruiter will automatically send a letter to the organization following their discussions. The letter will include a proposal and specify the terms and conditions under which the organization and the recruiter will work. In addition, personnel is frequently asked to sign and return a copy of the letter.

2:1.5A Employment Agency Fee Agreement

FEE AGREEMENT

Subject to your agreement to the terms and conditions contained herein, ________________ Company agrees to pay to you a referral fee, as more fully described herein, for each job candidate employed by ________________, for not less than 30 days, as a direct result of your referral to ____ of such candidate.

1. Prior to referring a candidate to ________________, you will, in addition to verifying the candidate's former or current employment, verify that the candidate has permission to accept employment in the United States. Upon request from ________________, you agree to provide written confirmation of such verification, in form satisfactory to ________________.

2. Company shall have sole discretion, taking into account any factors of its choosing, to accept or reject any such candidate for employment. ________________ shall have no obligation to discuss with or provide reasons for its decisions with respect to any candidate, whether before or after the commencement of employment of such candidate, to you, the candidate, or any other party.

3. If a candidate referred to ________________ by you is employed as a direct result of such referral, ________________ will conditionally pay to you a referral fee, which fee will be deemed to be fully earned by you on the ninety-first day of the candidate's continuous employment with ________________ in accordance with the following schedule:

Initial Annual Base Salary	*Fee*
$10,000 to 10,999	10% of initial annual base salary
11,000 to 11,999	11% of initial annual base salary
12,000 to 12,999	12% of initial annual base salary
13,000 to 13,999	13% of initial annual base salary
14,000 to 14,999	14% of initial annual base salary
15,000 to 15,999	15% of initial annual base salary
16,000 to 16,999	16% of initial annual base salary
17,000 to 17,999	17% of initial annual base salary
18,000 to 18,999	18% of initial annual base salary
19,000 to 19,999	19% of initial annual base salary
20,000 or above	20% of initial annual base salary

4. If the employment of a candidate employed by ________________ as a direct result of a referral by you terminates, for any reason, prior to the ninety-first (91st) day following the commencement of such employment, you agree to refund the unearned portion of the fee in accordance with the following schedule:

	Refund
Within 30 days of starting date	Full
After 30 days but within 60 days of starting date	2/3
After 60 days but within 90 days of starting date	1/3

5. No amendment, modification, or waiver of any of the terms of this agreement, or any consent to any departure from the terms of this agreement, shall be effective unless approved in writing by the party to be charged, and shall not by any act, delay, omission, or otherwise be deemed to have waived any provision of this agreement.

6. This agreement may be terminated at any time by either party hereto upon written or oral notice to such effect from one party to the other; provided, however, that no such termination shall be effective with respect to rights and obligations of the parties hereto arising prior to the effective date of such termination.

7. This agreement shall be governed by, and construed in accordance with, the laws of the state of ________________.

By: ____
Name Title

Accepted and agreed to:

Agency

By: ____
Name Title

2:1.5B EEO Compliance Statement

EQUAL EMPLOYMENT OPPORTUNITY COMPLIANCE STATEMENT

1. ________________ will not discriminate against any applicant for employment because of race, creed, color, sex, age, national origin, or handicap. This agency agrees to post in conspicuous places, available to applicants for employment, notices setting forth the provisions of this nondiscrimination clause.

2. This agency will, in all solicitations or advertisements for employees placed by or on behalf of ________________, state that all qualified applicants will receive consideration for employment without regard to race, creed, color, sex, age, national origin, or handicap.

3. In the event of this agency's noncompliance with the nondiscrimination clauses or with any of such rules, regulations, or orders, our working agreement may be canceled, terminated, or suspended.

________________________ ____________ ________________________
Signature Date Name

____

________________________ ________________________
Position Address

2:2 Employee Evaluations and Discipline

As with employment applications, so too with evaluations, many companies seem to borrow evaluation forms from other corporations or professional associations or books, with little thought as to whether the criteria on those evaluations measure anything meaningful or useful to their particular organizations or departments. Thoughtless evaluations that nevertheless affect pay and promotion, can lead to accusations of job discrimination while poorly conceived and constructed evaluations can hurt employment morale without providing useful information for either the manager or the subordinate being evaluated.

In the area of employee discipline, there are two predominate schools of thought today. First, there is the traditional, or punitive disciplinary approach where rules are laid down for employees to follow, and when they violate those rules, employees are punished. Typically, discipline follows a three or four step procedure: (1) verbal warning, (2) written warning, (3) suspension without pay, and (4) finally, job termination.

By contrast, many companies are adopting so-called affirmative discipline programs. The philosophy underlying an affirmative discipline program is that the employer and employee can agree together on the parameters of proper job performance. Under this model, instead of a written warning, an employee may be asked to participate in a written evaluation of that employee's shortcomings and the means and methods for correcting those shortcomings. This evaluation then becomes a sort of contract which both sides sign, and to which the employee is expected to adhere going forward. Similarly, instead of a suspension without pay, an affirmative discipline program typically will allow for a day off with pay during which the employee is expected to decide whether continuing in the job is in his or her best interests.

Similarly, new approaches to employee attendance and absenteeism have been developed in recent years. The most noteworthy is the so-called no-fault attendance policy. Under this type of policy, an employee can have a specified number of absences, before that employee's job is in jeopardy. There is no need for the employer or the employee to fuss with considerations about whether a particular absence is excused or unexcused, justified or unjustified.

Affirmative discipline and no-fault attendance policies are not for every organization.

2:2.1 Employee Performance Appraisals

The performance appraisal process is initiated by management. Frequently, appraisals are considered necessary, but they are often implemented only because everyone else is using them. Before taking steps to establish a performance appraisal process, an organization should determine whether one would actually be appropriate.

Introducing a performance appraisal form without caution may be harmful to the organization in terms of lost morale, and may also lead to costly litigation. Sometimes organizations are unaware that performance appraisals are considered tests and thus are subject to the same legal scrutiny as the tests used for recruitment. In addition, the process must be fair and open to question by staff members who feel "slighted" because of the way in which they were treated. Of course, employees may still claim that they were discriminated against in their performance appraisals, even if the appraisal process seems to be beyond reproach.

A performance appraisal program is inherently flawed for other reasons as well. When employees are evaluated, they put total responsibility for the appraisal on the person who is evaluating them. The person doing the evaluations, meanwhile, holds the environment accountable for any performance discrepancies. Also, the whole performance appraisal process operates under the assumption that no one is perfect. People, being people, have a hard time accepting criticism.

Nevertheless, a performance appraisal program has many important purposes. These, as well as the basic forms used by an appraisal program, are discussed in this section.

Reasons for maintaining a performance appraisal program include:

- To measure an employee's performance.
- To identify training needs or other ways to improve an employee's performance (for example, job, equipment, or motivational changes).
- To ensure orderly succession. Performance appraisals determine the potential of current employees to take on additional responsibilities and what training methods may be used or future assignments given to help them do so. Thus, if a lack of sufficient ability or potential among current staff is determined, strategies can be implemented for hiring outside the organization.
- To determine appropriate and equitable performance-based (or merit) increases.
- To motivate employees by providing feedback and goals for them.
- To allow supervisors to tell subordinates how they can do tasks more effectively.
- To eliminate subjective and arbitrary personnel decisions.

2:2.1A Trait-Based Appraisal Forms

Quality of work, productivity, initiative, dependability, interpersonal relations, and so forth, are all categories that may be analyzed on a trait-based appraisal form. Trait-based appraisals, such as the sample included (2:2.1A[1]) have two advantages. First, forms can be developed quickly. Second, they can be used for all positions.

The trait-based appraisal also has its disadvantages. One is that it does not define observable employee job behavior. It refers to potential predictors of performance rather than to performance itself. Thus, it does not provide employees with sufficient feedback nor does it allow for goal setting. As a result, employees are not shown how to maintain or improve their performance. Another major disadvantage of the trait-based appraisal form is that more than likely it will be rejected by the courts if introduced by management as documentation in support of job-related action (for example, the firing of an employee).

The following form is an example of a trait-based evaluation form.

TRAIT-BASED PERFORMANCE APPRAISAL

PERFORMANCE EVALUATION AND RECOMMENDATIONS FOR IMPROVEMENT

Employee: **Type of Review:**

Department: **Review Date:**

Job Title: **Last Review Date:**

Directions: Please indicate the appropriate level of performance for each area of the performance evaluation. When the evaluation is complete, a copy should be given to the employee. For each rating other than "Satisfactory," please make a comment(s) citing specific examples to justify the rating and include recommendations for improvement where appropriate. Use additional sheets whenever necessary.

Absences

Number of Incidents	Number of Days

Evaluation Criteria	Rating, Comments and Recommendations

1. **Initiative.** The degree to which the employee acts independently in new as well as everyday situations; the extent to which the employee sees what needs to be done and does it without being told.

   ☐ **Excellent**
   Little or no supervision needed. Highly resourceful in new situations.

   ☐ **Good**
   Thinks and acts independently. Resourceful in familiar situations.

   ☐ **Satisfactory**
   Initiative is satisfactory. Requires occasional supervision in routine situations.

   ☐ **Below Standard**
   Requires frequent instruction and close supervision.

   ☐ **Unsatisfactory**
   Must be told everything. Takes no personal initiative.

2. **Productivity.** The actual work output of the employee—relative to standards (if established), output of peers. Consider what the employee *actually* produces rather than what the employee may be capable of producing.

   ☐ **Excellent**
   Definitely a "top" producer. Consistently completes assignments ahead of deadlines.

   ☐ **Good**
   Produces more than most—above average. Sometimes completes assignments ahead of deadline.

   ☐ **Satisfactory**
   Output definitely meets requirements. Occasionally beats deadlines.

PERFORMANCE EVALUATION AND RECOMMENDATIONS FOR IMPROVEMENT page 2

Evaluation Criteria	Rating, Comments and Recommendations
☐ **Below Standard** Low output—below average. Sometimes meets deadlines, often is late.	
☐ **Unsatisfactory** Extremely low output—definitely not acceptable. Rarely meets deadlines.	
3. **Quality.** Freedom from errors and mistakes; accuracy, quality, of work in general.	
☐ **Excellent** Consistently highest possible quality. Final product virtually perfect.	
☐ **Good** Sometimes perfect work. Usually few errors and mistakes.	
☐ **Satisfactory** Quality acceptable—with some mistakes but of a tolerable level.	
☐ **Below Standard** Barely meets minimum standards. Frequent mistakes, improvement needed.	
☐ **Unsatisfactory** Excessive errors and mistakes. Very poor quality.	
4. **Effort.** The degree to which the employee does the best to be a top employee (without regard to how effective the employee may be). Consider conscientiousness and motivation.	
☐ **Excellent** Intensely motivated. Exerts maximum effort.	
☐ **Good** A hard worker. Exerts more effort than most.	
☐ **Satisfactory** Satisfactory effort.	
☐ **Below Standard** Low motivation. Could do better.	
☐ **Unsatisfactory** Effort exerted only when forced to do so.	
5. **Dependability.** The extent to which the employee can be relied upon to be available for work and do it properly. The degree to which the employee is reliable, trustworthy and persistent.	
☐ **Excellent** Completely reliable. Even goes beyond limits of tasks with little or no supervision when a need is perceived to do so.	

PERFORMANCE EVALUATION AND RECOMMENDATIONS FOR IMPROVEMENT page 3

Evaluation Criteria	Rating, Comments and Recommendations
☐ **Good** Usually reliable and persistent in spite of most difficulties.	
☐ **Satisfactory** Trustworthy but needs direction at times. If choice is between getting support or trying risk alone, will get support.	
☐ **Below Standard** Sometimes unreliable. Avoids responsibility. Seems to be satisfied to "get by."	
☐ **Unsatisfactory** Gives up easily. Frequently unreliable. Does not wish to assume responsibility.	
6. **Job Knowledge.** Knowledge of techniques, processes, procedures, services, equipment and materials required to do the job.	
☐ **Excellent** An authority on own tasks and superior knowledge of related jobs.	
☐ **Good** Well informed about present tasks and related jobs.	
☐ **Satisfactory** Satisfactory knowledge of his/her job and sufficient knowledge of related jobs.	
☐ **Below Standard** Minimum knowledge for current position. Additional training necessary.	
☐ **Unsatisfactory** Complete lack of knowledge to perform work properly. Training will not help.	
7. **Interpersonal Relations.** Effectiveness in accomplishing tasks by working with others (e.g., peers, superiors, customers).	
☐ **Excellent** Always works effectively with others and has exceptional social skills. Always seems to have the exact words for any situation. Keen insight into people and readily adapts to them.	
☐ **Good** Usually works well with others. Usually demonstrates awareness and consideration of others' viewpoints.	
☐ **Satisfactory** Acceptable relations with others. May have some difficulty communicating intricate or technical information but otherwise gets along with others.	

PERFORMANCE EVALUATION AND RECOMMENDATIONS FOR IMPROVEMENT page 4

Evaluation Criteria	Rating, Comments and Recommendations
☐ **Below Standard** Occasionally causes conflict with others in the implementation of an assignment.	
☐ **Unsatisfactory** Usually creates a hostile environment whenever interaction with others is necessary to complete an assigned task.	
8. Supervision. (Rate only if employee has been doing supervisory work.) Effectiveness in planning, organizing, delegating, and controlling the work of subordinates and winning their cooperation. General effectiveness in getting work done through subordinates.	
☐ **Excellent** Has mastered skills of supervision. Gets maximum production and cooperation. General effectiveness in getting work done through subordinates.	
☐ **Good** Better than most in getting work done through others. Effective.	
☐ **Satisfactory** Gets work done through others but sometimes "takes over him/herself."	
☐ **Below Standard** Has difficulty as a supervisor. Improvement needed. Often ends up doing the work instead.	
☐ **Unsatisfactory** Lacks ability to supervise at this time.	

Summary/Overall Rating (use additional sheet if necessary):

Supervisor's Signature ____________________ Date ____________________

Employee Comments (use additional sheet if necessary):

Employee's Signature ____________________ Date ____________________

Note: Employee's Signature is for acknowledgement that he/she has reviewed the evaluation and does not indicate approval and agreement with the statements provided.

Officer-In-Charge's Signature ____________________ Date ____________________

Group Head's Signature ____________________ Date ____________________

2:2.1B Results/Outcome-Based Appraisal Forms

Many organizations have attempted to tie performance to outcomes that are agreed on in advance. This process is commonly known as management by objectives (MBO). Rather than focusing on traits, the MBO approach emphasizes performance objectives that can be measured in terms of results. The following form is an example of a results/outcome-based appraisal form.

A Management By Objectives (MBO) approach to performance appraisal is a technique that has been used by major corporations throughout the United States since the early 1970's, coinciding with the infusion of MBA graduates into various staffing functions in these organizations. These MBA's were able to influence their institutions to switch from a "process" orientation to a results environment and to increase the corporation's emphasis on profitability while identifying the multi-faceted ways to determine that profitability.

Unlike the trait-based form, this one lends itself to objectivity. Because the evaluator and the employee being evaluated agree beforehand on the goals and objectives that the employee must meet, both have a clearer understanding of the expected outcome at the start of the rating period. And the subordinate, therefore, is more committed to the attainment of the agreed-on objective.

The MBO approach has become so popular that it is frequently used by major corporations, as well as smaller ones. The results so far have been mixed. Major problems in the programs have included:

Lack of flexibility: Frequently, when goals are set at the beginning of the cycle, business conditions or priorities change during that cycle and, because of other demands for attention, the objectives committed to at the beginning of the cycle are not adjusted to reflect the changing circumstances.

Lack of feedback: For management by objectives to be truly effective, it is essential that meetings take place throughout the cycle to determine whether or not the person being evaluated is on target in meeting his/her objectives and whether or not adjustments should be made.

Lack of support systems: Frequently the targets and objectives are inconsistent with the basis for providing awards and recognition to the person being evaluated. This has a debilitating effect and causes the approach to lose credibility.

Ineffective objectives: The key to the program is the development of appropriate objectives. It is not sufficient that these be consistent with the overall objectives of the organization but also that they be realistic and challenging. Failure to provide effective objectives will allow problems to creep into and undermine the program. Unrealistic goals will negatively affect morale, while goals too easily attainable will weaken the entire program by demotivating key staff members.

Emphasis on the wrong objectives: Encouraging, for instance, the solicitation of new accounts while paying no attention to the loss of current accounts will communicate to incumbents that their results will be measured on only a portion of those duties for which they should be rewarded.

Lack of evaluator training: As important as training is for the evaluation of trait or behavioral performance, effective training is even more important in a results approach. In fact the approach is as much a management tool as an appraisal instrument and as such demands a team of committed individuals who are able to implement the program.

An overly political environment: Some environments, regardless of results, support the perception by staff members that those who are favored get ahead while those who aren't don't. The results achieved in a results-based system make this "fact" all the more obvious.

Lack of organizational commitment: After the program has been introduced, signs may appear indicating that management is not committed to the approach. Even though the program is underway, the perception begins to take hold resulting in tension and skepticism that detracts from the program's opportunities for success.

The following form is an example of a results/outcome-based appraisal form.

RESULTS/OUTCOME-BASED PERFORMANCE APPRAISAL

Performance Planning and Review Worksheet
Name
Title
Department
Employment Date
Date Assigned
Period Covered
Date Discussed with Employee
Prepared by

RESULTS/OUTCOME-BASED PERFORMANCE APPRAISAL **page 2**

I—PERFORMANCE PLAN

The Performance Plan should focus on the 6 to 8 significant objectives planned for the year. Indicate target date for completion and note how performance will be measured. Assign a weight to each objective. Additional work relating to ongoing responsibilities should be summarized in one objective which should be assigned a weight of not more than 15%. Total weight of all objectives should equal 100%. List objectives in descending order of importance based on the assigned weight.

No.	Objectives	Weight
Employee's Signature	Date	100%
Signature & Title of Employee's Immediate Supervisor	Date	
Signature & Title Next Level of Supervision	Date	

RESULTS/OUTCOME-BASED PERFORMANCE APPRAISAL **page 3**

II—PROGRESS REVIEW

Record any additions or changes to the Performance Plan (Section I). Indicate any changes in the weighting of the objectives. Review and document employee's progress to date toward attaining each objective.

No.	Objectives	Weight
		100%

Date of mid-year Progress Review: ____________________

RESULTS/OUTCOME-BASED PERFORMANCE APPRAISAL page 4

III—PERFORMANCE REVIEW

Indicate what results were achieved during the year, being as specific as possible. Where objectives were not met, note the specific reason. Include a review of all significant work, whether or not it was planned.

RESULTS/OUTCOME-BASED PERFORMANCE APPRAISAL

page 5

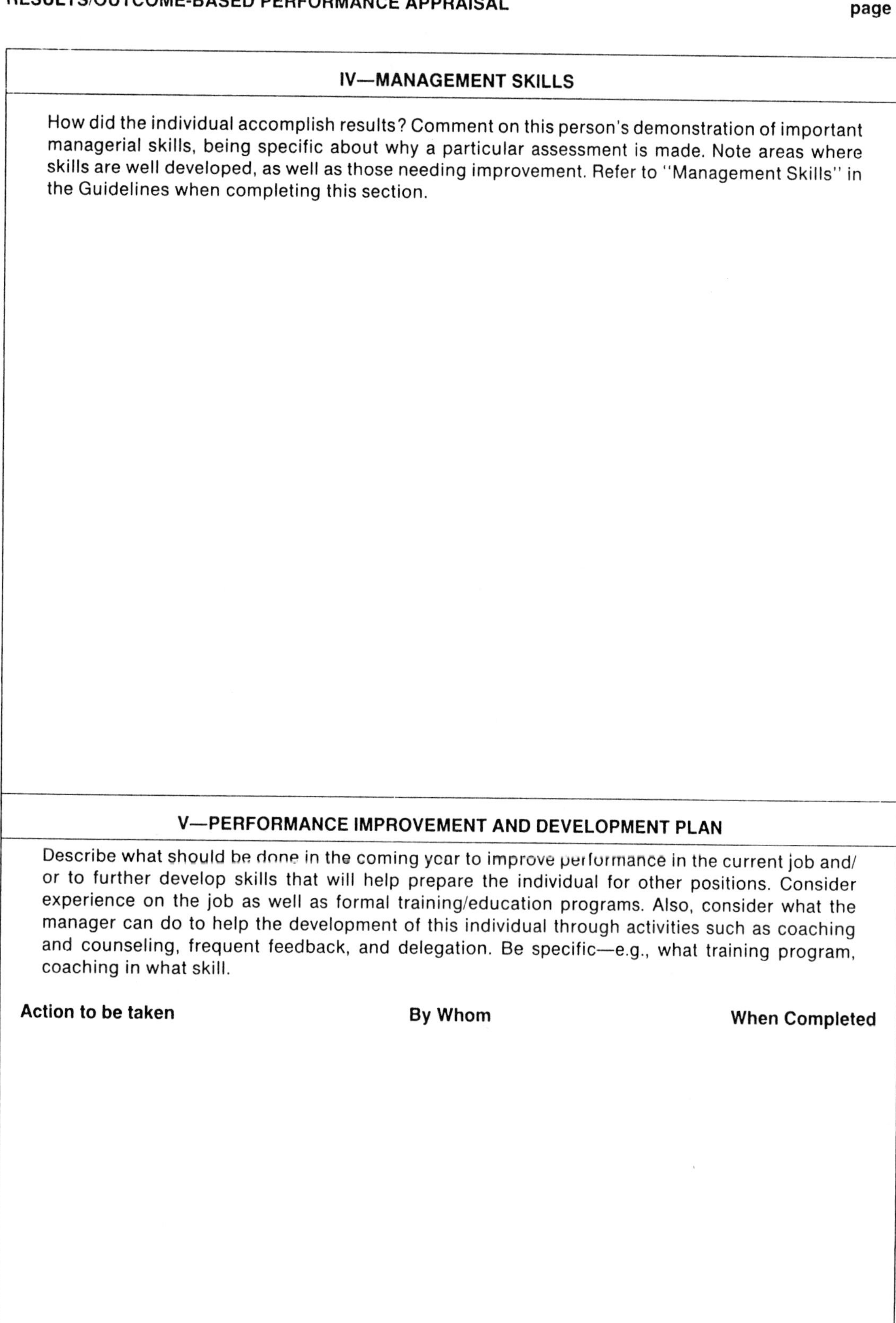

IV—MANAGEMENT SKILLS

How did the individual accomplish results? Comment on this person's demonstration of important managerial skills, being specific about why a particular assessment is made. Note areas where skills are well developed, as well as those needing improvement. Refer to "Management Skills" in the Guidelines when completing this section.

V—PERFORMANCE IMPROVEMENT AND DEVELOPMENT PLAN

Describe what should be done in the coming year to improve performance in the current job and/or to further develop skills that will help prepare the individual for other positions. Consider experience on the job as well as formal training/education programs. Also, consider what the manager can do to help the development of this individual through activities such as coaching and counseling, frequent feedback, and delegation. Be specific—e.g., what training program, coaching in what skill.

Action to be taken	By Whom	When Completed

RESULTS/OUTCOME-BASED PERFORMANCE APPRAISAL **page 6**

VI—OVERALL RATING OF PERFORMANCE

- ☐ Accomplishments in all areas far exceeded expectations for position, both in terms of results and the manner in which they were achieved. This rating should be reserved for truly exceptional performance.
- ☐ Accomplishments exceeded expectations for position in most areas and fully met the requirements in all others. Work performed in a highly effective manner.
- ☐ Performance fully met expectations for position in most areas and exceeded expectations in some others. Employee is effective both in achieving results and in demonstrating a competent level of management skills.
- ☐ Overall results achieved met the basic expectations for the position. While performance in one or two areas may have fallen slightly below expectations, this was balanced by performance above expectations in others.
- ☐ Performance falls short of fully meeting expectations for position in several areas. Attention required to bring performance up to an acceptable level.
- ☐ Does not meet minimum expectations for position. If performance does not improve within the time specified and discussed with the employee, the employee should be moved out of the position.

VII—SIGNATURES AND COMMENTS

Appraiser: Your signature indicates that you have discussed this review with your employee.

Signature ______________________________ Date ____________________

Employee: Your signature indicates that you have read this form and that your manager has reviewed your performance with you. It does not necessarily indicate your agreement with everything that was written or discussed. Use the space below for additional comments.

Signature ______________________________ Date ____________________

Appraiser's Manager: Your signature indicates that you have reviewed and concur with this appraisal.

Signature ______________________________ Date ____________________

Comments:

2:2.1C Behavior Criteria-Based Appraisal Form

The third major type of performance appraisal is based on work-related behaviors. This appraisal concentrates on evaluating specific, observable behavior directly affecting job performance. It can be used to measure productivity and compliance with policies (for example, absenteeism, punctuality). This performance appraisal rates the specific performance of employees with respect to the specific requirements and responsibilities of their positions. The behavior criteria-based appraisal analyzes an employee's behavior in terms of his or her cost-saving or profit-gaining activities.

Behavior-criteria forms are position specific. For example, the sample behavior-criteria form provided on the next page evaluates the performance behavior of secretaries and/or typists. This, of course, is a major disadvantage of this type of appraisal, since much time and effort must be used in designing a behavior-criteria appraisal form for each position.

The following form is an example of a behavior criteria-based appraisal form.

BEHAVIOR CRITERIA-BASED PERFORMANCE APPRAISAL

Secretary/Typist

Employee Name	Department
Job Title	Date of Last Review
Reviewer's Name	Time in Position

Preparing the Report

This report is designed to help managers appraise each employee based on particular and distinct characteristics of each position.

To be most effective, the report must be prepared in a careful and thorough manner. To serve this end, here are some suggestions.

- Consider only one item at a time.
- Base your ratings on direct knowledge and employee performance on the job.
- Have the ratings reflect typical current performance. At the same time avoid being influenced by recent instances of success or failure which are not typical or by past performance which has now changed.
- Concentrate on evaluating specific, observable behavior that directly affects job performance.
- If possible, have some other manager in your area prepare an independent report and compare the two appraisals.
- Completion of this report will be an occasion for discussing job progress with each employee. You should show the report to the employee. You may find it of great value to give the employee a blank report for a self-evaluation. Both you and the employee will benefit by comparing and discussing the evaluations.
- Use the "Comments" section on the last page for amplification, additions or explanations.

Performance Appraisal Form **page 2**

Below is a list of categories specifically relevant to the secretary/typist positions. Determine the weight appropriate for each category and then multiply that weight by the rating given for the incumbent's performance during the time period for the appraisal. Keep in mind total weight for all categories selected should equal 100.

The rating for each category is on a scale of 0 to 5. Each level is established with a numerical value in the column on the left hand side of the page. For each category where the lowest level of performance is indicated, written documentation is required. The highest possible score is 400 points. Ratings are as follows: Outstanding: 352–400; Commendable: 278–350; Competent: 212–276; Minimal/Acceptable: 152–210; Unsatisfactory: 0–150.

I. Knowledge of Department Functions (Secretaries only)	**Rating × Weight =**
0 Work falls below minimum acceptable performance. (document) 1 Knows basic functions of most sections in department. Routine calls and inquiries promptly directed. 2 Understands functions of each section in department and can refer customers and calls to proper areas. Can identify applications for opening various services. Uses files to locate customer information. 3 Knowledge of most department services and procedures. Able to use available resources to resolve customer requests. 4 Answers questions on all services. Calls and inquiries never misdirected. Able to handle basic questions if boss or other employee is unavailable.	☐
II. Dictation (Secretaries only)	**Rating × Weight =**
0 Work falls below minimum acceptable performance. (document) 1 Dictation inadequate for routine assignments. Speed is below organization standard. 2 Dictation skills are acceptable for routine work. Speed equals organization standard (80–90 wpm). 3 Takes dictation of a more complex nature. Work consistently accurate. Speed clearly above organization standard. 4 Demonstrates proficient dictation skills superior to organization standard.	☐
III. Customer Service	**Rating × Weight =**
0 Work falls below minimum acceptable performance. (document) 1 Courteous to customers. Answers questions if asked. Does not always screen telephone calls or customers. Recognizes only a few regular customers. 2 Serves as a central information point for customers. Answers questions in a polite, friendly manner. Recognizes regular customers. Generally demonstrates good telephone techniques. Comes to the assistance of waiting customers. 3 Courteous to customers both in person and by phone even during difficult situations. Customers rarely kept waiting. 4 Promotes the organization and its services. Recognizes major accounts and their principals.	☐

Performance Appraisal Form	page 3
IV. Quantity 0 Work falls below minimum acceptable performance. (document) 1 Output below expected level. Has occasional difficulty completing tasks within the same day. Frequently misses deadlines. Usually some work backlogged. 2 Output approximately equal to expected levels. Completes all tasks within the same day. 3 Output clearly above the expected levels. Completes work within deadlines. Able to assist others in duties. 4 Output far superior to expected levels. Consistently has time to develop customer service, or to assist as needed in other areas.	**Rating × Weight =** ☐
V. Typing & Correspondence 0 Work falls below minimum acceptable performance. (document) 1 Completed tasks are occasionally without proper format or neatness. Proofreads work. Some work is returned for correction. Deadlines sometimes missed. Typing is less than organization standard. 2 Work is completed in proper format and is neat. Proofreads all assignments. Work is rarely returned for correction. Meets deadlines. Typing speed equals organization standard. 3 Work is thoroughly prepared and submitted correctly. Completes tasks well within deadline. Typing skills above organization standard. 4 Completed tasks consistently error free. Demonstrates proficient typing skills superior to organization standards.	**Rating × Weight =** ☐
VI. Business English 0 Work falls below minimum acceptable performance. (document) 1 Has difficulty applying proper use of the English language and its rules (spelling, grammar, vocabulary, punctuation). 2 Demonstrates adequate use of the English language and grammatical rules. 3 Has good command of the English language. Demonstrates proficient editing skills. 4 When required, composes original correspondence.	**Rating × Weight =** ☐
VII. Cooperation 0 Work falls below minimum acceptable performance. (document) 1 Reluctant to take on new tasks or assist in usual situations. Often has excuses when asked to help. 2 Cooperates when called upon. 3 Always available to assist department or co-workers in any situation. 4 Exhibits a spirit of teamwork and assumes leadership in promoting cooperation. Able to resolve conflict without assistance.	**Rating × Weight =** ☐

Performance Appraisal Form **page 4**

VIII. Attendance & Punctuality (Recorded from Employee Attendance Record. Be sure to review accuracy of the Attendance Record.)

Rating × Weight = ☐

Attendance

	Total Incidents (Chargeable)	Total Days (Chargeable)
0	6 or more	12 or more
1	4–5	8–11
2	2–3	5–7
3	1	1–4
4	0	0

Punctuality

Rating × Weight = ☐

	Total Lost Time:
	Tardiness Incidents
0	31 or more
1	21–30
2	11–20
3	1–10
4	0

Total Points: ☐

Comments (Use extra sheets if necessary)

Prepared by ______________________ Date __________

Reviewed by ______________________ Date __________

Employee Remarks (Use extra sheets if necessary)

Employee Signature Date __________

2:2.1D New Staff Progress Report

Frequently, an evaluation form is used during the first three months of a staff member's employment. Although the form can be used along with any of the three approaches discussed previously, the progress report is usually traits-analysis oriented. The form on the following page is an example of a new staff member progress report.

The form, to be completed three times during the employee's first three months of work, must be signed by the staff member being reviewed. The purpose is to remind both supervisors and subordinates, right from the start, that the performance appraisal form is being used to encourage two-way communication.

PERFORMANCE APPRAISAL FOR NEW STAFF

NEW STAFF MEMBER PROGRESS REPORT

STAFF MEMBER NAME	DEPARTMENT	TITLE	DATE HIRED
TO THE SUPERVISOR: This report will be sent to you 3 times during the staff member's first three months with the company. After 3 weeks, 6 weeks, and 10 weeks you will be asked to rate the progress of the staff member on each factor, using the codes that appear below. Please complete each report, discussing your staff member's progress with him/her, and return to the Human Resources Department.	1ST REPORT Please complete this column and return to Human Resources by:	2ND REPORT Please complete this column and return to Human Resources by:	3RD REPORT Please complete this column and return to Human Resources by:
QUALITY Accuracy, neatness, and completeness of work assigned			
QUANTITY Output of work, considering newness of assignment			
UNDERSTANDING Ability to learn, grasp concepts essential to the work, and follow instructions			
INITIATIVE Ability to work independently with a minimum of supervision			
COOPERATION Ability to work well with co-workers, supervisors, customers, etc.			
SUITABILITY Do attitude, personality, and temperament appear appropriate for this kind of work? (Does the person match the job?)			
ATTENDANCE (Rate as either "M" or "D")			
PUNCTUALITY (Rate as either "M" or "D")			

Staff member's signature/date	Staff member's signature/date	Staff member's signature/date
Manager's signature/date	Manager's signature/date	Manager's signature/date

E = Exceeds Expectations M = Meets Expectations D = Does Not Meet Expectations

2:2.3 Rules of Employee Conduct

Employers must establish concrete guidelines that clearly define what an employer considers appropriate on-the-job behavior. Without the clear definition of acceptable employee behavior, attempts at even the most progressive discipline programs will not achieve the employer's stated evaluation and discipline guidelines. The following documents provide examples of comprehensive employee rules of conduct.

2:2.3A Sample Rules of Work and Conduct (Traditional)

The following rules of employee conduct are drafted along the traditional lines of employee discipline and reflect a conservative attitude towards monitoring and disciplining the workplace.

Rules Of Work And Conduct

The Company has established rules of work and conduct that are to be practiced by employees during their employment with the firm. The following pages will explain these rules and also outline undesirable conduct which may result in disciplinary action and/or termination. It is hoped that this outline will provide you with a better understanding of what is expected of you and make this employment association mutually rewarding.

These rules are intended as guidelines and are not necessarily inclusive. Should these rules of work and conduct require future revision, employees will be informed of all changes. All employees are encouraged to inquire with their supervisor and personnel for any clarification necessary concerning these rules.

The Company's philosophy in regard to disciplinary action and termination is based on counseling and progressive discipline. Except in cases justifying immediate suspension or termination, employees who breach the rules and regulations of the Company and have been employed for at least ninety days, will be subject to progressive discipline. Infractions need not be of the same rule to result in discipline at the next step. The progressive procedure is as follows:

First offense	—	Verbal warning
Second offense	—	Written warning
Third offense	—	Second warning and/or suspension
Fourth offense	—	Further disciplinary action including discharge

Corrective Discipline

Unless special circumstances exist, violation of any of the following rules will result in corrective discipline:

1. Willful neglect of duty.
2. Abusive language or conduct directed at a supervisor or other employee.
3. Fighting, horseplay, disorderly or unsafe conduct on Company premises.
4. Leaving job at any time without permission of a supervisor and clocking out.
5. Loansharking, gambling, working numbers on Company premises.
6. Excessive absenteeism, lateness or early quits.
7. Using the Company telephone at any time without prior permission of a supervisor; using the pay phone during working time (not including break and meal times).

8. Bad attitude or offensive personal conduct, condition or appearance resulting in an adverse effect on the Company's work, safety and health or employee morale.
9. Poor performance or productivity.
10. Negligence or carelessness which causes or could cause damage to equipment, to others or create a safety hazard.
11. Posting, altering or removing any matter on bulletin boards or Company property unless specifically authorized; defacing walls or bulletin boards or other Company property.
12. Selling, distributing materials, soliciting or collecting contributions for any purpose on Company premises in violation of the no solicitation policy.
13. Loafing, loitering, or unnecessary absence from work station or other abuse of working time.
14. Performing personal work on Company time or equipment without permission.
15. Failure to report accidents immediately.
16. Violation of safety rules.
17. Failure to call in daily when sick, or to supply a doctor's note to the Company by the fourth lost working day.

Immediate Suspension or Dismissal

The following conduct is prohibited and will result in immediate suspension or discharge.

1. Any form or threat of physical assault of a supervisor or business visitor of the Company.
2. Being under the influence of, using, selling, distributing or possessing alcohol or a controlled drug during working time, whether on or off the premises. If an employee is suspected of being under the influence of alcohol or a drug in violation of this rule, the employee will be removed from the premises and taken to a medical facility for testing. The employee will not be permitted to work for the balance of the shift. If the employee refuses to be tested, s/he will be discharged for insubordination. If the test result is negative (less than one half the level used by the state police to determine driving under the influence), the employee will be compensated for any lost time at his base rate of pay and returned to work. If the test result is one half the standard but less than the standard, the employee will not be compensated for any lost time, but sent home and given a warning under the corrective discipline system. If the test result is positive (equals or exceeds the standard), the employee will be discharged.
3. Theft or dishonesty, including a breach of Company security or confidentiality, punching another employee's time card, falsification of any business record or the giving of a false excuse for absence from work.
4. Conviction of a crime (arrest for the alleged Commission of a felony may result in an unpaid suspension until the charge is resolved or an independent investigation is completed).

5. Intentional damage to the property of the Company, another employee or business visitor of the Company.
6. Unprovoked assault on another employee during working hours or on Company property or the use of a weapon in any fight on Company property.
7. Carrying or otherwise possessing firearms or other deadly weapons on the premises.
8. Absence from work for three consecutive work days without proper notification.
9. Willful violation of plant safety rules which endangers the safety of any person or Company property.
10. Endangering the premises by carelessness which could cause fire.
11. Concealing defective work.
12. Refusal to perform work assigned by a supervisor or willful disobedience of a reasonable instruction or direction of a supervisor.
13. Deliberate interference with or delaying or restricting of production or the production of others.

Any violation not listed above that the Company deems serious may result in disciplinary action or discharge.

Review of Disciplinary Action

The Company wants to be a good place for you to work. From time to time, however, it is necessary for us to remind employees of their responsibilities. This is usually done through warnings set up by our discipline system. Unfortunately, in a few cases the warnings go unheeded or an employee commits an act so serious that employment must be terminated for the good of the Company and the remaining employees. We recognize the special importance of those decisions. For this reason, we have implemented a procedure available to all employees to review termination decisions.

If an employee is involuntarily terminated for cause and the employee believes the decision of the supervisor was unwarranted, the employee may request a review of the discharge by a special Review Board made up of three peer (exempt or non-exempt) employees and two supervisors. The employee who wishes to use this procedure must inform the Personnel Director of this desire by the end of the next regularly scheduled work day after the day of discharge. Within two workdays thereafter, the Personnel Director will place in a container the names of all peer employees with five or more complete years of Company service. The employee will draw three names and those employees will serve on the Board. At the same time, the Personnel Director will place the names of all non-involved supervisors in a container and the employee will draw two names. These supervisors will also serve on the Board. The Personnel Director will be the non-voting chairperson of the Board and will act as the coordinator.

Within two work days after the selection of the Board members, the Board will meet to examine all of the facts involved in the discharge and to listen to witnesses. The employee or his/her peer representative may appear before the Board and present any information or arguments they desire. The Board may request the production of any document relating to the facts and summon any witness. The issues before the Board will be "whether the facts establish by the weight of credible evidence that a violation of a rule occurred and whether the employee's discharge followed the disciplinary procedure." All decisions of a Board will be by simple majority and secret ballot. Decisions will be final and binding on both the employee and the Company. If the Board's decision is that the employee's discharge was not supported by the facts, the employee will be reinstated to his/her regular job without loss of pay and the discharge will be removed from his/her record.

Employee Representation

The Company believes that no employee should be denied the opportunity to have someone else present at any discipline conference with a supervisor. Consequently, any employee who wishes to have another employee present and speak on his/her behalf at any discipline meeting may simply request it. Only employees with more than five complete years of service with the Company can be a representative, however, and representatives can serve in that capacity only once in any twelve month period. The Personnel Director will assist an employee in obtaining a representative, if s/he wishes. Only a person employed by the Company can be a representative.

Employee Acknowledgment

This will acknowledge the receipt and review of the Company's rules of work and conduct.

______________________________ ______________________________

Signature Date

2:2.3B Sample Code of Conduct (Progressive)

The following sample code of conduct is drafted to reflect a nontraditional approach to employee discipline and reflects a progressive, pro-active attitude towards monitoring and disciplining the workplace.

Code of Conduct

Employee Responsibilities

As an employee of the Company you have responsibilities. Most of these, such as regular and prompt attendance, good productivity and a pleasant and cooperative attitude, are known to everyone. Other responsibilities, however, may not occur to people. The Company believes it is helpful, therefore, to specify as clearly as possible all types of conduct which are unacceptable and which may result in the termination of employment. Giving this information is part of our responsibility to you as an employee. It is hoped that this will help you have a more satisfying employment experience because it will better enable you to know what is expected by the company.

The following conduct is prohibited and will result in immediate termination of employment:

1. Any form of threat of physical assault of a super-visor or business visitor of the company.
2. Being under the influence of, using, selling, distributing or possessing alcohol or a controlled substance (*e.g.*, marijuana, narcotics, barbiturates) during working time, whether on or off the premises. If an employee is suspected of being under the influence of alcohol or a drug in violation of this rule, the employee will be removed from the premises and taken to a medical facility for testing. The employee will not be permitted to work for the balance of the shift. If the employee refuses to be tested, he or she will be discharged for insubordination. If a test result is negative, the employee will be compensated for any lost time at his base rate of pay. The standard the Company will use to determine whether an employee has violated this rule is the standard used by the motor vehicle department for determining whether someone is "under the influence." For alcohol, this would be a blood alcohol level of 0.1.

   A "negative" test is one which results in a level of the substance of less than one-half of the standard. For alcohol, this would be a blood alcohol count of 0.049 or less.

   A level of substance of between one-half the standard (for alcohol, a count of 0.050 or 0.099) indicates conduct which is irresponsible and threatening to the safety of equipment, product and other employees and the employee him or herself. Such conduct will be disciplined as a violation of a Progressive Discipline Rule and the employee will be sent home without pay for the balance of the shift.
3. Theft or dishonesty, including a breach of company security or confidentiality, punching another employee's time card, falsification of any business record or the giving of a false excuse for absence from work.

4. Conviction of a crime (arrest for the alleged commission of a felony may result in an unpaid suspension until the charge is resolved).
5. Intentional damage to the property of the company, another employee or business visitor of the Company.
6. Unprovoked assault on another employee during working hours or on company property or the use of a weapon in any fight on company property.
7. Carrying or otherwise possessing firearms or other deadly weapons on the premises.
8. Absence from work for three consecutive workdays without proper notification.
9. Willful violation of plant safety rules which endangers the safety of any person or company property.
10. Refusal to perform work assigned by a supervisor or willful disobedience of a reasonable instruction or direction of a supervisor.
11. Deliberate interference with or delaying or restricting of production or the production of others.

Violation of any of the following rules will subject an employee to progressive discipline: (Absenteeism and tardiness are covered by the separate attendance policy.)

1. Willful neglect of duty.
2. Abusive language or conduct directed at a supervisor or other employee.
3. Fighting, horseplay, disorderly or unsafe conduct on company premises.
4. Temporarily leaving the company during working time without permission of a supervisor or other employer representative and clocking out. (Leaving the company without permission and clocking out for more than one-half of a shift will be considered a voluntary quit and job abandonment.)
5. Loansharking, gambling, working numbers on company premises.
6. Failure to be ready to work and at the assigned work station on time following rest and meal periods or leaving the job prior to the wash-up time.
7. Using the company telephone at any time without prior permission of a supervisor; using the pay telephone during working time (not including break and meal times).
8. Bad attitude or offensive personal conduct resulting in an adverse effect on the company's work, safety and health or employee morale.
9. Poor performance or productivity.
10. Negligence or carelessness which causes or could cause damage to equipment or create a safety hazard.
11. Posting, altering or removing any matter on bulletin boards or company property unless specifically authorized.
12. Abuse of or conduct indicating an intent to abuse the attendance policy.
13. Selling, distributing materials, soliciting or collecting contributions for any purpose on company premises without prior permission.
14. Loafing, unnecessary absence from work station or other abuse of working time.
15. Performing personal work on company time or equipment without permission.

16. Failure to turn your production record in to your foreman daily at the end of the shift.
17. Failure to report accidents immediately.
18. Violation of safety rules.

2:2.4 Absenteeism

Absenteeism is one of the most common but easily controlled employee problems. This section presents two types of absenteeism control policies. The first, at 2:2.4A, presents a no-fault absenteeism policy while the second, at 2:2.4B, provides an example of an absenteeism control policy with excuses.

2:2.4A Sample No-Fault Absenteeism Control Policy

The following absenteeism policy provides employees with a stated number of allowed absences. Once this number is exceeded the employee is subject to termination and, as such, it represents a conservative approach to controlling absences.

Sample No-Fault Absenteeism Control Policy

Attendance Policy

The Company has a no-fault system for the control of absenteeism, tardiness and early quits. It is a no-fault system because there are no excused absences. Except for previously scheduled absences, such as military leaves, jury duty, bereavement leave, scheduled sick leave, vacation, suspensions, plant closures, or holidays, you are counted absent if you are not at work. If you are late for work by any amount, regardless of the cause, you are tardy. If you leave work early, regardless of the cause or whether a supervisor has given permission, you have left early. Tardiness is any time you are not ready to work at the scheduled starting time.

The system allows you twelve occurrences of absence, tardiness or authorized early quits in a rolling twelve-month period. At the thirteenth occurrence, your employment will be terminated for unacceptable attendance. If an absence involves a series of consecutive days due to a legitimate illness (unscheduled sick leave) and the Company is adequately notified, the series will only count as one occurrence. However, we must receive satisfactory proof of the illness and compliance with all other requirements for an unscheduled sick leave or each day of the series will be counted as a separate occurrence. A doctor's note may be some evidence of illness, but such notes are not conclusive evidence. The Company reserves the right to reject any particular note or all of the notes from any particular doctor when it believes that the employee may not have been ill or that the doctor's procedures are not adequate.

Under the rolling twelve-month system, the disciplinary step is determined by the number of occurrences during the twelve months preceding the latest occurrence of absenteeism, lateness or early quit. In this fashion, occurrences become inactive on their anniversary date and will not be used in determining the step of discipline. As a result, an employee may repeat a specific step.

For example, an employee may accumulate six occurrences in the twelve months beginning October 1, 1990. If the employee has another occurrence on October 1, 1991, his record, nevertheless, still will be six occurrences on that date. The October 1, 1990 occurrence will have become inactive. The employee will receive another first written warning on October 1, 1991 because he has once again accumulated six occurrences.

In addition to the opportunity to cleanse your attendance record offered by the rolling twelve month feature of this system, the company will automatically make inactive the oldest occurrence in the twelve month period preceding the completion of each three consecutive months of perfect attendance, to a maximum of four per year (one for each complete three month period). As a result, an employee who has accumulated six occurrences in three months can reduce his occurrence level to five if he has no occurrences for three months following his sixth, four if he has no occurrences for six months, and so on.

Doctors' notes or any other kind of medical excuse will not avoid an occurrence. An occurrence will result from any and all absences as defined in this policy, even if the absence is due to an illness or injury. You have the responsibility to notify the Company if you are going to be late or absent. Notification must be a minimum of one (1) hour prior to your scheduled starting time. Failure to properly notify the Company will result in an assessment of an additional occurrence for a total of two occurrences for that absence.

Vacation days may not be used to avoid an occurrence. No absence, lateness or early quit can or will be excused. There will be no exceptions. The number of allowed occurrences is high enough to permit a reasonable amount of illness and personal business. Save your occurrences. You may need them sometime for an emergency. Your supervisor cannot give anyone any special treatment. Acceptance of overtime creates an obligation to work the time scheduled just like a regular shift and lateness and absenteeism will be treated as if the overtime were a regular workday.

The following disciplinary action will be taken upon accumulation of occurrences:

Six Occurrences	First Written Warning
Eight Occurrences	Second Written Warning
Eleven Occurrences	Three Days Suspension—to start at a time convenient to the Company within one week of the notice.
Thirteen Occurrences	Discharge

Occurrences will accumulate as follows:

1. Lateness of 15 minutes or less	—	½ occurrence
2. Authorized early quit or lateness of more than 15 minutes	—	1 occurrence
3. Absence	—	1 occurrence
4. Absence of two or more days due to any reason other than proven illness or incapacitating accident	—	1 occurrence for each day absent
5. Absence with failure to call office at least one hour before scheduled shift begins	—	2 total occurrences

After three consecutive days of absence, due to illness, you must present a doctor's statement of care and releasing you to return to work. The statement must be signed by the doctor who treated you, and must be on the doctor's stationery to return to work.

In unusual circumstances, where the thirteenth occurrence is due to a cause outside the control of the employee and a discharge would be unreasonable in light of the employee's total record and conduct, the Plant Manager of the Company may review the case and void the discharge. Such an action, however, will be taken only in exceptional cases where the application of the system would create an overall injustice and the employee has not acted irresponsibly in accumulating prior occurrences.

Remember, save your occurrences, since you may need them for an actual inability to come to work. An employee who has not been responsible and saved occurrences may face termination for excessive absenteeism even though his last occurrence may be due to an unavoidable incident or condition. This system will allow an absenteeism rate of more than twice the national average. However, an employee who abuses the system and unnecessarily accumulates occurrences risks not having any to be used in the event of an emergency or other actual inability to work. Because six absences in twelve months is close to the national average, we have begun the warnings at that point. Warnings should be understood by you as notices that your attendance has fallen below the national average and that you should take special care to save your occurrences in the event you may need them.

2:2.4B Sample Absenteeism Control Policy With Excuses

The following absenteeism policy provides for corrective discipline action in the event an employee's absenteeism gets out of control. As such, it represents a more pro-active approach to controlling absences than the one at 2:2.4A.

Sample Absenteeism Control Policy With Excuses

Prompt attendance on the job is an important part of the performance of employee responsibilities. Absence and tardiness not only disturb the smooth functioning of the employee's job but also inconvenience and interfere with other interrelated jobs and functions of the Company. Good attendance is a condition of continued employment.

1. Definitions:
   a. Lateness: anytime an employee is not at his/her work station, dressed and ready to work on time at the beginning of the shift or after any break or meal period.
   b. Excused Lateness: anytime an employee is late but provides a properly documented excuse satisfactory to the employee's supervisor.
   c. Unexcused Lateness: anytime an employee is late and fails to have a satisfactory excuse.
   d. Early Quit: anytime an employee leaves work before the end of a shift.
   e. Excused Early Quit: anytime an employee has permission from his/her supervisor to leave work early.
   f. Unexcused Early Quit: anytime an employee leaves work before quitting time without the prior permission of a supervisor.
   g. Absence: anytime an employee is not at work for an entire shift.
   h. Excused Absence: anytime an employee is absent but provides a properly documented excuse satisfactory to the employee's supervisor.
   i. Unexcused Absence: anytime an employee is absent and fails to provide a properly documented excuse satisfactory to his/her supervisor.
2. Reporting off: All employees must notify their department head or immediate supervisor of their expected lateness or absence and provide a verbal reason prior to the beginning of the employee's shift. Subsequent written documentation supporting the reason for the lateness or absence may be required. Except in rare and unusual cases, a failure to report off prior to the beginning of a shift will render the lateness or absence "unexcused," regardless of any later justification or reason which may be offered. An excuse will not be given until the reason is properly considered by the supervisor; reporting off will not be an automatic excuse.
3. Unexcused lateness, absences and early quits: Excessive unexcused lateness, absenteeism and early quits will be subject to discipline procedures. All lateness and early quits will result in the docking of pay. While each employee deserves to be treated as an individual, as a general guideline, excessive unexcused tardiness is defined as more than one unexcused lateness in any rolling month period, and excessive unexcused absenteeism is defined as one unexcused absence in any rolling three-month period.

Unexcused early quits are not acceptable at any time and will result in immediate implementation of the discipline procedures under the Code of Conduct.

4. Excused absences, lateness, early quits: Although an employee's absences, latenesses and early quits may be excused, it is possible that an accumulation of these occurrences will render an employee so undependable that his/her employment should be terminated. In these cases, the employee will receive discipline and the supervisor will attempt to work out a solution to the problem in order to avoid the further accumulation of an unacceptable number of excused absences, latenesses and/or early quits.
5. Job abandonment: An employee is considered to have abandoned his/her job if he/she has been absent from work for three consecutive work days without proper notification. Job abandonment is considered to be a voluntary resignation.

2:2.5 Employee Discipline Programs

Discipline programs can range from the traditional form of purely punishing employees as a way to correct behavior to nontraditional progressive, proactive discipline programs that are participatory in nature. This section provides examples of a punitive system with progressive corrective discipline programs as well as a sample punitive discipline plan with a corrective action policy and progressive discipline system.

2:2.5A Sample Employee Warning Notice Form

EMPLOYEE WARNING NOTICE

Name of Employee ______________________________

Dept./Location ______________________________

Job Description ______________________________

You Are Hereby Warned About: ______________________________

VIOLATION: ______________________________

____

____

____

____

OTHER: ______________________________

____

____

____

____

ACTION: Employee Counseling ______________________________

First Warning ______________________________

Second Warning ______________________________

Final Warning ______________________________

DISCIPLINE: None ______________________________

Suspension ______________ From: ______________ To: ______________

Discharge ______________ Effective Date: ______________

Employee's Signature ______________________________

Signature and Title of Department Head/Supervisor

____

Date Issued ______________ Personnel Dept. ______________

2:2.5B Sample Punitive System with Progressive Corrective Discipline Program

Punitive System

Progressive Corrective Discipline

Purpose

The Company views progressive, corrective discipline as a method which allows employees to correct any improper work habits or conduct through self-control. As a result, the company follows a uniform four-step discipline procedure consisting of:

1. Oral Warning;
2. Written Reprimand;
3. Disciplinary Suspension; and
4. Discharge.

A consistent application of this policy and a thorough documentation of all violations is essential for the effectiveness of the program.

Scope

This policy applies to all employees of the Company exclusive of exempt personnel.

Procedure

1. When an employee's improper attitude, unacceptable conduct, poor performance, or violation of company work rule(s) warrants discipline, the immediate supervisor initiates the disciplinary action. However, prior to invoking a disciplinary action, the supervisor is to confront the employee with the facts and allow the employee to respond to the situation. In a department represented by a union, the employee may request that a union representative be in attendance. This meeting serves notice to the employee that improper attitude, unacceptable conduct, poor performance, or violation of company rule(s) has occurred and that the employee has a right to respond.

The burden of justifying the disciplinary action rests with the supervisor.

The supervisor should ensure that the following exists at all times in the unit for which he/she is responsible:

   a. The employee is informed of all Company rules and regulations which may affect him/her on the job.
   b. The employee knows how to do the job.
   c. The employee knows how well he/she is doing the job.
   d. Nothing beyond the employee's control is preventing him/her from doing the job.

2. If the supervisor is assured the preceding conditions exist and it appears a violation of the Code of Conduct has taken place, it is the supervisor's

responsibility to get all the facts. The supervisor should take an appropriate investigatory approach to learn exactly what happened, keeping notes as to precisely what was said by each person as well as precise answers to questions such as the following:

a. What, when, why and where the alleged violation occurred?
b. Who was involved?
c. Whether the action was habitual in nature or an isolated incident?
d. Which company policy is involved?
e. What is the employee's past overall record?
f. Whether any mitigating circumstances exist?
g. Whether the offense is governed in any manner by the language of the current labor agreement? (if applicable)
h. Whether the incident was a malicious act, the result of negligence or accidental?
i. How serious is the violation?
j. What precedents are there in handling similar situations?
k. What is the attitude of the employee?

3. Is the penalty appropriate to the offense? Each case must be considered individually, based on the facts and circumstances involved, the employee's length of service, and the employee's past conduct record during the prior nine to twelve months. If any disciplinary action is to be effective, the following principles are extremely important:
   a. Consistency among employees without any favoritism shown, as well as consistency with the individual.
   b. No offense should be overlooked by Company management.
   c. Emphasis must be on correction of the problem rather than punishment of the individual.
   d. Employee must be allowed to maintain his or her self respect.
   e. Progressively increase the seriousness of the discipline, if the problem is not resolved.
   f. Recognition of employee changes in behavior and becoming a more responsible employee.
4. *Oral Reprimand:* The employee is to be given an oral reprimand when his/her improper attitude, unacceptable conduct, poor performance, or violation of Company work rule(s) occurs. Following the investigation procedure outlined above, the supervisor is to confront the employee with the facts and allow the employee to respond to them. Oral warnings, counseling, or cautionings are essential to help employees correct themselves, thereby leading to self-discipline. Every oral reprimand is to include notice to the employee that continued violations will result in further disciplinary action. Following the issuance of the oral reprimand, the supervisor is to document the nature of the violation(s) including: time, date, and place of both the offense and disciplinary conference. The documentation is to be retained by the supervisor in the department. No documentation is to be sent to Human Resources. The union, when applicable, should be informed that the oral reprimand has been given.
5. *Written Reprimand:* The employee is to be given a letter of written reprimand for a second offense of the same nature that occurs within twelve months from

the date of an oral reprimand or if the nature of the violation warrants more than an oral warning but not a suspension or discharge. The letter of written reprimand is discipline and has specific applications that differentiate it from a written warning. (See Section I).

Prior to issuing a written reprimand, the nature of the offense is to be discussed with the employee in detail, stating clearly the reasons why the improper attitude or unacceptable conduct cannot be allowed to continue. The employee is to be given an opportunity to respond to the charges. The letter of written reprimand should state the material facts of the case: nature, date, time and place of violation(s) and that there was a prior oral warning. The original of this letter is to be handed to the employee, with copies sent to Human Resources and, when applicable, a copy hand-delivered to the union Representative.

6. *Disciplinary Suspension:* The employee is to be given a disciplinary suspension for a third offense that occurs within twelve months from the date of the letter of reprimand. This suspension is to be for three working days. After doing an investigation, the supervisor is to confront the employee with the facts surrounding the misconduct and the employee is to be given an opportunity to respond to these charges.

   The facts of the case, including history of past offenses, are to be carefully documented. A letter is to be sent to the employee which explains the intent and nature of the disciplinary suspension. Copies of the letter are to be sent to Human Resources and, when applicable, given to the employee's union representative.

7. *Discharge:* If all efforts at corrective discipline fail, the final action is discharge. This action is to be taken after an investigation reveals that an offense has occurred within twelve months from the date of the disciplinary suspension.

   The circumstances surrounding a discharge should be discussed with Human Resources prior to the discharge. In addition, a conference is to be held with the employee in order to explore the reasons for the discharge, including the history of past offenses and details of the current misconduct. This due process procedure also allows the employee to respond to the charges.

   After these conferences have been held, a follow-up letter is to be sent directly to the employee's home. Copies of this letter are to be forwarded to Human Resources and, when applicable, to the employee's union representative.

8. *Accelerating Discipline:* Under extreme conditions, the disciplinary process may be accelerated, depending upon the gravity of the offense. The standard against which the gravity of personal misconduct is tested is: "Can you chance the offense happening again?" If the infraction cannot be tolerated and may be a threat to the health or safety of any employee, an accelerated penalty may be imposed due to the gravity of the misconduct and in order to deter him/ her from repeating it.

9. *Written Warning:* There are three instances in which a written warning is issued instead of a written reprimand. These are:

   a. Incompetence not due to the employee's fault;

   b. Chronic absence for *bona fide* illnesses;

   c. Accident proneness beyond the fault of the employee or due to physical incapacity.

In such cases, the employee should be given an oral warning or counseling first. This should be followed by a written warning indicating that the substandard performance or work violation is not acceptable. The written warning should be self-contained in that it should indicate the correction needed and the circumstances under which the cause may result in termination.

2:2.5C Sample Punitive System with Corrective Action Policy and Progressive Discipline Policy

Punitive Discipline Plan

Corrective Action Policy and Progressive Discipline System

Corrective Action Policy

Purpose

To recognize the importance of early identification and prompt, coordinated action by line supervisors and Human Resources staff in the successful resolution of employee performance problems.

Scope

Applies to all employees.

Policy

Line supervisors are to achieve safe, efficient operations in their sections by ensuring that job performance by employees meets expectations. Supervisors will address problems that could or do impact on performance in a timely, constructive, and corrective manner. The handling of potentially serious problems will be coordinated with Human Resources.

Procedure

1. At the first indication of a potentially serious employee performance problem, supervisors will consult with their departmental personnel representative, and conduct a constructive interview with the employee to accomplish the following:
   a. Employee understanding of job responsibilities, performance standards, and importance of the job.
   b. Employee awareness of the problem.
   c. Determine the cause if possible and identify the corrective action that must be taken.
   d. Provide assurance of appropriate assistance and support.
2. If there is a reason to believe that the problem may be a continuing one of a serious nature, the supervisor will:
   a. Inform his higher management.
   b. Contact the Manager–Training and Development for guidance regarding corrective action.
      (1) In the event that training is appropriate, supervisors will initiate training efforts.
      (2) In the evident that formal counseling is appropriate, the "Employee Counseling Program" will be followed.
   c. Inform the appropriate Union official, where a Bargaining-Unit employee is involved, of the nature of the problem and corrective action being taken

so that the Union may act as appropriate with the employee toward the goal of resolving the problem.

3. In the event that discipline is anticipated, contact the Director of Personnel for guidance and concurrence. Refer to "Progressive Discipline Program."
4. Supervisors will ensure that they (1) keep their higher levels of management, the Manager–Training and Development, and the Union appropriately informed in a timely manner, (2) provide the employee with periodic evaluations of progress, and (3) have thorough records showing the nature of the problem and corrective actions that they have taken.

Progressive Discipline Program

Purpose

To provide a uniform approach to the administration of discipline in accordance with the principle that discipline is corrective in nature.

Procedure

1. Except when immediate action is required, before disciplining any employee beyond the Oral Reprimand level, supervisors should inform their higher management and obtain guidance and concurrence from the Director of Personnel. Guidance will include advice for the preparation of Written Reprimands and suspensions and termination memoranda.
2. It is advisable to have a second member of management present at all disciplinary sessions above the Oral Reprimand level.
3. Union employees have the right to Union representation at any level of discipline when they so request.
4. Discipline should be administered equitably and progressively. This section outlines the steps of progressive discipline:
   a. *Oral Reprimand:* If an employee's behavior violates any of the non-summary rules in the Code of Conduct, a supervisor must issue an Oral Reprimand. A record of the Oral Reprimand must be placed in the employee's file and a copy of that record given to the employee and, if applicable, to the employee's union steward.
   b. *Written Reprimand:* If an employee violates more than two different non-summary rules in a rolling six month period or the same non-summary rule in a rolling twelve month period, a supervisor must issue a Written Reprimand to the employee. The Written Reprimand will be placed in the employee's file with copies to the employee, to the employee's union steward (if any) and to the Director of Personnel. A Written Reprimand can be issued only after a conference with the employee.
   c. *Suspension Without Pay:* Any violation of any of the non-summary rules by any employee who was issued a Written Reprimand within the prior twelve months and any violation of the same non-summary rule which caused the issuance of the Written Reprimand within the 24 months prior to the issuance of the Written Reprimand will result in a Suspension Without Pay for three consecutive working days to be selected at the Company's discretion for sometime within the two weeks following the issuance of the notice of suspension. No Suspension Without Pay can be issued without approval of the Director of Personnel after a meeting with the employee.

d. *Termination:* If an employee violates any of the non-summary rules within 24 months of having been issued a Suspension Without Pay, the employee will be terminated. No Termination can occur without the approval of the Director of Personnel after a meeting with the employee.

5. If an employee commits any Summary offense as stated in the Code of Conduct, he/she will be suspended immediately, pending investigation of the facts and a decision regarding termination. A decision regarding termination will be made by the Director of Personnel (or designee) within ten working days from the commencement of the suspension.

2:3 Grievance Procedures

The models offered in this section range from a simple open door policy to procedures which mimic those typically required under a collective bargaining agreement with a labor union. In deciding what best fits your organization, the following considerations (at a minimum) should be taken into account:

1. The size and sophistication of your organization;
2. The corporate culture and past history of handling grievances and disputes; and
3. The state employment law, particularly (a) whether the adoption of a grievance procedure contractually binds you to follow it and (b) whether use of a grievance procedure will shield you from subsequent employment litigation.

2:3.1 Open-Door Policies

Open-door policies can either be informally or formally stated. In either case their goal is to allow employees to express complaints and have them brought to the attention of the appropriate member of the management team. The policy at 2:3.1 provides an example of an informal open-door policy. The policy at 2:3.2 is an example of a more formally stated policy.

2:3.1A Sample Informal Open-Door Policy

The following open-door policy is an example of an informal yet pro-active method of resolving conduct disputes while maintaining a cohesive workforce.

Open Door Policy—
Statement Of The Basic Relations

The basic approach to employee relations at [NAME OF EMPLOYER] reflects the belief that each person, unless proven otherwise, commands the full respect and trust of the Company and his or her fellow employees. It is presented at the outset that employees are concerned for their family, their security, their community and their personal dignity. Employees are essentially more willing to understand and work for the objectives of a company .hat, in turn, understands and respects their concerns. It is a matter of mutual fulfillment.

The basic approach in effect says that the Company and the individual have mutually sustaining purposes. In particular, the Company recognizes that individual contribution is not unrelated to individual needs, values and security.

The emphasis of this approach is upon teamwork, upon employee involvement in matters that affect them, upon the concept that all members of the team share the responsibility for the effectiveness of the operation and for contributing to and sharing the benefits of a mature and successful industrial climate.

Concepts such as probationary period, break schedules, an exhaustive list of rules, clock cards and time clocks, are not part of our program.

Simply stated, this program implies and is constructed to mean that the individual who is being or has been selected to join our team, is going to be a responsible, active and vital member of [EMPLOYER].

Plant Harmony

Since a cornerstone of the Company's employee relations approach is mutual respect and trust, there is a natural way of treating people . . . and that is "Treat others as you would like to be treated if your roles were reversed."

This is basically an honor system in which each individual makes a commitment to the entire group.

In the event of individual conduct disrespectful to any member of the group, the incident will be reviewed by the team leader with the individual to ascertain the pertinent facts and circumstances. If a problem does exist, counseling or aid will be provided to help overcome or resolve the situation. The nature and extent of counseling and aid will vary with the individual circumstances.

Under this approach, an individual employee is not asked to suffer any of the increasingly punitive "corrective" steps leading to suspensions traditionally found in industry. Rather, the objective is to arrive at a common understanding of conduct respectful of and responsible to the group and to the operation. Thereafter, the individual is entrusted to discipline himself/ herself to that common understanding. If experience clearly demonstrates that the individual's standards cannot co-exist with the rights of the group, then the employee will be terminated. The emphasis of this whole program is not "discipline" but the kind of understanding in which discipline is not necessary.

It should be emphasized that this approach is not a matter of "letting everyone do what they want." Nothing can be more disconcerting. This is an approach of "concern." When anything happens indicative of a problem or unfairness to fellow employees, the matter is DISCUSSED AND SOLUTIONS SOUGHT IMMEDIATELY with genuine faith that the individual, if disrespectful, can and will maturely correct his or her own course. Experience has shown to date that this kind of adult relationship not only uncovers prompt solutions but tends to lead those very few people uncomfortable with self-control to separate themselves voluntarily.

"Open" Policy

Freedom of expression among all members of the Company, regardless of your level in the organization, is an important prerequisite in making the Company's philosophy work.

Anytime you have an idea, a suggestion, a complaint, or a problem, feel free to call it to the attention of your Team Leader/Department Manager. Listening to what you have to say is an important part of his or her job.

If you are not satisfied with the outcome of your discussion, your Team Leader will help you arrange a prompt meeting with the Department Manager or Plant Manager.

If for some reason you prefer to initiate a particular discussion with the Department Manager, Employee Relations Manager, any other department head or Plant Manager instead of with your Team Leader, feel free to do so.

2:3.1B Sample Formal Open-Door Policy

The following open-door policy is an example of a traditional, formal method for resolving employee complaints and/or disputes.

Open Door Policy

Purpose

The purpose of this procedure is to provide a thorough, expeditious, and objective assessment of employee complaints, identify their causes, investigate any corrective actions which may be required, and respond to the complainants indicating that reviews were conducted with a position that either the complaint was ill-founded, or corrective action will be initiated.

Scope

This procedure outlines the steps for investigating and responding to complaints submitted by all employees to the Chairman, President and other Corporate Officers, including Operating Group heads.

Responsibility

Line management of Operating Groups is responsible for investigation and resolution of employee complaints which are received by Corporate Officers. Responsibility for answering such complaints is as follows:

> For complaints directed to the Chairman, President or other Officers not in the Groups, the Group Head prepares a written response to the complainant for the officer's signature. Copy is sent to the Corporate Vice President, Personnel and Organization Planning.

Complaints sent to Corporate Officers in Groups are to be answered by the Officer directly to the complainant with copy to the Corporate Vice President, Personnel and Organization Planning.

Personnel organizations within the Unit assist line management in the investigation and resolution of complaints.

The Corporate Vice President, Personnel and Organization Planning carries out further investigation of complaints to Officers as may be required.

Procedure

1. *Receipt of Complaint and Acknowledgement:* Employee complaints directed to Corporate Officers will be acknowledged to the complainant by the Officer receiving the complaint as soon as possible after receipt. A copy of the complaint is sent to the Corporate Vice President, Personnel and Organization Planning for information purposes.
2. *Forward to Appropriate Personnel Unit:* The Chairman, President or Executive Vice President receiving the complaint will forward it to the head of the Group in which the complainant is or was employed. In case of complaints directed to Corporate Officers within a Group, the complaint will be forwarded directly to the responsible Operating Unit Manager by the Officer.
3. *Investigation:* The complaint will be investigated by the next higher level of line management in the organization from which the complaint originated,

i.e., a complaint originating from a branch would be investigated by a Region, complaints from a Region investigated by a Group, etc.

4. *Response Time:* Response time on complaints will not exceed two weeks from receipt in the appropriate Operating Head's office. If for some reason the response cannot be made on the due date, a memo is to be directed to the Corporate Officer explaining the delay and establishing a new due date.
5. *Response to Complainant:* The Group head shall prepare a response to the complaint for the signature of the Chairman, President or other responsible Officer. If the complaint was directed to the Officer within the Group, that Officer shall reply directly to the complainant. All answers will convey the proper tone and will contain sufficient information to cover major points raised in the complaint. Copies of all answers are forwarded to the Vice President, Personnel and Organization Planning.
6. *Interviews:* In all cases, the employee filing the complaint should be interviewed, as well as the manager of that employee. Copies of the interview record should be part of the package forwarded to the Officer.
7. *Corporate Personnel Involvement:* In cases where an Officer or the Vice President, Personnel and Organization Planning feels that the complaint has not been satisfactorily investigated, or in cases which have Corporate-wide implications, or are extremely serious in nature, Corporate Personnel will directly investigate the complaint, including on-site interviews with the complaining employee and management, and issue its findings to the appropriate Officer, Operating Group head and Personnel Manager.

Tips On Using Open Door

1. Be sure your complaint is serious and not trivial. Performance appraisals, down-grades, compensation, benefits, affirmative-action matters are all serious; parking-space allotments, loose vacation days, office furnishings are not.
2. Go as high as you feel is necessary. All levels of management are open to you, but experience shows "Open Door" works quickest when your complaint is directed to an executive in your own organization.
3. Put your complaint in writing. A brief memo or letter, one page at most, will do. There is no special form to fill out.
4. Say up front who you are, what you are, and where you are, then focus on the nature of your complaint. That way, the recipient can find out quickly who is involved and what it is about.
5. Set out what you have done thus far to resolve the problem. Have you talked with your boss? With your boss's boss? To personnel? With what results? If you haven't heard anything in two or three weeks, say so.
6. Stick to the facts as you perceive them and avoid editorializing. Your complaint will be resolved more on its merits than on your pungent prose.
7. Give a copy of your complaint to your boss. First-line management is charged with helping you use Open Door, and can best do so if kept informed along the way—even if your boss is part of the problem.
8. Discuss overt signs of retaliation with personnel. You're guaranteed the right to air a perceived grievance without future risk, and personnel is there to help see this is done.

2:3.2 Grievance Appeal Procedures

Grievance procedures are designed to allow employees a means of recourse when they feel they have not been treated in accordance with stated company policy. This section provides an example of a generic grievance procedure plus a grievance procedure with a designated employee hearing officer appeal system.

2:3.2A Sample Designated Officer Appeal Policy and Generic Grievance Procedure

Designated Officer Appeal Policy

Grievance Procedure

In the normal operation of any company, problems or questions may arise. In addition, rumors often float around that may cause misunderstanding. In most instances, your supervisor will be able to give a prompt answer to your questions and will assist in solving your problems. However, your supervisor can only help you if you make your problem known. Should you feel you are treated unfairly, or that a problem is not being handled properly or that you need a question answered, you are invited to make use of the following policy:

FIRST, if a problem arises, we urge you to have an open discussion with your immediate supervisor before it affects your work or work atmosphere. Your supervisor has a responsibility to both you and the Company to solve problems as they arise; however, without your help your supervisor may not even be aware that a problem exists.

SECOND, if after a meeting with your supervisor, you still feel there are points that need further clarification or you are dissatisfied with the solution suggested by your supervisor, you may request a meeting with the [SECOND LEVEL OFFICER]. The [SECOND LEVEL OFFICER] will meet with you and discuss the matter within [   ] days. The [SECOND LEVEL OFFICER] will promptly investigate the matter and give you a written answer.

THIRD, if the problem remains unresolved, you may request the [SECOND LEVEL OFFICER]'s assistance in referring it to: [THIRD LEVEL OFFICER].

A written summary of the above investigation and meeting will be submitted for you by the [THIRD LEVEL OFFICER] along with any additional information you may desire to send. In addition, a personal meeting will also be arranged with [TOP OFFICER] during his/her next visit at your request.

FOURTH, if you have made the above-mentioned efforts concerning your problem and still feel it is unresolved, the Chairman of the Board of the Company will review your problem and have an independent investigation made of the matter. His answer will be a final resolution.

We are anxious to help with any problem and urge the above procedure. If you do not appeal your problem to any of the next levels, the resolution of the last step will be presumed to have been satisfactory to you.

Formal Grievance Management Appeal Committee System

Grievance Procedure

1. *Grievance Rights and Privileges.* The Company has established a grievance procedure designed to provide all personnel, other than those employed in a supervisory capacity, with a means of recourse when they feel they have not been treated in accordance with company policy. The procedure is also available to probationary personnel in all matters other than termination.

   The Company Grievance Procedure is administered by the Employee Relations office. You may obtain advice and assistance from the staff in this office in the processing of any grievance.

   The findings and results of the grievance procedure will be made available to the courts or any agency where the aggrieved is seeking further relief or adjustment.

2. *General Grievance Procedure.* A grievance is a statement or claim by you that the company has violated an express term of this handbook to your disadvantage. Any grievance must be presented orally or in writing to the immediate supervisor within seven days of the event resulting in the grievance or within seven days of the date you became aware of the violation. A grievance will not be considered unless prepared within the above seven-day time limit. The supervisor will attempt to adjust the matter as equitably as possible and will render a decision within seven days from the date the grievance was presented.

   If the supervisor's disposition of the matter is not satisfactory to you, the following procedure is available:

   a. Administrative Appeal—Within seven days after receipt of the supervisor's decision, you will obtain from and present to Employee Relations a grievance form which will contain a clear, concise, written statement of the problem, together with the decision rendered by the supervisor and the desired remedy or correction expected of the company.

      You may obtain assistance from the Employee Relations office in preparing the statement. After obtaining four typewritten, dated copies of the Grievance Notice, signed by you, Employee Relations will leave one copy with you, forward one copy to the organization head, one copy to the proper administrative officer, and retain the fourth copy for its files.

      Employee Relations will investigate the grievance impartially by consulting with you, the organization head and administrative officer and by referring to other appropriate sources of information.

      If Employee Relations considers it advisable, a conference will be held between you, the organization head or administrative officer, and an Employee Relations representative to discuss the grievance in an effort to reach a mutually satisfactory adjustment.

      In the absence of a satisfactory disposition of the matter in conference, the administrative officer will, within seven days after the date of the Grievance Notice, render a decision on the form provided for that purpose and forward one copy each to you, the organization head and Employee Relations, who retains the fourth copy.

   b. Management Appeals Committee—If you are not satisfied with the decision of the administrative officer, an appeal may be presented to the appropriate Employee Relations office within seven days after receipt of the decision. Such appeal will be heard by the Management Appeals Committee. You may obtain assistance from Employee Relations in preparing the Notice of Appeal. Reasons for the appeal must be stated in a clear, concise manner. Employee Relations will forward a typewritten copy of the Notice of Appeal and all documents pertinent to the proceedings to each member of the Management Appeals Committee. This Committee will be composed of a division officer, the corporate vice president of Industrial Relations, and the senior Industrial Relations executive of the appropriate division.

No grievance appeal will be considered at a meeting of the Management Appeals Committee unless it has been filed for at least four days before the meeting. You will be encouraged to appear at the meeting.

The Committee will render its decision in writing within 14 days after the meeting at which the appeal is considered. A signed copy of this decision will be delivered to you and the decision will be final.

2:3.2B Employee Represented Formal Grievance Procedure and Designated Employee Hearing Officer Appeal System

Noncontract Employee Grievance Procedure

The Vice President–Industrial Relations is primarily responsible for the policies and procedures in this section.

Statement Of Purpose

This grievance procedure is established to ensure that the policies of the Company are applied to its employees in fair, reasonable and nondiscriminatory fashion. It is not intended as a mechanism for questioning the content or advisability of policies. Thus, if you have a complaint involving the manner in which a Company policy has been applied to you, this procedure is the proper channel for registering that complaint. If you have a complaint relating to the content or advisability of a policy, you should register your complaint instead by sending a letter describing it (with a copy of the letter to your immediate supervisor) to your local Personnel office. That office will then carefully evaluate your complaint, act upon it if appropriate, and advise you in writing of its ultimate disposition.

The core of a good working relationship is open and direct communication. This procedure is not intended to limit that communication but rather to provide for a remedy when a frank discussion has failed to solve a problem. To that end it is expected that any employee who has a question or a complaint about his working conditions will meet with his supervisor and request an explanation. Only if that discussion fails to resolve the problem may an employee initiate Step 1 of the procedure. Similarly, with respect to a complaint involving the content or advisability of a policy, the employee may write to the local Personnel office only after meeting with a supervisor and requesting an explanation of the policy in question.

Eligibility

This procedure is available to any full-time or regular part-time employee, not covered by a collective agreement, who has completed his probationary period. This procedure is not available when in conflict with local laws and is not applicable in those countries where collective agreements or laws or government regulations provide procedures for the settlement of employee complaints or disputes.

Basic Regulations

1. The grievance procedure consists of three steps and is initiated as outlined in Step 1, Paragraph C.1.a. STEP 1 MUST BE INITIATED WITHIN FIFTEEN BUSINESS DAYS OF THE DATE ON WHICH THE CAUSE OF THE GRIEVANCE IS KNOWN TO THE EMPLOYEE OR COULD REASONABLY BE EXPECTED TO HAVE BEEN KNOWN.
2. Company supervisory personnel will not discriminate against an employee who invokes the grievance procedure nor against his representative or any witness called to testify in any hearing or investigation in connection therewith. The Personnel offices will monitor grievances to ensure compliance with this provision.

3. A grievant who desires to be assisted by another employee in processing his grievance may select another noncontract employee of the Company to assist him. The selected employee may decline such assistance for any reason and the grievant shall then be free to make an alternate selection. The grievant shall advise the Company of his selection in writing.
4. Complaints involving selection of an employee for promotion or the granting or withholding of merit pay increases will not be considered under the grievance procedure.
5. All hearings and investigations will be conducted during regular day working hours insofar as possible. Employees participating in the grievance procedure shall not suffer any loss of normal pay but shall not be compensated for participation during nonworking hours.
6. Any grievance not presented by the employee within the time limits prescribed, or any extension thereof, shall be considered automatically settled on the basis of the last decision.
7. In any time set forth in these instructions the term "business days" means Monday through Friday exclusive of Company-recognized holidays. Any of the time limits specified herein may be extended by mutual agreement.
8. The grievant together with all other employees who participate in the grievance proceedings, including participation before the System Board of Adjustment, will not suffer loss of pay as provided in Paragraph B.5 above. In addition, the Company will reimburse such persons for reasonable and actual expenses incurred in traveling to and participating in the Step 3 hearing. All expenses incurred in connection with the retention of outside counsel or the use of non-Company witnesses will be borne solely by the grievant.
9. If a grievance is appealed to the System Board of Adjustment as outlined in Paragraph C.3.b.2., the charges for preparation of a transcript and the fees of the neutral party will be borne by the Company.
10. In all steps, a copy of the answer may be either presented to the employee personally or sent to him by certified mail, return receipt requested. Filing of a grievance and appeal shall be either by personal delivery or by certified mail, return receipt requested, to the appropriate Company representative, within the specified time limit.
11. An employee who desires to file a grievance may call upon his local Personnel office for any information he requires pertaining to the administration of this procedure or for any policy or procedure information which he deems pertinent to his grievance. However, no Personnel representative will be eligible to serve on the System Board of Adjustment, except for the Vice President–Industrial Relations (or his designee) as provided in Paragraph C.3.b. of this section nor will any such representative be eligible to represent a grieving employee in the processing of his grievance.
12. The appropriate Personnel office will be responsible for notifying the supervisors of all employees to be involved in a grievance proceeding, including witnesses; the grievant's representative; and if applicable, the grievant's appointee to the Board.

Procedures

Step 1

1. The employee's grievance must be in writing and three copies must be personally delivered or mailed by certified mail, return receipt requested, to the employee's immediate supervisor within the time limit specified in Paragraph 8.1. (The immediate supervisor referred to in this procedure is the first level of management to whom the grieving employee reports.) The employee will forward one copy to the appropriate Personnel office for its investigation and retain one copy for his own file.
2. The supervisor will meet with the employee and any noncontract employee he has designated to assist him, consider the facts and answer in writing on the form within fifteen business days after receipt. The supervisor will return the original copy of the form to the employee, retain one copy for his file and forward one copy to the appropriate Personnel office.

Step 2

1. If the employee is not satisfied with the answer in Step 1, he may appeal by filing in writing with the appropriate Personnel office within five business days after receipt of the Step 1 answer.
2. Within five business days of receipt of the appeal, the Personnel office will designate a Hearing Officer to preside over an informal hearing. If the grievant knows of or has any reason for recommending the selection or exclusion of a particular individual, the grievant should include it in a letter with his appeal. However, final discretion in selection of the Hearing Officer rests with the appropriate Personnel office.
3. Within fifteen business days of receipt of the appeal, the Hearing Officer so designated shall meet with the employee, the noncontract employee representative previously authorized by him in writing and the first level supervisor. The Hearing Officer shall, within fifteen business days of the date of the hearing, give a written answer to the grievant by returning two copies of it to the employee and forwarding one copy together with copies of the Step 1 grievance and answer to the appropriate Personnel office. The Hearing Officer shall also send one copy to the grievant's supervisor. The decision of the Hearing Officer will be final.

2:3.4 Employee Counseling, Discipline and Peer Review Policies, and Employee Surveys

One goal of a proactive discipline program is to provide counseling to employees that fail to perform their duties or conduct themselves responsibly in order to achieve the solutions to the problems. Another method of correcting substandard behavior is to establish a peer review committee that is responsible for communicating problems to employees and applying corrective measures in a less threatening manner. This section provides an example of a peer review policy as well as a model peer review system of disciplinary actions. Finally, this section provides an employee survey that can be used by employers to gain valuable information on how to improve the corporate work environment.

2:3.4A Model Employee Counseling and Affirmative Discipline Policy

Employee Counseling And Affirmative Discipline

Purpose

To establish a program through which employees are assisted in their performance of responsibilities through affirmative and supportive counseling.

Policy

It is the policy of [NAME OF EMPLOYER] to assist and encourage employees in the performance of their responsibilities as employees. This policy involves the definition of and notice to employees of their responsibilities through the publication of standards of appropriate conduct, the establishment of procedures and guidelines for the affirmative counseling of employees who fail to perform their duties or conduct themselves responsibly and for achieving the solutions to problems. This policy also incorporates procedures by which employees may resolve disputes concerning the performance of their duties or conduct.

Responsibilities

Employees: Employees have responsibilities to the Company. Most of these, such as regular and prompt attendance, good productivity and a pleasant and cooperative attitude, are assumed by everyone. Other responsibilities, however, may not occur to all people. The Company believes it is helpful, therefore, to specify as clearly as possible all types of conduct which are unacceptable and which may result in the termination of employment. Giving employees this information is part of the Company's responsibility to its employees. It is hoped that this will help employees have a more satisfying employment experience because it will better enable them to know what is expected by the Company. A complete list of employee responsibilities is attached to this policy as Appendix A.

Department Head/Supervisor: It is the responsibility of the Department Head and/or Supervisor to assist and counsel employees in the performance of their responsibilities. This counseling must be in accordance with established procedures and conducted in an affirmative manner for the purpose of assisting employees to retain employment. The Department Head should solicit assistance and advice from the Personnel Department when presented with a difficult or unusual situation.

Personnel Department: It is the responsibility of the Personnel Department to define the parameters of permissible conduct; to monitor the operation of the procedures to ensure consistency and conformance to policy; to provide guidance to Department Heads and Supervisors; to provide additional counseling to employees; and to facilitate the grievance procedure.

Affirmative Discipline (AD) Procedure

AD is a procedure for handling and solving problems caused by employee conduct which falls below an acceptable standard of behavior. It is non-punitive in the sense that employees are not punished for violating rules but counselled and helped by supervisors to avoid similar conduct in the future. While some conduct may result in the immediate termination of an individual's employment (summary action), most unacceptable conduct will result in AD procedures. AD procedures involve the participation of the supervisor with the employee to resolve the problem that is causing the unacceptable conduct and the opportunity of the employee to improve while continuing active employment. The steps of AD are as follows:

First Meeting: In the event an employee engages in any unacceptable conduct (commits a non-summary offense) the supervisor will meet with the employee to work out a solution to the problem. This first meeting will not result in any formal or written agreement on a solution but a note will be made by the supervisor and a copy of the note will be given to the employee. If the solution is successful and no other failure to fulfill responsibilities occurs within twelve months, this incident will be removed from the employee's record.

Second Meeting: If, however, a second incident of unacceptable conduct occurs within the twelve months, the supervisor will again meet with the employee. Because the second incident indicates that a more serious problem may exist, the supervisor will develop with the employee a new solution to the problem and ask the employee to sign it. The employee's signature will indicate an agreement to the solution and intention to use it as the basis for fulfilling responsibilities. Again, if no other incident of unacceptable conduct occurs within twelve months from the last, both the first and second incidents will be removed from the employee's record.

Decision Day: If a third occurrence of unacceptable conduct takes place within twelve months of the second, a serious question will exist as to whether the employee wishes to continue employment at the Company. It may be that his/her life style or attitudes make it impossible to satisfactorily fulfill all of the responsibilities of an employee of the Company. The supervisor will tell the employee to stay away from his/her job for a day to consider whether he/she wishes to continue as an employee. If after the Decision Day off the employee chooses to remain employed at the Company, it will be with the understanding that he/she will satisfactorily fulfill all employee responsibilities. The Decision Day off will be *with* pay because the Company does not want the employee to think of this decision time as punishment. The Company hopes that every employee who is given decision time off will decide to continue employment. After the decision day off the employee must indicate whether he/she has decided to continue employment or quit. If the employee's decision is to continue, the supervisor and employee must develop a written solution to whatever difficulty the employee may be having which has been preventing responsible conduct. When a satisfactory solution is worked out, the employee must sign it. A form for this purpose will be provided (See Appendix B).

As in earlier steps, if there is no reoccurrence of unacceptable conduct within twelve months of the Decision Day off, the employee's record will be cleared. However, if another unacceptable incident occurs within the twelve months, it will indicate an inability or unwillingness to be a responsible employee and employment will be terminated.

Attendance Policy

Prompt attendance on the job is an important part of the performance of employee responsibilities. Absence and tardiness not only disturb the smooth functioning of the employee's job but also create inconveniences and interfere with other interrelated jobs and functions of the Company.

Good attendance is a condition of continued employment.

Definitions:

1. Lateness: anytime an employee is not at his/her work station, dressed and ready to work on time at the beginning of the shift or after any break or meal period.
2. Excused lateness: anytime an employee is late but provides a properly documented excuse satisfactory to the employee's supervisor.
3. Unexcused lateness: anytime an employee is late and fails to have a satisfactory excuse.
4. Early quit: anytime an employee leaves work before the end of a shift.
5. Excused early quit: anytime an employee has permission from his/her supervisor to leave work early.
6. Unexcused early quit: anytime an employee leaves work before quitting time without the prior permission of a supervisor.
7. Absence: anytime an employee is not at work for an entire shift.
8. Excused absence: anytime an employee is absent but provides a properly documented excuse satisfactory to the employee's supervisor.
9. Unexcused absence: anytime an employee is absent and fails to provide a properly documented excuse satisfactory to his/her supervisor.

Reporting off: All employees must notify their department head or immediate supervisor of their expected lateness or absence and provide a verbal reason prior to the beginning of the employee's shift. Subsequent written documentation supporting the reason for the lateness or absence may be required. Except in rare and unusual cases, a failure to report off prior to the beginning of a shift will render the lateness or absence "unexcused" regardless of any later justification or reason which may be offered. An excuse will not be given until the reason is properly considered by the supervisor; reporting off will not be an automatic excuse.

Unexcused lateness, absences and early quits: Unexcused lateness, absenteeism and early quits will be handled as follows:

- First Occurrence—first AD counseling (lateness and early quits to be docked from pay)
- Second Occurrence within twelve months—second AD counseling (lateness and early quit to be docked from pay)
- Third Occurrence within twelve months—Decision day off with pay (lateness and early quit to be docked from pay)
- Fourth Occurrence within twelve months—Termination

Because the system is based upon a rolling twelve months, a step in the procedure may be repeated. However, Decision Day can occur only once in any twelve month period. If the Decision Day step is reached more than once in a twelve month period, it is replaced by a final written warning co-signed by the employee.

Excused absences, lateness, early quits: Although an employee's absences, latenesses and early quits may be excused, it is possible that an accumulation of these occurrences will render an employee so undependable that his/her employment should be terminated. In these cases, the employee will receive AD counseling and the supervisor will attempt to work out a solution to the problem of the employee to avoid the further accumulation of an unacceptable number of excused absences, latenesses and/or early quits.

Job abandonment: An employee is considered to have abandoned his/her job if he/she has been absent from work for three consecutive work days without proper notification. Job abandonment is considered to be a voluntary resignation.

Superior Review

If at any time an employee believes that he/she has been unable to reach a satisfactory solution to a problem with a supervisor or disputes the facts stated as the bases for any counseling or Decision Day off, the employee may meet and discuss the situation with the personnel director. The personnel director will review the facts and conduct an independent investigation, if the employee requests and/or will work with the employee to reach a satisfactory solution.

If the employee is still unable to reach a satisfactory solution to the problem or believes he/she is being treated unfairly, he/ she may have the entire situation reviewed by any of the vice presidents of the Company the employee wishes. The employee simply informs the personnel director of a desire for this superior review and the identity of the vice president to examine the situation. All of the documents and information will be given to the vice president and a final solution will be worked out at that time.

Appeal

If an employee's employment is terminated, the employee may appeal the termination to a Decision Board for final consideration.

The Decision Board will be made up of three employees and two first line supervisors. All members of the Board will be chosen for the one case only. Employees in the same production unit or area (subject to the same first line supervisor), any supervisors involved in the case and the employee's direct supervisor may not be on the Board. The employee members of the Board shall be chosen by lot from all other non supervisory employees with more than five completed years of seniority. The supervisor members of the Board shall be chosen by lot from all non-involved first time supervisors.

The Decision Board members will hear anything the employee or any of the employee's witnesses may wish to say and will explore all of the other facts brought to their attention. In this process, the employee may choose to be represented by someone selected by him/her through the Representation Procedure, described later.

The Decision Board will decide whether the termination of employment was justified under the policy or rule. The Decision Board will not be allowed to alter, change or modify any policy or rule. The decision of the Board will be final and binding on the Company and employee. If the decision of the Board is that the termination was unjustified, the employee will be reinstated to full employment. If the decision of the Board is that the termination was appropriate, the termination will stand. The Board members must vote by secret ballot and can only state whether the termination was unjustified or justified. The decision of the Board will be by a simple majority. For convenience only, the personnel director will serve as a non-voting chairman of the Board.

Representation Procedure

At any time from the second incident of unacceptable conduct through proceedings before the Decisional Board an employee may select any first line supervisor who is not involved with the issue and not the employee's direct or indirect supervisor as a representative. This representative will be present with the employee at all meetings with the employee's supervisor and before the Decision Board to help the employee reach a solution to the problem or to ensure that all of the facts are considered. The representative will also be available to the employee at reasonable times to discuss the situation. These discussions will be confidential and will not be related to any other person in the Company, unless the employee specifically authorizes it. Representatives are instructed that they are to act only on behalf of the employee and are prohibited from discussing anything related to the employee's situation with any other person unless the employee is present or has specifically authorized it.

Appendix A
Code of Conduct

Summary Offenses

The following conduct is prohibited and will result in the termination of employment:

1. Any form of physical assault or severe verbal abuse of a supervisor, another employee or business invitee of the Company.
2. Being under the influence of, using or possessing alcohol or a controlled substance (e.g., marijuana, narcotics, barbiturates) during working hours (including lunchtime, dinner and break periods whether on or off the premises), or using alcohol or a controlled substance at any time just prior to working hours.
3. Theft or dishonesty, including a breach of Company security or confidentiality, punching another employee's time card, falsification of any business record or the giving of a false excuse for absence from work.
4. Intentional damage to the property of the Company, another employee or business invitee of the Company.
5. Unprovoked assault on another employee or the use of a weapon in any fight with another employee during working hours or on Company property.
6. Carrying or otherwise possessing firearms on the premises.
7. Absence from work for three consecutive workdays without proper notification.
8. Insubordination, willful neglect of duty or disobedience of reasonable instructions or directions issued by a supervisor or other representative of the employer. This includes the refusal to work overtime and the refusal to sign any AD statement.

Non-Summary Offenses

The following types of conduct are considered unacceptable and will result in AD procedures:

1. Abusive language or conduct directed at a supervisor, other employee or business invitee of the Company.
2. Fighting, horseplay, disorderly or unsafe conduct on Company premises.
3. Leaving the Company during scheduled working hours without permission of a supervisor or other employer representative.
4. Loan sharking, gambling, working numbers on Company premises.
5. Failure to follow absentee notification procedure.
6. Violation of the Company's no solicitation rule.
7. Bad attitude resulting in an adverse effect on the Company's work or employee morale.

8. Poor performance or productivity.
9. Negligence or carelessness which causes or could cause damage to equipment, others or create a safety hazard.
10. Unsatisfactory attendance or the abuse of or conduct indicating an intent to abuse the attendance policy.

Appendix B

After my Decision Day with pay, I have decided that I want to remain employed by [NAME OF EMPLOYER]. To do this, I understand that I must fulfill my responsibilities as an employee. One of these responsibilities is to comply with the Code of Conduct, specifically [state here the rules previously violated].

I have discussed with my supervisor the reasons why I have had difficulty in the past and agree that in the future [state here the agreed upon solution].

I also understand that this is my last chance. If I violate any rule in the Code of Conduct at any time within the next twelve months, my employment will be terminated. If I conduct myself responsibly by not violating any of the rules within the next twelve months, my record will be cleaned.

______________________	______________________
Supervisor	Employee

2:3.4B Sample Peer Review System

Peer Review System
Review of Disciplinary Actions

[NAME OF EMPLOYER] wants to be a good place for you to work. For this reason, we try to be fair to all of our employees. We think that fairness is one of our responsibilities to you. From time to time, it is necessary for us to remind employees of their responsibilities. This is usually done through warnings set up by our discipline system. Unfortunately, in a few cases the warnings go unheeded or an employee commits an act so serious that employment must be terminated for the good of the Company and the remaining employees. We recognize the special importance of those decisions and the particular need at those times to be fair. For this reason, we are implementing a procedure available to all employees to review all termination decisions.

The procedure involves a Review Committee made up of three regular employees and two first line supervisors. If a majority of the Committee votes to uphold the discharge, the termination stands. If the Committee votes to overturn the discharge, the termination will be reversed and the employee will be returned to his regular job with no loss of pay. The decision of the Committee will be final and cannot be reversed by the Company. The following four paragraphs explain how the procedure works.

If an employee is terminated for any reason, he or she may request the personnel director to call a Review Committee meeting. This request must be made by the end of the working day after the day of discharge. On the next regular working day the names of all employees in the company who have five or more years of seniority will be placed in a container. The personnel director will draw one name. That employee will then draw three names. These three people will be members of the Review Committee. The names of all first line supervisors will be placed by the personnel director in a separate container and the appealing employee will draw three names. The employee may choose which two of those three people will be the two supervisory members of the Review Committee. If any of the Committee members do not wish to serve or were directly involved in the facts on which the termination was based, new names will be drawn for their replacement.

On the next work day, the Review Committee will meet. The non-voting chairperson of the Committee will be the personnel director. The personnel director will present to the Committee all of the documents involved in the case and a report of the facts. The employee involved may be present at this and all subsequent meetings. In addition, the employee may call any witnesses he or she wishes and may choose any other employee to represent or be with him or her at all meetings.

The Committee may call any witnesses it wants to hear and ask for any relevant documents to be produced.

When the Committee has heard all of the evidence it wishes to hear or which the involved employee has presented, the Committee will vote by secret ballot. The single question to be answered by the Committee is "Should this employee have been discharged under the rules?" If a majority of the Committee votes "Yes," the employee's termination will stand. If a majority of the Committee votes "No," the termination is reversed and the employee will return to work the next day with all back pay. The Committee cannot invalidate a rule or reduce the discharge to a suspension. The Committee's decision is limited to whether the rule was violated and the discharge of the employee was justified by the facts and under the procedure.

If you have any questions about how this policy is intended to operate, feel free to discuss it with either the personnel director or the plant manager.

2:3.4C Sample Employee Survey

This survey is to find out about your place of work: what you think about it and how it can be made better. The results of this Study will be used by [EMPLOYER] to identify those things which are good and those things which are not so good about working at this Company.

While your answers to the questions will be completely confidential, the results will be discussed in group meetings so that we can all participate in making improvements. No one in the Company will ever be able to look at your answers. All answer sheets will be tabulated by an independent company and only the overall results will be discussed.

If this survey is to be helpful, it is important that you answer each question honestly. This is not a test and there are no right or wrong answers. Some questions ask you to agree or disagree with a description of things at the Company. Others ask for your opinion.

You will notice that some of the same questions are asked several different ways. This is not meant to trick you. We do this to determine how well our different questions measure the same ideas.

We thank you in advance for your cooperation and hope you find the survey interesting.

I.N.D. Surveys

Part I

The following information is needed to help us analyze the data. All of your responses are strictly confidential. Individual responses will not be seen by anyone within the Company.

Select One:

1. Are you
   a. full time
   b. part time — Answer ________________

2. Do you work at
   a. [DIVISION ONE]
   b. [DIVISION TWO] — Answer ________________

3. What is your current pay range?
   a. $______ – $______
   b. $______ – $______
   c. $______ – $______
   d. $______ – $______ — Answer ________________

4. How long have you been employed by this Company?
   a. less than 1 year
   b. 1-5 years
   c. 6-10 years
   d. over 10 years — Answer ________________

5. How many permanent full time jobs have you had before working for this Company?
   a. None
   b. 1 to 2 previous jobs
   c. 3 to 4 previous jobs
   d. 5 to 6 previous jobs — Answer ________________

6. How long have you been performing your present job (even though your pay level may have changed)?
   a. less than 1 year
   b. 1 to 2 years
   c. 3 to 4 years
   d. 5 or more years — Answer ________________

7. How long has it been since you bid for or otherwise were promoted to a higher rated job?
   a. less than 1 year
   b. 1 to 2 years
   c. 3 to 4 years
   d. 5 or more years
   e. never — Answer ________________

Part II

The questions in this part ask you:

- How much you AGREE with things

or

- How IMPORTANT things are

or

- How OFTEN things happen

You will answer each question by circling a number.

	strongly disagree	disagree	undecided	agree	strongly agree
A.					
1. The information I receive from management is usually accurate	1	2	3	4	5
2. When changes are made, the employees usually lose out in the end	1	2	3	4	5
3. In this Company, it is sometimes unclear who has the authority to make a decision	1	2	3	4	5
4. It is really not possible to change things around here	1	2	3	4	5
5. In general, I like working here	1	2	3	4	5
6. People here feel you can't trust supervisors	1	2	3	4	5
7. People here feel you can't trust the owner	1	2	3	4	5

	strongly disagree	disagree	undecided	agree	strongly agree
8. My pay is fair considering what other companies in this area pay	1	2	3	4	5
9. Employees do not have much of a chance to influence what goes on in this Company	1	2	3	4	5
10. Management is flexible enough to make changes when necessary	1	2	3	4	5
11. I often think about quitting	1	2	3	4	5
12. If I could find another job which paid about the same as this one, I would quit	1	2	3	4	5
13. All in all, I am satisfied with my pay	1	2	3	4	5
14. All in all, I am satisfied with the fringe benefits I receive	1	2	3	4	5
15. People in this organization will do things behind your back	1	2	3	4	5
16. The people I work with generally do a good job	1	2	3	4	5
17. I have confidence that the management will try to do as much for the employees as it reasonably can	1	2	3	4	5

	strongly disagree	disagree	undecided	agree	strongly agree
18. I feel I am really a part of this Company	1	2	3	4	5
19. I look forward to coming to work each day	1	2	3	4	5
20. In general, the employees here try to get along and work together	1	2	3	4	5
21. My supervisor lets me know just what is expected of me	1	2	3	4	5
22. My supervisor encourages me to help in developing new or better ways to do my job	1	2	3	4	5
23. My supervisor maintains high standards for performance	1	2	3	4	5
24. My supervisor expects more from me than what is reasonable	1	2	3	4	5
25. My supervisor does not understand what it is like to do my job all day	1	2	3	4	5
26. My supervisor treats all employees in my work area equally	1	2	3	4	5
27. My supervisor treats me fairly	1	2	3	4	5

	strongly disagree	disagree	undecided	agree	strongly agree
28. My supervisor gives me adequate feedback about how well I do my job	1	2	3	4	5
29. My supervisor asks my opinion about how to solve work related problems	1	2	3	4	5
30. My job is challenging	1	2	3	4	5
31. It always seems I have too much work to do	1	2	3	4	5
32. The work I do on my job is meaningful to me	1	2	3	4	5
33. It is important to me that my work is of high quality	1	2	3	4	5
34. I do not have enough training to do my job well	1	2	3	4	5
35. I know what I will be doing from day to day	1	2	3	4	5
36. I have too much work to do everything well	1	2	3	4	5
37. My job makes good use of my abilities	1	2	3	4	5
38. Doing my job well gives me a feeling that I've accomplished something worthwhile	1	2	3	4	5
39. I have all the skills I need to do my job	1	2	3	4	5

	strongly disagree	disagree	undecided	agree	strongly agree
40. I work hard	**1**	**2**	**3**	**4**	**5**
41. Considering my skills and the effort I put into my job, I am satisfied with my pay	1	2	3	4	5
42. On my job, I know exactly what is expected of me	1	2	3	4	5
43. I will probably look for a new job in the next year	1	2	3	4	5

44. Please rate the amount of effort you put out in the performance of your job during an average work day.

1	2	3	4	5
no effort		*some effort*		*extreme effort*

45. Please rate the amount of skill you believe your job takes.

1	2	3	4	5
no skill		*some skill*		*great skill*

B. Different people want different things from their job. Here is a list of things a person could think are important. How important is each of the following to you?

	little or no importance		moderately important		extremely important
46. How important is the friendliness of the people you work with?	1	2	3	4	5
47. How important is the amount of pay you get?	1	2	3	4	5
48. How important is paid time-off?	1	2	3	4	5
49. How important is the availability of overtime?	1	2	3	4	5

	little or no importance		moderately important		extremely important
50. How important is it for you to have a sense of accomplishment from your job?	1	2	3	4	5
51. How important is the respect you receive from the people who supervise your work?	1	2	3	4	5
52. How important is it that the owners of the Company care about you and the quality of your worklife?	1	2	3	4	5

C. Here are some things that could happen to people who do their work *well*. How likely is it that each of these things would happen to you?

	very unlikely		somewhat likely		very likely
53. How likely is it that you will be promoted or given a better job if you perform well?	1	2	3	4	5
54. How likely is it that you will be recognized as a good performer if you do well?	1	2	3	4	5
55. How likely is it that you will receive any special benefit from doing your job well?	1	2	3	4	5
56. How likely is it that you will be disciplined if you perform your job poorly?	1	2	3	4	5

D. Here are some things that could happen to people when they do their jobs *poorly*. How likely is it that each of these things would happen to you?

	very unlikely		somewhat likely		very likely
57. How likely is it that you won't be promoted or given a better job if you perform poorly?	1	2	3	4	5
58. How likely is it that you will not get a benefit or cash reward if you perform your job poorly?	1	2	3	4	5
59. How likely is it that you will be disciplined if you perform your job poorly?	1	2	3	4	5

E. How much pride do you feel about each of the following?

	No pride at all	Not very much pride	Some pride	Quite a bit of pride	A great deal of pride
60. My job performance	1	2	3	4	5
61. The quality of the Company's product in general	1	2	3	4	5
62. My job	1	2	3	4	5
63. The Company	1	2	3	4	5

F.

	strongly disagree	disagree	undecided	agree	strongly agree
64. I feel my job is secure from layoff	1	2	3	4	5
65. People sometimes get disciplined or fired unfairly	1	2	3	4	5
66. Employees around here get a second choice	1	2	3	4	5
67. Supervisors are always looking over our shoulders trying to catch us doing something wrong	1	2	3	4	5
68. Supervisors really don't care about the employees as people.	1	2	3	4	5
69. There is a great deal of pressure put on me for high quality work	1	2	3	4	5
70. My job keeps me busy	1	2	3	4	5
71. My ideas on how to do my job better are not considered	1	2	3	4	5
72. I am welcome to discuss any problem with the President of the Company	1	2	3	4	5

	strongly disagree	disagree	undecided	agree	strongly agree
773. When I express dissatisfaction with my job or the workplace in general I can count on my supervisor to try to help	1	2	3	4	5
74. There is little chance for promotion in this Company	1	2	3	4	5
5. There is nothing I can do to affect whether or not I get a promotion	1	2	3	4	5
76. New employees do not get proper training	1	2	3	4	5
77. People who are applying for jobs here are not qualified	1	2	3	4	5
78. Management here frowns on transferring to other jobs	1	2	3	4	5
79. Management here is not concerned with improving employee satisfaction with their jobs	1	2	3	4	5
80. Promotions around here are not related to job performance	1	2	3	4	5
81. I am not sure what factors determine whether you get a promotion	1	2	3	4	5

THANK YOU

Chapter 3

Coping With Labor Unions

While union membership has steadily declined from a peak of 35 percent of the American workforce in the 1950s to less than 20 percent today, an organized workforce remains a fact of life for many employers. Yet, organized labor's assertion that its membership will increase in the next decade seems reasonable because employees have become increasingly concerned about their job security due to (1) continued competition from abroad and (2) the declining economy and the resulting large number of employee terminations in order to achieve corporate "rightsizing." Should a group of employees be approached by or attempt to organize a union to represent them, employers must be aware of the statutory mandates and prohibitions that apply to labor organizations. Generally, the rights conferred to labor unions and the employees whom unions represent are derived under the authority of the National Labor Relations Act (NLRA). Section 3:1 covers how the NLRA resticts employers' actions and, in turn, what permissable behavior employers and their supervisors can engage in when confronted with a union organizing drive. Section 3:1 covers the collective bargaining process between employers and unions once employees have successfully managed to organize. Finally, Section 3:3 covers the procedures of the National Labor Relations Board (NLRB) in resolving disputes between employers and unions.

3:1 Union Organizing Drives

The National Labor Relations Act (NLRA) has established various procedures and specified certain events that must take place when employees seek union affiliation. (See Q. 113–Q. 134 and Q. 117S–Q. 127.1S.) The NLRA also restricts actions and statements of employers (including the employer's managers and supervisors) when confronted with a union organizing drive so that the process will not be unduely hindered. (See Q.119, Q. 120, Q. 124, and Q. 125.) For example, employers may neither promise any benefit if the union were not to be elected, nor threaten any reprisal if the union were to sustain a majority. The National Labor Relations Board (NLRB) is the independent governmental agency that is empowered by Congress to enforce NLRA. Among its many duties, the NLRB must accept representation petitions filed by labor unions and employees, investigated the validity of those petitions, and conduct secret ballot elections. If the union should win a secret ballot election, the NLRB has the authority to certify that union as the bargaining representative for that group of employees. (See Q. 135–Q. 159 and Q. 135.1S–Q. 175.1S for a discussion of the collective bargaining process.)

However, the mere existence of the NLRA and NLRB does not mean that an employer must resign itself to an organized workforce. Unions lose more elections than they win; thus, the chances of winning are probably high enough for an employer to invest the time and money necessary to conduct an effective campaign to win employees back from the union. (See Q. 134.) In fact, a company that vigorously opposes unionization enjoys a substantially better chance of defeating a union than a company that does not address the issue of organizing.

Section 3:1.1 presents a model supervisor's guide on personnel relations and labor law. This supervisor's guide is intended to serve as a blueprint for employer behavior during a union organizing drive. It is comprehensive in its coverage of union organizing drives. It contains substantive information regarding unions and the process of union organizing drives, it effectively communicates the importance of the status, role, and proper behavior of supervisors as members of management during a union organizing drive, and it contains samples of acceptable, effective communication from an employer to its employees when attempting to defeat a union election campaign.

3:1.1 Model Supervisor's Guide On Personnel Relations And Labor Law

The following is an example of a supervisor's guide covering personnel relations including management conduct during a union organizing drive. As noted in its introduction, this guide is intended to be a source of quick, general answers to specific questions and problems that may arise should a union organizing drive occur. Why should a non-union company consider preparing such a guide *before* being faced with an organizing drive? For several reasons. First, because employer behavior is subject to a series of prohibitions under the National Labor Relations Act. These prohibitions extend to the employer's supervisors and managers as well. For example, a employer should *not* do the following:

- Interrogate employees about their interest in the union or union activities;
- Discharge or otherwise punish employees who are trying to organize for the union;
- Make threats or promises to employees; or
- Conduct surveillance of employees at organizing meetings or other union activities.

All members of an employer's management team must be aware *before the fact* that engaging in prohibited behavior during a union organizing drive can lead to charges of "union busting" or engaging in unfair labor practices.

A second reason for developing this type of supervisor's guide is that a significant number of union organizing drives fail. Therefore, a company that vigorously opposes unionization enjoys a substantially better chance of defeating a union than a company that does not address the issues of organizing. The first step in vigorously opposing unionization should be to conduct a meeting of supervisors and managers to explain their role in defeating unionization as well as how they should and should not conduct themselves during the drive. This guide is designed to help accomplish that first step.

Supervisor's Guide On Personnel Relations And Labor Law

Introduction

This Supervisor's Guide on Personnel Relations and Labor Law is prepared for your use in dealing with everyday personnel relations and with labor union organizing.

It is intended to be a source of quick, general answers to specific questions and problems which may arise and if you familiarize yourself with it and use it for quick reference, you will have the ability to solve many of the more common problems as they occur, and will know when to seek more advice on those not covered.

It is no secret that labor unions are engaging in massive organizational drives throughout the entire country. Their membership is down and they have lost much of their political power. A recent study reveals that fewer than 1 out of every 4 American workers belongs to a labor union. For this reason, unions are spending millions each year to get more people. Supervisors are often the reason a union is successful or unsuccessful.

Today's professional union organizer is highly trained, well informed and knows exactly what he wants to accomplish and how he wants to accomplish it. This makes it imperative that all supervisors be well informed.

You As A Supervisor

It is important that every supervisor realizes the importance of their actions as part of the company's management team. Below is a discussion of the various roles and responsibilities that accompany a supervisory position. A thorough understanding of these roles and responsibilities is critical, not only in the event of a union organizing drive, but also in the context of the day-to-day, ongoing management of the company. Fulfilling your role as supervisor effectively is the best way to ensure that the company's employees are satisfied with and secure in their jobs. This, in turn, is the best defense against an organized workforce.

Your Status

Under the National Labor Relations Act, all employees of the Company are divided into two groups—labor and management.

You are a supervisor and, as such, are a part of management. As supervisors, there are several things you should never forget:

1. You are the front line managers of our Company; the people who, with the employees for whom you are responsible, really make it go.
2. The employees regard you as the connecting link between the administration and themselves.
3. You are the primary leaders to whom the employees under your supervision look for pay raises and promotions, for a fair scheduling of work, for special treatment in cases of personal hardship, and for discipline and impartial treatment.

4. Under the law, you are the legal agents of all of management. This means that what you say or do is the same under the law as what the Administrator of the Company says or does.

Leadership

Let's take a frank look at ourselves as front line supervisors. It is only natural that the employees get their strongest impression of management from their supervisors. They see you and deal with you every work day. Therefore, it is most important that the image they have of you be good.

Many case studies in labor management affairs have shown that front line supervision is all-important. This is not to say that you are due all the credit, or all the blame in specific circumstances. Rather, it is to say that you share a large part of the responsibility if union problems develop and, most importantly, that management cannot possibly relate to all of the employees as it might wish, or should, without you. Union organization is always based on one or both of two ideas:

1. That management is mistreating the employees either through insufficient wages or through unfair or discriminatory work practices.
2. That even if wages are all right and working conditions are fine, the only way to obtain security and protection is through a union; that is, job insurance.

Management Mistreatment

The traditional argument that unions have used to stir up support is that management mistreats the rank and file employee. We are all familiar with the old stories about basement sweatshops, company guards beating people, unsafe conditions in coal mines, the 16-hour day, the company store, child labor, and all the rest. These things were bad and needed correction. They were corrected and not just by unions. Managers became smarter, laws were passed, and good sense directed that happy and fairly treated employees were the best. These conditions haven't existed since World War I. Nevertheless, unions have continued for over forty years to try to scare people by arousing the spectre of management mistreatment and have attempted to take all of the credit for eliminating gross abuses of power by managers.

Job Insurance

Examination of hundreds of union organizational pamphlets shows that although some organizers are still using the scare techniques, most of them are getting smarter and using the "soft sell." The scare tactics are now used only for background. In other words, unions don't actively try to scare. They admit that sweatshop conditions no longer exist, but they now imply that "if you don't join the union, all of the bad conditions may come back." They don't do this by saying that if you don't join the union, Congress will repeal all of the laws it has passed for the last 50 years, or that fine managers of great businesses will reinstate the 15-hour day at 15 cents an hour; or that discipline will be enforced with a billy club. Of course, that would be ridiculous, and union organizers aren't that crude. They take a smoother approach to try to get the same thing across.

For example, unions stress "discrimination." They tell the employees that if the union gets in, no longer will they be subject to the whim of a supervisor or his favoritism. This may be a potent argument. Let's examine it carefully.

Most workers are convinced, if they are making a decent salary, that their company is a good one. To them it is a source of pride to be working for a successful organization, and the bigger and more successful the organization, the better. The gripes they have are usually directed at the front line supervisor. Workers commonly say that the policies of the Company are all right but the trouble is that the supervisors don't carry them out.

If employees don't understand the method of pay, the scheduling or division of work; if they see favored treatment given some employees; if they experience harsh, inconsistent, unpredictable or apparently unjustified discipline; if management seems to be unsympathetic about their personal problems, it isn't the president or the vice president who gets the blame. The fault is fixed on you—the person in charge of the job.

There are two points to be learned here:

1. Whoever gets the blame, the result is the same—union success.
2. *Humanics* are as important as *mechanics*.

You must be certain to handle most of these problems before they arise, and that when they do arise, to deal with them fairly and promptly. Remember, a union cannot do anything to make an employee's job more secure but eliminate unfair treatment. If an employee must be disciplined or discharged for good cause, a union cannot prohibit it. If a reduction in force is required, a union can't stop it.

Self-Examination

Examine yourself today. If you have been wrong, don't be afraid to admit it. We all hate to say, "I don't know the answer" or, "I was wrong, but I'll get it straightened out." Leadership requires us to be honest with ourselves and to clear up any past situations which may be smoldering.

Many of us came up from the ranks. Periodically, think back to how it was when you were in the ranks and try to analyze the situation. One reason you are supervisors is your ability to think ahead and to find the reasons for trouble.

Principles Of Leadership In Supervision

Much has been written about leadership principles. Much more could be written. The aim of these principles is just to serve to remind us of things we already know.

Your Leadership Role In Relation To The Company

While you are directly responsible for the day-to-day management of specific department(s) and employees, your actions as a supervisor reflect on the company as a whole. Therefore, you should:

1. Support with honesty the policies laid down by the Company;
2. Promote the Company by speaking well of it and bragging about past performances;
3. Be a morale builder;
4. Help develop a good organization by building employees who will carry on in future years;
5. Make suggestions concerning the improvement of efficiency and personnel relations;

6. Promote economy and prevent waste;
7. Maintain the highest standards of efficiency;
8. Enforce and practice all safety rules and regulations of the Company;
9. Protect and preserve Company property at all times; and
10. Be a good citizen off duty.

Your Leadership Role In Relation To Immediate Superiors

In dealing with immediate superiors you should:

1. Cooperate with them;
2. Obey orders and carry out instructions in detail, and inform your superior of changes in conditions or personnel problems;
3. Report occurrences or conditions fully and accurately;
4. Be courteous and respect the position of your superior as you wish to be respected by those you supervise;
5. Make suggestions for improvements;
6. Try to relieve your superior of details; and
7. Assume full responsibility for your area.

Your Leadership Role In Relation To Allied Supervisors

In dealing with allied supervisors you should:

1. Cooperate with all supervisors on the same level;
2. Exchange ideas for the good of the Company;
3. Talk positively about all Company affairs;
4. Treat them with courtesy, respect, and tolerance;
5. If invited, counsel with them on personal matters;
6. Help them look good in their work and to those whom they supervise;
7. Never belittle an associate for the sake of personal gain;
8. Let the employees know that you have confidence in their supervisor; and
9. Always be fair and honest.

Your Leadership Role In Relation To Subordinates

1. Treat them with consideration and remember at all times to respect their feelings;
2. Honestly represent them to management when necessary;
3. Interpret Company policies to them;
4. Be an example, both on and off duty;
5. Be generous with praise where deserved;
6. Be considerate and positive with discipline;
7. *Be consistent in all of your treatment of all employees and always avoid favoritism*;
8. Help them develop themselves;
9. Judge them honestly and never let personalities enter into your judgment;
10. Develop their confidence by being fair and loyal to them;

11. Try to place employees according to their ability and temperament;
12. Never pass the buck;
13. Support your employees by assuming full responsibility for their work;
14. Be interested and sympathetic in their personal problems; and
15. *Be predictable.*

What The Employees Expect Of You

Just as you set goals for and have expectations of your employees, those employees have the right to expect certain expectations of you, which you must keep in mind if you hope to develop a satisfied, secure and motivated workforce. Some expectations that employees have of you include:

1. To keep them busy without driving them;
2. To know their capabilities, individually, and to judge them honestly;
3. To teach them thoroughly and correctly;
4. To maintain discipline;
5. To insist upon safety in detail;
6. To be willing to discuss individual grievances and to handle them fairly;
7. To insist upon high standards of work;
8. To be a good workman yourself as well as a good supervisor;
9. To be well-liked and to have the respect of your superiors and allied supervisors; and
10. To know your own job thoroughly.

The Labor Law

A general understanding of the federal labor laws is necessary for you to represent the company effectively. Below is a brief description of the present labor law as well as a more detailed discussion of "protected activities" and "prohibited activities," which are the portions of the law that directly affect you as a supervisor.

Federal Labor Act

The first federal labor law was known as the "Wagner Act" and was passed in 1935. The law was amended in 1947 by the "Taft-Hartley Act." The law was amended again in 1959 by the "Landrum-Griffin Act." The 1947 and 1959 amendments were necessary to stop union abuses which had been exposed by Congressional hearings. The basics of the present law are discussed below:

Purpose

To regulate relations between management and labor in businesses affecting interstate commerce. The Act makes a sharp distinction between management and labor. It is supposed to reduce strife between the two and sets up certain rules regulating union organization.

Coverage

It applies to all of our employees.

Main Parts

The main parts of the Act are contained in Section 7, known as "Protected Activities" and Section 8, known as "Prohibited Activities."

Protected Activities

These are rights which are given to employees and they are not just for union employees. For instance, any group of employees who get together for any purpose concerning their work conditions are given these rights. They are:

1. The right of self-organization;
2. The right to form, join, or assist labor organizations;
3. The right to bargain collectively through their chosen representatives;
4. The right to engage in concerted activities for the purpose of bargaining as a group or for other mutual aid or protection; and
5. *The right to refuse to join, form or assist labor organizations.*

Prohibited Activities

The employer (and remember, this includes all supervisors) is prohibited from:

1. Interfering with the above rights of employees or coercing them;
2. Assisting or interfering with the formation of a labor organization or contributing money to it;
3. Discriminating against any person in hiring or firing in order to discourage union membership;
4. Punishing an employee for giving testimony; and
5. Refusing to bargain with the chosen representative of the employees.

A violation of either a protected or a prohibited activity is called an "unfair labor practice." Unions can also commit unfair labor practices.

Union Unfair Labor Practices

The following are examples of how a union can commit an unfair labor practice. Such practices include:

1. To restrain or coerce employees in exercising their protected rights;
2. To attempt to cause an employer to discriminate against an employee;
3. To refuse to bargain with the employer;
4. To engage in secondary boycotts, which is to try to get an employer or his employees to stop dealing with another employer; and
5. To extort, charge exorbitant fees, etc. and other matters that are similar.

Special Comment

An employer has the right to hire or fire for any reason so long as it is not on account of union activities or on the basis of an individual's race, sex, religion, etc. Sometimes union organizers will tell employees that they can't be fired if they belong to a union or even during an organizational campaign. Sometimes organizers will tell an employee to notify his supervisor that he is engaged in union activity for two reasons: (1) in order to put the entire Company on notice of such activity so that any firing can be tied to union activities; (2) in order to bait the supervisor into firing him.

Warning

Any firing or layoff during union organizational activity is dangerous and should be cleared with your immediate supervisor, except in emergencies such as insubordination, drunkenness, serious violation of safety rules, failure to report for work, etc. There are three reasons for this:

1. Unions sometimes try to drum up discharge cases to aid their organizing effort so that they appear to be defending all the employees;
2. Unions take credit if it is finally determined that the firing was discriminatory and the Company has to reinstate the person with back pay for the time off; and
3. Unions can be recognized as a representative of employees without an election if it is finally determined that the firing was discriminatory and that the act so created an atmosphere of fear among the employees that a fair election could not be conducted.

Union Representation Procedures

Unions have the right to try to convince employees to join them and to permit them to be their representative for collective bargaining and in grievances. Unions can attempt to organize employees in many ways. Common methods are:

1. Picket the Company to advertise;
2. Pass out leaflets outside the Company to advertise;
3. Contact employees in their homes or by telephone; and
4. Provide leaflets and other materials to sympathetic employees who campaign inside the Company.

If a union secures signed cards authorizing them as the representative of a majority of the employees in a group with common interest, it may demand to be recognized by the employer as the bargaining agent for all of the employees in that group. The employer can then voluntarily recognize the union and bargain with it. However, if the employer has a good faith doubt that the union actually has authorization cards from a majority of the employees the employer believes are in a group with common interests, or has a good faith doubt that the cards were obtained fairly, it can refuse to recognize the union. If the employer refuses to voluntarily recognize the union, the union may file a charge with the Regional Office of the National Labor Relations Board for the area and ask the Board to certify the union as the representative of the employees. The Union could also file a petition with the Board asking that it conduct an election among the employees in the group sought to determine whether the union represents a majority of those employees. A petition must be supported by cards signed by at least 30% of the employees, and these cards state that the employees want the union to represent them.

If the union files a charge (called an unfair labor practice charge for refusing to bargain with the union), the union must show that it in fact represents a majority of the employees in the unit and that the Employer has no good faith doubt as to its majority status. If the Board determines that there is sufficient evidence that what the union is charging is true, it will file a complaint against the Employer. A hearing on the complaint will be conducted and, if the union's charge is sustained, the Employer will be obligated to recognize and deal with the union.

If the union files a petition for an election, the Employer can agree that the unit of employees is appropriate for bargaining and consent to an election. If that happens, an election is scheduled to take place usually in about 30 days.

If the Employer does not agree that the cards submitted in support of the petition are enough or are valid, that the unit of employees requested is appropriate for bargaining or that everything else is proper, a hearing will be conducted by the Board. If the Board determines that an election should take place, it will schedule one, usually, again, within the next 30 days. At the election, the union must get a majority of the eligible employees to vote in its favor. If there is a tie vote, no majority has been established and the union loses the election.

If for any reason the union's petition is dismissed, it may file another at anytime. If an election is conducted and the union loses, however, another election cannot be held in that unit of employees again for at least 12 months.

Once an election is scheduled but before it is held, the Employer and union campaign to the employees, trying to convince them to vote against or for the union. Much of the remainder of this Guide concerns what you can and cannot do during this campaign period. First, you should know what unionization means; how you can recognize the beginnings of an organizational drive; and why your Employer believes that the employees are better off not having a union.

What Does Union Representation Mean Legally?

The legal implications of union representation are:

1. That all of the employees in the bargaining unit, except supervisors, have transferred to the union all of their rights to negotiate or talk to Company officials and other supervisors about their wages, holidays, hours and schedules of work, vacation, insurance, overtime, and every other thing related to wages, hours or conditions of work.
2. That this representation will continue for at least a year, and probably longer.
3. That the union will represent all employees in the bargaining unit, whether they voted for the union or not.

What Else Does Representation Mean?

Other implications of union representation that you should be aware of are:

1. That one of the employees will be appointed by the union to the favored position of steward and all matters must go through him—all gripes or complaints or requests.
2. That the employees will have to conform to national union policies.
3. Those who are members will have to pay dues every month.
4. That special money assessments, requests and per capita taxes will be made for fighting funds, strike funds for other companies, politics, etc.

Authorization Cards

Authorization cards are postcard size, and unions get employees to sign them in order to prove the unions' majority status. Regardless of what the union organizer tells the employees to get them to sign one of these cards, they are not simple requests to have an election. Rather, they are membership cards and, by signing one, an employee says he or she wants to be a member of the union. These cards are used in two different ways by the unions.

Under certain circumstances, the union organizer will present cards signed by a majority of employees and demand recognition on the basis of the cards alone. If a union organizer or any employee should present a stack of cards and ask that you examine them for any reason, you should refuse to do so. Immediately thereafter, you should inform your immediate superior of what has happened.

The reason you should not examine the cards presented to you, no matter how curious you may be, is simple. Your inspection of the cards can be used later by the union to support a charge that the Employer does not have a good faith doubt as to the majority status of the union because one of its supervisors looked at the authorization cards and could see that a majority of the employees in the unit had signed them. Remember, you don't know whether any of the cards may have been forged and you don't know what the union organizer may have said to an employee to get a signature by undue or fraudulent means.

If a union is unable to use the cards to gain recognition in the above manner, they may also be used to support the petition for an election. As stated above, cards signed by only thirty per cent of the employees are sufficient to obtain an NLRB election. However, unions rarely file such petitions unless they have cards from substantially more than a majority of the employees.

A supervisor cannot ask to see the cards and cannot try to get them revoked. If, however, an employee shows him one or asks his advice in any way about one, he can discuss it and tell the truth about it. Legally, an authorization card has no binding effect whatsoever. An employee may revoke it and, should an election be held, he may vote any way he chooses, whether he signed a card or not. The best way to revoke it is to vote against the union.

The Election

The election is absolutely secret and is conducted and supervised by the Labor Board. Each employee in the bargaining unit will receive a ballot which asks the employee to state, by marking a "Yes" or "No" box, whether the employee wants to be represented by the union. The employee will mark the ballot in a totally secret place, usually a closed, windowless room or an actual voting booth. A union representation election is very much like political elections in that there must be no electioneering within the immediate vicinity of the polling place, votes cast by those who are drunk or receive improper help are invalid. Also, ballots which are marked in such a fashion that the intent of the voter cannot be absolutely determined are void.

The voting process is that employees who desire to vote line up outside the polling area. The employee in front identifies himself to the people sitting at a table. Usually there are three such people; one observer for the union (always an employee within the proposed unit), one observer for the Company (a non-supervisory, non-unit employee—usually someone out of the payroll, bookkeeping or clerical staff) and the observer for the Labor Board. Since the employee who is the union observer is not working, the employer need not pay him or her regular wages. Usually, the Union would pay the observer the equivalent of the wages lost. Payments larger than this can be improper as a form of a bribe and could cause the entire election to be voided.

After the prospective voter states his/her name and, possibly, clock number, the observers each check his/her name off the voter eligibility list which has been supplied by the employer as a list of all employees within the proposed unit. If the employee's name is on the list, he or she is given a ballot and they go into the voting booth or room and mark it. The employee than deposits the ballot in the ballot box. The employee must then leave the area. If the employee's name is not on the list, he/she is still given a ballot and is allowed to vote, but the ballot is impounded until the Labor Board determines whether the employee was eligible to vote. Occasionally the union or Company observer may challenge the eligibility of someone whose name is on the list because they may be a supervisor or otherwise not eligible. They will still be permitted to vote, but their ballot will be impounded until after the Labor Board determines the employee's eligibility.

Impounded ballots may never be counted. The issues of eligibility will be resolved by the Labor Board only if the impounded ballots will possibly change the outcome.

After the election is over and the polls are closed, the Labor Board Agent, assisted by the union and employer observers, will immediately count the ballots. The counting of ballots is done in public and anyone may attend. If the union receives the vote of a *majority of those voting*, it will have won. If the vote is tied or a majority is cast for *NO union*, the union will have lost.

The Labor Board will then wait 5 days to see if the loser will file objections to the election on the basis that the election was unfair. If no objections are filed or, if filed, dismissed as without merit—the election results are final. If the union wins, the union represents the employees and the employer must bargain with it. If the union loses, it cannot have another election for 12 months.

If the objections are sustained, the election will be rerun. However, if the union is the one who objects and the conduct about which the union complains is such that the Labor Board believes a fair election cannot be held, the union will be declared the winner. For this to happen, the Labor Board must conclude that what the employer did was so bad that the effects cannot be dispelled sufficiently to permit a fair election. Examples of such conduct are threats of mass discharge if the union wins or threats of going out of business if the union wins.

Significantly, the election is determined by the number of votes cast, not the number of eligible voters. Consequently, it is extremely important that everyone votes. For example, if there are 200 eligible voters but only 100 vote and 51 vote for the union, the union will win and be entitled to represent the employees. In this case, 51 voters will have decided the issue for all 200 employees.

The Campaign

After an election date is set but before the election is actually held, both the employer and union are free to campaign to the employees and try to convince them to vote against or for union representation. This period is critical because it is the time an employer can demonstrate to the employees why the union is unnecessary or even bad for them. What the employer and union do during this period is closely conscribed and, if improper or unfair, can be the basis for objections to the election.

Generally, the employer cannot offer a benefit or threaten a loss of a benefit to get an employee to vote "NO UNION." The union cannot threaten or grossly mislead the employees to get them to vote for them.

The instruments used by the employer and union are handbills, letters, posters, meetings and one-on-one conversations.

There are, however, some techniques not available to a union and some not available to the employer. For instance, the union may visit or telephone the employees in their homes and the employer cannot. On the other hand, the union cannot hold employee meetings on the premises of the employer while the employer can compel the employees to attend meetings during working hours.

Without question, however, the most important instrument is the supervisor. The most effective campaigning can be done by a supervisor in private conversations with individual employees.

Solicitation

This term means any method used by the union to induce employees to join. There are two kinds of solicitation:

1. By outside organizers; and
2. By employees on the inside.

Our Company has a no-solicitation rule and this means that outsiders (non-employees) may not come on Company property and pass out literature or talk union. This also means that all other outside solicitations, such as insurance, charity, etc., are similarly barred. This does not apply to supply, service or any other third party service personnel. However, if third party service people solicit for the union, they can be barred.

As to your own employees, you can prohibit union talk during work time provided you enforce the no-solicitation rule uniformly. Work time is for work. You cannot interfere on the employees' own time—lunch, coffee breaks, etc. Even during an employee's non-work time, you can stop solicitation in any area directly associated with work.

New Employees

It is extremely important that each new employee be greeted by his immediate supervisors and that he be given essential information. This initial impression is important to show him that this is a Company made up of good and competent people with good equipment and that the Company is interested in him. Remember, most of his impressions of the Company are gained from you!

Information To New Hires

In many cases, the information that should be communicated to new hires will be contained in the company's employee handbook. However, rather than assuming that the new hire will read the employee handbook immediately, supervisor's should be sure that they directly cover the following information:

1. History of the Company. How it started. Who the officers are. What it has done and expects to do.
2. Names of all the supervisors with whom they may have contact. If possible, meet each one personally. Make sure employee knows where he will get his orders.
3. Have him meet all of the department employees personally.

4. Hours of work and schedules.
5. Rates of pay and overtime.
6. Tools and equipment.
7. General discussion of Company and department rules.
8. Safety rules and practices.
9. How and when he is paid.
10. Absences: excused, due to injury on or off job, personal reasons, sickness.
11. Insurance, vacations, compensation and other benefits. Make sure he understands.
12. If he is inexperienced, make sure he gets competent and sympathetic instruction on how to do the job.
13. He will be your employee and our employee. Let's be sure he is informed and do our best to make him satisfied in his work. We will all benefit.

Summary

Unions are usually successful only where there are conditions present which are substandard or unfair or where employees can be convinced that their future is insecure.

Front line supervisors are the most important managers in opposing the union. They accomplish their mission by being informed and by good work and fair treatment. Union organizers are well informed. Supervisors owe it to themselves and the Company to be at least as well informed as organizers. Correct information gives self-confidence and makes the employee confident in their supervision. Good personnel methods are all important!

3:1.2 Employer Communication to Employees Regarding Union Organizing Drives

Dear Fellow Employee:

We have recently learned that the [UNION] is trying to get our employees to sign authorization cards. We feel very strongly that you do not need a union. We have worked very hard to provide fair and excellent working conditions for our employees. You now have good wages and fringe benefits without paying union dues or initiation fees, and without exposing yourselves to fines, assessments, and the possibility of strikes. Not one of you has lost one day's pay to get any of this.

Some of you may not be familiar with union organizing tactics. The union organizer's purpose is to get you to sign a union authorization card. **YOU SHOULD BE ON YOUR GUARD!** Why? As a means of answering this question, we have drawn up a series of questions and answers:

What is an authorization card?

It is a signed statement that an employee wants the union to be his or her collective bargaining agent.

Does signing a card obligate you?

Yes. It is a legal obligation.

What may the union do with the cards it collects?

There are two possibilities:

1. If the union gets cards signed by 30 percent of our employees, it can petition the National Labor Relations Board for an election, *but*
2. If the union gets cards signed by a majority of our employees, it may send us a letter asking us to bargain. (It may send us copies of the cards in its possession—some unions do.)

If the union gets cards signed by a majority and asks the company to bargain, must the company do so?

No.

What can the union do if the company refuses to bargain in these circumstances?

The union has two choices:

1. It can call an immediate strike for recognition; or
2. It can request an election.

What about the company's "no-solicitation" rule?

Solicitation by employees is prohibited during working time. In particular, this rule prohibits the solicitation of signatures on union authorization cards when either the person soliciting or being solicited is on work time.

Should you sign a card?

We don't think you should. Why? It legally *signs away* to the union your right of choice of representation. After you have had an opportunity to learn the facts about the union, you may decide you don't want it to represent you. *By signing a card now, you may be giving up your right to vote against the union if you should later change your mind.*

Don't believe the union solicitor who states any of the following:

"This card is only to get an election or more information."

"A majority of employees has already signed."

"You must sign a card to vote."

"It will cost you more if you don't join now."

"If you don't sign now, you won't have your jobs after we win."

REMEMBER: Do not sign a card unless you are willing to accept all the consequences and obligations of union membership.

Very truly yours,

3.2 Collective Bargaining Agreements

Once the NLRB has certified a union as the bargaining representative for a group, or "bargaining unit" of employees (see Q. 135) an employer has a legal duty to bargain in good faith with the union. (See Q. 137 and Q. 137.1**S**) The result of this good-faith bargaining is a Collective Bargaining Agreement, commonly called a labor contract, which is an agreement reached between an employer and a union that sets forth the terms and conditions of employment for the employees in the bargaining unit. The collective bargaining agreement is reached through a process of collective bargaining in which the union and the employer are required to bargain over certain mandatory subjects (*e.g.*, wages, benefits, and working hours); if the two parties bargain to impasse on these mandatory subjects, the employer may then unilaterally implement its last, best, and final offer. In the process of bargaining, the employer and the union also negotiate non-mandatory subjects, but neither party is required to bargain to impasse in these areas.

Section 3:2.1 is just one example of a sample collective bargaining agreement. Different factual situations will warrant very different contractual provisions Therefore, this sample should be adapted carefully to reflect an individual employer's situation before presenting it as a example of good-faith bargaining.

3:2.1 Collective Bargaining Agreement

AGREEMENT made and entered into as of this _____ day of _________, 19___ by and between [NAME OF EMPLOYER], (hereinafter referred to as the "Company") of [ADDRESS], and [NAME OF BARGAINING REPRESENTATIVE] (hereinafter referred to as the "Union") of [ADDRESS] for itself and acting on behalf of the employees of the Company now and to be employed (hereinafter designated as "Employees").

WITNESSETH

WHEREAS, it is the purpose of this Agreement to establish equitable employment conditions and an orderly system of employee-employer relationships which will facilitate cooperative solutions of mutual problems and to avoid interruptions and interferences with the operations of the Company.

NOW, THEREFORE, in consideration of the mutual covenants herein contained, the parties hereto agree as follows:

ARTICLE I

Recognition of The Collective Bargaining Unit

Section 1.1.
Pursuant to certification issued by the National Labor Relations Board in Case No. _____, as modified hereafter, the Company recognizes the Union as the sole and exclusive collective bargaining representative of the full-time employees employed by the Company within a unit comprised of [DESCRIPTION OF BARGAINING UNIT].

Section 1.2.
Whenever the word "employees" is used in this Agreement, it shall mean the employees in the bargaining unit defined in Section 1.1.

[*Note: Use the following alternative paragraph in the case of voluntary recognition of the union by the company.*]

ARTICLE I

Recognition of The Collective Bargaining Unit

Section 1.1.
The Company recognizes the Union as the sole and exclusive collective bargaining representative of the full-time employees employed by the Company within a unit comprised of [DESCRIPTION OF BARGAINING UNIT].

Section 1.2.
Whenever the word "employees" is used in this Agreement, it shall mean the employees in the bargaining unit defined in Section 1.1.

ARTICLE II

Union Security

No employee, as a condition of employment, shall be required to be or become a member of or pay dues to the Union.

[*Note: Use the following alternative paragraph when there is to be a maintenance of membership.*]

ARTICLE II

Union Security

Section 2.1.
All employees who are or may become members of the Union on the thirtieth (30) day following the effective date hereof or on any date thereafter shall remain members of the Union in good standing as a condition of employment for the duration of this Agreement, provided that all employees who may be or may become members of the Union may withdraw their membership in the Union during the period beginning with the fifteenth (15) day before the termination of this Agreement and extending to the day of the termination of this Agreement.

Section 2.2.
Membership in good standing shall mean only that the employee remains current in the payment of all dues and general fees required by the Union.

Section 2.3.
Within thirty (30) days from the date of written notification by the Union that any employee member of the Union is not a member in good standing, the Company shall terminate that employee's employment.

Section 2.4.
The Union shall indemnify and save the Company harmless against any and all claims, demands, suits and other forms of liability that may arise out of or by reason of action taken or not taken by the Company in compliance with the provisions of this Article.

[*Note: Use the following alternative paragraph when there is to be a modified maintenance of membership.*]

ARTICLE II

Union Security

Section 2.1.
All employees who are or may become members of the Union on the thirtieth (30) day following the effective date hereof or on any date thereafter shall remain members of the Union in good standing as a condition of employment for the duration of this Agreement, provided that all employees who may be or may become members of the Union may withdraw their membership in the Union during the period beginning with the fifteenth (15) day before the termination of this Agreement and extending to the day of the termination of this Agreement. Any employee

employed on or after [DATE CHOSEN BY THE PARTIES] and who successfully completes his/her probationary period shall be required to become and remain a member in good standing of the Union, provided that any such employee may withdraw his/her membership in the Union during the period beginning with the fifteenth day before the termination of this Agreement and extending to the day of the termination of this Agreement.

Section 2.2.

Membership in good standing shall mean only that the employee remains current in the payment of all dues and general fees required by the Union.

Section 2.3.

Within thirty days from the date of written notification by the Union that any employee member of the Union is not a member in good standing, the Company shall terminate that employee's employment.

Section 2.4.

The Union shall indemnify and save the Company harmless against any and all claims, demands, suits and other forms of liability that may arise out of or by reason of any action taken or not taken by the Company in compliance with the provisions of this Article.

ARTICLE III

Check-Off

Section 3.1.

Upon the receipt from an employee of a written authorization in the form as attached hereto as Exhibit A, the Company shall, pursuant to each authorization, deduct a standard amount of dues and fees from the wages due said employee and remit monthly to the Union the regular dues and standard fees so authorized.

Section 3.2.

The Union shall indemnify and save the Company harmless against any and all claims, demands, suits and other forms of liability that may arise out of or by reason of any action, claim, demand or suit by any person which may involve or be in whole or in part based upon the collection or deduction of any money by the Company and remitted to the Union pursuant to this Article or which may involve or be in whole or in part based upon the use of any moneys by the Union which may have been collected or deducted by the Company and remitted to the Union pursuant to this Article.

Section 3.3.

The Company shall not be required to make check-off deductions for employees who 1) terminate employment, 2) transfer out of the bargaining unit, 3) are laid off, 4) are on an excused leave of absence, or 5) lawfully revoke the check-off authorization.

ARTICLE IV

Union Activities

Section 4.1.
No employee or Union representative shall engage in any Union activity, including the distribution of literature, which interferes with the employee's performance of work or the performance of work by another employee except as provided in the grievance procedure of this Agreement.

Section 4.2.
A Union representative shall be permitted to visit the Company for the purpose of discussing a specific grievance with the employees directly involved or the Company. The General Manager shall be notified by the Union representative either prior to or immediately upon entering the Company. No Union representative will be permitted in any production area unless specific prior permission is given by the General Manager or his designee.

ARTICLE V

Management's Rights

Section 5.1.
The functions and responsibilities of Management are retained and vested exclusively in the Company except as otherwise specifically abridged or modified by the express provisions of this Agreement. The rights reserved to the Company include all matters of inherent managerial policy.

Section 5.2.
The Company reserves the right to establish and administer policies and procedures, training, operations, services, and maintenance; to hire, to promote, to transfer, furlough, and recall employees to work, to reprimand, suspend, discharge or otherwise discipline employees for just cause; to determine the number of employees and duties to be performed by them; to maintain the efficiency and effectiveness of employees; to establish, expand, reduce, appoint, combine, consolidate, or abolish any job classification, department, operation, or service; to determine staffing patterns and areas worked; to introduce new equipment and supplies; to control and regulate the use of facilities, supplies, equipment, and other property of the Company; to determine the number, location and operation of divisions, departments and other units of the Company; the assignment of work, the qualifications required and the size and composition of the work force; to make or change reasonable Company rules, regulations, policies and practices, and otherwise to help the Company attain and maintain full operating efficiency and effectiveness and direct the work force; to determine or change the starting and quitting time and the number of hours worked; to assign and transfer employees to other departments, unit or jobs—as operations may require.

The above-set-forth Management Rights are by way of example and not by way of limitation.

Section 5.3.

Nothing herein contained is to be construed to mean that any employee or group of employees has inherent rights to a particular task or job, nor is their work restricted to a particular task or job.

ARTICLE VI

Probationary Employees

Section 6.1.

Newly hired employees shall be considered probationary for a period of six months from the date of employment. The Company, upon notice to the employee and Union, may extend the probationary period for any newly hired employee an additional thirty days.

Section 6.2.

During or at the end of the probationary period, the Company may discharge any such employee at will and such a discharge shall not be subject to the grievance and arbitration provisions of this Agreement.

ARTICLE VII

Grievance Procedure

Section 7.1.

A grievance shall be defined as any complaint, dispute, controversy or disagreement which one or more employees or which the Union has against or with the Company. Grievances shall be processed and disposed of in the following manner:

STEP I An employee and/or the Union representative for the employee shall take up any grievance with the employee's Supervisor within forty-eight hours from the events giving rise to the grievance, preferably in writing. The Supervisor shall give an answer to the employee and/or the Union representative within forty-eight hours after the presentation of the grievance.

STEP II If the grievance is not settled in Step I, the grievance may, within five days after the answer in Step I or upon the expiration of the five day period, whichever comes first, be presented in Step II. When grievances are presented in Step II, they have to be in a writing signed by the grievant and the Union representative and presented to the General Manager of the Company. A grievance so presented shall be answered by the Company in writing within five days after its presentation.

STEP III If the grievance is not settled in Step II, it shall proceed as provided in Article VII hereof.

Section 7.2.

All time limits shall be exclusive of Saturdays, Sundays and holidays and may be extended by agreement.

Section 7.3.

Any disposition of any grievance from which no appeal is taken by the Union or employee within the time limits shall be deemed resolved and thereafter shall not be considered subject to the grievance and arbitration provisions of this Agreement.

Section 7.4.

A grievance which affects a substantial number or class of employees and which the Company representative designated in Step I lacks authority to settle may be initially presented within five days from the events giving rise to it by the Union representative at Step II.

Section 7.5.

The Union shall designate one steward and one alternate steward who shall be allowed reasonable time during the scheduled working hours to represent employees during disciplinary interviews or who have initiated or wish to initiate a grievance. The investigation of grievances or possible grievances, however, shall not be conducted during scheduled working hours except to the extent specific leave for that purpose is granted by the steward's or alternate steward's supervisor. Any time spent in the processing of grievances or representing employees with grievances which is outside the regularly scheduled working hours for the steward or alternate steward shall not be compensated for by the Company as time worked.

ARTICLE VIII

Arbitration

Section 8.1.

Within ten days after completion of Step II of the grievance procedure (Saturdays, Sundays and holidays excepted), a grievance which has not been resolved may be referred to arbitration by the Representative of the Local Union by giving notice to the Company and the American Arbitration Association.

Section 8.2.

The notice by the Local Union to the American Arbitration Association shall request a list of arbitrators, the selection of an arbitrator and an arbitration in accordance with the Rules of the American Arbitration Association governing labor arbitrations.

Section 8.3.

The arbitrator shall not have jurisdiction to add to, modify, vary, change or remove any terms of this Agreement.

Section 8.4.

The decision of the arbitrator shall be final and binding upon the Company, the Union and the employees covered by the Agreement.

Section 8.5.

The arbitrator shall make his findings and render his decision based upon the substantial weight of the evidence presented at a hearing at which the normal rules of evidence shall govern.

Section 8.6.

This section of the Agreement shall not survive the termination date hereof.

Section 8.7.
The expenses of the arbitration and the arbitrator's fee shall be apportioned between the parties by the arbitrator.

ARTICLE IX

Strikes And Lockouts

Section 9.1.
There shall be no strikes during the term of this Agreement. It is specifically agreed that no employee shall engage in nor shall the Union instigate, authorize or sanction any slowdown, interruption of work, interference with work, "sick out," "job action," or other form of strike activity whether primary, secondary or sympathetic in nature.

Section 9.2.
In the event any of the acts mentioned in Section 9.1 occur, the Union shall immediately take all action within its power to stop such activity, including, but not by way of limitation, sending notices to and conducting meetings with the employees for the purpose of urging them to cease the prohibited activity and informing them that such activity is prohibited by the Agreement and, unless halted immediately, will result in discipline by the Union (including fines and loss of membership). It is further understood that should any employee engage in any of the above-prohibited acts, the Company retains the right to take disciplinary action toward any and all of those employees taking part in such activity. Discipline taken pursuant to this section shall not be subject to the arbitration provisions of this Agreement except on the question of whether the employee actually engaged in the prohibited activity.

Section 9.3.
There shall be no lockouts during the term of this Agreement.

ARTICLE X

Discipline And Discharge

Section 10.1.
The Company shall have the right to discharge, suspend or otherwise discipline any employee for just cause.

Section 10.2.
The Company will notify the Union Steward in writing of any discharge or suspension within twenty-four hours from the time of the discharge or suspension. If the Union Steward desires to contest the discharge or suspension, he shall give written notice thereof to the Company within five days from the date of receipt of notice of discharge or suspension. In such event, the dispute shall be submitted and determined under the grievance and arbitration procedure set forth in this Agreement, commencing with Step II of the grievance machinery.

Section 10.3.
All time limits shall be deemed exclusive of Saturdays, Sundays and holidays.

Section 10.4.

Any discipline (including suspension) or discharge levied against any employee must be effected within a reasonable period of time after the Company has become aware of the occurrence giving cause for the discipline or discharge.

Section 10.5.

All minor infractions on an employee's record shall be cleared after one year from the date of their occurrence.

Section 10.6.

Except in cases justifying immediate discharge, employees who breach the rules and regulations of the Company or commit other acts justifying discipline shall be governed by the following progressive discipline system:

First Offense	—	Oral warning;
Second Offense of the same nature	—	Written warning;
Third Offense of the same nature	—	Suspension without pay;
Fourth Offense of the same nature	—	Discharge.

ARTICLE XI

No Discrimination

Section 11.1.

Neither the Company nor Union shall discriminate against any employee by reason of race, creed, color, national origin, sex, non-job related disability, age, veteran status or activity or lack of activity on behalf of the Union.

Section 11.2.

It is the specific intent of the Union and Company that complaints against the Company concerning the alleged violation of this Article must be processed through the grievance and arbitration procedure and that the remedies provided by this Agreement shall be exclusive, final and binding on all parties.

ARTICLE XII

Seniority

Section 12.1.

Seniority shall be defined as the length of time an employee has been continuously employed in any capacity by the Company.

Section 12.2.

Seniority shall commence after the completion of the probationary period and shall be retroactive to the date of hire.

Section 12.3.

Seniority will not be lost but shall not continue to accrue during periods of authorized leaves of absence, medical leaves of absence or layoff.

Section 12.4.

Seniority shall be lost when an employee:

a. quits, resigns or retires;

b. is discharged for just cause;

c. is laid off for a period of 6 consecutive months;

d. fails to report to work following recall from layoff or a decision of an arbitrator reinstating an employee who was discharged within five days after being notified by telegram or registered mail at the last address in the Company's records or fails to inform the Company within twenty-four hours after being notified by telegram or registered mail at the last address in the Company's records as to his/her intent to return to employment. Failure to effect delivery of the notice as provided herein shall be construed as a voluntary quit;

e. fails to return at the end of a leave of absence, or vacation or any extension thereof;

f. is employed by another employer during a leave of absence except for military duty or when such employment is approved by the Company;

g. fails to return following disciplinary suspension;

h. is absent for twelve consecutive work hours without notifying the office of the Manager of the Company.

Section 12.5.

Resignations and Layoff.

a. Employees are required to give two (2) weeks notice of resignation. Vacation time cannot be taken during the two weeks following a notice of resignation, unless specifically agreed to by the Company. In the event an employee fails to give the required two weeks notice, the accrued vacation pay to which the employee may otherwise be entitled will be forfeited on a day for day basis.

b. In the event it is necessary for the Company to reduce the number of employees, temporary and probationary employees shall be laid off first, and any additional layoffs shall be in the inverse order of seniority, provided the employees remaining in service are as qualified and have as much ability to perform the work that remains to be done. Part-time employees must be willing and able to perform the work available to avoid layoff.

c. The Company will notify the affected employees and the Union as far in advance of the layoff as possible.

Section 12.6.

Recall. Whenever a vacancy occurs, employees who are on layoff shall be recalled in accordance with their seniority in reverse order in which they were laid off, provided that they have the qualifications and apparent ability to perform the available work.

Section 12.7.
Seniority Lists.

a. Seniority lists shall be posted on the bulletin board by the Company on January 1 and July 1 of each year and furnished to the Union.

b. Separate lists shall be prepared for full and part-time employees.

ARTICLE XIII

Transfers And Change In Status

Section 13.1.
Posting. The Company agrees to post available positions within the bargaining unit on the bulletin board. The posting shall remain for a minimum of three calendar days prior to the filling of such positions unless an emergency requires a lesser period of time, in which case, the lesser period of time will be included in the notice. It is understood that the Company will endeavor to post vacancies as soon as it becomes aware of them.

Section 13.2.
Permanent Transfers. In the event a vacancy occurs in a department and more than one qualified employee bids to fill that vacancy, the most qualified employee shall be entitled to transfer. Where no differences in qualifications exist, the employee with the most over-all seniority shall be entitled to transfer.

Section 13.3.
Probation After Transfer. Permanent transfers shall be for an initial probationary period of sixty working days. During or at the end of this period, the employee may return or be returned to his original job. In such a case, the job shall be reposted and the employee who was returned to his original job shall be disqualified from bidding on it. For the purpose of this section, only days actually worked shall be counted as working days.

Section 13.4.
Temporary Transfers. For the purpose of filling a job while it is temporarily vacant due to a leave of absence, vacation, pending completion of the posting process or any other reason, the Company may temporarily transfer any employee into the job.

ARTICLE XIV

Employee Personnel File

Section 14.1.
Personnel Practices. Any employee whose job performance or conduct becomes subject to evaluation shall have the right to participate in review of such an evaluation. Evaluation of any employee shall be signed by the employee.

Section 14.2.
Personnel File. Employees may inspect the contents of their personnel file under the following terms and conditions:

a. They must make an appointment with the Director of Personnel or the Director's designee;
b. Nothing may be removed from the file;
c. Nothing may be written by the employee on any papers in the file;
d. No pre-employment materials may be inspected; and
e. The review must be conducted within the presence of a representative of the Company.

ARTICLE XV

Health And Safety

Section 15.1.
The Company agrees to comply with the federal and state safety laws and to provide first aid supplies for minor injuries or ailments.

Section 15.2.
Employees are required to adhere strictly to all reasonable and/or legally mandated safety rules and regulations and a violation of the safety rules will be cause for discipline.

Section 15.3.
The Union and employees agree to give the Company notice of any allegedly unsafe condition and a reasonable opportunity to correct it prior to reporting the condition to a federal or state safety authority.

Section 15.4.
No employee may refuse to perform a task which he asserts to be unsafe unless the task or condition presents an immediate danger of serious injury.

ARTICLE XVI

Telephones

The Company will continue to make available to the employees a pay telephone, provided that, except in an emergency, no employee may use the telephone during working hours without the prior permission of his supervisor.

ARTICLE XVII

Hours Of Work

Section 17.1.
The normal hours of work shall consist of forty hours in a seven-day pay period beginning at 12:00 a.m. Sunday and ending at 11:59 p.m. Saturday, one week hence.

Section 17.2.

The normal workday shall be eight and one half consecutive hours per day which shall include a one-half hour unpaid lunch period and two ten minute paid break periods.

Section 17.3.

The Company reserves the right to alter the regular starting and quitting times to accommodate operational needs.

Section 17.4.

Employees who work more than twelve consecutive hours within a twenty-four hour period will be granted an additional one-half hour unpaid lunch period.

ARTICLE XVIII

Unpaid Leaves Of Absence

Section 18.1.

Medical Leave. All employees shall receive unpaid leaves of absence for periods of disability due to pregnancy, illness or injury as follows:

a. Whenever an employee becomes disabled, ill or injured, or can reasonably anticipate a future temporary disability, the employee shall furnish the Company with a certificate from a physician stating the nature of the illness, injury or disability, that the employee is physically incapable of continuing his/her normal job duties and the anticipated date upon which the employee is expected to be medically capable of resuming his/her normal job duties and, in the case of pregnancy, the expected date of delivery. An employee who is pregnant shall be permitted to continue to work through the term of the pregnancy or for as long as her condition may permit without adversely affecting the health of herself or the unborn child or the normal performance of her job duties.

b. To determine the right of an employee to a leave of absence under this Section or any extension thereof or right or obligation to return to work from a medical leave, the Company may require the examination of any employee by a physician designated by the Company and a certification from the physician that continued or resumption of employment will not adversely affect the health of the employee and/or unborn child and that the employee is capable of safely performing his/her normal job duties. In the event the employee is not so certified, he/she may be required to begin or continue the medical leave of absence.

c. Medical leaves shall not exceed six months and will be without pay. Extensions of the leave may be granted upon written request by the employee and proof of continued medical disability. Any employee who wishes to return to work must so notify the Company in writing at the time the medical leave commences and reaffirm his/her intent in writing at least thirty days before the date of return.

d. Seniority for benefit purposes shall not accrue but will be frozen as of the date the leaves commence.

Section 18.2.

Military Leave. Leaves of absence for the performance of duty with the U.S. Armed Forces or with the Reserve component thereof shall be granted in accordance with applicable law.

Section 18.3.

Educational Leave. Upon request by the employee and agreement by the Company, an educational leave to further professional growth and advancement shall be granted up to twelve months with no loss of seniority and other rights. However, seniority for benefit purposes shall not accrue during the period of the absence. The Company may deny a request for leave under this Section when the operations of the Company do not permit the absence of the employee at the times requested or where the employee cannot establish the job relatedness of the courses or degree program which he/she is intending to take.

Section 18.4.

Return to Work.

a. An employee on an unpaid leave of absence who returns within one month of the date of the commencement of the leave will be reinstated to his/her former or like job in accordance with his/ her seniority.

b. An employee on an unpaid leave of absence which extends beyond one month but less than six months shall be entitled to his/her former or similar job, if such a position is available at the time the employee desires to return to work. In the event that the regular job of the employee is occupied by another employee at the time the employee returns to work, and a similar job is available, the returning employee shall have the option of filling the job which is available or his/her regular job with the other employee being transferred to the other job. If the employee's former job or a similar job is not available at the time the employee desires to return to work, the employee shall be placed on a preferred waiting list and be given the first available position for which he is qualified. At that time, if his former job is occupied by another employee, he shall have the right to occupy his former job with the other employee being transferred to the other job.

ARTICLE XIX

Vacations

Section 19.1.

Employees shall be entitled to the following vacations with pay:

a. After completion of probation, employees earn vacation benefits retroactive to 60 days after the date of employment at a rate of one day per month up to a maximum of ten days. Employees are not entitled to take this vacation until after the first June 1 which occurs after the completion of the probation period. At that time, employees may take whatever vacation days have been earned.

b. Beginning with the first June 1 after the employee completes his probation, the employee will earn vacation to be taken after the next June 1 at a rate of one day per month to a maximum of ten days plus a bonus day for each completed twelve months of employment as of June 1 of any year.

Section 19.2.

Vacations may be scheduled within each production unit at any time throughout the year as requested by the employee, provided the operations of the Company are not adversely affected by the absence of the employee at the time desired. When two or more employees in the same production unit who are relatively equally qualified desire the same vacation period but not all can be spared by the Company without adversely affecting operations, the employee with the most seniority shall be given the vacation period.

Section 19.3.

Vacation pay shall be based on the employee's base rate of pay.

Section 19.4.

Upon separation from employment or loss of seniority for any reason other than discharge for cause, an employee shall receive payment for all vested but unused vacation entitlement. For the purpose of this section, an employee on leave of absence shall not be considered to have separated from his employment until after the permitted length of the leave is exceeded or he notifies the Company of his intent not to resume his employment, whichever comes first.

Section 19.5.

Vacation requests must be made by employees by February 1 of every year for the vacation year beginning June 1. Vacation requests by employees shall be acted upon by the Company by March 1. Employees who fail to make a vacation request within the time specified herein shall lose their right to exercise their seniority for vacation selection purposes as against any person who had made a timely request and shall be restricted to the times available on a first come first serve basis.

Section 19.6.

With the prior agreement of the employee's supervisor, an employee may be permitted to take vacation in units of single days (to a maximum of three per year), provided that, except in cases of prolonged illness or injury qualifying under the medical leave section, an employee may not substitute or use vacation days for illness.

ARTICLE XX

Holidays

Section 20.1.

All full-time employees are entitled to the following holidays with pay:

Scheduled Holidays:

New Year's Day	Labor Day
Memorial Day	Thanksgiving Day
Independence Day	Christmas Day

Personal Days: Four

Section 20.2.

An employee working on any of the scheduled holidays set forth in Section 20.1 shall receive holiday pay in addition to premium pay for the hours worked that day.

Section 20.3.

To qualify for holiday pay, an employee must work the entire last scheduled work day prior to and the entire next scheduled work day after the holiday.

Section 20.4.

If one of the holidays set forth in Section 20.1 falls within the employee's vacation period, he/she shall be given one day's pay in lieu of the additional day.

Section 20.5.

An employee who is scheduled to work on any holiday and fails to do so shall lose the holiday and holiday pay.

Section 20.6.

If a holiday falls on a Saturday, the previous Friday shall be celebrated as the holiday. If a holiday falls on a Sunday, the following Monday shall be celebrated as the holiday.

Section 20.7.

Personal holidays may be taken as operations permit and must be approved by the employee's immediate supervisor at least two weeks in advance.

Section 20.8.

Holiday pay shall be eight times the employee's base rate of pay.

ARTICLE XXI

Sick Days

Section 21.1.

Sick days are defined as days when employees are prevented from working due to illness or non-work related injury and for which they receive their regular pay. Employees become eligible for sick days upon completion of the probationary period. Sick days accrue at the rate of one-half day per month and can be taken in half-day increments. Sick days may be accumulated from year to year to a maximum of thirty days.

Section 21.2.

In the event of the termination of any employee, whether voluntary or involuntary, accumulated sick days will not be paid.

Section 21.3.

The Company will have a right to demand at any time a physician's note giving the medical reason for the employee's absence prior to allowing the employee to return to work or to the paying for any time not worked as a sick day. In addition, employees who are absent three or more consecutive work days in all cases will be required to submit a physician's note giving the medical reason for the employee's absence prior to returning to work and to receiving payment for any of the days as sick days. Employees out more than seven consecutive days for medical reasons will be placed on a medical leave of absence. Employees who take sick days but who are not ill or injured will be guilty of dishonesty and theft and subject to immediate discharge.

Section 21.4.

Accrued vacation days may not be substituted for sick days.

ARTICLE XXII

Jury Duty

Any employee who is prevented from working on a regularly scheduled workday due to mandatory service on a jury shall be paid by the Company the difference between the employee's regular straight time rate of pay for the scheduled hours missed and the payment received for jury service, provided the employee presents evidence of the amount paid for the jury service and has given notice to the Company of his order to appear for jury service within three work days of the receipt thereof and cooperated with the Company in any attempt it may make to have him excused. In the event an employee is directed to report or is excused from active jury duty at a time which will reasonably permit the employee to perform at least one complete hour of work, the employee will work the available time.

ARTICLE XXIII

Bereavement Leave

The Company will grant employees who have completed probation up to three days with pay in the event of a death in the employee's immediate family (spouse, children, parents, brothers or sisters), provided that the days must be contiguous, include the day of the funeral, and be days when the employee was scheduled to work. In the event of the death of an employee's grandparents or in-laws, the employee will be granted the day of the funeral with pay, provided that the day is one for which the employee was scheduled to work and the employee actually attends the funeral.

ARTICLE XXIV

Wages

Effective ______________, 19___ there will be an across- the-board increase to the wages of each employee of _____ percent.

ARTICLE XXV

Overtime

Section 25.1.

All hours worked by an employee in excess of forty hours in any week shall receive compensation at 1½ times the employee's regular rate of pay. Overtime payments shall not be duplicated for the same hours worked under any of the terms of this

Agreement, and to the extent that hours are compensated for at overtime rates under one provision, they shall not be counted as hours worked in determining overtime under any other provision.

Section 25.2.

The Company may assign employees to perform overtime work. Overtime will not be assigned when qualified volunteers are available. Overtime shall be divided as equally as possible among the employees qualified to do the work required.

Section 25.3.

Except as provided below, vacation time and holidays only shall be considered as time worked for the purpose of calculating overtime.

ARTICLE XXVI

Shift Differential

Section 26.1.

Employees on the second shift shall have $_____ added to their base rate of pay as a shift differential premium.

Section 26.2.

Employees on the third shift shall have $_____ added to their base rate of pay as a shift differential premium.

ARTICLE XXVII

Report Pay

When employees report for work and no work is available, they shall be paid for four (4) hours work at the employee's applicable rate and may be retained on the premises and assigned tasks other than their regular tasks without reduction in their regular rate of pay or the rate of pay of the assigned task, whichever is higher.

ARTICLE XXVIII

Insurance Benefits

The Company will continue its present insurance coverages.

ARTICLE XXIX

Separability

It is understood and agreed that all agreements herein are subject to applicable laws now or hereafter in effect. If any provision of this agreement contravenes the laws or regulations of the United States or of the State of _________, such provision shall be null and void. The remainder of the provisions of the Agreement shall continue in full force and effect.

ARTICLE XXX

Conclusiveness Of Agreement

The Company and the Union acknowledge that during the formal discussions which preceded this Agreement, both parties had an unlimited right and opportunity to make proposals with respect to any matter not removed by law from the area of formal discussions and that the agreements arrived at are set forth in the Agreement. Both parties, for the duration of this Agreement, each voluntarily and unequivocally waive the right and agree that the other shall not be obligated to negotiate with respect to any subject or matter included in or omitted from the Agreement, irrespective of whether the subject was mentioned or discussed during negotiations.

ARTICLE XXXI

Duration

This Agreement shall continue in full force and effect from the ______ day of __________, 19____, and shall remain in effect until and including the ______ day of __________, 19____, and shall continue in full force from year to year thereafter unless and until either of the parties hereto shall give to the other party sixty days written notice prior to the end of the original term of the Agreement or any extension thereof of an intention to terminate the contract at the end of the original or then current term. Failure to give the notice as required herein shall be conclusive evidence of the intent and desire of the parties to continue this Agreement for another year on its same terms and the said Agreement shall be automatically renewed. To constitute a written notice for the purpose of this Section, the writing must be certified mail, return receipt requested and must specify the provisions the party desires to modify or terminate and, if modification is desired, the nature thereof.

IN WITNESS WHEREOF, the parties hereto have set their hands and seals the day and year first above written.

FOR THE COMPANY	FOR THE UNION
______________________________	______________________________

3.3 National Labor Relations Board Forms

The National Labor Relations Board (NLRB) is the administrative body that is responsible for determining (1) whether a sufficient number of workers want to the represented by a union and (2) adjudicates allegations that either an employer or a union representing its members has violated the National Labor Relations Act. The ballot at 3:3.1A is an example of the form that should be used when employees vote on whether they want to be represented for purposes of collective bargaining. The form at 3:3.1B is an example of the form that should be used when employees vote for their collective bargaining representative.

Violations of the National Labor Relations Act are often referred to as unfair labor practices and the form used to file an unfair labor practice charge is included at 3:3.2.

If employees who elect a union to represent them in collective bargaining become disenchanted with that union, the employees may file what is called a "Decertification Petition." The Decertification Petition must be initiated and encouraged by employees only; any employer involvement in the decertification process will be considered an unfair labor practice and will void the Decertification Petition. Once the majority support for Decertification is evident, the union may be decertified by the National Labor Relations Board. A sample of a petition that the NLRB uses for decertification is found at 3:3.3.

3:3.1 Collective Bargaining Forms

The following forms should be used when employees are in the process of determining whether they want collective bargaining representation and, if so, by whom.

3:3.1A Form for Determining Collective Bargaining Representation

UNITED STATES OF AMERICA
National Labor Relations Board
FORM NLRB-707N2 (RC, RM, RD CASES) (4-84)

OFFICIAL SECRET BALLOT

For certain employees of

Janco Computer Services, Inc.

Do you wish to be represented for purposes of collective bargaining by -

Local

MARK AN "X" IN THE SQUARE OF YOUR CHOICE

YES	NO
☐	☐

DO NOT SIGN THIS BALLOT Fold and drop in ballot box.
If you spoil this ballot return it to the Board Agent for a new one.

3:3.1B Form for Electing Collective Bargaining Representation

UNITED STATES OF AMERICA
National Labor Relations Board

OFFICIAL SECRET BALLOT

For certain employees of

This ballot is to determine the collective bargaining representative, if any, for the unit in which you are employed.

MARK AN "X" IN THE SQUARE OF YOUR CHOICE

Local	NEITHER	Local
☐	☐	☐

FORM NLRB-707N3 (RC, RM, RD CASES) (5-80)

DO NOT SIGN THIS BALLOT. Fold and drop in ballot box.
If you spoil this ballot return it to the Board Agent for a new one.

GPO 869 485

3:3.2 Form to Make Charge Against Labor Union

FORM EXEMPT UNDER 44 U.S.C. 3512

FORM NLRB-508
(8-83)

UNITED STATES OF AMERICA
NATIONAL LABOR RELATIONS BOARD
CHARGE AGAINST LABOR ORGANIZATION OR ITS AGENTS

DO NOT WRITE IN THIS SPACE	
Case	Date Filed

INSTRUCTIONS: File an original and 3 copies of this charge and an additional copy for each organization, each local, and each individual named in item 1 with the NLRB Regional Director of the region in which the alleged unfair labor practice occurred or is occurring.

1. LABOR ORGANIZATION OR ITS AGENTS AGAINST WHICH CHARGE IS BROUGHT

a. Name	b. Union Representative to contact
c. Telephone No.	d. Address *(street, city, state and ZIP code)*

e. The above-named organization(s) or its agents has *(have)* engaged in and is *(are)* engaging in unfair labor practices within the meaning of section 8(b), subsection(s) *(list subsections)* ______________________ of the National Labor Relations Act, and these unfair labor practices are unfair practices affecting commerce within the meaning of the Act.

2. Basis of the Charge *(be specific as to facts, names, addresses, plants involved, dates, places, etc.)*

3. Name of Employer		4. Telephone No.
5. Location of plant involved *(street, city, state and ZIP code)*		6. Employer representative to contact
7. Type of establishment *(factory, mine, wholesaler, etc.)*	8. Identify principal product or service	9. Number of workers employed

10. Full name of party filing charge

11. Address of party filing charge *(street, city, state and ZIP code)*	12. Telephone No.

13. DECLARATION

I declare that I have read the above charge and that the statements therein are true to the best of my knowledge and belief.

By ______________________________ ______________________________
(signature of representative or person making charge) *(title or office, if any)*

Address ______________________________ ______________ ______________
(Telephone No.) *(date)*

WILLFUL FALSE STATEMENTS ON THIS CHARGE CAN BE PUNISHED BY FINE AND IMPRISONMENT

3:3.3 Sample Decertification Petition

FORM NLRB-502 (11-64)

UNITED STATES OF AMERICA
NATIONAL LABOR RELATIONS BOARD

FORM EXEMPT UNDER 44 U.S.C. 3512

PETITION

DO NOT WRITE IN THIS SPACE
CASE NO
DATE FILED

INSTRUCTIONS.—Submit an original and four (4) copies of this Petition to the NLRB Regional Office in the Region in which the employer concerned is located.
If more space is required for any one item, attach additional sheets, numbering item accordingly.

The Petitioner alleges that the following circumstances exist and requests that the National Labor Relations Board proceed under its proper authority pursuant to Section 9 of the National Labor Relations Act.

1. Purpose of this Petition *(If box RC, RM, or RD is checked and a charge under Section 8(b)(7) of the Act has been filed involving the Employer named herein, the statement following the description of the type of petition shall not be deemed made.)*
(Check one)

- ☐ RC-CERTIFICATION OF REPRESENTATIVE —A substantial number of employees wish to be represented for purposes of collective bargaining by Petitioner and Petitioner desires to be certified as representative of the employees.
- ☐ RM-REPRESENTATION (EMPLOYER PETITION)—One or more individuals or labor organizations have presented a claim to Petitioner to be recognized as the representative of employees of Petitioner.
- ☐ RD-DECERTIFICATION — A substantial number of employees assert that the certified or currently recognized bargaining representative is no longer their representative.
- ☐ UD-WITHDRAWAL OF UNION SHOP AUTHORITY—Thirty percent (30%) or more of employees in a bargaining unit covered by an agreement between their employer and a labor organization desire that such authority be rescinded.
- ☐ UC-UNIT CLARIFICATION—A labor organization is currently recognized by employer, but petitioner seeks clarification of placement of certain employees: *(Check one)* ☐ In unit not previously certified ☐ In unit previously certified in Case No. ______
- ☐ AC-AMENDMENT OF CERTIFICATION—Petitioner seeks amendment of certification issued in Case No. ______
Attach statement describing the specific amendment sought.

2. NAME OF EMPLOYER	EMPLOYER REPRESENTATIVE TO CONTACT	PHONE NO

3. ADDRESS(ES) OF ESTABLISHMENT(S) INVOLVED *(Street and number, city, State, and ZIP Code)*

4a. TYPE OF ESTABLISHMENT *(Factory, mine, wholesaler, etc.)*	4b. IDENTIFY PRINCIPAL PRODUCT OR SERVICE

5. Unit Involved *(In UC petition, describe PRESENT bargaining unit and attach description of proposed clarification.)*
Included
Excluded

6a. NUMBER OF EMPLOYEES IN UNIT
PRESENT ______
PROPOSED (BY UC/AC) ______

6b. IS THIS PETITION SUPPORTED BY 30% OR MORE OF THE EMPLOYEES IN THE UNIT?* ☐ YES ☐ NO
*Not applicable in RM, UC, and AC

(If you have checked box RC in 1 above, check and complete EITHER item 7a or 7b, whichever is applicable)

7a. ☐ Request for recognition as Bargaining Representative was made on .... *(Month, day, year)* and Employer declined recognition on or about .... *(Month, day, year)* *(If no reply received, so state)*

7b. ☐ Petitioner is currently recognized as Bargaining Representative and desires certification under the act.

8. Recognized or Certified Bargaining Agent *(If there is none, so state)*

NAME	AFFILIATION
ADDRESS	DATE OF RECOGNITION OR CERTIFICATION

9. DATE OF EXPIRATION OF CURRENT CONTRACT, IF ANY *(Show month, day, and year)*	10. IF YOU HAVE CHECKED BOX UD IN 1 ABOVE, SHOW HERE THE DATE OF EXECUTION OF AGREEMENT GRANTING UNION SHOP *(Month, day, and year)*
11a. IS THERE NOW A STRIKE OR PICKETING AT THE EMPLOYER'S ESTABLISHMENT(S) INVOLVED? YES .... NO	11b. IF SO, APPROXIMATELY HOW MANY EMPLOYEES ARE PARTICIPATING?

11c. THE EMPLOYER HAS BEEN PICKETED BY OR ON BEHALF OF .... *(Insert name)* A LABOR ORGANIZATION, OF .... *(Insert address)* SINCE .... *(Month, day, year)*

12. ORGANIZATIONS OR INDIVIDUALS OTHER THAN PETITIONER (AND OTHER THAN THOSE NAMED IN ITEMS 8 AND 11c), WHICH HAVE CLAIMED RECOGNITION AS REPRESENTATIVES AND OTHER ORGANIZATIONS AND INDIVIDUALS KNOWN TO HAVE A REPRESENTATIVE INTEREST IN ANY EMPLOYEES IN THE UNIT DESCRIBED IN ITEM 5 ABOVE (IF NONE, SO STATE)

NAME	AFFILIATION	ADDRESS	DATE OF CLAIM *(Required only if Petition is filed by Employer)*

I declare that I have read the above petition and that the statements therein are true to the best of my knowledge and belief.

.... *(Petitioner and affiliation, if any)*

By .... *(Signature of representative or person filing petition)* .... *(Title, if any)*

Address .... *(Street and number, city, State, and ZIP Code)* .... *(Telephone number)*

WILLFULLY FALSE STATEMENT ON THIS PETITION CAN BE PUNISHED BY FINE AND IMPRISONMENT (U.S. CODE, TITLE 18, SECTION 1001)

GPO 883-920

Chapter 4

Employment Discrimination

Discrimination in employment has been illegal in the workplace since the passage of Title VII of the 1964 Civil Rights Act. Additional Acts and Executive Orders have expanded and supported the scope and strength of Civil Rights. Many organizations have recognized that it is good business practice to have an environment free of discrimination.

The EEOC, which is empowered to review and make determinations, has standard guidelines and reporting procedures to assist organizations to achieve compliance. This chapter provides sample forms which include an EEOC Determination Notice, an EEO Compliance Statement, an EEO-1 Reporting Form, Anti-Discrimination and Sexual Harassment Policy, a Sample Employment Agency Letter, and a Sample Vendor letter.

4:1 Anti-Discrimination Agency Forms

The Equal Employment Opportunity Commission ("EEOC") is the administrative agency charged with processing allegations of employment discrimination arising under Title VII of the 1964 Civil Rights Act and the Americans with Disabilities Act, among others. Once a charge is filed with the EEOC, the parties engage in a fact-finding conference which enables the EEOC agent to get a more complete picture of the validity of the charge. The EEOC then renders a decision, finding that the complainant's charge either is unfounded or presents a valid question of discrimination.

This section presents samples of notices and correspondence that are required by the EEOC when complying with its mandates.

4:1.1 EEO Compliance Statement and Form EEO-1

The Employer Information Report EEO-1 must be filed annually by all employers that have 100 or more employees and are covered by Title VII of the Civil Rights Act of 1964. Companies that have 50 or more employees and that are federal contractors subject to Executive Order 11246 (affirmative action) are required to file as well.

The first page of the EEO-1 form is for company identification. The second page requires the employer to break down the total number of employees by job category, sex, and ethnic background. The form provides an opportunity for organizations to annually review and recognize potential problems and make improvements in the following year.

4:1.1A EEO Compliance Statement

EEO COMPLIANCE STATEMENT

EQUAL EMPLOYMENT OPPORTUNITY COMPLIANCE STATEMENT

1. ________________ will not discriminate against any applicant for employment because of race, creed, color, sex, age, national origin, or handicap. This agency agrees to post in conspicuous places, available to applicants for employment, notices setting forth the provisions of this nondiscrimination clause.

2. This agency will, in all solicitations or advertisements for employees placed by or on behalf of ________________, state that all qualified applicants will receive consideration for employment without regard to race, creed, color, sex, age, national origin, or handicap.

3. In the event of this agency's noncompliance with the nondiscrimination clauses or with any of such rules, regulations, or orders, our working agreement may be canceled, terminated, or suspended.

______________________________ ______________ ______________________________
Signature Date Name

____

______________________________ ______________________________
Position Address

4:1.1B Employer Information Report EEO-1

EMPLOYER INFORMATION REPORT EEO-1

Joint Reporting Committee

- Equal Employment Opportunity Commission
- Office of Federal Contract Compliance Programs (Labor)

EQUAL EMPLOYMENT OPPORTUNITY

EMPLOYER INFORMATION REPORT EEO–1

Standard Form 100
(Rev 5-84)
O.M.B. No. 3046-0007
EXPIRES 5-31-86
100-212

Section A—TYPE OF REPORT

Refer to instructions for number and types of reports to be filed.

1. Indicate by marking in the appropriate box the type of reporting unit for which this copy of the form is submitted (MARK ONLY ONE BOX).

(1) ☐ Single-establishment Employer Report

Multi-establishment Employer:

(2) ☐ Consolidated Report (Required)

(3) ☐ Headquarters Unit Report (Required)

(4) ☐ Individual Establishment Report (submit one for each establishment with 50 or more employees)

(5) ☐ Special Report

2. Total number of reports being filed by this Company (Answer on Consolidated Report only) ______

Section B—COMPANY IDENTIFICATION *(To be answered by all employers)* — OFFICE USE ONLY

1. Parent Company

a. Name of parent company (owns or controls establishment in item 2) omit if same as label — a.

Name of receiving office | Address (Number and street) — b.

City or town | County | State | ZIP code | b. Employer Identification No. ☐☐☐☐☐☐☐☐☐

OFFICE USE ONLY

2. Establishment for which this report is filed. (Omit if same as label)

a. Name of establishment — c.

Address (Number and street) | City or Town | County | State | ZIP code — d.

b. Employer Identification No. ☐☐☐☐☐☐☐☐☐ (Omit if same as label) — e.

Section C—EMPLOYERS WHO ARE REQUIRED TO FILE *(To be answered by all employers)*

☐ Yes ☐ No 1. Does the entire company have at least 100 employees in the payroll period for which you are reporting?

☐ Yes ☐ No 2. Is your company affiliated through common ownership and/or centralized management with other entities in an enterprise with a total employment of 100 or more?

☐ Yes ☐ No 3. Does the company or any of its establishments (a) have 50 or more employees AND (b) is not exempt as provided by 41 CFR 60–1.5, AND either (1) is a prime government contractor or first-tier subcontractor, and has a contract, subcontract, or purchase order amounting to $50,000 or more, or (2) serves as a depository of Government funds in any amount or is a financial institution which is an issuing and paying agent for U.S. Savings Bonds and Savings Notes?

→ If the response to question C–3 is yes, please enter your Dun and Bradstreet identification number (if you have one): ☐☐☐☐☐☐☐☐☐

☐ Yes ☐ No 4. Does the company receive financial assistance from the Small Business Administration (SBA)?

NOTE: If the answer is yes to questions 1, 2, or 3, complete the entire form, otherwise skip to Section G.

NSN 7540–00–180–6384

EMPLOYER INFORMATION REPORT EEO-1

page 2

SF 100 Page 2

Section D—EMPLOYMENT DATA

Employment at this establishment—Report all permanent full-time or part-time employees including apprentices and on-the-job trainees unless specifically excluded as set forth in the instructions. Enter the appropriate figures on all lines and in all columns. Blank spaces will be considered as zeros.

JOB CATEGORIES		NUMBER OF EMPLOYEES										
			MALE					FEMALE				
		OVERALL TOTALS (SUM OF COL. B THRU K)	WHITE (NOT OF HISPANIC ORIGIN)	BLACK (NOT OF HISPANIC ORIGIN)	HISPANIC	ASIAN OR PACIFIC ISLANDER	AMERICAN INDIAN OR ALASKAN NATIVE	WHITE (NOT OF HISPANIC ORIGIN)	BLACK (NOT OF HISPANIC ORIGIN)	HISPANIC	ASIAN OR PACIFIC ISLANDER	AMERICAN INDIAN OR ALASKAN NATIVE
		A	B	C	D	E	F	G	H	I	J	K
Officials and Managers	1											
Professionals	2											
Technicians	3											
Sales Workers	4											
Office and Clerical	5											
Craft Workers (Skilled)	6											
Operatives (Semi-Skilled)	7											
Laborers (Unskilled)	8											
Service Workers	9											
TOTAL	10											
Total employment reported in previous EEO-1 report	11											

(The trainees below should also be included in the figures for the appropriate occupational categories above)

Formal On-the-job trainees												
White collar	12											
Production	13											

NOTE: Omit questions 1 and 2 on the Consolidated Report.

1. Date(s) of payroll period used:

2. Does this establishment employ apprentices?
   1 ☐ Yes 2 ☐ No

Section E—ESTABLISHMENT INFORMATION *(Omit on the Consolidated Report)*

1. Is the location of the establishment the same as that reported last year?
   1 ☐ Yes 2 ☐ No 3 ☐ No report last year

2. Is the major business activity at this establishment the same as that reported last year?
   1 ☐ Yes 2 ☐ No 3 ☐ No report last year

OFFICE USE ONLY

3. What is the major activity of this establishment? (Be specific, i.e., manufacturing steel castings, retail grocer, wholesale plumbing supplies, title insurance, etc. Include the specific type of product or type of service provided, as well as the principal business or industrial activity.)

f.

Section F—REMARKS

Use this item to give any identification data appearing on last report which differs from that given above, explain major changes in composition or reporting units and other pertinent information.

Section G—CERTIFICATION *(See Instructions G)*

Check one
1 ☐ All reports are accurate and were prepared in accordance with the instructions (check on consolidated only)
2 ☐ This report is accurate and was prepared in accordance with the instructions.

Name of Certifying Official	Title	Signature	Date

Name of person to contact regarding this report (Type or print)	Address (Number and street)				
Title	City and State	ZIP code	Telephone Area Code	Number	Extension

All reports and information obtained from individual reports will be kept confidential as required by Section 709(e) of Title VII

WILLFULLY FALSE STATEMENTS ON THIS REPORT ARE PUNISHABLE BY LAW, U.S. CODE, TITLE 18, SECTION 1001

4:1.2 Affirmative Action Report

Affirmative action encompasses the steps employers take to offset imbalances in the workforce caused by past discriminatory practices (as defined by the categories established in the Civil Rights Act of 1964). To implement affirmative action, employers must:

- Consider the current staff composition (by EEO categories);
- Project job openings for the next year;
- Determine proper EEO levels (by job categories); and
- Commit to an action plan that improves staff composition (by EEO category), so that it accurately reflects the "availability pool" of the geographical location.

An affirmative action report (Form 4:1.2A) is used to plan affirmative action programs. The form can serve as the basis for the development of an affirmative action plan (whether the organization is required to develop one or not). The affirmative action plan monitors an organization's progress in removing staff imbalances resulting from past discriminatory practices and is a good business practice as well.

Organizations with over 50 employees that are federal contractors doing over $50,000 worth of government contract work annually are required to have a written affirmative action program.

4:1.2A Affirmative Action Report

EEO Code Number	AFFIRMATIVE ACTION REPORT	Location
Period Ending 19		Submitted by
		Date

1	2				3				4	5				6				7				8			
JOB CATEGORIES	NUMBER OF EMPLOYEES PREVIOUS PERIOD				NUMBER OF EMPLOYEES CURRENT PERIOD				NUMBER OF PERMANENT VACANCIES IN THIS PERIOD	NUMBER OF APPLICATIONS RECEIVED				NUMBER OF APPLICANTS INTERVIEWED				NUMBER OF APPLICANTS HIRED				NUMBER OF TRANSFERS FROM OTHER LOCATIONS			
	WHITE		MINORITY		WHITE		MINORITY			WHITE		MINORITY		WHITE		MINORITY		WHITE		MINORITY		WHITE		MINORITY	
	M	F	M	F	M	F	M	F		M	F	M	F	M	F	M	F	M	F	M	F	M	F	M	F
Officials and Managers																									
Supervisors																									
Professionals																									
Technicians																									
Sales Workers																									
Office and Clerical																									
Craftsmen (skilled)																									
Operatives (semiskilled)																									
Laborers (unskilled)																									
Service Workers																									
Total																									

Explanatory Notes

Column 2: Number of Employees Previous Period. Number of employees from last semiannual report.
Column 4: Number of Permanent Vacancies in This Period. Vacancies are defined as job openings resulting from one or both of the following:

- Jobs that become vacant as a result of any personnel action, where a replacement is required; and
- Newly created jobs.

AFFIRMATIVE ACTION REPORT

page 2

EEO Code Number	AFFIRMATIVE ACTION REPORT	Location
Period Ending 19		Submitted by
		Date

9	10				11				12				13				14				15				16				17			
JOB CATEGORIES	NUMBER OF PROMOTIONS TO CATEGORY				NUMBER OF PROMOTIONS WITHIN CATEGORY				NUMBER OF TERMINATIONS				NO. OF TRANSFERS TO OTHER LOCATIONS				NUMBER OF TEMPORARY LAYOFFS				NUMBER OF RECALLS				AFFIRMATIVE ACTION PROGRAM GOALS ESTABLISHED				AFFIRMATIVE ACTION PROGRAM GOALS ATTAINED TO DATE			
	WHITE		MINORITY		WHITE		MINORITY		WHITE		MINORITY		WHITE		MINORITY		WHITE		MINORITY		WHITE		MINORITY		WHITE		MINORITY		WHITE		MINORITY	
	M	F	M	F	M	F	M	F	M	F	M	F	M	F	M	F	M	F	M	F	M	F	M	F	M	F	M	F	M	F	M	F
Officials and Managers																																
Supervisors																																
Professionals																																
Technicians																																
Sales Workers																																
Office and Clerical																																
Craftsmen (skilled)																																
Operatives (semiskilled)																																
Laborers (unskilled)																																
Service Workers																																
Total																																

Explanatory Notes

Column 10: Number of Promotions to Category. When an individual advances from a lower grade to a higher grade and the new job title is classified under a different EEO Category, the promotion should be reflected in this column.

Column 11: Number of Promotions Within Category. When an individual advances from a lower grade to a higher grade within the same EEO category, the promotion should be reflected in this column. A rate progression based on time in the job is not counted as a promotion.

Column 14: Number of Temporary Layoffs. All employees on temporary layoff should be reflected in this column and included in column 3 (Number of Employees Current Period). This applies until such employees lose their recall rights under the collective bargaining agreement (hourly); or until their three-month layoff period expires (salaried). When either of the above occurs, the employees should be included only in column 12 (Number of Terminations).

Column 15: Number of Recalls. All employees recalled from temporary layoff and reinstated to the payroll should be reflected in this column and included in column 3 (Number of Employees Current Period).

Column 16: Affirmative Action Program Goals Established. Goals are for the current calendar year.

Column 17: Affirmative Action Program Goals Attained to Date: Goals for December 31 reporting period are for full calendar year.

4:1.3 Employment Discrimination Complaints

If any employee complains of employment discrimination based on race, creed, age, sex, national origin, disability, sexual orientation, or affectional preference, the complaint should be filed in writing. Form 4:1.3A can be used for this purpose. Organizations should make employees aware that they do not have to tolerate discrimination of any kind. Employees are warned that, when confronted with some form of discrimination, they must immediately make the organization aware of it by completing a form like Form 4:1.3A.

In answer to the complaint, which the organization should address promptly, a personnel representative interviews the employee and reports the results on Form 4:1.3B.

Finally, the EEOC issues a formal determination of its findings like the one at 4:1.3C.

4:1.3A Employment Discrimination Complaint Form

COMPLAINT FORM: EMPLOYMENT DISCRIMINATION
INFORMAL COMPLAINT OF EMPLOYMENT DISCRIMINATION

This form may be used to report discrimination related to race, creed, age, sex, national origin, disability, sexual orientation, or affectional preference. Please print or type.

Case Number ______________________

Your Name ______________________
(Mr., Mrs., Ms., Miss)

Title ______________ Department ______________________

Address ______________________________ Telephone ______________

Basis of the alleged discrimination:

Race ____ Color ____ Creed ____ National Origin ____ Sex ____ Age ____

Disability ____ Sexual Orientation/Affectional Preference ____

Who discriminated against you? Give the title, name, and department of the person(s) that you believe discriminated against you.

Name ______________________ Title ______________ Department ______________
(use extra sheet if necessary)

Date, time, and location where the alleged discrimination occurred.

____

____

Did anyone else witness the alleged act of discrimination? If so, provide:

Name ______________________ Title ______________ Department ______________

Explain what act or acts were done to you. How were other persons treated differently? (Use extra sheet if necessary)

____

____

____

What corrective action do you wish taken in your behalf regarding your complaint?

____

____

Signature ______________________________ Date ______________

4:1.3B Report on Complaint of Employment Discrimination

INTERVIEW REPORT ON INFORMAL COMPLAINT OF EMPLOYMENT DISCRIMINATION

Equal Employment Opportunity Unit Case # ____________

Interview Conducted by ____________

Case Assigned To ____________

Location Of Interview ____________

Date ____________ Time Began ____________ Time Ended ____________

Name ____________ Sex* ____________ Race* ____________

Age* ____________ Disability* ____________ Religion* ____________

National Origin* ____________

Sexual Orientation or Affectional Preference* ____________

Title ____________

Social Security # ____________ Department ____________

Address ____________

____________ Telephone ____________

Immediate Supervisor (of person interviewed) ____________

Details: (Use Additional Sheet If Necessary)

____

____

____

At the beginning of each interview, the following is to be read to each person interviewed:

"I want to inform you that by making this complaint at this office, this does not preclude you from, nor do you forfeit your right of, making and filing a formal complaint with any human rights agency."

____
Signature of EEO Investigator/
Counselor Conducting Interview

*For completion as applicable to the particular complaint.

4:1.3C Sample EEOC Determination Notice

Equal Employment Opportunity Commission

Charge Number ________

Charging Party:

Respondent:

DETERMINATION

Under the authority vested in me by the Procedural Regulations of the Equal Employment Opportunity Commission (EEOC), I issue the following Determination as to the merits of the subject charge filed under Title VII of the Civil Rights Act of 1964, as amended (Title VII).

All requirements for coverage have been met. Charging Party alleged that he was discriminated against in violation of Title VII in that [Statement of Allegations].

Respondent denies the allegations and states that [Statement of Employer's Defense].

Documentation submitted and interviews conducted support [ ]'s position with respect to the subject allegations [Statement of Findings.]

Based on this analysis, I have determined that the evidence obtained during the investigation does [not] establish a violation of the statute.

This Determination does not conclude the processing of this charge. If the [Non-prevailing Party] wishes to have this Determination reviewed, he must submit a signed letter to the Determinations Review Program which clearly sets forth the reasons for requesting the review and which lists the Charge Number and [Opposing Party's] name and must attach a copy of this Determination to the letter. These documents must be personally delivered or mailed (postmarked) on or before ________ to the Determinations Review Program, Office of Program Operations, EEOC, 1801 L. Street, N.W., Washington, D.C. 20507. It is recommended that some proof of mailing, such as a certified mail receipt, be secured.

If the [Non-prevailing Party] submits a timely request for review by the date shown above, the Commission will review this Determination. Upon completion of the review, the [Non-prevailing Party] and [Opposing Party] will be issued a final determination which will contain the results of the review and what further action, if any, the Commission may take. The final determination will also give notice, as appropriate, of the [Non-prevailing Party's] right to sue.

If the [Non-prevailing Party] does not request a review of this Determination by ________, this Determination will become final and the following day, the processing of this charge will be complete and the charge will be dismissed. (This letter will be the only notice of dismissal and the only notice of the [Non-prevailing Party's] right to sue which will be sent by the Commission.) FOLLOWING DISMISSAL, THE [NON-PREVAILING PARTY] MAY ONLY PURSUE THIS MATTER FURTHER BY FILING SUIT AGAINST THE [OPPOSING PARTY(S)] NAMED IN THE CHARGE IN FEDERAL DISTRICT COURT WITHIN 90 DAYS OF THE EFFECTIVE DATE OF DISMISSAL. Therefore, in the event a request for review is not made, if a suit is not filed by _________, the [Non-prevailing party's] right to sue will be lost. The Commission's regulations governing no cause determinations are printed in Title 29, Code of Federal Regulations, Section 1601.19.

______________________________ ______________________________
Date District Director

Enclosure: (to [Non-prevailing Party])
Information Sheet on Filing Suite in Federal Court

Date of Mailing: _________________

4:2 Non-Discrimination Statements

Employers in the United States with fifteen or more employees are required to conform to the mandates of Title VII of the 1964 Civil Rights Act. As such, employers must provide equal employment opportunities to employees and applicants of all races, genders, creeds, and disability status. In order to inform employees and applicants that your organization adheres to a policy of non-discrimination, it is advisable to post or disseminate non-discrimination statements. The following are examples of statements and policies that indicate that employers will provide equal employment opportunities, will not tolerate sexual harassment in the workplace, and will accommodate disabled employees and applicants. The EEOC also requires that an equal employment opportunity notice be posted, and a copy of that notice is included in this section.

4:2.1 Sample Anti-Discrimination and Sexual Harassment Policy

Policy Against Discrimination And Sexual Harassment

[EMPLOYER] is an equal opportunity employer that does not discriminate in hiring, promotion, or other employment decisions on the basis of race, sex, religion, national origin, age, or non-job-related disability. The [EMPLOYER'S] equal opportunity policy includes the absolute prohibition of sexual harassment of any kind in the workplace.

This prohibition applies to all employees and extends not only to sexual favors as a condition of employment or promotion, but likewise to any behavior tending to create a hostile working environment for employees of either sex.

Any person working at this [EMPLOYER] who believes s/he is a victim of sexual harassment should immediately bring the matter to the attention of her or his immediate supervisor. If that supervisor is the source of the sexual harassment, the complaint may be brought to the firm's Personnel Director or the General Manager, as the harassed individual sees fit.

No matter to whose attention the complaint is brought, [EMPLOYER] is committed to the following:

1. The complaint will be investigated promptly, and if found to have merit, immediate steps will be taken to end the harassment.
2. The complaint and the complainant's identity will be revealed within the firm strictly on a "need to know" basis, and under no circumstances will the complainant be subjected to retaliation for having registered the complaint.

If anyone has any questions concerning this policy now or in the future, s/he should feel free to raise them in confidence with the Personnel Director.

4:2.2 Independent Contractor Compliance Statements

Employers should also obtain EEOC compliance statements from independent contractors such as recruiting services, suppliers, vendors and subcontractors. The two letters that follow are examples of the types of statements that should be obtained.

4:2.2A Recruiting Service Compliance Statement

(company letterhead)

____
(name)

____
(street)

______________________________ Date
(city, etc.)

Dear _________:

The company is dedicated to complying with its legal and ethical obligations as an equal opportunity employer. The company has an on-going commitment, through affirmative action programs, to hire and develop the best people available, based on job-related qualifications. Our recruiting and hiring procedures are free of discrimination based on race, religion, color, sex, age, national origin, handicap, or veteran status.

We request your vigorous support in our affirmative action efforts as they relate to providing employment opportunity for minority groups, women, handicapped individuals, and veterans. Our continued use of any referral agency depends on that agency's full compliance with equal employment opportunity requirements. We expect that your agency will refer qualified applicants to us for any job opening listed without regard to race, religion, color, sex, age, national origin, handicap, or veteran status.

Please express the concurrence of your agency in this nondiscriminatory policy by signing a copy of this letter and returning it. A duplicate is enclosed for your convenience. Thank you.

Very truly yours,

____
EEO Manager

We concur with the nondiscriminatory policy stated in your letter.

By: ______________________________ Dated: ______________________________

4:2.2B Supplier, Vendor, Subcontractor Compliance Statement

(company letterhead)

____
(name)

____
(street)

________________________________ Date
(city, etc.)

Dear ________:

As your firm is well aware, the company and its wholly owned subsidiaries are equal opportunity employers.

Pursuant to Executive Order 11246 as amended, the Vocational Rehabilitation Act, and the Vietnam Era Veterans Act you are advised that under the provisions of government contracting and in accordance with these laws, contractors and subcontractors are obligated to take affirmative action to provide equal employment opportunity without regard to race, religion, color, national origin, age, sex, handicap, or veteran's status.

We expect to see our commitment to equal opportunity employment reflected in the racial and sexual composition of your firm's workforce and urge a vigorous affirmative action program to overcome underutilization.

Please indicate your agreement by signing the enclosed copy and returning it to us. Thank you.

Sincerely,

____
EEO Manager

We agree with the policy stated in your letter.

By: ____________________________ Date: ____________________________

4:3 Affirmative Action Policies

Executive Order 11246 requires employers who contract with the federal government to be non-discriminatory in their employment decisions and to engage in affirmative action to increase the employment opportunities of protected classes. The Office of Federal Contract Compliance Program ("OFCCP") enforces Executive Order 11246. The Executive Order requires government contractors to prepare written affirmative action programs, and failure to do so can result in the OFCCP's debarring of government contractors from receiving government contracts.

The following are model affirmative action programs that can be adapted to your specific organization.

4:3.1 Sample Minority Affirmative Action Program

The Affirmative Action Policy that follows is designed to satisfy the equal opportunity and affirmative action responsibilities under Executive Order 11246 regarding minorities. Separate programs for disabled persons and veterans follow it.

Affirmative Action Program
For
[NAME OF EMPLOYER]

Corporate EEO-1 Identification Number:______________________________

Facility Dun & Bradstreet Identification Number:

Inclusive dates of the Affirmative Action Program:

From ______________________ to ________________________
(Month, Day, Year) (Month, Day, Year)

Program completed,
read and
approved by:

(Telephone Number)

Location of Corporate Headquarters:

Corporate Chief Executive Officer:

Corporate EEO Officer: ______________________________
(Name and Title)

____
(Telephone Number)

Corporate Dun & Bradstreet Identification Number:

Preface

This Affirmative Action Program ("AAP") is designed to satisfy the equal employment opportunity/affirmative action responsibilities under Executive Order 11246, as amended, and the implementing rules and regulations of the Secretary of Labor. A separate Affirmative Action Program for disabled persons and disabled veterans of the Vietnam Era has been adopted.

A. Confidentiality

This Affirmative Action Program contains confidential information which is subject to the provisions of 18 USCS § 1905. *Chrysler Corp. v. Brown*, 441 U.S. 281 (1979). Copies of this Affirmative Action Program and all related appendices, documents and support data are made available on loan to the U.S. Government, and upon the request of the government, on the condition that the government holds them totally confidential and does not release copies to any persons whatsoever. This Affirmative Action Program and its appendices and other supporting documents contain much confidential information which may reveal, directly or indirectly, the Company's plans for business and geographical expansion and contraction. The Company considers this Affirmative Action Program to be exempt from disclosure, reproduction, and distribution under the Freedom of Information Act upon the grounds, among others, that such material constitutes (1) personnel files, the disclosure of which would constitute a clearly unwarranted invasion of personal privacy, which are exempt from disclosure under 5 USCS § 552(b)(6); (2) confidential, commercial or financial information, which is exempt from disclosure under 5 USCS § 552(b); (3) investigatory records compiled for law enforcement purposes, the production of which would constitute an unwarranted invasion of personal privacy, which are exempt from disclosure under 5 USCS § 552(b)(7)(C); and, (4) matters specifically exempted from disclosure by state, which are exempt from disclosure under 5 USCS § 552(b)(3). Notice is hereby given of a request pursuant to 41 CFR § 60-60.4(d) that portions of this program be kept confidential.

Thus, the Company wishes to make it clear that it does not consent to the release of any information contained in this Affirmative Action Program under the Freedom of Information Act or otherwise. If the U.S. Government, or any agency or subdivision thereof, is considering a request for release of this program under the Freedom of Information Act, request is hereby made that the government immediately notify the Chief Executive Officer of the Company of any and all Freedom of Information Act requests received by the government or any other contemplated release of this Affirmative Action Program by the government which relates to information obtained by the government from this Company. The Company further requests that everyone who has any contact with this Affirmative Action Program, or its supporting appendices, documents, and other data, treat such information as totally confidential and that such information not be released to any person whatsoever. Retention or disclosure of information relating to identifiable individuals may also violate the Privacy Act of 1974.

B. Program Terminology

The terms "utilization analysis," "underutilization," and "problem area," appearing in this Affirmative Action Program, are terms the Company is required to use herein by government regulations. The criteria used in relation to these terms are those specified by the government. These terms have no independent legal or factual significance whatsoever. Although we will use the terms in total good faith in connection with the Affirmative Action Program, such usage does not necessarily signify that the Company agrees that these terms are properly applied to any particular factual situation.

Whenever the term "goal" is used, it is expressly intended that it "should not be used to discriminate against any applicant or employee because of race, color, religion, sex, or national origin," as stated in 41 CFR § 60-2.30.

This Affirmative Action Program is not intended to create any rights in any person or entity other than the relevant contracting government entity.

C. Reliance on EEOC's Guidelines on Affirmative Action

Although the Company does not believe any violation of Title VII of the 1964 Civil Rights Act exists, it has developed this Affirmative Action Program in accordance with and in reliance upon the EEOC's Guidelines on Affirmative Action, 29 CFR § 1608.

I. Reaffirmation Of Equal Employment Opportunity Policy

In issuing this Affirmative Action Program, we affirm our commitment and pledge our full support to equal employment opportunity for all persons, regardless of race, color, religion, sex or national origin in compliance with Executive Order 11246.

Recognizing equal opportunity can only be achieved through implementation of a viable affirmative action program, our AAP sets forth specific affirmative action and equal employment opportunity responsibilities of managers, supervisors, and all employees. All employees are expected to make reasonable efforts to carry out their AAP responsibilities in spirit as well as in letter to assure that equal opportunity is available to all. We further expect all employees to demonstrate sensitivity to and respect for all other employees and to demonstrate commitment to the Company's equal employment opportunity and affirmative action objectives.

Attached to this AAP is a copy of the Chief Executive Officer's letter in which he reaffirms the Company's Equal Employment Opportunity Policy. Copies of this reaffirmation, as well as the Equal Employment Opportunity Policy, are conspicuously posted so that employees may be informed of its content.

Equal Employment Opportunity Policy

1. The Company, through responsible managers, shall recruit, hire, train, and promote in all job titles without regard to race, color, national origin, religion, sex, physical disability, age or status as a disabled veteran of the Vietnam Era, except where sex or age is a *bona fide* occupational qualification.
2. Managers shall ensure that all other personnel actions such as compensation, benefits, Company sponsored training, transfer, demotion, termination, layoff, return from layoff, and social recreation programs shall be administered without regard to race, color, national origin, religion, sex, physical disability, age or status as a disabled veteran or veteran of the Vietnam Era, except where sex or age is a *bona fide* occupational qualification.
3. Managers shall base employment decisions on the principles of equal employment opportunity and with the intent to further the Company's affirmative action program goals.

4. Managers shall take affirmative action to ensure that minority group individuals, females, veterans of the Vietnam Era and qualified disabled persons and disabled veterans are hired and that these employees are encouraged to aspire for promotion and are considered as promotional opportunities arise.

II. Dissemination Of Policy

In order to ensure that all employees, applicants for employment, and others are aware that this Company is an Equal Opportunity Employer and of its official policy on Equal Employment Opportunity, the following steps are taken and will continue to be undertaken as prescribed in the following:

A. Internal Dissemination

1. The policy of Equal Employment Opportunity is published in the Company's [Employee Handbook/Industrial Relations Manual].
2. [At least once each year, the EEO policy is published in Company newsletters intended for the general reading of management and employees.]
3. The Company shall conduct EEO meetings at least twice a year. The EEO policy is thoroughly explained—its intent, the individual responsibility of managers and supervisory personnel for effective implementation, and the chief executive officer's attitude toward EEO.
4. Employees have been notified of the existence of the Company's Affirmative Action Program and EEO policy through the President's letter posted on key bulletin boards. For example, employees are advised that all aspects of employment, including job opportunity, training programs and social events, will be available to all without regard to race, color, religion, sex, national origin, disability, age, or veteran status. Additionally, employees will be advised to contact supervisors concerning problems they have including those involving discrimination questions.
5. The EEO program and policy have been included in all employee orientation programs and is communicated to applicants. This will assure that all present and new employees will be able to avail themselves of the program's benefits.
6. Articles covering the benefits of EEO programs, career promotions, and other items of career interest to minority and female employees are included in any relevant company publications.
7. The EEO policy and the reaffirmation statements described above are conspicuously posted in the following areas: [ ].
8. When employees are featured in product or consumer advertising, in employee handbooks or similar publications, both nonminority and minority men and women are pictured.
9. The Company communicates to employees the existence of its affirmative action program and makes available such elements of this program as will enable employees to know of and avail themselves of its benefits.

B. External Dissemination

1. All recruiting sources are informed each year of the Company's EEO policy. These sources are requested to recruit and refer minorities and women for all openings. The list of recruiters is constantly studied and evaluated to deter-

mine the effectiveness of the sources. Where the record indicates lack of cooperation, the recruiting source is eliminated and new sources are added.

2. The Equal Employment Opportunity clause and the requirements of Executive Order 11246, as amended, are included in all covered purchase orders, contracts, etc.
3. Through the use of various techniques and media, minority and female organizations, community agencies, secondary schools and colleges having a high representation of minorities and women, and other interested groups are kept aware of the Company's EEO policy.
4. Whenever employees are pictured in consumer, public relations or help wanted advertising, minority and nonminority men and women will continue to be depicted.
5. The existence of the Affirmative Action Plan will be communicated to prospective employees. Any elements of this program that will enable prospective employees to take advantage of the program will be made available to them.

III. EEO Responsibilities

The execution and implementation of Corporate policy in this plan will be administered by Company staff as outlined below:

A. President

Overall responsibility for equal employment opportunity and affirmative action program compliance for the Company is vested in the President.

The President has assigned to the Corporate EEO Officer the authority and responsibility for implementing and monitoring the overall EEO Program. The responsibilities include, but are not limited to:

1. Developing policy statements, affirmative action programs, and internal and external communication techniques.
2. Assisting management in the identification of problem areas and arriving at solutions to problems, and establishing goals and objectives.
3. Designing and implementing audit and reporting systems that will:
   a. Measure the effectiveness of the Company's programs.
   b. Indicate need for remedial action.
   c. Determine the degree to which the Company's goals and objectives have been attained.
4. Serving as liaison between the Company and enforcement agencies.
5. Serving as liaison between the Company and minority organizations, women's organizations, and community action groups concerned with employment opportunities of minorities and women.
6. Keeping management informed of the latest developments in the EEO area.
7. Reporting the status of the EEO Program alone with recommendations to the President at the end of each quarter.
8. Investigating all formal charges of discrimination and participating in conciliation negotiations with government agencies.
9. Coordinating all compliance reviews scheduled by the Office of Federal Contract Compliance Programs.

10. Ensuring that an Affirmative Action Program is adopted and effectively implemented each year.
11. Conducting regular discussions with managers, supervisors, and employees to ensure that the Company's EEO Policy and AAP objectives are being followed.
12. Informing managers and supervisors that their work performance is being evaluated, in part, on the basis of their EEO efforts and results, and evaluating managers and supervisors on those factors.
13. Requiring managers and supervisors to take actions to prevent racial, ethnic, religious and sexual harassment of employees.
14. Ensuring the Company's continued compliance with the OFCCP's Sex Discrimination Guidelines and Guidelines on Discrimination Because of Religion or National Origin.
15. Ensuring that minority and female employees are afforded a full opportunity and are encouraged to participate in all Company sponsored educational, training, recreational, and social activities. Ensuring that all facilities, such as locker rooms and rest rooms, are comparable for both sexes.
16. Performing an EEO analysis of special programs, such as social and recreational activities, and training programs; and developing procedures and counseling employees to ensure that all employees are hired, promoted, or transferred without regard to race, color, religion, sex, national origin, age, disability, or veteran status.
17. Reviewing all technical forms (such as application forms and posters) for compliance with federal regulations.
18. In order to measure and ensure the effectiveness of the EEO program, conducting quarterly audits, as appropriate, of training programs, hiring and promotional patterns, and qualifications of all employees to ensure that minorities and women are given full opportunity for advancement.

IV. Internal Audit And Reporting System

The Company's Audit and Reporting System has been designed to:

1. Measure the effectiveness of the program.
2. Indicate those areas where remedial action is needed.
3. Determine the degree to which the Company's goals and objections have been obtained.

The audit system will provide for maintenance of the following records:

1. An applicant log, which will show the date, name of applicant, race, sex, veteran status, disability status, referral source, interview date (if any), EEO-1 category of position applied for, and final disposition.
2. Summary data of job offers, hires, permanent promotions, resignations, discharges, layoffs, and training programs by job group, disability status, veteran status, sex and minority group identification for the twelve (12) month period immediately preceding the new plan year.

3. Summary data of applicant flow by EEO-1 categories, disability status, veteran status, sex and minority group identification for twelve (12) month period immediately preceding the new plan year.

The audit system at the Company will include periodic reports, by the EEO Coordinator indicating efforts to achieve EEO goals. The supervisors will indicate any current or foreseeable EEO problem areas and outline suggestions for solutions. If problem areas arise, the supervisor will report them to the EEO Coordinator immediately.

1. The EEO Coordinator will discuss any problems relating to managers' implementation of the programs such as high rejection ratios, frequent EEO charges, or harassment problems. The EEO Coordinator will also audit the total selection and placement process, including promotion, transfer and termination patterns.
2. The EEO Coordinator periodically will report the status of the Company's Affirmative Action Program to the President. The President will take any remedial steps which are necessary to provide for the effective implementation of the program.

V. Development And Execution Of Affirmative Action Program

All personnel involved in recruiting, selection, promotion, discipline, and related processes will be trained on the Company's affirmative action objectives; equal employment opportunity laws, regulations, and court decisions; and job-related personnel practices.

The Company will develop programs to facilitate the attainment of the numerical goals which have been set to increase the utilization of minorities and women in the Company. The following programs or policies will be among those implemented to facilitate appropriate utilization of minorities and women at all levels of the Company's workforce, and to ensure that all Company employment policies and procedures are strictly job-related.

A. Job Descriptions, Specifications, and Requirements.

Staff has been assigned to:

1. Conduct detailed analyses of position descriptions to ensure that they accurately reflect position functions.
2. Evaluate worker specifications for each job classification by department using job performance criteria. Specifications will be free from bias with respect to race, color, religion, sex, disability or national origin, except where sex is a *bona fide* occupational qualification. If any requirements screen out a disproportionate number of minorities or women, these requirements will be carefully evaluated with respect to their relationship to actual job performance and business necessity.
3. Make available approved position descriptions and worker specifications to all members of management involved in the recruiting, screening, selection, and promotion processes; and distribute copies to all recruiting sources.

B. Recruitment Practices.

Staff has been assigned to conduct the following types of recruitment activities:

1. Include the phrase "Equal Opportunity/Affirmative Action Employer H/V" in all printed employment advertisements.
2. Place help wanted advertising, if used, in the minority news media and women's interest media.
3. Disseminate information on job opportunities and the Company's affirmative action objectives to organizations representing minorities and women and employment development agencies.
4. Actively encourage minority and women employees to refer applicants.
5. Send minority and women employees to participate in career days, job fairs, and related activities in their communities.
6. Recruit actively at secondary schools, junior colleges and colleges with predominantly minority or female enrollments, where recruiting is done at schools.
7. Participate, when appropriate, in special employment programs, summer jobs for minority youth, work-study programs for male and female students, etc.
8. Ensure that referral agencies used, if any, are referring minorities and women in a nondiscriminatory manner.

C. Selection Practices.

Staff has been assigned to take the following actions, among others, to ensure that the Company's selection process is job-related and to eliminate any artificial barriers to the employment and promotion of minorities and women that may be identified.

1. Review the Company's job application and other pre-employment forms to ensure that inquiries are job-related.
2. Evaluate the total selection process to ensure that it is free from bias and does not hinder the Company's ability to attain its affirmative action goals.
3. Evaluate selection methods that have a disparate impact on minorities or women to ensure that they are job-related and necessary.
4. Train personnel interviewers on proper techniques, inquiries, and documentation, and the Company's affirmative action objections.
5. Analyze unscored selection procedures, such as application forms, background checks, interviews, and physical examinations for possible discrimination against or exclusion of minorities or women, and eliminate any procedure having adverse impact if it is not strictly job related.

D. Promotional and Training Practices.

Staff has been assigned to take the following types of actions to prepare minorities and women for promotion and assist employees in advancing to jobs which offer more responsibility, challenge, and further opportunity for advancement.

1. Post promotion opportunities, when appropriate.

2. Offer career counseling to assist employees in identifying promotion opportunities, training and educational programs to enhance promotability, and opportunities for job rotation or transfer.
3. Administer the employee performance evaluation program, which is designed to assist employees in meeting performance standards, in a non-discriminatory manner.
4. Evaluate requirements for promotion on job-related criteria and ensure that minorities and women are not required to possess higher qualifications than others.
5. Require supervisory personnel to explain promotion selection decisions when minority or women employees are among the candidates rejected for advancement opportunities.

E. Supervisory and Disciplinary Practices.

Staff has been assigned to take the following actions to assist supervisors in meeting their affirmative action program responsibilities:

1. Develop and periodically review forms and instructions on supervisory practices, such as interviews, employee evaluations, counseling, training, and discipline.
2. Offer training for supervisors on the Company's affirmative action objectives and job-related personnel practices.

F. Facilities, Benefits, and Rules.

Staff has been assigned to take the following actions to ensure that the Company's facilities are desegregated and its benefits programs and rules are nondiscriminatory.

1. Verify that Company facilities and Company-sponsored social and recreational activities are desegregated and all employees are actively encouraged to participate.
2. Review the Company's employee benefits plans, coverages, and administration procedures to ensure that they do not inadvertently discriminate illegally because of race, color, religion, sex, disability, national origin, or age.
3. Review the Company's rules to ensure that they do not inadvertently discriminate illegally because of race, color, religion, sex, disability, national origin or age.

VI. Compliance With Sex Discrimination Guidelines

The Company fully complies with all applicable requirements of the OFCCP Sex Discrimination Guidelines.

A. Recruiting and Advertising.

1. The Company recruits employees of both sexes for all jobs (except where sex is a *bona fide* occupational qualification).

2. Employment advertisements do not express a sex preference (except where sex is a *bona fide* occupational qualification for the job). The Company does not place advertisements in columns headed "Male" or "Female."

B. Job Policies and Practices.

1. The Company's Equal Employment Opportunity Policy expressly states that the Company does not discriminate against employees or employment applicants based on sex.
2. The Company affords employees of both sexes an equal opportunity to compete for any available job for which they are qualified (except where sex is a *bona fide* occupational qualification).
3. The Company does not discriminate on the basis of sex in employment opportunities, wages, hours, benefits, or other conditions of employment.
4. The Company makes no employment distinctions between married and unmarried persons of either sex.
5. The Company does not deny employment to applicants with young children.
6. The Company does not terminate or force any employees below age 70 to retire on account of age; optional retirement ages are the same for men and women.
7. The Company provides and maintains appropriate physical facilities for both sexes.
8. The Company does not rely on state "protective laws" to deny female applicants or employees any jobs for which they are qualified.
9. The Company's maternity leave policy meets the requirements of the Pregnancy Discrimination Act amendment to Title VII of the 1964 Civil Rights Act: employees and applicants for employment are not denied employment, promotion, or training because of pregnancy, childbirth, or related medical conditions. Disabilities caused or contributed to by pregnancy, childbirth, or related medical conditions, for all job-related purposes, are treated the same as disabilities caused or contributed to by other medical conditions under the Company's health insurance (disability insurance) and sick leave plans. Written and unwritten employment policies and practices involving matters such as the commencement and duration of leave, the availability of extensions, the accrual of seniority and other benefits and privileges, reinstatement, and payment under the Company's health (and disability) insurance and sick leave plans, are applied to disability due to pregnancy, childbirth or related conditions on the same terms and conditions as they are applied to other disabilities.

C. Seniority System

The Company's seniority lines and seniority lists are not segregated by sex.

D. Wages.

1. The Company's wage schedules are not related to or based on the sex of employees.
2. The Company does not restrict employees of one sex to certain job classifications; the Company makes all jobs available to all qualified employees without regard to sex.

E. Affirmative Action.

1. The Company takes affirmative action to recruit women to apply for all job vacancies. Advertisements used to solicit applicants indicate that women will be considered equally with men for jobs.
2. The Company does not make selection decisions based on sex in any Company sponsored training programs; the Company takes affirmative action to ensure that both sexes have equal access to all training programs.

F. Sexual Harassment and Favors

It is against Company policy for any manager or supervisor to use official authority in making sexual advances toward employees over whom the manager or supervisor is authorized to make or recommend personnel actions; in granting, recommending or refusing to take any personnel action because of sexual favors; or taking or failing to take a personnel action as reprisal against any employee for rejecting or reporting a sexual advance. The Company will take corrective action against any employee who it knows violated this policy. Employees, likewise, are warned against making unwarranted advances toward co-workers. Employees are encouraged to report incidents of sexual harassment at work by supervisors, co-workers, or even those nonemployees who come upon the worksite with permission. There are remedial procedures with respect to personal privacy of those involved.

VII. Compliance With Guidelines On Discrimination Because Of Religion Or National Origin

The Company fully complies with all applicable requirements of the Guidelines on Discrimination because of Religion or National Origin.

A. Equal Employment Opportunity Policy.

1. The Company's Equal Employment Opportunity Policy expresses its commitment to prohibit discrimination based on religion or national origin against applicants or employees in employment, upgrading, demotion, transfer, recruitment, recruitment advertising, layoff, termination, rates of pay and other forms of compensation, and selection for training, including apprenticeship.
2. The Company's policy reflects its commitment to take affirmative action to ensure that applicants are employed and employees are treated during employment without regard to their religion or national origin.

B. Personnel Practices.

1. The Company's employment practices, including those affecting top and middle management levels, afford fair consideration for job opportunities to members of the various religious and ethnic groups.
2. The Company undertakes appropriate outreach and positive recruitment activities to ensure that it does not discriminate on the basis of religion or national origin, including, as appropriate:
   a. Communicating internally the Company's obligation to provide equal employment opportunity without regard to religion or national origin in a

manner which fosters understanding, acceptance, and support among the Company's executive, management, supervisory and other employees, and encourages them to take the necessary action to aid the Company in meeting this obligation.

b. Utilizing internal monitoring procedures to ensure that the Company's obligation to provide equal employment opportunity without regard to religion or national origin is being fully implemented.

c. Informing all employees periodically of the Company's commitment to equal employment opportunity for all persons, without regard to religion or national origin.

d. Enlisting the assistance and support of all recruitment sources for the Company's commitment to provide equal employment opportunity without regard to religion or national origin.

e. Reviewing employment records to determine the availability of promotable and transferable members of various religious and ethnic groups.

f. Establishing meaningful contacts with religious and ethnic organizations and leaders for such purposes as advice, education, technical assistance, and referral of potential employees, if problems come to the Company's attention which can be alleviated by such contacts.

C. Religious Accommodation

The Company accommodates the religious observances and practices of employees and prospective employees, unless the Company is unable to reasonably accommodate an employee's or prospective employee's religious observance or practice without undue hardship on the conduct of the Company's business.

VIII. Consideration Of Minorities And Women Not In The Workforce

The following are some of the means by which the Company will consider minorities and females not currently in the workforce who have the requisite skills and who can be recruited through affirmative action measures:

1. Minorities and females within our present workforce are advised of vacancies when they occur and are requested to refer minorities and/or females they know who might be interested in employment.
2. When contacting referral agencies, those agencies are requested to seek out and refer both minorities and females not currently in the workforce.
3. Vocational schools are advised of vacancies so that their current student body, not currently in the workforce, will be advised of employment opportunities when they occur.
4. In addition, organizations promoting the interest of minority group members and women will be contacted in seeking applicants from among those not currently in the workforce.

IX. Participation In Community Action Programs

All employees, and managers in particular, are encouraged by the Company to take the following community oriented actions, among others, to enhance employment opportunities of minorities and women:

1. Serve on community relations boards, merit employment councils, and similar activities.
2. Support vocational guidance institutes, vestibule training programs and similar activities.
3. Assist secondary schools and colleges, upon request, and as feasible, in programs designed to enable minority and female graduates to compete in the open employment market on a more equitable basis.
4. Support programs developed by such organizations as the National Alliance of Business, the Urban Coalition, and other organizations concerned with employment opportunities for minorities and women.
5. Support child care, equal housing, and public transportation programs that might improve employment opportunities for minorities and women.

X. Internal Workforce Analysis

A workforce analysis by department has been conducted as required. [The forms that follow this AAP show all employees by department, job title, race and sex, from the highest paid to the lowest paid, including departmental or unit supervision. The pay rates or salary ranges have been coded.]

XI. Job Group Analysis

Job groups have been developed based upon the criteria of combining job titles with similar content, similar advancement opportunities, and similar compensation. Job groups have been developed that highlight, rather than obscure, underutilization and problem areas, if any.

[The forms that follow this AAP show a statistical breakdown of each group by race and sex and will be used in the utilization analysis.]

XII. Eight Factor Analysis/Utilization Analysis

A. Eight Factor Analysis

Pursuant to applicable regulations, the Company has considered each factor which is specified in such regulations in order to determine availability of protected class members. [As indicated below, we have determined that some factors are not applicable to our calculations.

We have considered factor 1.a. noted on the following forms, "Population in Labor Area-Minority," but have assigned it no weight because it does not take into account requisite skills or those people who are available for work. We have considered factor 1.b., "Women Seeking Employment," but it is not applicable because the available information is too broad (encompassing officials and managers, professionals and technicians) and makes no distinction for requisite skills needed in specific industries. Likewise, for factor 2, "Size of Unemployment Force," we have considered this factor, but it is not applicable because the available information is too broad and makes no distinction for requisite skills needed in specific industries. It also does not identify those available for work. With regard to factor 3, "Work Force in Immediate Labor Area," we have considered this factor but it is not applicable because the information is too broad and makes no distinction for requisite skills needed in specific industries. Regarding factor 7, "Training Institutions," we have considered this factor but it is not applicable because requisite skills here are developed through experience acquired by on-the-job training. Concerning Factor 8 "In-House Training," this factor has been considered in Factor 6, "Within Organization."]

B. Utilization Analysis

An analysis of all major job groups at the Company has been conducted [and is included in the forms following this AAP]. In making this analysis of our major job classifications and job groups, we have considered whether or not minorities and females are "underutilized." No underutilization was identified in job groups in which the shortfall is less than one or current utilization is within 80% of availability.

[In making our availability study, we have separately considered the availability of minorities and females by taking into account the utilization factors, both internal and external. In connection with the external utilization considerations, it is important to note that the statistical information is based upon the most recent census information available to us. It is also pertinent to note that the availability information provided us does not reflect the availability by job titles or job groups in our particular industry, but is rather broadly categorized. Further, it is not possible to determine with any precision the skills or abilities possessed by minority and female persons in the workforce so as to determine whether the particular classifications in the statistical data compare with the classifications that we have assigned present personnel in EEO-1 reporting or in grouping jobs by similar content, wage rates and opportunities. Our analysis of utilizations, availability and the establishment of goals is thus necessarily inexact, particularly as to "external" considerations. Promotables/transferables and training considerations permit much more exactness in "internal" determinations.]

XIII. Statement Of Goals

[Statement of job groups with underutilization and statement of goals with respect to those job groups for the coming year.]

XIV. Prior Year Affirmative Action Results

[Statement of prior year results with respect to attaining goals.]

XV. Identification Of Problem Areas

A. Composition of the Workforce

Workforce, job group, and utilization analyses have been conducted in accordance with government regulations. [Statement of results of analyses.]

B. Composition of Applicant Flow

The Company will maintain applicant flow records as required by the regulations.

C. Company-Sponsored Programs

All Company-sponsored programs are available in accordance with the Equal Opportunity Policy. [Statement of any identified problems.]

D. Workforce Attitude

Our experience supports the conclusion that there is no serious lack of support and commitment by all managers to implement the Company's EEO policy. Lack of support of the EEO/AAP by any manager will not be tolerated.

E. Technical Compliance Phase

All technical phases of compliance are being met. All required posters are exhibited where they may be viewed by applicants and employees. The required certification to recruitment sources will be sent annually if vacancies occur or are anticipated. Applicants and related employment data are maintained as required by federal legislation and guidelines.

4:3.1A Sample Equal Opportunity Reaffirmation

Reaffirmation Of Equal Opportunity Policy

[company letterhead]

Date:

TO: All Employees

[NAME OF EMPLOYER] is committed to the maximum utilization of all human resources and the goal of Equal Employment Opportunity. I wish to reaffirm that commitment and bring to the attention of all employees that these objectives are reflected in all aspects of our daily operations. When vacancies occur, we shall continue to recruit, hire, train, and promote in all job titles without regard to race, color, religion, national origin, sex, age or disability, except where age and sex are essential *bona fide* occupational requirements, or where disability is a *bona fide* occupational disqualification. Furthermore, we shall continue to provide Equal Opportunity for qualified disabled veterans and veterans of the Vietnam Era.

Every reasonable effort shall be made to ensure that all employment decisions, Company programs and personnel actions are administered in conformity with the principle of Equal Employment Opportunity. Each of us has a responsibility to support these objectives and to ensure that this policy is fully implemented within our organization. To this end, employees are expected to bring EEO problems to the attention of their supervisor. This is the right of each and every employee and management will ensure that there is no coercion, intimidation, or harassment of any employee who calls attention to such problems.

I have designated ________________ as the company's Equal Employment Opportunity Coordinator, and have charged [him/her] with the responsibility to maintain the necessary programs, records, and reports to comply with all government regulations, including the maintenance of monitoring procedures for our policy objectives. Affirmative Action Programs have been developed at this company. Any employee may review these programs on _________ between the hours of _____ and _____ by contacting ________________.

Just as we all share the responsibility for meeting the challenges of our business objectives, each of us must assume a leading role in making our Equal Employment Policy work effectively.

____

[EMPLOYER]

4:3.2 Sample Disabled Persons Affirmative Action Program

The Affirmative Action Policy that follows is designed to satisfy the equal opportunity and affirmative action responsibilities regarding disabled persons. It is meant to complement the program at 4:3.1.

Affirmative Action Program For Disabled Persons

I. Reaffirmation Of Company Policy Concerning Disabled Persons

The Company is committed to the goal of equality of opportunity in employment. To further this goal, there is need for a Company policy concerning affirmative action in providing employment opportunities to disabled persons.

There is a continuing need for managers to take affirmative action in providing employment opportunities for disabled persons. Managers must assure through action, accommodation and teaching that positive steps are being taken to comply with this policy and to meet the requirements of law, while achieving the stated objectives of the Company for continued profitable, responsible, growth and success.

Handicapped individual means any person who (1) has a physical or mental impairment which substantially limits one or more of such person's major life activities, (2) has a record of such impairment, or (3) is regarded as having such an impairment. For purposes of this definition, a disabled individual is "substantially limited" if he or she is likely to experience difficulty in securing, retaining or advancing in employment because of a disability.

The Chief Executive Officer has reaffirmed the Company's policy concerning disabled persons by letter which appears in Section I of the Company's affirmative action plan for women and minorities.

II. Equal Employment Opportunity Policy

1. The Company shall recruit, hire, upgrade, train and promote in all job titles without regard to race, color, religion, sex, national origin, age, disability or status as a disabled veteran or a veteran of the Vietnam Era, except where age and sex are essential *bona fide* occupational requirements, or where disability is a *bona fide* occupational disqualification.
2. Managers shall ensure that all other personnel actions, such as compensation, benefits, layoffs, returns from layoffs, Company-sponsored training, educational tuition assistance, and social and recreational programs, shall be administered without regard to race, color, religion, sex, national origin, age, disability or status as a disabled veteran or a veteran of the Vietnam Era, except where age and sex are essential *bona fide* occupational requirements, or where disability is a *bona fide* occupational disqualification.
3. Managers shall base employment decisions on the principles of Equal Employment Opportunity and with the intent to further the Company's EEO commitment.

4. Managers shall take affirmative action to ensure that minority group individuals, females, veterans of the Vietnam Era and qualified disabled persons and disabled veterans are introduced into the work force and that these employees are encouraged to aspire for promotion and are considered as promotional opportunities arise.

III. Dissemination Of Policy

In order to ensure that all employees, applicants for employment and others are aware that this establishment is an employer of the disabled and of its official policy on employment of disabled persons, the following steps have been taken and shall continue to be undertaken as described:

A. Internal Dissemination

1. The policy concerning employment of disabled persons is contained in the President's letter, which is posted and attached at the end of this AAP.
2. The Company shall conduct meetings at least annually to disseminate Company policy. These meetings shall include management and supervisory personnel and shall cover the policy concerning disabled persons, its intent and individual responsibility for effective implementation, as well as the Chief Executive Officer's attitude.
3. Employees have been notified of the existence of the Company's affirmative action program for disabled persons and the equal employment opportunity policy through the President's letter dated and posted on key bulletin boards. For example, employees are advised that all aspects of employment, including job opportunity, training programs, and social events, shall be available to all to the extent that a disability is not a *bona fide* disqualification. Further, employees are advised to contact the Equal Employment Coordinator with problems concerning disability discrimination.
4. The affirmative action program for disabled persons and the equal employment opportunity policy have been included in all employee orientation programs, including management training, and are being communicated to job applicants. This will assure that all present and new employees can avail themselves of the program's benefits.
5. The Company has communicated the existence of the Company's affirmative action program to employees and job applicants. Copies of the affirmative action program have been made available to all employees and applicants for employment upon request. The location of the plan, the hours when it is available, the equal employment opportunity Policy and the reaffirmative statements have been conspicuously posted.
6. When employees are featured in product or consumer advertising, employee handbooks or similar publications, disabled employees are depicted, subject to the individual's right to privacy.

B. External Dissemination

1. All recruiting sources, including state employment security agencies, educational institutions and social service agencies, have been informed of the Company policy concerning employment of disabled persons and have been

advised to actively recruit and refer qualified disabled persons for positions listed.

2. A statement relating to the equal opportunity requirements of the Rehabilitation Act, the Americans with Disabilities Act, and implementing regulations is made a part of all contracts, order forms and leases.
3. An effort shall be made to consider all qualified disabled persons not currently in the workforce who have requisite skills and can be recruited through affirmative action measures.

C. Outreach and Positive Recruiting

The Company has reviewed its employment practices to ensure that the personnel programs provide the required affirmative action for employment and advancement of qualified disabled individuals. In conjunction with these programs, should vacancies occur, the Company shall undertake appropriate outreach and positive recruiting activities such as those listed below:

1. Recruiting programs shall be established and the assistance of recruiting sources shall be enlisted, where applicable and feasible, from:
   - State Employment Services;
   - Vocational Rehabilitation Agencies;
   - State Rehabilitation Centers;
   - Easter Seal Rehabilitation Centers;
   - State Education Agencies;
   - Sheltered Work Shops;
   - Organizations Serving Retarded persons;
   - Social Service Organizations;
   - Service Clubs; and
   - College Placement Offices.
2. Should vacancies occur, the Company shall engage in recruiting programs at schools for disabled people in their area, such as schools for deaf or blind individuals. Contacts shall be made and fostered with the agencies listed above for advice, technical assistance and referral of potential employees. The Company must periodically review its workforce to determine the availability of promotable, qualified, disabled individuals and to determine whether their skills are being fully utilized and developed.

IV. Responsibilities

The development and execution of Company policy in this plan shall be administered as outlined below.

A. Equal Employment Opportunity Department

Overall responsibility for equal employment opportunity and affirmative action planning for the Company is vested in the EEO Officer.

In the exempt, non-exempt, and hourly categories, each manager is responsible for performance, results, and compliance with Company policy and affirmative action requirements.

The EEO Officer's responsibilities include:

1. Developing policy statements, affirmative action programs, and internal and external communication techniques.
2. Assisting line management in the identification and solution of problem areas.
3. Designing and implementing audit and reporting systems that will:
   a. Measure the effectiveness of the Company's programs;
   b. Indicate need for remedial action;
   c. Determine the degree to which the Company's objectives have been attained;
   d. Determine whether known disabled employees have had the opportunity to participate in all Company-sponsored training, recreational and social activities; and
   e. Ensure that the Company is in compliance with the Rehabilitation Act of 1973.
4. Serving as liaison between the Company and enforcement agencies.
5. Serving as liaison between the Company and organizations promoting the interests of disabled persons and arranging for the active involvement of Company representatives in these organizations.
6. Keeping management informed of the latest developments in the area of equal employment opportunity.
7. Encouraging voluntary self-identification of disabled employees.
8. Providing advice and counsel on the interpretation and implementation of this policy and proposed plans and programs.
9. Recommending policy to the Corporate Executive Office.
10. Researching and evaluating new concepts and approaches in the field of equal employment opportunity and employment of disabled persons.
11. Notifying both applicants and referral sources that the Company is an "Equal Opportunity Employer."
12. Ensuring that individuals with personnel selection authority are selected and trained to ensure the furtherance of the Company's objectives and policy with regard to the hiring and promotion of disabled individuals.
13. Taking affirmative steps to ensure a bias-free selection process and to encourage the application of qualified disabled individuals for available job openings.
14. Ensuring that job qualification requirements are made available to those managers involved in the employment process, *i.e.*, recruitment, screening, selection and promotion processes.
15. Assisting in recruiting efforts under the Company's outreach program.
16. Reviewing the qualifications of all employees to ensure that disabled persons are given full opportunities for transfers, promotions, and development. Making a reasonable effort to conduct on-the-job training programs for disabled individuals.

17. Providing career counseling, where appropriate, for all employees.
18. Auditing training programs, hiring and promotion patterns, and job accommodations for disabled persons to ensure that there are no impediments to the attainments of objectives.
19. Checking with managers, supervisors, and employees to see if the Company's policies are being followed.
20. Checking for compliance in the following areas:
    a. Whether posters are properly displayed;
    b. Whether facilities are designed to accommodate use by disabled employees; and
    c. Whether disabled persons are afforded a full opportunity, consistent with their abilities, and are encouraged to participate in all Company-sponsored educational, training, recreational, and social activities, including tuition refund programs.
21. Advising supervisors that their work performance is being evaluated on the basis of their equal employment opportunity efforts and results, as well as other criteria.
22. Advising supervisors of their responsibility to take actions to prevent harassment of employees placed through affirmative action efforts.
23. Determining the need for and developing the means of making job accommodations for qualified disabled employees or applicants.
24. Ensuring that the compensation received by disabled employees will not be reduced because of their receipt of income from other sources.
25. Develop annually an Affirmative Action Program and improve internal and external communication techniques.
26. Assist in the identification and solution of EEO problem areas.
27. Implement and audit, as may be necessary, a reporting system to evaluate the effectiveness of the program, including:
    a. Determining the degree of compliance with the policy and the job accommodations that are being made for disabled persons; and
    b. Defining and recommending any necessary remedial actions.
28. Serve as liaison between the Company and employment agencies.
29. Review all technical forms for compliance with federal regulations.
30. Measure and ensure the effective implementation of the Affirmative Action Program for disabled persons by conducting, as appropriate, audits of training programs, hiring and promotion, and qualifications of all employees to ensure that disabled persons are given full opportunity for advancement.

V. Audit And Reporting System

The Company's Audit and Reporting System has been designed to:

1. Measure the effectiveness of the affirmative action program for disabled individuals.
2. Indicate those areas where remedial action is needed.
3. Determine the degree to which the facility's objectives have been obtained.

4. Determine whether known disabled employees have had the opportunity to participate in all Company-sponsored training, recreational, and social activities.
5. Ensure that each facility is in compliance with the Rehabilitation Act of 1973 and the Americans with Disabilities Act.

The audit system will provide for maintenance of the following records:

1. An applicant log, which will show the date, name of applicant, race, sex, veteran status, disability status, referral source, interview date (if any), EEO-1 category of position applied for, and final disposition.
2. Summary data of job offers, hires, promotions, resignations, discharges, layoffs, and training programs by job group, sex and minority group identification disability status and veteran status, except in such instances where it can be demonstrated that it is not possible to maintain such records.

VI. Plan Of Action

A. Introduction

The Company views its AAP for employment of disabled persons as a results-oriented program designed to enhance the opportunities of qualified disabled workers. It recognizes that the ultimate success of this undertaking will be largely the result of the "good faith efforts" detailed in the plan of action section of the AAP. In the following paragraphs, the substance of the plan to convert commitments to measurable progress is outlined.

B. Recruiting

The Company will actively seek, when openings occur, qualified disabled persons for current and future employment. In order to improve recruitment and the flow of qualified disabled applicants, we will contact as appropriate those recruitment sources listed previously.

The Company will inform primary recruiting sources verbally and in writing, at least annually, of our EEO-handicapped policy and maintain a file of sources notified and acknowledgements received.

C. Tests

The Company uses only content valid skills tests of typing, dictation, transcription and machine operation ability. These tests are used only for jobs which require demonstrated skills.

D. Employment and Selection

The application record of each known disabled applicant for employment with the Company will identify every job for which the applicant was considered. If a disabled applicant is rejected for employment, a written statement shall be appended to the application record stating: the reasons for such rejections; a comparison of the applicant's qualifications with those of the person selected; and a description of the accommodations, if any, considered.

All employees engaged in hiring or other selection decisions are trained in EEO policy making. Results are reviewed periodically to check to see that EEO policy is being followed. The Company maintains an affirmative action file containing all applications for employment from disabled individuals. The AA file is maintained to check that:

1. Qualified disabled persons are applying;
2. There is a proper representation of disabled applicants for all jobs; and
3. Handicapped applicants are being given equal consideration for employment.

E. Promotions

The records of disabled employees are reviewed to assure that qualified individuals are given equal consideration as opportunities for upgrading, promotion, and transfer occur. Where additional training and experience would be helpful for advancement, management counsels and assists disabled employees.

The personnel file of each known disabled employee identifies every promotion and every training program for which the employee has been considered.

Where an applicant or employee is selected for hire, promotion, or training, and the Company undertakes any job accommodation on his or her behalf, or has previously instituted some accommodation which makes it possible for the Company to place such person on the job, a description of the accommodation shall be included in the employee's personnel record.

F. Training

Handicapped employees are given equal access to all training programs designed to enhance an employee's ability to assume positions of greater responsibility. Records of employee attendance at development training courses are maintained for two years. This information is reviewed periodically to assure that all employees have equal access regardless of disability.

Also, the Company's tuition reimbursement program is made available to all employees who wish to enhance their opportunity with the Company by continuing their formal education.

G. Facilities

In designing new construction and remodeling old facilities, the requirements of the Americans with Disabilities Act will be met.

H. Internal Complaint Review Procedure

The facility has established an internal review procedure for the processing of complaints alleging violations of the Rehabilitation Act of 1973 and the Americans with Disabilities Act.

Complaints referred to the U.S. Department of Labor or other EEO agencies under this Act shall be processed under the internal review procedure. The details of this procedure are available from the Facility EEO Coordinator.

I. Job Accommodation

The Company shall make every effort to accommodate the physical or mental limitations of disabled applicants and employees. In addition, if appropriate, the Company shall seek guidance from the various resource organizations that may be helpful in designing reasonable job accommodations for such applicants or employees. In determining the extent of the Company's job accommodation obligations, the following factors, among others, shall be considered:

1. Business necessity;
2. Financial cost and expenses.

4:3.2A Sample Statement of Compliance

Statement Of Compliance

(On Company letterhead)

TO APPLICANTS AND EMPLOYEES:

The Company is a government contractor subject to Section 503 of the Vocational Rehabilitation Act of 1973, as amended, and Section 402 of the Vietnam Era Veterans Readjustment Act of 1974, which require federal government contractors to take affirmative action to employ and advance in employment qualified disabled individuals, disabled veterans and veterans of the Vietnam Era. If you are a disabled person, a disabled veteran, or a veteran of the Vietnam Era, please advise if you would like to be considered under these affirmative action programs. Submission of this information is voluntary, and refusal or failure to provide it will not subject you to discharge, discipline or any other adverse treatment.

In order to assure proper placement of all applicants and employees who have a disability or are disabled veterans, we request you supply the information requested below to the Company. This information shall be kept confidential, except that supervisors, managers and safety and health personnel may be informed regarding any restrictions in the work or duties and any necessary job accommodations.

Please inform us about: (1) any mental or physical disability you have had or have currently which causes you to be disabled; (2) any special methods, skills or procedures which qualify you for positions that you might not otherwise be able to do because of your disability; and (3) the accommodations which you believe we could make to enable you to perform the job.

If you are a disabled veteran or a veteran of the Vietnam Era, we request that you supply us with a copy of your military record, discharge papers and any other relevant documentation in order to assure your proper placement.

Any employee who believes that he or she is being discriminated against because of mental or physical disability, or because he or she is a disabled veteran or veteran of the Vietnam Era, should discuss this matter with his or her immediate supervisor, or the EEO Coordinator, __________________.

The affirmative action programs for the disabled and disabled and Vietnam Era veterans are available for inspection.

Sincerely,

[NAME OF PRESIDENT]

4:3.3 Sample Disabled Veterans (Including Vietnam Era Veterans) Affirmative Action Program

The Affirmative Action Policy that follows is designed to satisfy the equal opportunity and affirmative action responsibilities regarding disabled veterans and disabled veterans of the Vietnam Era. It is meant to complement the program at 4:3.1.

Affirmative Action Program For Disabled Veterans And Veterans Of The Vietnam Era

I. Reaffirmation Of Company Policy Concerning Disabled Veterans And Veterans Of The Vietnam Era

The Company reaffirms that it will take affirmative action to employ and advance in employment qualified disabled veterans of the Vietnam Era.

For purposes of compliance, a Vietnam Era veteran is a person who: (1) served on active duty for more than 180 days between August 5, 1964, and May 7, 1975, and was discharged, or (2) was discharged or released from active duty for a service connected disability if any part of such active duty was performed between August 5, 1964 and May 7, 1975.

This affirmative action program applies to all employment practices, including, but not limited to, the following: hiring, upgrading, demotion or transfer, recruitment advertising, layoff or termination, rates of pay or other forms of compensation and selection for training.

II. Dissemination Of Policy

In order to ensure that all employees, applicants for employment, and others are aware that this establishment is an equal opportunity employer of disabled veterans and veterans of the Vietnam Era, the following steps have been taken and will continue to be taken:

A. Internal Dissemination

1. The policy concerning employment of veterans is contained in the President's letter (attached hereto), which is posted as noted in conspicuous locations.
2. The Company will conduct special meetings at least once each year to disseminate Company policy. These meetings shall include management and supervisory personnel and shall cover the policy concerning disabled veterans and veterans of the Vietnam Era, its intent, and individual responsibility for effective implementation, as well as the President's attitude.
3. Employees have been notified of the existence of the Company's affirmative action program for disabled veterans and veterans of the Vietnam Era and the Equal Employment Opportunity Policy through the facility manager's letter dated _____ and posted on key bulletin boards on _____. For example, employees are advised that all aspects of employment, including job opportunity, training programs, tuition refund, and social events are available to all, to the extent that physical or mental disability or disability is not a *bona fide* disqualification. Further, employees are advised to contact the Equal Employ-

ment Coordinator if they feel they are being discriminated against because of disability or veteran's status.

4. The affirmative action program for disabled veterans and veterans of the Vietnam Era and the Equal Employment Opportunity Policy have been included in all employee orientation programs, including management training, and are communicated to job applicants. This is to assure that all present and new employees can avail themselves of the program's benefits.
5. Copies of the full affirmative action program have been made available to all employees and applicants for employment upon request. The location of the plan and the hours when it is available, along with the Equal Employment Opportunity Policy and the reaffirmation statements have been conspicuously posted.

B. External Dissemination

1. All recruiting sources, including state employment security agencies, educational institutions, and social service agencies, have been informed of the Company policy concerning employment of disabled veterans and veterans of the Vietnam Era and have been advised to recruit actively and refer qualified veterans for positions listed.
2. Written notification has been sent to all contractors, subcontractors, vendors and suppliers requesting appropriate action on their part.
3. An effort shall be made to consider all qualified veterans not currently in the work force who have requisite skills and can be recruited through affirmative action measures.

III. Plan Of Action

The Affirmative Action Program for disabled veterans and Vietnam Era veterans includes the following measures:

- Review of personnel procedures to determine if these assure careful, thorough and systematic consideration of the job qualifications of known disabled veteran applicants and Vietnam Era veteran applicants for job vacancies filled either by hiring or promotion and of all training programs.
- Review of physical and mental job qualification requirements to ensure they are job-related, consistent with business necessity and the safe performance of the job.
- In determining the qualifications of a covered veteran, the Company shall consider only that portion of the military record, including discharge papers, relevant to the specific job qualifications for which the veteran is being considered.
- Reasonable accommodation will be made to the physical and mental limitations of a disabled veteran if such can be done without due hardship on the conduct of business.
- The policies and procedures established in compliance with provisions of the Vietnam Era Veterans Readjustment Act of 1974, and as outlined herein, will be communicated to all employees, reviewed with all levels of management and publicized in Company publications.

- The application form or personnel file of each known covered veteran will be annotated to identify each vacancy and each training program for which he/she was considered. In each case where a covered veteran is rejected for employment, promotion or training, a statement of the reasons will be included in the personnel file or appended application form.
- A record will be maintained of the hires, promotions and training provided to all covered veterans.
- All employment openings paying less than $_____ annually to be filled by external hiring will be listed with the appropriate office of the state employment service. The facility will complete and file all of the required quarterly reports on openings and hires.
- We will enlist the assistance of veterans groups and veterans service groups to the extent necessary to meet these Affirmative Action obligations.
- Disabled veterans and veterans of the Vietnam Era who wish to benefit from the Affirmative Action Program will be invited to voluntarily identify themselves to discuss employment opportunities or advancement. A sample of the solicitory letter can be found in the AAP for disabled persons.
- This program will be reviewed and updated annually.

4:3.3A Sample Disabled Veteran Compliance Statement

Statement Of Compliance

(On Company letterhead)

To Applicants And Employees:

The Company is a government contractor subject to Section 503 of the Vocational Rehabilitation Act of 1973, as amended, and Section 402 of the Vietnam Era Veterans Readjustment Act of 1974, which require federal government contractors to take affirmative action to employ and advance in employment qualified disabled individuals, disabled veterans and veterans of the Vietnam Era. If you are a disabled person, a disabled veteran, or a veteran of the Vietnam Era, please advise if you would like to be considered under these affirmative action programs. Submission of this information is voluntary, and refusal or failure to provide it will not subject you to discharge, discipline or any other adverse treatment.

In order to assure proper placement of all applicants and employees who have a disability or are disabled veterans, we request you supply the information requested below to the Company. This information shall be kept confidential, except that supervisors, managers and safety and health personnel may be informed regarding any restrictions in the work or duties and any necessary job accommodations.

Please inform us about: (1) any mental or physical disability you have had or have currently which causes you to be disabled; (2) any special methods, skills or procedures which qualify you for positions that you might not otherwise be able to do because of your disability; and (3) the accommodations which you believe we could make to enable you to perform the job.

If you are a disabled veteran or a veteran of the Vietnam Era, we request that you supply us with a copy of your military record, discharge papers and any other relevant documentation in order to assure your proper placement.

Any employee who believes that he or she is being discriminated against because of mental or physical disability, or because he or she is a disabled veteran or veteran of the Vietnam Era, should discuss this matter with his or her immediate supervisor, or the EEO Coordinator, ______.

The affirmative action programs for the disabled and disabled and Vietnam Era veterans are available for inspection.

Sincerely,

[NAME OF PRESIDENT]

Chapter 5

Immigration Reform and Control Act

Traditionally, as a result of the United States' professed policy of welcoming foreigners as prospective citizens, the nation has been considered a "melting pot" of cultures from all over the world. However, the government has stepped in to restrict immigration in order to prevent an adverse impact on the nation's economic and employment status. This chapter provides examples of the various types of documentation that employers are required to obtain in order to comply with recent immigration legislation.

5:1 Immigration Control Act Requirements

The Immigration Reform and Control Act of 1986 requires all employees who commenced employment after November 6, 1986, to furnish their employers with employment eligibility verification. For each employee hired after that date, a properly completed I-9 should be retained and made available upon request (should anyone from the federal government ever visit and ask to see these forms). This requirement applies to all employees, including U.S. citizens.

5:1.1 Sample Form I-9

ELIGIBILITY VERIFICATION: I-9

EMPLOYMENT ELIGIBILITY VERIFICATION (Form I-9)

1 EMPLOYEE INFORMATION AND VERIFICATION: (To be completed and signed by employee.)

Name: (Print or Type) Last	First	Middle	Birth Name
Address: Street Name and Number	City	State	ZIP Code
Date of Birth (Month/Day/Year)		Social Security Number	

I attest, under penalty of perjury, that I am (check a box):

☐ 1. A citizen or national of the United States.
☐ 2. An alien lawfully admitted for permanent residence (Alien Number A ____________).
☐ 3. An alien authorized by the Immigration and Naturalization Service to work in the United States (Alien Number A ____________, or Admission Number ____________, expiration of employment authorization, if any ____________).

I attest, under penalty of perjury, the documents that I have presented as evidence of identity and employment eligibility are genuine and relate to me. I am aware that federal law provides for imprisonment and/or fine for any false statements or use of false documents in connection with this certificate.

Signature	Date (Month/Day/Year)

PREPARER/TRANSLATOR CERTIFICATION (To be completed if prepared by person other than the employee). I attest, under penalty of perjury, that the above was prepared by me at the request of the named individual and is based on all information of which I have any knowledge.

Signature	Name (Print or Type)		
Address (Street Name and Number)	City	State	Zip Code

2 EMPLOYER REVIEW AND VERIFICATION: (To be completed and signed by employer.)

Instructions:
Examine one document from List A and check the appropriate box, ***OR*** examine one document from List B ***and*** one from List C and check the appropriate boxes. Provide the ***Document Identification Number*** and ***Expiration Date*** for the document checked.

List A Documents that Establish Identity and Employment Eligibility	List B Documents that Establish Identity	**and**	List C Documents that Establish Employment Eligibility
☐ 1. United States Passport ☐ 2. Certificate of United States Citizenship ☐ 3. Certificate of Naturalization ☐ 4. Unexpired foreign passport with attached Employment Authorization ☐ 5. Alien Registration Card with photograph	☐ 1. A State-issued driver's license or a State-issued I.D. card with a photograph, or information, including name, sex, date of birth, height, weight, and color of eyes. (Specify State)__________) ☐ 2. U.S. Military Card ☐ 3. Other (Specify document and issuing authority) __________		☐ 1. Original Social Security Number Card (other than a card stating it is not valid for employment) ☐ 2. A birth certificate issued by State, county, or municipal authority bearing a seal or other certification ☐ 3. Unexpired INS Employment Authorization Specify form # __________
Document Identification # __________	***Document Identification*** # __________		***Document Identification*** # __________
Expiration Date (if any) __________	***Expiration Date (if any)*** __________		***Expiration Date (if any)*** __________

CERTIFICATION: I attest, under penalty of perjury, that I have examined the documents presented by the above individual, that they appear to be genuine and to relate to the individual named, and that the individual, to the best of my knowledge, is eligible to work in the United States.

Signature	Name (Print or Type)	Title
Employer Name	Address	Date

U.S. Department of Justice
Immigration and Naturalization Service

EMPLOYMENT ELIGIBILITY VERIFICATION **page 2**

NOTICE: Authority for collecting the information on this form is in Title 8, United States Code, Section 1324A, which requires employers to verify employment eligibility of individuals on a form approved by the Attorney General. This form will be used to verify the individual's eligibility for employment in the United States. Failure to present this form for inspection to officers of the Immigration and Naturalization Service or Department of Labor within the time period specified by regulation, or improper completion or retention of this form, may be a violation of the above law and may result in a civil money penalty.

Section 1. Instructions to Employee/Preparer for completing this form

Instructions for the employee.

All employees, upon being hired, must complete Section 1 of this form. Any person hired after November 6, 1986 must complete this form. (For the purpose of completion of this form the term "hired" applies to those employed, recruited or referred for a fee.)

All employees must print or type their complete name, address, date of birth, and Social Security Number. The block which correctly indicates the employee's immigration status must be checked. If the second block is checked, the employee's Alien Registration Number must be provided. If the third block is checked, the employee's Alien Registration Number ***or*** Admission Number must be provided, as well as the date of expiration of that status, if it expires.

All employees whose present names differ from birth names, because of marriage or other reasons, must print or type their birth names in the appropriate space of Section 1. Also, employees whose names change after employment verification should report these changes to their employer.

All employees must sign and date the form.

Instructions for the preparer of the form, if not the employee.

If a person assists the employee with completing this form, the preparer must certify the form by signing it and printing or typing his or her complete name and address.

Section 2. Instructions to Employer for completing this form

(For the purpose of completion of this form, the term "employer" applies to employers and those who recruit or refer for a fee.)

Employers must complete this section by examining evidence of identity and employment eligibility, and:

- checking the appropriate box in List A ***or*** boxes in both Lists B and C;
- recording the document identification number and expiration date (if any);
- recording the type of form if not specifically identified in the list;
- signing the certification section.

NOTE: Employers are responsible for reverifying employment eligibility of employees whose employment eligibility documents carry an expiration date.

Copies of documentation presented by an individual for the purpose of establishing identity and employment eligibility may be copied and retained for the purpose of complying with the requirements of this form and no other purpose. Any copies of documentation made for this purpose should be maintained with this form.

Name changes of employees which occur after preparation of this form should be recorded on the form by lining through the old name, printing the new name and the reason (such as marriage), and dating and initialing the changes. Employers should not attempt to delete or erase the old name in any fashion.

RETENTION OF RECORDS.

The completed form must be retained by the employer for:

- three years after the date of hiring; or
- one year after the date the employment is terminated, whichever is later.

Employers may photocopy or reprint this form as necessary.

U.S. Department of Justice
Immigration and Naturalization Service

OMB #1115-0136
Form I-9 (05/07/87)

5:2 Applicant Information Form

Legislation further requires each employee to furnish proof of work eligibility within 72 hours after the commencement of employment. To expedite this process, personnel can provide each applicant with an applicant documentation checklist. Proof of eligibility will, therefore, be addressed at the start of the recruitment process, and there will be no surprises later.

Currently, consultants and temporary employees must also furnish documentation to establish their identity and employment eligibility, even if they are retained through a third party (e.g., a contract help agency) and that third-party employer is required to obtain (and retain) the same data.

Employment agencies and executive search firms are also required to obtain proof of eligibility. Agencies and search firms are held accountable for not doing so and are subject to the same legal penalties for noncompliance as are employers. However, they may be relieved of responsibility for the process if the employer takes full responsibility and provides the agencies and/or search firms with a letter to that effect.

Employers that assume full responsibility for verifying eligibility remove a burden that agencies should be accountable for. If an agency cannot confirm a candidate's eligibility to work and ensure that his or her documentation is in order, the agency should not present the candidate to the employer.

Applicant Information Form

Notice: Applicants who do not present proper documentation cannot be hired.

As a condition of employment with ________________, successful applicants will be asked to present one of the following documents before being hired:

1. U.S. passport (can be expired)
2. Certificate of U.S. Citizenship or Certificate of Naturalization
3. Unexpired foreign passport authorizing U.S. employment (with official impression by State Department)
4. Resident alien card or other alien registration card containing the applicant's identification, photograph, and authorization to work in the U.S.A.

If none of the above is available, successful applicants must present one of the following:

a. U.S.Social Security card
b. Certificate of birth in the U.S.
c. Certificate establishing U.S. nationality at birth

Applicants who present a Social Security card, U.S. birth certificate, or certificate of U.S. nationality must *also* present one of the following identification cards:

d. Valid U.S. driver's license containing photograph
e. Other state-issued identification card containing photograph

5:3 Employment Agency Eligibility Letter and Guarantee

This form is a proof of eligibility guarantee form letter that the employer can attach to the agency's fee agreement. This letter asks agencies to guarantee their participation in the verification process by having candidates bring a letter from the agency with them on the interview. The attestation of employment eligibility is the document that the applicant must bring to an employment interview.

It is not suggested that candidates furnish any proof at this time and, in fact, it may be dangerous to do so. The organization would be taking on a potential risk. If a candidate is not hired, he or she could claim that the job was not offered because of his or her citizenship status. Besides, asking this information from all applicants would be performing more than the law requires.

5:3.1 Employment Agency Eligibility Letter

Sample Letter To Agency
And Attestation Of Work Eligibility

[DATE]

Dear Sir/Madam:

As you are aware, Congress passed the Immigration Reform and Control Act, which requires employers and employment referral agencies to verify that the individuals they employ or refer are eligible to work in the United States. The implementing regulations of the Act also state that verification must be done prior to commencement of employment "and by individuals recruited for a fee or referred for a fee prior to recruitment or referral for employment in the United States."

To aid us in our compliance efforts, we ask that you prepare a statement on your company's letterhead that states you have verified the applicants' documents, what documents were presented, and that they appear to be authentic and correct. The referrals should then bring this statement, not their document(s) along on their interview. Our recruiters will not interview your candidates without the statement.

Attached for your information are the temporary forms we will use to process the new hires to conform with the 1-9 form.

Should your referral be extended an offer of employment, we would then ask him/her to show the necessary documents on his/her start date.

We would like this procedure to commence on [DATE].

Sincerely,

5:3.2 Employment Agency Eligibility Guarantee

ATTESTATION OF EMPLOYMENT ELIGIBILITY

On, ______________________ , ______________________________________ ,
(date) (Name of individual hired, recruited or referred)

presented to me the following document(s), which appeared genuine, to establish identity and authorization for employment in the United States. Unless the individual presents a document described in Part A of this form, he or she **must** present at least one document described in Part B and one document described in Part C.

☐ **A. One document establishes both identity and authorization for employment.**

- ☐ 1. United States passport.
- ☐ 2. Certificate of United States Citizenship.
- ☐ 3. Certificate of Naturalization.
- ☐ 4. U.S. Citizen identification card.
- ☐ 5. Unexpired foreign passport with an unexpired endorsement of the Attorney General authorizing the individual's employment in the United States.
- ☐ 6. Resident alien card which contains a photograph of the applicant.

Document ID # ____________________ Expiration date (if any) ____________________

☐ **B. One document establishes employment authorization:**

- ☐ 1. Social security card (which does not specify on its face that the card authorizes employment in the United States).
- ☐ 2. A certificate of birth in any State. The certificate must contain the given surname, name, date of birth, place of birth, date the birth record was filed, and an official seal or other certification by the official custodian of such record. Official custodian refers to the governmental agency with which the birth is registered.
- ☐ 3. Report of U.S. Citizen Birth Abroad, issued by the U.S. Department of State.
- ☐ 4. Form I-94 with employment authorization stamp.
- ☐ 5. ______________________________________
(Describe the document)

Document ID # ____________________ Expiration date (if any) ____________________

☐ **C. One document establishes identity:**

- ☐ 1. A state driver's license or ID card with a photograph or information, which includes full name, date of birth, height, weight, color of eyes, and residence address.
Specify State ______________________________________ .
- ☐ 2. U.S. Military card.
- ☐ 3. Other (Specify document and issuing authority) ____________________ .

Document ID # ____________________ Expiration date (if any) ____________________

A copy of each indicated document is attached hereto.

I declare under penalty of perjury and under the laws of the United States that the foregoing is true and correct.

____________________ ____________________ ____________
(Signature) (Name–Print or Type) (Title)

____________________ ____________________ ____________
(Employer Name) (Address) (Date)

5:4 I-9 Eligibility Documentation Chart

This form, an I-9 eligibility documentation chart, can be used by personnel as a quick reference during the eligibility verification process. It indicates what documents may be used to establish identification and work authorization. The most important column is the one on the far right. If new hires demonstrate possession of any of the items marked in this column, no other identification or work authorization documentation is required.

Personnel may consider making the furnishing of eligibility data a condition of employment. Personnel can warn applicants right from the start that failure to provide the necessary documents when employment commences will delay or remove the employment offer. It is also a good idea for the necessary documents to be obtained before employees report to work, although the law permits 72 hours to pass. If employees do not have adequate proof on the first day of employment, it may be difficult to obtain that information on the third day. Even if an organization is disciplined and its personnel department has solid credibility, problems and tension will result if a "good" employee persistently fails to provide the necessary documentation.

Any person given the authority can verify the eligibility documentation. The I-9 form is explicitly detailed. To ensure that employees responsible for obtaining the appropriate documentation have done so correctly, a photocopy of the documentation should be attached to the I-9 form. In fact, although not required, there are instructions on the form that specifically authorize the duplication of certain identification items (even though other items may not be duplicated for identification purposes).

Personnel should review all related materials on an ongoing basis to ensure completeness and accuracy of the entire eligibility verification process. Fines for noncompliance can be costly. Currently, they are $100 to $1,000 a day per employee found in violation.

Legal experts agree that under no circumstances should I-9 forms and their accompanying photocopied documentation be kept with employee personnel files. Rather, they should be chronologically stored in a different location, and kept for three years from the date of hire or one year after employment is terminated (whichever is later).

I-9 forms should be stored separately because they are the only documents that should be made available if employer's records are subjected to an inspection.

I-9 ELIGIBILITY DOCUMENTATION CHART

Documentation Acceptable to Establish Identity and Authorization to Accept Employment (8 C.F.R. §274a.2(b)(1)(v)(A), (B), (C))

Document	*Establish Identity (1)*	*Establish Work Authorization (2)*	*Both (1) and (2)*
U.S. passport			X
Certificate of U.S. citizenship (INS Form N-560)			X
Certificate of naturalization (INS Form N-550)			X
Unexpired foreign passport plus INS Form I-94			X
Alien registration receipt card (INS Form I-151, or I-551)			X
Temporary resident card (INS Form I-688)			X
Employment card (INS Form I-688A)			X
State driver's license	X*		
Social Security card (Valid for employment)		X	
Unexpired reentry permit (INS Form I-327)		X	
Unexpired refugee travel document (INS Form I-571)	X		
Certification of birth (Dept. of State Form FS-545)	X		
Certification of birth abroad (Dept. of State Form DS-1350)	X		
Original birth certificate or certified copy	X		

*The INS has requested suggestions and comments from the public for additional documents that may serve to verify an employee's identity.

Chapter 6

Employee Compensation

Employee compensation is a highly complex area involving legal wage restrictions that apply to a wide variety of occupations and compensation methods. This chapter provides sample forms and documents to help comply with the provisions of the Fair Labor Standards Act that apply to minimum wage and compensation for overtime, as well as the permissible exemptions from the minimum wage and overtime regulations.

6:1 Wage Records

Employers must follow certain guidelines when compensating their employees. Typically wages paid to employees are largely regulated by federal and state wage laws, which set minimum rates and overtime compensation that must be paid to the employees who fall under the protection of these statutes. This section provides samples of the various wage records that employers should maintain.

6:1.1 Form W-4

New staff members are placed on payroll the day they start work. As a part of in-processing, new employees are required to complete a W-4 Form so that the correct amount of federal income tax is withheld from their pay. The 1991 W-4 Form includes instructions and a worksheet to help employees make accurate calculations.

The form implies that the burden of accurate withholding is the employee's. If a W-4 is not completed, salary should not be paid, because the burden of accurate withholding then becomes the employer's.

Salary should never be paid if a Social Security number has not been obtained. The Social Security number is required for the withholding of income tax. Once salary is paid without the number, the legal burden of accurate withholding rests with the employer. In fact, it is beneficial to ask employees for their Social Security numbers right after they are hired. The Social Security card can also be used for I-9 purposes.

1991 Form W-4

Purpose. Complete Form W-4 so that your employer can withhold the correct amount of Federal income tax from your pay.

Exemption From Withholding. Read line 6 of the certificate below to see if you can claim exempt status. *If exempt, complete line 6; but do not complete lines 4 and 5.* No Federal income tax will be withheld from your pay. Your exemption is good for one year only. It expires February 15, 1992.

Basic Instructions. Employees who are not exempt should complete the Personal Allowances Worksheet. Additional worksheets are provided on page 2 for employees to adjust their withholding allowances based on itemized deductions, adjustments to income, or two-earner/two-job situations. Complete all worksheets that apply to your situation. The worksheets will help you figure the number of withholding allowances you are entitled to claim. However, you may claim fewer allowances than this.

Head of Household. Generally, you may claim head of household filing status on your tax return only if you are unmarried and pay more than 50% of the costs of keeping up a home for yourself and your dependent(s) or other qualifying individuals.

Nonwage Income. If you have a large amount of nonwage income, such as interest or dividends, you should consider making estimated tax payments using Form 1040-ES. Otherwise, you may find that you owe additional tax at the end of the year.

Two-Earner/Two-Jobs. If you have a working spouse or more than one job, figure the total number of allowances you are entitled to claim on all jobs using worksheets from only one Form W-4. This total should be divided among all jobs. Your withholding will usually be most accurate when all allowances are claimed on the W-4 filed for the highest paying job and zero allowances are claimed for the others.

Advance Earned Income Credit. If you are eligible for this credit, you can receive it added to your paycheck throughout the year. For details, get Form W-5 from your employer.

Check Your Withholding. After your W-4 takes effect, you can use **Pub. 919,** Is My Withholding Correct for 1991?, to see how the dollar amount you are having withheld compares to your estimated total annual tax. Call 1-800-829-3676 to order this publication. Check your local telephone directory for the IRS assistance number if you need further help.

Personal Allowances Worksheet

For 1991, the value of your personal exemption(s) is reduced if your income is over $100,000 ($150,000 if married filing jointly, $125,000 if head of household, or $75,000 if married filing separately). Get Pub. 919 for details.

A Enter "1" for **yourself** if no one else can claim you as a dependent . . . . . A ______

B Enter "1" if:
1. You are single and have only one job; or
2. You are married, have only one job, and your spouse does not work; or
3. Your wages from a second job or your spouse's wages (or the total of both) are $1,000 or less. . . B ______

C Enter "1" for your **spouse.** But, you may choose to enter "0" if you are married and have either a working spouse or more than one job (this may help you avoid having too little tax withheld) . . . . . C ______

D Enter number of **dependents** (other than your spouse or yourself) whom you will claim on your tax return . . . D ______

E Enter "1" if you will file as **head of household** on your tax return (see conditions under "Head of Household," above) . . E ______

F Enter "1" if you have at least $1,500 of **child or dependent care expenses** for which you plan to claim a credit . . . F ______

G Add lines A through F and enter total here . . . . . ▶ G ______

For accuracy, do all worksheets that apply.
- If you plan to **itemize or claim adjustments to income** and want to reduce your withholding, see the Deductions and Adjustments Worksheet on page 2.
- If you are **single** and have **more than one job** and your combined earnings from all jobs exceed $27,000 OR if you are **married** and have a **working spouse or more than one job,** and the combined earnings from all jobs exceed $46,000, see the Two-Earner/Two-Job Worksheet on page 2 if you want to avoid having too little tax withheld.
- If **neither** of the above situations applies, **stop here** and enter the number from line G on line 4 of Form W-4 below.

---------- **Cut here and give the certificate to your employer. Keep the top portion for your records.** ----------

Form **W-4** | Department of the Treasury | Internal Revenue Service

Employee's Withholding Allowance Certificate

▶ For Privacy Act and Paperwork Reduction Act Notice, see reverse.

OMB No. 1545-0010 | **1991**

1 Type or print your first name and middle initial	Last name	2 Your social security number
Home address (number and street or rural route)	3 Marital status: ☐ Single ☐ Married ☐ Married, but withhold at higher Single rate. **Note:** *If married, but legally separated, or spouse is a nonresident alien, check the Single box.*	
City or town, state, and ZIP code		

4 Total number of allowances you are claiming (from line G above or from the Worksheets on back if they apply) . . . 4 ______

5 Additional amount, if any, you want deducted from each pay . . . . . 5 $ ______

6 I claim exemption from withholding and I certify that I meet **ALL** of the following conditions for exemption:
- Last year I had a right to a refund of **ALL** Federal income tax withheld because I had **NO** tax liability; **AND**
- This year I expect a refund of **ALL** Federal income tax withheld because I expect to have **NO** tax liability; **AND**
- This year if my income exceeds $550 and includes nonwage income, another person cannot claim me as a dependent.

If you meet all of the above conditions, enter the year effective and "EXEMPT" here . . . . ▶ 6 19

7 Are you a full-time student? (**Note:** *Full-time students are not automatically exempt.*) . . . . . 7 ☐ **Yes** ☐ **No**

Under penalties of perjury, I certify that I am entitled to the number of withholding allowances claimed on this certificate or entitled to claim exempt status.

Employee's signature ▶ **Date ▶** , 19

8 Employer's name and address (**Employer:** Complete 8 and 10 **only if sending to IRS**)	9 Office code (optional)	10 Employer identification number

Form W-4 (1991) Page 2

Deductions and Adjustments Worksheet

Note: *Use this worksheet only if you plan to itemize deductions or claim adjustments to income on your 1991 tax return.*

1 Enter an estimate of your 1991 itemized deductions. These include: qualifying home mortgage interest, charitable contributions, state and local taxes (but not sales taxes), medical expenses in excess of 7.5% of your income, and miscellaneous deductions. (For 1991, you may have to reduce your itemized deductions if your income is over $100,000 ($50,000 if married filing separately). Get Pub. 919 for details.) . . . . . . 1 $______

2 Enter: { $5,700 if married filing jointly or qualifying widow(er); $5,000 if head of household; $3,400 if single; $2,850 if married filing separately } . . . . . . 2 $______

3 **Subtract** line 2 from line 1. If line 2 is greater than line 1, enter zero . . . . . . 3 $______

4 Enter an estimate of your 1991 adjustments to income. These include alimony paid and deductible IRA contributions . . 4 $______

5 **Add** lines 3 and 4 and enter the total . . . . . . 5 $______

6 Enter an estimate of your 1991 nonwage income (such as dividends or interest income) . . . . . . 6 $______

7 **Subtract** line 6 from line 5. Enter the result, but not less than zero . . . . . . 7 $______

8 **Divide** the amount on line 7 by $2,000 and enter the result here. Drop any fraction . . . . . . 8 ______

9 Enter the number from Personal Allowances Worksheet, line G, on page 1 . . . . . . 9 ______

10 **Add** lines 8 and 9 and enter the total here. If you plan to use the Two-Earner/Two-Job Worksheet, also enter the total on line 1, below. Otherwise, **stop here** and enter this total on Form W-4, line 4 on page 1 10

Two-Earner/Two-Job Worksheet

Note: *Use this worksheet only if the instructions for line G on page 1 direct you here.*

1 Enter the number from line G on page 1 (or from line 10 above if you used the Deductions and Adjustments Worksheet) . 1 ______

2 Find the number in **Table 1** below that applies to the **LOWEST** paying job and enter it here . . . . . . 2 ______

3 If line 1 is **GREATER THAN OR EQUAL TO** line 2, subtract line 2 from line 1. Enter the result here (if zero, enter "0") and on Form W-4, line 4, on page 1. **DO NOT** use the rest of this worksheet . . . . . . 3 ______

Note: *If line 1 is **LESS THAN** line 2, enter "0" on Form W-4, line 4, on page 1. Complete lines 4–9 to calculate the additional dollar withholding necessary to avoid a year-end tax bill.*

4 Enter the number from line 2 of this worksheet . . . . . . 4 ______

5 Enter the number from line 1 of this worksheet . . . . . . 5 ______

6 **Subtract** line 5 from line 4 . . . . . . 6 ______

7 Find the amount in **Table 2** below that applies to the **HIGHEST** paying job and enter it here . . . . . . 7 $______

8 **Multiply** line 7 by line 6 and enter the result here. This is the additional annual withholding amount needed 8 $______

9 Divide line 8 by the number of pay periods remaining in 1991. (For example, divide by 26 if you are paid every other week and you complete this form in December of 1990.) Enter the result here and on Form W-4, line 5, page 1. This is the additional amount to be withheld from each paycheck . . . . . . 9 $

Table 1: Two-Earner/Two-Job Worksheet

Married Filing Jointly		All Others	
If wages from **LOWEST** paying job are—	Enter on line 2 above	If wages from **LOWEST** paying job are—	Enter on line 2 above
0 - $4,000	0	0 - $6,000	0
4,001 - 8,000	1	6,001 - 10,000	1
8,001 - 12,000	2	10,001 - 14,000	2
12,001 - 17,000	3	14,001 - 18,000	3
17,001 - 21,000	4	18,001 - 22,000	4
21,001 - 26,000	5	22,001 - 45,000	5
26,001 - 30,000	6	45,001 and over	6
30,001 - 35,000	7		
35,001 - 40,000	8		
40,001 - 55,000	9		
55,001 - 75,000	10		
75,001 and over	11		

Table 2: Two-Earner/Two-Job Worksheet

Married Filing Jointly		All Others	
If wages from **HIGHEST** paying job are—	Enter on line 7 above	If wages from **HIGHEST** paying job are—	Enter on line 7 above
0 - $46,000	$320	0 - $26,000	$320
46,001 - 94,000	600	26,001 - 55,000	600
94,001 and over	670	55,001 and over	670

Privacy Act and Paperwork Reduction Act Notice.—We ask for the information on this form to carry out the Internal Revenue laws of the United States. The Internal Revenue Code requires this information under sections 3402(f)(2)(A) and 6109 and their regulations. Failure to provide a completed form will result in your being treated as a single person who claims no withholding allowances. Routine uses of this information include giving it to the Department of Justice for civil and criminal litigation and to cities, states, and the District of Columbia for use in administering their tax laws.

The time needed to complete this form will vary depending on individual circumstances. The estimated average time is: **Recordkeeping** 46 min., **Learning about the law or the form** 10 min., **Preparing the form** 70 min. If you have comments concerning the accuracy of these time estimates or suggestions for making this form more simple, we would be happy to hear from you. You can write to both the **Internal Revenue Service,** Washington, DC 20224, Attention: IRS Reports Clearance Officer, T:FP; and the **Office of Management and Budget,** Paperwork Reduction Project (1545-0010), Washington, DC 20503. **DO NOT** send the tax form to either of these offices. Instead, give it to your employer.

*U.S. Government Printing Office: 1990 — 265-083

6:1.2 Weekly Time Sheet and Attendance Records

The time that the employee ends work should be recorded before the employee calculates the total hours worked for the day, and, on Friday, the total for the week. This sheet should accurately reflect the hours at work and there should be no padding for time away from work, whether excused or not. For salaried employees, this never poses a problem. Encouraging employees to pad the sheet undermines responsibility in the organization and should never be condoned.

When an employee is allowed to leave early, he or she should sign out at the actual time he or she leaves. If the employee is salaried, this will not be a problem because he or she will not be "docked." If the person is an hourly employee leaving with management's consent, a notation should be made if that person is not to be docked.

If an employee is absent for any reason at all, a code (for example, 9 for sickness or 10 for leave of absence) must be recorded. If an absence occurs at the end of the week, the attendance clerk or supervisor should sign the time sheet for the employee. Otherwise, the employee must sign the time sheet and the person in charge must carefully read the sheet to ensure that the record is accurate. The record is then filed away in case a complaint arises.

All supervisors or line managers should keep an individual attendance sheet to record absences and latenesses:

- Form 5.02-B remains with the supervisor, who refers to it at the end of the week to make sure that the time sheet is accurate.
- Form 5.02-C is another example of an individual attendance sheet that line managers can use to record incidents of absence or tardiness as soon as they occur. The time that the employee arrives can be inserted in the boxes.

Either of these forms may be used separately by the payroll department to maintain a centralized record of all employee attendance. However, it is advisable that a separate form be maintained in the department where the employee is located to ensure accuracy of recordkeeping.

Often a monthly time card such as Form 5.02-D is used for salaried professionals. There is room on the back for professionals to request meal reimbursement. The time card must go to payroll when overtime meal money is authorized, if such is the organization's policy.

6:1.2A Weekly Time Sheet

WEEKLY TIME SHEET

Must be received in Payroll by 10:00 a.m. Monday

All notations should be made in ink.

Any corrections must be initialed.

Absences are to be indicated by the following codes:

With Pay
1—Sickness
2—Disability (to be indicated on 6th consecutive day absent
3—Personal Day
4—Vacation
5—Jury Duty
6—Military Duty
7—Marriage Leave
8—Death in Family

Without Pay
9—Sickness
10—Leave of Absence
00—Other

APPROVED BY MANAGER

Department ______

Week Ending ______

Initials & Signature (in numerical order)		Mon.	Tues.	Wed.	Thur.	Fri.	Total
	TIME IN	AM ☐ PM ☐ SHIFT ☐	AM ☐ PM ☐ SHIFT ☐	AM ☐ PM ☐ SHIFT ☐	AM ☐ PM ☐ SHIFT ☐	AM ☐ PM ☐ SHIFT ☐	
Employee Initials (with number)	TIME OUT						
	LESS LUNCH						
Employee Signature	TOTAL DAY						
	DAILY OVERTIME						
	TIME IN	AM ☐ PM ☐ SHIFT ☐	AM ☐ PM ☐ SHIFT ☐	AM ☐ PM ☐ SHIFT ☐	AM ☐ PM ☐ SHIFT ☐	AM ☐ PM ☐ SHIFT ☐	
Employee Initials (with number)	TIME OUT						
	LESS LUNCH						
Employee Signature	TOTAL DAY						
	DAILY OVERTIME						
	TIME IN	AM ☐ PM ☐ SHIFT ☐	AM ☐ PM ☐ SHIFT ☐	AM ☐ PM ☐ SHIFT ☐	AM ☐ PM ☐ SHIFT ☐	AM ☐ PM ☐ SHIFT ☐	
Employee Initials (with number)	TIME OUT						
	LESS LUNCH						
Employee Signature	TOTAL DAY						
	DAILY OVERTIME						
	TIME IN	AM ☐ PM ☐ SHIFT ☐	AM ☐ PM ☐ SHIFT ☐	AM ☐ PM ☐ SHIFT ☐	AM ☐ PM ☐ SHIFT ☐	AM ☐ PM ☐ SHIFT ☐	
Employee Initials (with number)	TIME OUT						
	LESS LUNCH						
Employee Signature	TOTAL DAY						
	DAILY OVERTIME						

6:1.2B Individual Attendance Record

INDIVIDUAL ATTENDANCE SHEET

19__

Fill in dates and indicate holidays for each month. Absences are to be indicated by the following codes:

With Pay

1—Sickness
2—Disability (to be indicated on 6th consecutive day of absence)
3—Personal Day
4—Vacation
5—Jury Duty
6—Military Duty
7—Marriage Leave
8—Death in Family

Without Pay

9—Sickness
10—Leave of Absence
11—Business
12—Other

JANUARY

Sun.	Mon.	Tue.	Wed.	Thu.	Fri.	Sat.

FEBRUARY

Sun.	Mon.	Tue.	Wed.	Thu.	Fri.	Sat.

MARCH

Sun.	Mon.	Tue.	Wed.	Thu.	Fri.	Sat.

APRIL

Sun.	Mon.	Tue.	Wed.	Thu.	Fri.	Sat.

MAY

Sun.	Mon.	Tue.	Wed.	Thu.	Fri.	Sat.

JUNE

Sun.	Mon.	Tue.	Wed.	Thu.	Fri.	Sat.

JULY

Sun.	Mon.	Tue.	Wed.	Thu.	Fri.	Sat.

AUGUST

Sun.	Mon.	Tue.	Wed.	Thu.	Fri.	Sat.

SEPTEMBER

Sun.	Mon.	Tue	Wed.	Thu.	Fri.	Sat.

OCTOBER

Sun.	Mon.	Tue.	Wed.	Thu.	Fri.	Sat.

NOVEMBER

Sun.	Mon.	Tue.	Wed.	Thu.	Fri.	Sat.

DECEMBER

Sun.	Mon.	Tue.	Wed	Thu.	Fri.	Sat.

6:1.2C Individual Attendance Form

INDIVIDUAL ATTENDANCE FORM
INDIVIDUAL ATTENDANCE RECORD, 1990

INDIVIDUAL ATTENDANCE FORM
INDIVIDUAL ATTENDANCE RECORD, 1990

Employee Name ________________ Department ________________

	1	2	3	4	5	6	7	8	9	10	11	12	13	14	15	16	17	18	19	20	21	22	23	24	25	26	27	28	29	30	31
January					W	W						W	W						W	W						W	W				
February		W	W						W	W						W	W						W	W							
March		W	W						W	W						W	W						W	W						W	W
April						W	W						W	W						W	W						W	W			
May				W	W						W	W						W	W						W	W					
June	W	W						W	W						W	W						W	W						W	W	
July						W	W						W	W						W	W						W	W			
August			W	W						W	W						W	W						W	W						
September	W						W	W						W	W						W	W						W	W		
October					W	W						W	W						W	W						W	W				
November		W	W						W	W						W	W						W	W						W	
December	W						W	W						W	W						W	W						W	W		
	1	2	3	4	5	6	7	8	9	10	11	12	13	14	15	16	17	18	19	20	21	22	23	24	25	26	27	28	29	30	31

6:1.2D Monthly Time Card: Salaried Employees

MONTHLY TIME CARD

Officer Attendance Report: 19__

Due to the requirements of our various benefit plans, it is both advantageous and important that we have an accurate record of each officer's attendance. Fill in days of the month and mark any holidays. Using the codes below the calendar, indicate only the days you were **not** present, then forward the card to payroll at the end of each month.

Please complete the reverse side if meal money is requested for overtime hours worked.

Signature below indicates review of both sides.

Officer's (Name & Employee Number)	Supervising Officer's

SUN	MON	TUE	WED	THU	FRI	SAT

Codes:
- V—Vacation
- M—Military
- S—Illness
- H—Holiday
- P—Personal Day
- B—Bank Business
- D—Death in Family
- C—Compensatory Day
- O—Other (Specify)

MONTHLY TIME CARD page 2

MEAL REIMBURSEMENT

Policy: Staff members will be paid a meal money supplement of $4.00 when daily overtime worked exceeds 2½ hours.

Please state below the dates and hours worked to qualify for reimbursement:

Date	Hours Worked From: To:	Date	Hours Worked From: To:	Meal Money

Total Meal Reimbursement ____________

6:1.3 Overtime Records

This section covers forms that are used to authorize the payroll department to pay employees overtime. The form discussed below can be used for both nonexempt employees, who by law are entitled to overtime pay, and exempt employees who, regardless of their FLSA status, are receiving overtime pay.

Personnel is usually responsible for determining who is eligible for overtime according to FLSA guidelines. Once that decision is made, it must be communicated to the employee, especially if he or she has been determined to be exempt. An exempt employee is not protected by the FLSA in the same way that a nonexempt employee is.

Paid overtime should be computed separately from the attendance record. It can be computed on another sheet, such as the summary overtime hours report (see 6:1.3A). This form, which is merely a summary of the overtime hours recorded on the time sheet, authorizes payroll to make overtime payments.

There is no request for the employee's signature on the overtime form, since the employee has already completed and signed the weekly time sheet. Another reason it is a good idea that the report be without the employee's signature is that it then guarantees that the supervisor is in control of the hours that his or her employees work.

Employees should not assume that they will be reimbursed for overtime that is not authorized in advance. It should be noted, whenever and wherever possible (for example, in the handbook, on the bulletin board, or with payroll stuffers), that only overtime authorized in advance will be paid.

If the time sheet is used to accurately record the time of arrival at the work station but not the actual start of work, then the time sheet and the overtime form may differ slightly. Under no circumstances, however, should the overtime form reflect a higher amount of hours than the time sheet.

The overtime sheet can be used to record "special overtime," which is overtime that requires premium pay (or is treated separately) because it is performed on a day other than a regular workday. Form 6:1.3B is an example of such a form used for this purpose.

The form is advantageous in that it is used for more than one day and thus helps keep paperwork to a minimum. The employee is required to sign this form because, unlike the overtime summary report, this overtime is not recorded on the basic attendance sheet. On the back of the sheet, the overtime policy may be noted as it is on the summary overtime hours report to ensure compliance and clear communication.

FLSA exemption test: Whenever new employees join an organization, the payroll department must be informed of whether the hire's overtime is to be determined at an exempt or a nonexempt rate. According to the law, nonexempt persons are entitled to overtime pay. Regardless of their salary levels, these employees are entitled to receive 1½ times their normal wages per hour for each hour they work over 40.

If an employee's status is determined to be exempt because the nature of the work performed is more administrative or professional and the starting base salary is over $13,000 a year, the organization may do what it wants in regard to paying the employee overtime. The law will have an impact only in those instances in which the organization's overtime policy is inconsistent in its application.

The Fair Labor Standards Act exemption test is used to determine eligibility to receive overtime pay. The form is to be completed by the supervisor and requires only a short amount of time to do. It is important that the personnel and payroll departments review the findings to ensure that the form has been completed properly. The final decision for the test usually rests with personnel.

Employees must always be informed by their supervisors of the results of their FLSA tests. To avoid a complaint that might lead to an audit, personnel should make sure that employees realize the fairness of this decision.

Whenever there is just cause, FLSA tests should be reviewed. A good time to review an FLSA test is when an employee's job description is being reviewed.

6:1.3A Overtime Hours Report

SUMMARY OVERTIME HOURS REPORT

Department ______________________

Week Ending ______________________

Minutes are to be entered as a decimal equivalent as shown below:			
08–22 minutes .25	23–37 minutes .50	38–52 minutes .75	53–60 minutes 1.00

	OVERTIME HOURS			
Employee Name and Number	36–40 Hours Worked Straight Time	Over 40 Hours Worked Time & One-Half	Total Meal Money	Reason for Overtime
Grand Total				

Approved by: ______________________________
(Manager)

OVERTIME POLICY

page 2

[Name of company] compensates each of its staff members in accordance with the regulations of the Fair Labor Standards Act and all other relevant federal, state, and city labor laws and regulations.

The following outlines [name of company] overtime policy:

Nonexempt Staff Members

Upon completion of 36–40 hours of the regularly scheduled workweek, these staff members are compensated on a straight-time basis.

Compensation is paid on a time-and-a-half basis for each hour worked over 40 during the regularly scheduled workweek.

Holiday/weekend compensation is paid on a time-and-a-half basis.

Exempt Staff Members

Upon completion of 40 hours of work during the regularly scheduled workweek, these staff members are compensated on a straight-time basis.

Holiday/weekend compensation is paid on a straight-time basis.

Official Staff Members

Members of the Official Staff do not receive compensation for overtime worked during the regularly scheduled workweek.

Holiday/weekend compensation is paid at a rate of $10.00 per day, with a compensatory day off with pay.

6:1.3B Overtime Hours Report: Weekends/Holidays

SPECIAL WEEKEND/HOLIDAY ATTENDANCE RECORD

Department ______________________

Week Ending ______________________

Minutes are to be entered as a decimal equivalent as shown below:			
08–22 minutes .25	23–37 minutes .50	38–52 minutes .75	53–60 minutes 1.00

Employee Name and Number	Day	In	Out	Less Lunch	Total Hours	Meal Money	Overtime Hours in Decimal Equivalent
	Sat.						
	Sun.						
	Hol.						
	Other						
	Sat.						
	Sun.						
	Hol.						
	Other						
	Sat.						
	Sun.						
	Hol.						
	Other						
	Sat.						
	Sun.						
	Hol.						
	Other						
	Sat.						
	Sun.						
	Hol.						
	Other						
					Grand Total		

Approved By: ______________________
(Manager)

6:1.3C FLSA Exemption Test

Form 4.08-A
FLSA EXEMPTION TEST

FAIR LABOR STANDARDS ACT EXEMPTION TEST

Name of Staff Member ____________________

Department ____________________

Job Title ____________________

Salary Grade ____________________

Please respond to each question by checking yes or no in the appropriate box.

Yes ☐ **No** ☐

1. Does the staff member customarily and regularly direct the work of two or more staff members, while primarily* managing a section/department?

Yes ☐ **No** ☐

2. Does the staff member customarily and regularly exercise discretion and independent judgment in his/her work that is directly related to the management policies or general business operations of the company or its customers?

If you answered yes to questions #1 or #2 STOP.

If your response was no, answer #3 below.

Yes ☐ **No** ☐

3. Does the staff member primarily* do work requiring invention, imagination, or talent in a recognized field of artistic endeavor, or work requiring consistent exercise of discretion and judgment in activities not covered by #2 above?

If #3 is no, check no and STOP.

If #3 is yes, check yes and answer A & B below.

Yes ☐ **No** ☐

A. Does the staff member do work primarily* requiring knowledge of an advanced type in a field of science or learning, customarily acquired by a prolonged course of specialized intellectual instruction and study, as distinguished from a general academic education?

Yes ☐ **No** ☐

B. Does the staff member do work primarily* concerned with teaching, instructing, or lecturing in the activity of imparting knowledge, and is the staff member employed and engaged in this activity as a teacher by the company?

*Primarily means 50% of the time.

Supervisor's Initials ____________ Date ______

Manager's Initials ____________ Date ______

6:2 Facsimiles of Notices To Be Posted

Legislation setting forth minimum wage requirements and child labor guidelines has been enacted by the U.S. Congress. The Department of Labor enforces the legislation, and requires that employers post summaries of the minimum wage and child labor laws. This section includes a facsimile of the required notice.

6:2.1 Minimum Wage/Child Labor Guidelines

NOTICE TO EMPLOYEES

Federal Minimum Wage

$3.80 per hour **Effective April 1, 1990** **$4.25** per hour **Effective April 1, 1991**

Most employees in the United States qualify for both minimum wage and overtime pay under THE FAIR LABOR STANDARDS ACT. Overtime pay may not be less than 1 1/2 times the employee's regular rate of pay for hours worked over 40 in one workweek.

Certain full-time students, student learners, apprentices, and workers with disabilities may be paid less than the minimum wage under special certificates issued by the Department of Labor.

Covered Employees

- Employees engaged in interstate commerce or in the production of goods for interstate commerce (i.e., goods that travel across state lines), regardless of the employer's annual volume of business.
- Employees who work for enterprises that have an annual gross volume of sales made or business done of over $500,000.
- Employees of hospitals, residential facilities that care for those who are physically or mentally ill or disabled, or aged, schools for children who are mentally or physically disabled or gifted, pre-schools, elementary and secondary schools, and institutions of higher education, regardless of the annual volume of business.
- Employees of public agencies.

Child Labor

An employee must be at least 16 years old to work in most non-farm jobs and at least 18 to work in non-farm jobs declared hazardous by the Secretary of Labor. Youths 14 and 15 years old may work outside school hours in various non-manufacturing, non-mining, non-hazardous jobs under the following conditions:
No more than—

3 hours on a school day or 18 hours in a school week;
8 hours on a non-school day or 40 hours in a non-school week.

Also, work may not begin before 7 a.m., or end after 7 p.m., except from June 1 through Labor Day, when evening hours are extended to 9 p.m. Different rules apply in agricultural employment.

Training Wage

A training wage of $3.35 per hour, or 85 percent of the applicable minimum wage, whichever is greater, may be paid to most employees under 20 years of age for up to 90 days under certain conditions. Individuals may be employed at this training wage for a second 90-day period by a different employer if certain additional requirements are met. No individual may be employed at the training wage, in any number of jobs, for more than a total of 180 days. Employers may not displace regular employees in order to hire those eligible for the training wage.

Tipped Employees

A tipped employee is one who regularly receives more than $30 a month in tips. Tips received by such employees may be counted as wages up to a certain percentage of the minimum wage. The minimum cash wage that employers must pay (from their own pockets) to tipped employees is $2.09 an hour effective April 1, 1990. It will rise to $2.13 an hour effective April 1, 1991. If an employee's hourly tip earnings (averaged weekly) added to this hourly wage do not equal the minimum wage, the employer is responsible for paying the balance.

Enforcement

The Department of Labor may recover back wages either administratively or through court action, for the employees that have been underpaid in violation of the law. Violations may result in civil or criminal action.

Civil money penalties of up to $1,000 per violation may be assessed against employers who violate the child labor provisions of the law or who willfully or repeatedly violate the minimum wage or overtime pay provisions. This law *prohibits* discriminating against or discharging workers who file a complaint or participate in any proceedings under the Act.

Note: Certain occupations and establishments are exempt from the minimum wage and/or overtime pay provisions.

Special provisions apply to workers in Puerto Rico and American Samoa.

Where state law requires a higher minimum wage the higher standard applies.

FOR ADDITIONAL INFORMATION CONTACT the Wage and Hour Division office nearest you - - listed in your telephone directory under United States Government, Labor Department.

The law requires employers to display this poster where employees can readily see it.

U.S. Department of Labor
Employment Standards Administration
Wage and Hour Division
Washington D.C. 20210

WH Publication 1088
Revised April 1990

Chapter 7

Employee Fringe Benefits

Although employers generally are not required by law to provide fringe benefits to employees, there are sound personnel reasons for doing so. A well-thought-out fringe benefit plan can give employers a competitive edge in attracting and retaining qualified employees. This chapter covers the various legal requirements that apply to various employee benefits plans including pension plans, worker's compensation, health insurance benefits as well as vacation time.

7:1 Employer Sponsored Pension Plan

Employer sponsored pension or retirement plans are the most popular type of employee fringe benefit. However, the legal requirements that apply to pension plans [see Q. 321–Q. 375] also make them expensive and complex to administer. The plan and trust agreement that follows provides an example of a sample plan restatement, which also serves to illustrate the requirements for establishing a new plan because the process for adopting a new plan is identical to restating an existing plan.

7:1.1 Comparison of Plan Characteristics

Plan Feature	Profit Sharing	Money Purchase	Defined Benefit
1. Is a contribution required every year?	No	Yes	Yes; but might be $0
2. Must the contribution be paid in quarterly installments?	No	No	Yes
3. Must the contribution be actuarially determined?	No	No	Yes
4. Is the plan subject to minimum funding standards?	No	Yes	Yes
5. Is the plan subject to PBGC requirements?	No	No	Yes
6. Are benefits related to the amount of contribution(s) with respect to each participant?	Yes	Yes	No
7. Does the employer take risk of poor investment performance?	No	No	Yes
8. How are forfeitures treated?	They may be used to reduce employer contributions or may be reallocated to remaining participants.	They may be used to reduce employer contributions or may be reallocated to remaining participants.	They must be used to reduce employer contributions.
9. Are in-service distributions possible prior to retirement age?	Yes	No	No
10. Is full vesting required if contributions formally cease?	Yes	Yes; The answer is generally "yes," but because money purchase plans may now reallocate forfeitures, the answer might be "no" (see IRS Publication 6678 (4/81).	Yes
11. Must contributions be related to profits?	No	No	No
12. Can the plan include a 401(k) arrangement?	Yes	No	No

13. May participants direct their own investments?	Yes	Yes	No
14. Might the plan be written to avoid the joint and survivor annuity requirements?	Yes	No	No
15. Can health or accident insurance be provided under the plan?	Yes	No	No
16. What is the maximum contribution as a percentage of compensation?	15	25	n/a

7:1.2 Plan And Trust Agreement

Sample Corporation
Money Purchase Plan and Trust

Money Purchase Plan And Trust Agreement

AGREEMENT made this 15th day of December, 1990, between Sample Corporation, a corporation organized and existing under the laws of the State of New York (hereinafter referred to as the "Sponsor"), and [President], [Secretary], and [Trustee] (hereinafter referred to as the "Trustees").

WITNESSETH

WHEREAS, the Sponsor desires to restate its Money Purchase Plan and Trust;

NOW, THEREFORE, in consideration of the mutual covenants herein contained, it is agreed by and between the Sponsor and the Trustees as follows:

MONEY PURCHASE

TABLE OF CONTENTS

ARTICLE II—ADMINISTRATION

ARTICLE III—ELIGIBILITY

ARTICLE IV—CONTRIBUTIONS

ARTICLE V—BENEFITS

ARTICLE VI—ALLOCATION

ARTICLE VII—TRUSTEES

ARTICLE VIII—AMENDMENT AND TERMINATION

ARTICLE IX—PROVISIONS RELATING TO THE COMPANY

ARTICLE X—CLAIMS PROCEDURE

ARTICLE XI—MISCELLANEOUS

ARTICLE XII—POLICIES

ARTICLE XIII—PROVISIONS RELATING TO INSURER

ARTICLE XIV—ROLLOVERS

ARTICLE XV—LOANS TO PARTICIPANTS

ARTICLE XVI—TOP HEAVY PLAN REQUIREMENTS AND ADMINISTRATION

Article I

Definitions

Whenever used in this Agreement, the following terms shall have the meanings set forth:

1.01—Account Balance means the net amount that has been credited to the Participant's Account, including any sub-account thereunder attributable to employee contributions pursuant to Section 4.06.

1.02—Adjustment Factor means the cost of living adjustment factor prescribed by the Secretary of the Treasury under Section 415(d) of the Code for years beginning after December 31, 1987, as applied to such items and in such manner as the Secretary shall provide.

1.03—Administrator means Sample Corporation. The Administrator shall be deemed a named fiduciary for purposes of Section 402(a) of ERISA.

1.04—Alternate Payee means any spouse, former spouse, child, or another dependent of a Participant who is recognized by a Qualified Domestic Relations Order as having a right to receive all, or a portion of, the benefits payable under this Plan with respect to the Participant.

1.05—Anniversary Date means each January 1 after the Effective Date of the Restatement.

1.06—Annual Addition means, effective for Limitation Years beginning after December 31, 1986, the annual increase in the value of a Participant's Account attributable to Employer contributions; (ii) Employee contributions pursuant to Section 4.06; (iii) forfeitures; (iv) amounts allocated, after March 31, 1984, to an individual medical account, as defined in Section 415(l)(2) of the Code, which is part of a pension or annuity plan maintained by the Employer, and (v) amounts derived from contributions paid or accrued after December 31, 1985, in taxable years ending after such date, which are attributable to post-retirement medical benefits, allocated to the separate account of a key employee, as defined in Section 419A(d)(3) of the Code, under a welfare benefit fund, as defined in Section 419(e) of the Code, maintained by the Employer.

For this purpose, any excess amount applied under Section 6.03(c) in the limitation year to reduce employer contributions will be considered annual additions for such limitation year.

1.07—Annuity Starting Date means the first day of the first period for which an amount is paid to the Participant as an annuity, or, in the case of a benefit not payable in the form of an annuity, the first day on which all events have occurred which entitle the Participant to such benefit. The Annuity Starting Date for a Beneficiary is defined in Article V.

1.08—Beneficiary means any person, estate, or trust designated in writing by a Participant to receive any payments on the death of such Participant, subject to the requirements of Article V.

1.09—Board means the Board of Directors of the Company, if the Company is incorporated.

1.10—Break-in-Service means a period of one or more consecutive One Year Breaks-in-Service. An Employee will not be deemed to have had a Break-in-Service when the Employee is on a Leave of Absence or a Maternity or Paternity Leave of Absence.

1.11—Code means the Internal Revenue Code of 1986, as amended.

1.12—Company means Sample Corporation or any other corporation or business organization which assumes the obligations of maintaining this Plan and Trust. Company also means any successor to the Company. The Company shall be deemed a named fiduciary for purposes of Section 402(a) of ERISA.

1.13—Compensation, unless otherwise defined by a particular provision of this Plan, means compensation paid by the Employer to the Participant during the Plan Year that is required to be reported as wages on the Participant's Form W-2. Compensation means Earned Income in the case of a self-employed individual.

Compensation also includes compensation that is not currently includible in the Participant's taxable income by reason of the application of Sections 125, 402(a)(8), 402(h)(1)(B), or 403(b) of the Code.

The annual compensation of each Participant taken into account under the plan for any Plan Year beginning after December 31, 1988 shall not exceed $200,000 as adjusted by the Secretary at the same time and in the same manner as under Section 415(d) of the Code. In determining the compensation of a Participant for purposes of this limitation, the rules of section 414(q)(6) of the Code shall apply, except in applying such rules, the term "family" shall include only the Spouse of the Participant and any lineal descendants of the Participant who have not attained age 19 before the close of the year. If as a result of the application of the preceding sentence, the adjusted $200,000 limitation is exceeded, then (except for purposes of determining the portion of compensation up to the integration level if this Plan provides for permitted disparity under Section 6.01) the limitation shall be prorated among the affected individuals in proportion to each individual's compensation as determined under this section prior to the application of this paragraph.

1.14—Earliest Retirement Age means the earliest date on which, under the terms of the Plan, a Participant may elect to receive retirement benefits.

1.15—Early Retirement Date means the Anniversary Date coincident with or next following the date on which the Participant has (i) attained age 55 and (ii) completed at least 7 Years-of-Service. A Participant who meets the service requirement, but separates from service before he meets the age requirement, will be entitled to receive his benefit upon satisfaction of the age requirement.

1.16—Earned Income means the net earnings from self-employment in the trade or business with respect to which the Plan is established, for which personal services of the individual are a material income-producing factor. Net earnings are reduced by contributions by the Employer to a qualified Plan to the extent deductible under Section 404 of the Code. For taxable years beginning after December 31, 1989, net earnings will be computed with regard to the employer deduction under Code Section 164(f).

1.17—Effective Date means January 1, 1986. The Effective Date of the Restatement means January 1, 1989.

1.18—Employee means any person employed by the Company, including anyone on Leave of Absence.

Effective with the first day of the first Plan Year beginning after December 31, 1986, Employee also means, to the extent required by regulations, any employee of the employer(s) maintaining the plan or any other employer required to be aggregated with such employer under Code Sections 414(b), (c), (m), and (o), and the term Employee shall also include any leased employee deemed to be an employee of any such employer pursuant to Code Sections 414(n) and (o) and the regulations thereunder.

1.19—Employer means Sample Corporation and any other corporation, partnership, proprietorship or any other business entity which, with the approval of the Company, adopts the Plan, including any successor to any Employer resulting from a merger, consolidation, or other form of reorganization of the business of the Employer.

Effective with the first day of the first Plan Year beginning after December 31, 1986, Employer also means, for the purposes of crediting Years-of-Service under Article III and Article V, as well as for aggregating benefits and compensation under Article XVI, any member of a controlled group of corporations or businesses under common control, as defined in Code Sections 414(b) and (c), with the Employer.

Effective with the first day of the first Plan Year beginning after December 31, 1986, Employer also means any member of an affiliated group as defined in Section 414(m) of the Code to the extent required by the regulations thereunder, and Employer shall also mean any other entity to the extent it is required to be aggregated with the Employer pursuant to regulations under Code Section 414(o).

Employer also means any predecessor to the Employer to the extent specified in the definition of "Years-of-Service" below.

1.20—Entry Date means January 1 and July 1 during each year in which this Plan remains in effect.

1.21—ERISA means the Employee Retirement Income Security Act of 1974, as amended.

1.22—Family Member means an individual described in Section 414(q)(6)(B) of the Code.

1.23—Highly Compensated Employee means an individual described in Section 414(q) of the Code and the regulations thereunder.

1.24—Hour-of-Service means:

a. Each hour for which an Employee is directly or indirectly paid or entitled to payment by the Employer for the performance of duties. These hours shall be credited to the Employee for the computation periods in which the duties are performed; and
b. Each hour for which an Employee is directly or indirectly paid or entitled to payment by the Employer for reasons other than for the performance of duties (such as vacation, sickness, or disability), whether or not the employment

relationship has terminated. These hours shall be credited to the Employee for the computation period or periods in which the period during which no duties are performed occurs, beginning with the first unit of time to which the payment relates. No more than 501 Hours-of-Service shall be credited under this paragraph for any single continuous period. Hours under this subparagraph shall be calculated and credited pursuant to Section 2530.200b-2(b) and (c) of the Department of Labor Regulations, which are incorporated by this reference.

c. Each hour for which back pay, regardless of mitigation of damage, has been either awarded or agreed to by the Employer. These hours shall be credited to the Employee for the computation period or periods to which the award or agreement pertains rather than the computation period in which the award, agreement, or payment was made.

d. Hours-of-Service will be credited for employment with other members of an affiliated service group (under Code Section 414(m)), a controlled group of corporations (under Code Section 414(b)), or a group of trades or businesses under common control (under Code Section 414(c)) of which the adopting Employer is a member, and any other entity required to be aggregated with the Employer pursuant to Code Section 414(o) and the regulations thereunder.

Hours-of-Service will also be credited for any individual considered an Employee for purposes of this Plan under Code Section 414(n) or Code Section 414(o) and the regulations issued thereunder.

1.25—Initial Eligibility Computation Period means the twelve consecutive month period that commences on the date the Employee first completes an Hour-of-Service.

1.26—Insured means a person on whose life a policy has been issued.

1.27—Insurer means a legal reserve life insurance company which shall issue a policy pursuant to this Agreement.

1.28—Leave of Absence means (a) a period of absence from employment authorized by the Employer either with or without pay, for a period not in excess of 2 years, if the Employee returns to the active employ of the Employer at or prior to termination of such period of absence. Such periods of absence shall be granted by the Employer on a uniform and nondiscriminatory basis to all Employees similarly situated; (b) a period of absence from employment for vacation or jury duty; (c) a period of absence from employment for service in the Armed Forces of the United States, provided the Employee returns to the active employ of the Employer within 90 days of the date upon which the Employee is first eligible to be discharged or separated from active service or such longer period during which his employment rights are protected by law; and (d) a period of absence from employment because of temporary disability, illness or injury, provided the Employee returns to the active employ of the Employer upon the determination of the Employer that he is no longer temporarily disabled, ill or injured.

1.29—Limitation Year for purposes of Code Section 415 means the twelve consecutive month period ending December 31.

1.30—Maternity or Paternity Leave of Absence means an absence from work for any period by reason of the Employee's pregnancy, birth of the Employee's child, placement of a child with the Employee in connection with the adoption of such child, or any absence for the purpose of caring for such child for a period immediately following such birth or placement.

1.31—Nonforfeitable Right means the unconditional entitlement of a Participant or his Beneficiary to a portion of his Account Balance pursuant to Article V.

1.32—Non-Highly Compensated Employee means any Employee of the Employer who is neither a Highly compensated Employee nor a Family Member.

1.33—Normal Retirement Age means, in the case of each Participant, the later of age 65 (not to exceed 65) or the fifth anniversary of the first day of the Plan Year in which the Participant commenced participation in the Plan.

1.34—Normal Retirement Date means in the case of each Participant, the Anniversary Date coincident with or next following the Participant's attainment of his Normal Retirement Age.

1.35—One Year Break-in-Service means a Plan Year during which a Participant is credited with 500 or fewer Hours-of-Service.

In the case of a Maternity or Paternity Leave of Absence, Hours-of-Service shall be credited for the computation period in which the absence from work begins, only if such credit is necessary to prevent the Employee from incurring a One Year Break-in-Service, or, in any other case, in the immediately following computation period. The Hours-of-Service credited for a Maternity or Paternity Leave of Absence shall be those which would normally have been credited but for such absence, or, in any case in which the Administrator is unable to determine such hours normally credited, eight Hours-of-Service per day. The total Hours-of-Service required to be credited for a Maternity or Paternity Leave of Absence shall not exceed 501.

1.36—Owner-Employee means an individual who is a sole proprietor, or who is a partner owning more than 10 percent of either the capital or profits interest of the partnership.

1.37—Participant means an Employee who has met all the eligibility requirements (including the Entry Date requirement) of Article III. An individual ceases to be a Participant when he separates from service and receives a distribution of all the benefits to which he is entitled under the Plan. An individual who separates from service and who is entitled to no benefits is deemed to receive a distribution of all the benefits to which he is entitled under the Plan when he incurs a One-Year Break-in-Service.

1.38—Participant's Account means the account established and maintained by the Administrator for each Participant' s allocable share of the Trust Fund.

1.39—Plan means the plan and trust embodied in this Agreement, as amended from time to time, which shall be called the Sample Corporation Money Purchase Plan and Trust.

1.40—Plan Year means a twelve-month period beginning on January 1 and ending on December 31.

1.41—Policy means any annuity, pension, income, or insurance policy or contract issued by an insurer.

1.42—Qualified Domestic Relations Order means a judgement, decree, or order issued under a State's domestic relations law that (1) provides for child support, alimony payments, or marital rights to a spouse, child, or other dependent of a Participant, (2) creates or recognizes the existence of an Alternate Payee's right to, or assigns to an Alternate Payee the right to, receive all or a portion of the benefits payable with respect to a Participant under this Plan, and (3) satisfies the requirements of Code Section 414(p).

1.43—Qualified Joint and Survivor Annuity means an immediate annuity for the life of a Participant with a survivor annuity for the life of his Spouse which is not less than one-half of, or greater than the amount of, the annuity payable during the joint lives of a Participant and his Spouse; and which is the actuarial equivalent of a single life annuity for the life of the Participant. The percentage of the survivor annuity under the Plan shall be 100 percent.

1.44—Qualified Pre-Retirement Survivor Annuity means a Survivor Annuity for the life of the Surviving Spouse of the Participant, the single-sum actuarial value of which is 100 percent of the Participant's Account Balance as of the date of death.

1.45—Rollover Contribution Account means a Participant's Account which consists of the Participant's rollover contributions plus earnings and less losses.

1.46—Self-Employed Individual means an individual who has earned income for the taxable year from the trade or business for which the Plan is established, or an individual who would have had earned income but for the fact that the trade or business had no net profits for the taxable year.

1.47—Spouse (Surviving Spouse) means the spouse or surviving spouse of the Participant, provided that a former spouse will be treated as the spouse or surviving spouse and a current spouse will not be treated as the spouse or surviving spouse to the extent provided under a Qualified Domestic Relations Order.

1.48—Trust or Trust Fund means all cash, investments, and other properties held and owned by the Trustee under this Agreement.

1.49—Trustee means the Trustee(s) named above and any successor Trustee(s).

1.50—Valuation Date means the last day of the Plan Year.

1.51—Vested Interest means that portion of a Participant's Account Balance to which he has a Nonforfeitable Right.

1.52—Vested Participant means any Participant who has a Nonforfeitable Right to any portion of his Account Balance.

1.53—Year-of-Participation means a Plan Year during which a Participant completes 1,000 Hours-of-Service as a Participant.

1.54—Year-of-Service means a Plan Year in which an Employee has been credited with at least 1,000 Hours-of-Service.

If the Employer maintains the Plan of a predecessor Employer, service for such predecessor Employer shall be treated as service for the Employer.

For purposes of determining eligibility to participate under Article III and vesting under Article V, Years-of-Service shall include Years-of-Service credited with respect to other members of an affiliated service group (under Code Section 414(m)), a controlled group of corporations (under Code Section 414(b)), or a group of trades or businesses under common control (under Code Section 414(c)) of which the adopting Employer is a member, and any other entity required to be aggregated with the Employer pursuant to Code Section 414(o) and the regulations thereunder.

An Employee's Years-of-Service while working within a particular classification of Employees that is (or is not) eligible for coverage under the terms of this Plan shall not be disregarded for purposes of Article III and Article V of this Plan in the event that (1) such Employee's job classification changes or (2) this Plan is amended with respect to coverage of such a job classification.

Except as may be provided under Section 3.04, if an Employee who has no Vested Interest incurs one or more consecutive One-Year Breaks-in-Service, Years-of-Service for purposes of Article III and Article V shall not include any Years-of-Service attributable to such prior service if the number of consecutive One Year Breaks-in-Service equals or exceeds the greater of (a) five, or (b) the aggregate number of Years-of-Service before such period of consecutive One Year Breaks in-Service. Any Years-of-Service disregarded under the preceding sentence will not be taken into account in applying the rule stated in the preceding sentence to a subsequent Break-in-Service by such Employee. The provisions of this paragraph are referred to as the *Rule of Parity*.

If an Employee is credited with his first Hour-of-Service on other than the first day of a Plan Year, he will be credited with a Year-of-Service for purposes of Article III if he completes 1,000 Hours-of-Service during his Initial Eligibility Computation Period. Whether or not the 1,000 hour requirement is met in the Initial Eligibility Computation Period, succeeding eligibility computation periods shall be Plan Years, beginning with the Plan Year in which falls the first anniversary of the date the Employee was first credited with an Hour-of-Service.

Article II

Administration

2.01 Assignment of Administrative Authority

The Plan shall be administered by the Administrator specified in Article I. The Trustee is charged with the administration of the Trust Fund under this Agreement.

2.02 Powers and Duties

The Trustee and Administrator shall administer this Agreement in accordance with its terms and shall have all powers necessary to carry out its provisions. They shall interpret the Agreement and shall determine all questions arising in the administration, interpretation, and application of it. Any such determination shall be conclusive and binding on all persons.

2.03 Records and Reports

The Trustee and Administrator shall keep records of all proceedings and accounts and shall keep all such books of account, records, and other data as may be necessary for proper administration of the Plan. They shall notify the Company of any action taken, and when required, shall notify any other interested person or persons.

2.04 Payment of Administrative Expenses

The Administrator shall receive no compensation for acting as such, but may be reimbursed from the Trust Fund for any reasonable expenses, including reasonable counsel and accounting fees, incurred in the administration of the Plan and Trust.

2.05 Liability of Trustee and Administrator

The Trustee and Administrator shall not incur any liability for any action or failure to act in connection with the administration of this Plan and Trust unless if in acting, or failing to act, he or they did not exercise the care, skill, prudence and diligence under the circumstances then prevailing that a prudent man acting in a like capacity and familiar with such matters would use in the conduct of an enterprise of a like character with like aims.

2.06 Liability Insurance

The Trustee and Administrator may use Trust Funds for the purchase of insurance to cover liability or losses occurring by reason of the act or omission to act of the Trustee, the Administrator, or of any delegate fiduciary; provided, however, that the terms of any insurance policy so purchased permits recourse by the insurer against the Trustee and Administrator, or the delegate fiduciary in the event of the breach of a fiduciary obligation by any of the aforementioned parties.

2.07 Agent for Service of Legal Process

The Administrator shall be deemed to be the agent designated for the service of legal process.

2.08 Authorized Appointments

The Administrator may appoint such consultants, specialists, qualified public accountants, investment advisors and other persons as he deems necessary or desirable in order to properly administer the Plan. No person may serve in such capacity if such service would violate Section 411 of ERISA.

2.09 Required Filings

The Administrator shall file with the Department of Labor and the Secretary of the Treasury such reports as may be required under the provisions of ERISA and the regulations thereunder.

2.10 Reports to Participants and Beneficiaries

The Administrator shall furnish each Participant and each Beneficiary such information, summaries and reports as may be required by the provisions of ERISA and the regulations thereunder.

Article III

Eligibility

3.01 Determination of Eligibility

The Administrator shall determine the eligibility of each Employee for participation in the Plan pursuant to the terms of this Agreement, on a nondiscriminatory basis. Such determination shall be conclusive and binding upon all persons. All eligible Employees shall complete any forms necessary for participation within the time prescribed by the Administrator.

3.02 Designation of Beneficiaries

Every Participant may designate a Beneficiary and successor Beneficiary to receive any death benefits provided under the Plan and such retirement benefits payable after his death as may be elected under Section 5.06. Such designations may be changed from time to time by the Participant (in accordance with the provisions of Section 5.06) by filing a new designation with the Administrator.

If any Participant shall fail to designate a Beneficiary for the purpose of this paragraph, the Administrator shall designate Beneficiaries in his behalf as follows: (1) the Participant's Spouse shall be so designated, if living, otherwise (2) the Participant's living children in equal shares, or if there are no living children, (3) the Participant's estate.

Neither the Employer nor the Administrator (or any Trustee) shall be named a Beneficiary.

3.03 Conditions of Eligibility

Any Employee who is a Participant in the Plan on the Effective Date of this Restatement shall continue to participate. Any nonunion Employee who had attained age 21 and completed one Year-of-Service before or as of the Effective Date of the Restatement shall commence participation in the Plan on the Effective Date of the Restatement. Any other current or future nonunion Employees shall participate on the Entry Date coincident with or next following the satisfaction of the age and service requirements.

Eligibility to participate, or to continue participation, shall not be curtailed or denied on account of the attainment of any age beyond twenty-one years.

Notwithstanding anything in this Section to the contrary, no Employee shall be admitted to this Plan if he is no longer an Employee on the Entry Date as of which his admission to participation would otherwise have become effective.

A nonunion Employee is any Employee who is not working pursuant to a collecting bargaining agreement under which retirement benefits were the subject of good faith negotiations.

3.04 Participation Upon Rehire

If an Employee who separated from service before becoming a Participant is rehired, he shall participate as of his date of reemployment if he has satisfied the eligibility requirements of Section 3.03 (including the Entry Date requirement).

If a Participant is rehired (i.e., the individual has a Vested Interest in the Plan when he is rehired), he shall continue participating in the Plan.

If a former Participant is rehired (i.e., the individual does not have a Vested Interest in the Plan when he is rehired), he shall become a Participant on his date of rehire unless his Break-in-Service causes his prior Years-of-Service to be disregarded under the Rule of Parity, in which case he shall be treated as a new

Employee. (The Rule of Parity is defined in the definition of Year-of-Service in Article I.)

3.05 Additional Requirements Regarding Owner-Employees

If this plan provides contributions or benefits for one or more Owner-Employees who control both the business for which this Plan is established and one or more other trades or businesses, this Plan and the plan established for the other trades or businesses must, when looked at as a single plan, satisfy Code Sections 401(a) and (d) for the employees of this and all other trades or businesses.

If the Plan provides contributions or benefits for one or more Owner-Employees who control one or more other trades or businesses, the employees of the other trades or businesses must be included in a plan which satisfies Sections 401(a) and (d) and which provides contributions and benefits not less favorable than provided for Owner-Employees under this plan.

If an individual is covered as an Owner-Employee under the plans of two or more trades or businesses which are not controlled and the individual controls a trade or business, then the contributions or benefits of the employees under the plan of the trades or businesses which are controlled must be as favorable as those provided for him or her under the most favorable plan of the trade or business which is not controlled.

For purposes of the preceding paragraphs, an Owner-Employee, or two or more Owner-Employees, will be considered to control a trade or business if the Owner-Employee, or two or more Owner-Employees together:

1. Own the entire interest in an unincorporated trade or business; or
2. In the case of a partnership, own more than 50 percent of either the capital interest or the profits interest in the partnership.

For purposes of the preceding sentence, an Owner-Employee, or two or more Owner-Employees shall be treated as owning any interest in a partnership which is owned, directly or indirectly, by a partnership which such Owner-Employee, or such two or more Owner-Employees, are considered to control within the meaning of the preceding sentence.

Article IV

Contributions

4.01 Employer Contributions to the Plan

With respect to each Plan Year, the Employer shall contribute an amount equal to 25 percent (not to exceed 25 percent) of the Compensation of all Participants in the Plan.

In the event a Participant separates from service prior to the end of the Plan Year, or completes less than one Year-of-Service during the Plan Year, no contribution shall be made on his behalf. If, however, the Plan fails to meet the coverage requirements under Code Section 410(b)(1)(B) during the Plan Year because of the operation of the preceding sentence, then effective for Plan Years beginning after December 31, 1989, a contribution will be made on behalf of all Participants who are employed on the last day of the Plan Year. If the Plan would still fail the coverage requirements under 410(b)(1)(B) after application of the preceding sentence, then a contribution will be made on behalf of all Participants, other than Participants who terminated during the Plan Year with less than 501 Hours-of-Service.

In no event shall Employer contributions exceed the amount deductible from the Employer's income under Section 404 of the Code, or any statute of similar import. Unless the Employer provides otherwise (by formal resolution) at the time a contribution is made, all contributions are conditioned on their deductibility.

4.02 Timing of Employer Contributions

The Employer shall pay its contribution to the Trustee on or before the date prescribed by law for filing the Employer's federal income tax return (including any extension of such date) for the fiscal year in respect of which such contribution is made.

4.03 Exclusive Benefit; Refund of Contribution

All contributions made by the Employer shall be for the exclusive benefit of the Participants and their Beneficiaries, and such contributions shall not be used for, nor diverted to, any purpose other than for the exclusive benefit of the Participants and their Beneficiaries (including the costs of maintaining and administering this Plan and the Trust). Notwithstanding the foregoing, if (i) any contribution is made to the Trust Fund and this Plan shall initially fail to satisfy the qualification requirements of Section 401(a) of the Code, (ii) a contribution, or any portion thereof, is made to the Trust Fund under a mistake of fact, or (iii) a contribution is conditioned upon the deductibility of the contribution under Section 404 of the Code, to the extent that such deduction is disallowed, then such contributions shall be returned to the Employer within one year after the date of denial of qualification of the Plan or Trust, the payment of the contribution, or the disallowance of the deduction, as the case may be.

4.04 Participant's Accounts

The Administrator shall establish and maintain an account in the name of each Participant, to which the Trustee shall credit the Employer's contribution on each such Participant's behalf and each Participant's share of the net earnings or the net losses of the Trust Fund.

4.05 Forfeitures

All forfeitures occurring during a Plan Year shall be applied to reduce the Employer's Contribution for such Plan Year. If forfeitures for any Plan Year exceed the contribution due for such year, any remaining balance shall be used to reduce contributions in succeeding Plan Years. Forfeitures shall occur on the earlier to occur of: (a) the date the Participant receives a cash-out distribution of his Vested Account Balance; or (b) the date the Participant incurs a period of five consecutive One-Year Breaks-in-Service.

4.06 Employee Contributions

Effective with the first day of the first Plan Year beginning after December 31, 1986, no mandatory or voluntary contributions (other than rollover contributions under Article XIV) are provided for under this Plan, except to the extent that this Plan is a restatement of a prior Plan that required or permitted Employee contributions. In other words, no new employee contributions will be made to the Plan. Any such previous contributions shall be held in a separate account for each Participant who made such contributions.

4.07 Prohibition Against Age Discrimination

Effective with the first day of the first Plan Year beginning after December 31, 1987, employer contributions shall not be discontinued or decreased because of the Participant's attainment of any age.

4.08 Waiver of Funding

In the event that the minimum funding requirement for a particular Plan Year has been waived in whole or part, then an Adjusted Account Balance shall be established for each Participant which shall reflect the Account Balance the Participant would have had, had the waived amount been contributed.

1. The Adjusted Account Balance shall remain in effect until such time as the value of the Participant's Account equals the value of the Participant's Adjusted Account Balance.
2. The excess of the value of each Participant's Adjusted Account Balance over the value of the Participant's Account Balance will be credited with earnings of 5 percent annually.
3. In the year after the waiver is granted, the waiver payment to be made by the Employer shall equal at least the amount necessary to amortize over 15 years, at 5 percent annual interest, the excess of the sum of the Adjusted Account Balances over the total value of the Trust Fund attributable to Employer contributions. In the next year, the excess for such subsequent year, if any, is amortized over 14 years. In each succeeding year the amortization period is reduced by one year. The Employer may, however, make such larger payments at any time as the Employer deems appropriate.
4. An unallocated Waiver Suspense Account shall be created, to which all payments designed to reduce the waived deficiency shall be made. If at the time of a distribution, the nonforfeitable portion of a Participant's Adjusted Account Balance exceeds that Participant's Actual Account Balance, that Participant will receive the larger amount but only to the extent that there are then funds in the unallocated Waiver Suspense Account to cover the excess. If a Participant is not able to receive a total distribution of the entire nonforfeitable portion of his Adjusted Account Balance, such Participant shall receive subsequent distributions derived from future waiver payments.

When the total value of the Trust Fund equals the sum of the Adjusted Account Balances, the Waiver Suspense Account shall be allocated to the affected Participants so that each Participant's Actual Account Balance equals that Participant's Adjusted Account Balance.

Article V

Benefits

5.01 Normal or Early Retirement

When a Participant retires on his Early, Normal, or Deferred Retirement Date, the value of the proportionate interest of such Participant in the Trust Fund shall be determined as set forth in Article VI, as of the Valuation Date coincident with or next following such retirement date or as soon as practicable thereafter, and such value shall be computed by including the Employer's contribution with respect to the Plan Year in which the Participant retired.

5.02 Deferred Retirement

A Participant may continue in the employ of the Employer beyond the Normal Retirement Date in which event the Employer shall make further contributions to the Trust Fund on account of compensation paid to such Participant. At actual retirement, such Participant shall be entitled to receive benefits pursuant to Section 5.01.

5.03 Disability Retirement

A Participant who, any time prior to his Normal or Early Retirement Date, incurs a disability of either physical or mental character which, in the opinion of a physician selected by the Trustee, renders him permanently disabled from satisfactorily performing the duties of his employment with the Employer, shall be permitted to retire. His retirement benefit shall be the one hundred percent of his Account Balance as of the Valuation Date preceding such determination of disability. Any payment thereof shall be made pursuant to Section 5.06.

5.04 Death Benefit

Subject to the provisions of Section 5.06, 5.07, and 14.03, in the event that a Participant shall die prior to termination of service or retirement, his Beneficiary shall be entitled to receive one hundred percent of his Account Balance, as well as any death benefits payable under any policy which has been purchased on the life of the Participant.

5.05 Vesting

If a Participant shall for any reason other than death, disability, or retirement, cease to be employed by the Company, such terminated Participant and his Beneficiary(ies) shall have a Nonforfeitable Right to a percentage of the value of the Participant's Account Balance attributable to Employer contributions in the manner scheduled below for the number of Years-of-Service after attaining age 18. Years-of-Service completed prior to the Effective Date of the Plan shall not be taken into account.

Number of Years-of-Service	*Vested Percentage*
Less than 3	0%
3	20%
4	40%
5	60%
6	80%
7	100%

A Participant's nonforfeitable percentage shall in no event be less than the percentage required by Section 8.01(c) in the event of an amendment or restatement of the Plan.

For the purpose of computing service and Breaks-in-Service included in the determination of Nonforfeitable Percentage, the vesting computation period shall be the Plan Year. In the case of any Employee who has any One Year Break-in-Service, Years-of-Service before such break shall not be taken into account until he has completed a Year-of-Service after his return.

If any Participant incurs a period of five consecutive One Year Breaks-in-Service, Years-of-Service after such five-year period shall not be taken into account for purposes of determining the nonforfeitable percentage of the portion of the Participant's Account Balance attributable to Employer contributions that accrued before such five year period.

Notwithstanding anything herein to the contrary, an actively employed Participant shall be 100 percent vested in his Account Balance upon attainment of his Normal Retirement Age, or if earlier, upon his Early or Disability Retirement Date.

A Participant always has a Nonforfeitable Right to 100 percent of the portion of his Account Balance attributable to his Employee, Contributions pursuant to Section 4.06, and Rollover Contributions pursuant to Article XIV.

If a Participant who is entitled to less than 100 percent of his Account Balance separates from service and receives a cash-out distribution, the Plan shall provide the Participant with a repayment option. If the Participant resumes covered employment with the Employer and repays to the Plan the entire amount of the distribution, the Participant's Account Balance at the time of the initial distribution, both the amount distributed and the amount forfeited, unadjusted by subsequent gains and losses, will be restored. The Plan requires that such repayment by the Participant be completed before the earlier of (a) five years after the first date on which the Participant is subsequently reemployed or (b) the close of the first period of five consecutive one year Breaks-in-Service commencing after the distribution.

5.06 Timing and Method of Payment of Vested Benefits

All amounts vested in a Participant pursuant to this Agreement shall be paid upon the Participant's attainment of his Early, Normal, or Deferred Retirement Date, or after he shall have become totally disabled pursuant to Section 5.03. Amounts payable to Vested Participants who have separated from service may be paid as of the Valuation Date following the date on which the Participant incurs a One Year Break-in-Service. Notwithstanding the foregoing, if a Participant's Account Balance is immediately distributable within the meaning of Regulation Section 1.417(e)-l, no distribution shall be made unless the consent requirements of this Section are complied with.

Cash-out distributions: The Administrator may direct the Trustee to cash-out a retired Participant's entire Account Balance in a lump-sum distribution. The Administrator shall treat all persons similarly situated in a uniform and nondiscriminatory manner.

The Administrator may direct the Trustee to cash-out an actively employed Participant's Account Balance in a lump-sum distribution if such Participant has attained his Normal Retirement Age. The Administrator shall treat all persons similarly situated in a uniform and nondiscriminatory manner.

The Administrator may direct the Trustee to cash-out the entire nonforfeitable portion of a terminated Participant's Account Balance in a lump sum distribution. If the value of such distribution is zero, the terminated Participant shall be deemed to have received a distribution of such vested balance. The forfeitable portion of the

Participant's Account Balance will be treated as a forfeiture. The Administrator shall treat all persons similarly situated in a uniform and nondiscriminatory manner.

Effective with the first day of the first Plan Year beginning after December 31, 1986, if a cash-out distribution is made after the Annuity Starting Date, or if the amount of a cash-out distribution exceeds $3,500., then the Participant and the Participant's Spouse (if the Participant is married at the time of the cash-out distribution) must consent in writing to the cash-out distribution; or, if the cash-out distribution is payable to a Surviving Spouse, the Surviving Spouse must consent in writing to the cash-out.

Immediately-distributable benefits: Effective with the first day of the first Plan Year beginning after December 31, 1986, if a benefit is payable to any Participant while such benefit is immediately distributable (as defined below), and the value of the Participant's Nonforfeitable Account Balance (derived from Employer and, pursuant to Section 4.06, Employee Contributions) exceeds (or at the time of any prior distribution exceeded) $3,500., the Participant and the Participant's Spouse (or if either the Participant or the Participant's Spouse has died, the survivor) must consent in writing, within the 90-day period ending on the Annuity Starting Date, to the commencement of benefits.

a. 1. Notice: The Administrator shall notify the Participant and the Participant's Spouse of the right to defer any distribution until the Participant's Account Balance is no longer immediately distributable. Such notification shall include a general description of the material features, and an explanation of the relative values of, the optional forms of benefit available under the Plan in a manner that would satisfy the notice requirements of Section 417(a)(3), and shall be provided no less than 30 days and no more than 90 days prior to the Annuity Starting Date.

Notwithstanding the foregoing, only the Participant need consent to the commencement of benefits in the form of a qualified joint and survivor annuity while the Account Balance is immediately distributable. Neither the consent of the Participant nor the Participant's Spouse shall be required to the extent that a distribution is required to satisfy Code Section 401(a)(9) or 415.

An Account Balance is immediately distributable if any part of the Account Balance could be distributed to the Participant (or Surviving Spouse) before the Participant attains (or would have attained if not deceased) the later of Normal Retirement Age or age 62.

b. 1. The qualified joint and survivor annuity: The benefits of a Vested Participant having a Spouse living on the Annuity Starting Date shall be paid in the form of a Qualified Joint and Survivor Annuity unless, within ninety days prior to such date, the Participant elects in writing not to receive such annuity. The benefits of an unmarried Participant shall be paid in the form of a life annuity unless the Participant elects otherwise in accordance with these procedures. A Participant may elect to have such annuity distributed upon attainment of the earliest retirement age under the plan.

Effective with the first day of the first Plan Year beginning after December 31, 1986, the election not to receive the Qualified Joint and Survivor Annuity shall not take effect unless the Spouse of the Participant consents in writing to such election, such election designates a beneficiary (or another form of benefits) which may not be changed without Spousal consent, the Spouse's consent acknowledges the effect of such election, and the consent to such election is witnessed by a Plan representative or a notary public. Notwithstanding the foregoing, subsequent designations may be made without Spousal consent if the consent obtained from the Spouse acknowledges that the Spouse has the right to limit consent (1) to a specific beneficiary or (2) to a specific form of benefit, and that the Spouse voluntarily elects to relinquish both of such rights.

The election shall, however, be given effect if it is established to the satisfaction of a Plan Representative that the consent required cannot be obtained because there is no Spouse, because the Spouse cannot be located, or because of such other circumstances as may be prescribed by regulations.

Any consent by a Spouse (or finding that the consent cannot be obtained) shall be effective only with respect to the Spouse in question.

b. 2. Notification and explanation of plan benefits during election period: Prior to, or at the commencement of an election period of ninety days prior to a Participant's Annuity Starting Date, the Administrator shall furnish to such Participant a written notification comprised of the following:

(i) The terms and conditions of the Qualified Joint and Survivor Annuity, including a general description or explanation of the relative financial effect of such annuity (and any other payment option under the Plan) on such Participant;

(ii) The Participant's right to make, and the effect of, an election not to take the Qualified Joint and Survivor Annuity Form of Benefit;

(iii) The rights of the Participant's Spouse to consent to such election in the manner described;

(iv) The right to revoke, and the effect of such a revocation of an election.

No Participant shall be required to make an election under this Section unless he has received from the Administrator such written notification.

c. 1. Qualified pre-retirement survivor annuity: Notwithstanding the provisions of Section 5.04, benefits derived from both Employer and Employee contributions payable to a Vested Participant having a Spouse living on the date of the Participant's death shall be paid in the form of a Qualified Pre-Retirement Survivor Annuity unless during the election period the Participant elects in writing to waive such annuity.

Effective with the first day of the first Plan Year beginning after December 31, 1986, the consent of the Participant's Spouse to such election not to take the Qualified Pre-Retirement Survivor Annuity shall be required to be given in the manner and under the conditions as specified in Section 5.06(b) with respect to the Qualified Joint and Survivor Annuity. A written notification and explanation (comparable to that required in Section 5.06 (b)), of the Qualified Pre-Retirement Survivor Annuity shall be furnished to the Participant during the applicable period. For purposes of the notice requirement, the applicable period means, with respect to a particular Participant, whichever of the following periods ends last: (1) the period beginning with the first day of the Plan Year in which the Participant attains age 32 and ending with the close of the Plan Year preceding the Plan Year in which the Participant attains age 35; (2) a reasonable period after the individual becomes a Participant; (3) a reasonable period after Code Section 417(a)(5) ceases to apply to such Participant; (4) a reasonable period after Section 401(a)(11) of the Code applies to the Participant; and (5) a reasonable period after separation from service in the case of a Participant who separates before attaining age 35.

For purposes of applying the preceding paragraph, a reasonable period ending after the enumerated events described in (2), (3) and (4) is the end of the two-year period beginning one year prior to the date the applicable event occurs, and ending one year after that date. In the case of a Participant who separates from service before the Plan Year in which age 35 is attained, notice shall be provided within the two-year period beginning one year prior to separation and ending one year after separation. If such a Participant thereafter returns to employment with the Employer, the applicable period for such Participant shall be redetermined.

The period during which a Participant may elect out of a Qualified Pre-Retirement Survivor Annuity or revoke such an election is the period that begins on the first day of the Plan Year in which the Participant attains age 35 and ends on the date of the Participant's death. If a Participant separates from service before the first day of the Plan Year in which he attains age 35, the election period shall begin on the date of separation.

c. 2. Revocability of election: An election made during any election period provided in this Section may be revoked in writing during such period and new elections may be made during such period.

c. 3. Annuity starting date: The Annuity Starting Date for the Surviving Spouse in the case of the Qualified Pre-Retirement Survivor Annuity shall not be later than the month in which the Participant would have attained the Earliest Retirement Age under the Plan. The Spouse can, however, direct that payments shall commence within a reasonable time after the Participant's death. Notwithstanding the foregoing, if the Qualified Pre-Retirement Survivor Annuity is immediately distributable within the meaning of Regulation Section 1.417(e)-1, no payment shall commence unless the consent of the Spouse is obtained in accordance with the procedures described in this Section.

c. 4. Effect of break-in-service: A Break-in-Service during any election period provided in this Section will neither invalidate a previous election or revocation nor prevent a subsequent election from being made or revoked.

d. One-year marriage requirement: The Spouse of a Participant who would otherwise be entitled to a Survivor Annuity shall not be entitled to receive such annuity unless the Participant and such Spouse were married throughout the one-year period ending on the earlier of the Participant's Annuity Starting Date or the date of the Participant's death.

However, in the case of a Participant who marries within one year of the Annuity Starting Date, for the purposes of a Qualified Joint and Survivor Annuity, if the Participant and the Spouse have been married for at least one year on or before the date of the Participant's death, then such Participant and such Spouse shall be treated as having been married for at least one year.

e. Spouse as required beneficiary: The Participant will be required to notify the Administrator of any change in marital status. It shall also be the responsibility of the Participant to advise the Administrator that the Participant and the Spouse have been married for one year so that the Administrator may make any changes required to effect the Qualified Joint and Survivor Annuity if the Participant and Spouse do not waive it.

f. Effect of a qualified domestic relations order: If a former Spouse of a Participant is entitled to receive a portion of the Participant's benefit under a Qualified Domestic Relations Order as defined in Article I, the Qualified Joint and Survivor Annuity and Qualified Pre-Retirement Survivor Annuity requirements shall not apply unless they are consistent with the Order.

The Plan shall not be required to provide a Qualified Joint and Survivor Annuity or a Qualified Pre-Retirement Survivor Annuity to the Spouse of a Participant's former Spouse.

g. Coordination with the fiduciary standards of ERISA: The Trustee and Plan Administrator shall at all times act under the fiduciary standards of ERISA with respect to this Section. Should the Trustee or Plan Administrator so acting, receive a notarized spousal consent, valid on its face, which the Trustee and Administrator have no reason to believe is invalid, or if the Participant asserts that the Spouse's consent cannot be obtained, then the Plan will not be liable for payments to the Surviving Spouse should such consent form or assertion be invalid. In addition, this paragraph shall act to relieve a third party payor from such liability for payments to a Surviving Spouse as long as the third party payor either relies on a Trustee or Administrator who acts in accordance with such standards, or acts in accordance with such standards in its own right.

h. Survivor annuity requirements: Effective with the first day of the first Plan Year beginning after December 31, 1986, the Survivor Annuity requirements set forth in this Section shall apply to benefits derived from both Employer and Employee contributions, to the extent that the latter are provided for under Section 4.06.

i. Optional forms of distribution: Subject to the provisions of this Section, a Participant, with the consent of his Spouse, may, prior to attaining his Normal Retirement Date, direct the Administrator to pay out his Account Balance in a form other than the form described in Subsection (b). Such direction shall be in writing and shall be delivered to the Administrator within the election periods described in Subsections (b) and (c). Any optional form of distribution under this Section shall be the Actuarial Equivalent of such Participant's Normal Retirement Benefit and shall also be the equivalent of any other form of payment under this Section. The optional forms of distribution under the Plan are:

1. Payment in a Lump Sum
2. Payment in equal monthly, semi-annual, or annual installments over a period of not less than three nor more than ten years; and
3. Payment under, or delivery of, a paid-up nontransferable annuity contract, provided it does not guarantee payments for a period longer than the life expectancy of the Participant or the Participant and his Spouse.

Any option mentioned above shall require the present value of the projected payments to the Participant to be at least 50 percent of the present value of the total projected payments to both the Participant and his Beneficiary.

j. Payment of benefits: Unless the Participant otherwise elects, and subject to the provisions of Section 5.08 the payment of benefits to the Participant shall begin not later than sixty days after the end of the Plan Year in which the latest of the following events occurs:

1. The Participant reaches Normal Retirement Age.
2. The Participant reaches the tenth anniversary of his Plan Participation.
3. The Participant terminates service.

Notwithstanding the foregoing, the failure of a Participant and Spouse to consent to a distribution while a benefit is immediately distributable, within the meaning of Regulation Section 1.417(e)-1, shall be deemed to be an election to defer commencement of payment of any benefit sufficient to satisfy this Section.

5.07 Required Distribution of Benefits

a. 1. Distribution date: Unless a transitional rule under Subsection (b) below applies, a Participant's benefits shall be distributed to him not later than the April 1st of the calendar year following the calendar year in which he attains age 70½. Alternatively, distributions to a Participant must begin no later than such calendar year and must be made over the life of the Participant (or lives of the Participant and a designated Beneficiary) or over a period not exceeding the life expectancy of the Participant (or the life expectancies of the Participant and a designated Beneficiary).

a. 2. Life expectancy: For the purposes of paragraph (a)(1) above, the life expectancy of the Participant and the Participant's Spouse (in the case of payments other than a life annuity) may be redetermined on an annual basis.

a. 3. Death of participant after distributions begin: Notwithstanding any provision in this Agreement to the contrary, if a Participant dies before his entire interest has been distributed to him and the distribution was structured under the terms of paragraph (a) (1) above, then the remaining portion of his interest shall be distributed in the same manner and over the same period as the manner of distribution in effect as of the date of the Participant's death.

a. 4. Death of participant before distributions begin: However, if a Participant dies prior to the date the distribution of his interest was to begin, then the entire interest of the Participant shall be distributed within five years after the date of the Participant's death.

a. 5. Payments to beneficiary: Notwithstanding paragraph (a)(4), if any portion of the Participant's interest is payable to a designated Beneficiary, and the distributions begin not later than one year after the date of the Participant's death, then such portion may be distributed over a period not extending beyond the life expectancy of such designated Beneficiary.

In addition, in the case of a Spouse as the designated Beneficiary, the date that the distribution of the Participant's interest must begin may not be later than April 1st of the calendar year following the later of the calendar year in which the Participant would have attained age 70½ or the calendar year in which the Participant would have been eligible to retire on his Normal Retirement Date.

a. 6. Incidental death benefits requirement: Any distributions required by the Incidental Death Benefit requirements shall be treated as a distribution made in accordance with the provisions of this Section.

Exceptions:

b. 1. The mandatory commencement of distributions to Participants and/or to a named Beneficiary pursuant to this Section shall not apply provided (i) that prior to January 1, 1984, a Participant (including Five Percent (5%) Owners) made a written designation providing for the commencement of distributions at a later date, and (ii) further providing for a method of distribution of the benefit which satisfies the provisions of Code Section 401(a)(9) as in effect prior to the enactment of the Tax Equity and Fiscal Responsibility Act of 1982 (including rules relating to incidental death benefits). Any written designation, if made, shall be binding upon the Plan Administrator.

b. 2. If the exception provided in Paragraph (b)(1) above does not apply, in the case of a Participant who had attained age 70½ before January 1, 1988, benefit distributions may not commence later than April 1st of the calendar year following the later of: (i) the calendar year in which the Participant attains age 70½, or (ii) the calendar year in which the Participant retires.

b. 3. Paragraph (b)(2) shall not apply to any Participant who is a Five Percent (5%) Owner (as defined in Code Section 416(i)) at any time during: (i) the Plan Year ending with or within the calendar year in which such owner attains age 66½, and (ii) any subsequent Plan Year.

c. 1. This Section shall at all times be administered in accordance with regulations issued under Code Section 401(a)(9), which are hereby incorporated by this reference.

ARTICLE VI

Allocation

6.01 Allocation of the Employer Contributions

The Employer contribution for each Plan Year shall be allocated as of the close of such Plan Year to the account of each Participant who is an Employee as of the close of such Plan Year and who has completed at least one Year-of-Service during the Plan Year. If, however, the Plan fails to meet the coverage requirements under Code Section 410(b) during the Plan Year because of the operation of the preceding sentence, then effective for Plan Years beginning after December 31, 1989, an allocation will be made on behalf of all participants who are employed on the last day of the Plan Year. If the Plan would still fail the coverage requirements under Code Section 410(b)(1)(B) after application of the preceding sentence, then a contribution will be allocated to all Participants, other than Participants who terminated during the Plan Year with less than 501 Hours-of-Service.

Subject to the other Sections of this Article, the Employer Contribution will be allocated to each Participant in an amount equal to 25 percent of his Compensation.

6.02 Allocation of Earnings or Losses of the Fund

The Trustee, as of the end of each Plan Year, shall determine the net worth of the assets of the Trust Fund and report such valuation to the Employer in writing. In determining such net worth, the Trustee shall evaluate the assets of the Trust Fund at their fair market value as of such Valuation Date, and shall deduct all expenses for which the Trustee has not yet obtained reimbursement from the Employer or from the Trust Fund. Such Valuations shall not include any current contributions made by the Employer.

As of each Valuation Date, the net earnings or losses shall be credited or debited to each Participant's Account in the ratio that each Participant's Account bears to the total of all Participants' Accounts on that date, excluding any contribution made by the Employer for the Plan Year in which such Valuation Date falls, so that the total of all Participants' Accounts will equal the net worth of the Trust as of each Valuation Date.

6.03 Maximum Annual Addition to a Participant's Account

Except as otherwise provided in this Article, effective with the first day of the first Plan Year beginning after December 31, 1986, the maximum Annual Addition that may be contributed or allocated to a Participant's Account under the Plan for any Limitation Year shall not exceed the limitations of Code Section 415 and the regulations thereunder, which are hereby incorporated by this reference.

Special Rules.

If, in any year, an allocation would exceed the maximum that is permitted, the excess shall not be allocated. Such excess balance shall be placed in a suspense account.

Any amount allocated to the suspense account shall be reallocated in the next Limitation Year among all Participants. Any leftover amount shall be used to reduce Employer contributions in the next and, if necessary, subsequent Limitation Years.

No additional contribution shall be made to the Plan until the suspense account has been depleted.

The amount allocated to the suspense account shall not be credited with gains, losses or other income.

6.04 Limitation in Case of More Than One Plan for Same Employee

In any case in which an individual is a Participant in both a Defined Benefit Plan and a Defined Contribution Plan, both maintained by the same Employer, such Participant shall first accrue his benefit under the Defined Benefit Plan.

In any case in which an individual is a Participant in both a Profit Sharing Plan and a Money Purchase Plan, both maintained by the same Employer, such Participant shall first receive an allocation of any contribution under the Profit Sharing Plan.

6.05 Prohibition Against Age Discrimination

Effective with the first day of the first Plan Year beginning after December 31, 1987, the allocation of Employer Contributions and Trust Earnings (and Forfeitures, if applicable), shall not be discontinued or decreased because of the Participant's attainment of any age.

ARTICLE VII

Trustees

7.01 Establishment and Acceptance of Trust

The Trustee agrees to receive any contribution paid to him by the Employer in cash or such other property that the Trustee finds acceptable. All contributions so received and the income therefrom shall be managed and administered pursuant to the terms of this Agreement. The Trustee hereby accepts the Trust created hereunder and agrees to perform the duties assigned to him under this Agreement.

7.02 Investment of Trust Fund

a. The Trustee shall invest and reinvest the principal and income of the Trust and keep the Trust invested, without distinction between principal and interest, in securities or in other property, real or personal, wherever situated, including, but not limited to, common and preferred stocks, bonds , mortgages, and other evidences of indebtedness or ownership, and ordinary life insurance, term life insurance, universal life insurance or annuity contracts.

1. For purposes of this Section, ordinary life insurance contracts are contracts with both nondecreasing death benefits and nonincreasing premiums. If such contracts are purchased, less than one-half of the aggregate Employer Contributions allocated to any Participant will be used to pay the premiums attributable to them.
2. Term and Universal Life—no more than one-fourth of the aggregate Employer Contributions allocated to any Participant will be used to pay the premiums on term life insurance contracts, universal life insurance contracts, and all other life insurance contracts which are not ordinary life.
3. Combination—the sum of one-half of the ordinary life insurance premiums and all other life insurance premiums will not exceed one-fourth of the aggregate Employer Contributions allocated to any Participant.

In no event shall the Plan continue ordinary life insurance protection to the Participant beyond retirement.

b. If it is prudent to do so, the Trustee may invest and reinvest the principal and income of the Trust in "qualifying employer real property" and "qualifying employer securities" within the meaning of Sections 407(d)(4) and 407(d)(5) of ERISA.

c. All such investments are to be made for the benefit of the Trust and the Participants under the Plan. In making such investments, the Trustee shall exercise the care, skill, prudence and diligence under the circumstances then prevailing that a prudent man acting in a like capacity and familiar with such matters would use in the conduct of an enterprise of a like character and with like aims. Except with respect to investments in "qualifying employer securities" and "qualifying employer real property," the Trustee shall diversify investments of the Trust so as to minimize the risk of large losses, unless under the circumstances it is clearly prudent not to do so.

7.03 Powers of Trustee

The Trustee shall have the following powers and authority in the administration and investment of the Trust:

a. To invest and reinvest the principal and income of the Trust in such securities and other property as a prudent man would believe to be sound and suitable investments for the Trust;

b. To deposit any or all amounts in the Trust Fund with an Insurer for payment of interest thereon;

c. To retain in cash or on deposit with a bank, such amount of funds as a prudent man would deem advisable, and the Trustee shall not be required to pay any interest on such uninvested funds;

d. To sell, exchange, convey, transfer or dispose of, to lease for any period of time, and to grant options with respect to, any property at any time held by him at such prices and upon such terms as a prudent man would deem advisable;

e. To borrow monies and to hypothecate any property to secure repayment of any loan and to repay any loan, provided that loans and repayments shall be made pro rata on all properties and on all accounts of the same class and type;

f. To execute, acknowledge and deliver any and all documents and other instruments that may be necessary or appropriate in the exercise of the powers granted under this Agreement;

g. To cause any investment of the Trust to be registered in his name as Trustee, or in the name of a nominee, or to retain any investment unregistered;

h. To exercise any options appurtenant to any securities for the conversion thereof into securities, or to exercise any rights to subscribe for additional securities and to make any and all necessary payments therefor;

i. To join in, or oppose, any plan of reorganization, recapitalization, consolidation, merger, liquidation, mortgage foreclosure, sale or lease of a corporation, as a prudent man would deem advisable, and to accept any securities which may be issued upon adoption of any such plan;

j. To vote, in person or by proxy, any securities held by him;

k. To purchase insurance policies or annuity contracts, to make or cause to be made proper application for any such insurance policies or annuity contracts to be purchased as herein provided, and to hold all such insurance policies and/ or annuity contracts in Trust pursuant to the terms of this Agreement;

l. To enforce any right, obligation or claim, and in general to protect in any way the interest of the Trust, and, if a prudent man would consider such action in the best interests of the Trust, to abstain from the enforcement of any right, obligation or claim which at any time may be held by him;

m. To compromise and settle any claim or controversy;

n. To receive assets from another qualified Plan pursuant to Article XIV;

o. To do all proper acts which a prudent man would deem necessary or desirable and to exercise any and all powers of a Trustee which a prudent man would deem in the best interest of the Trust.

p. Other provisions notwithstanding, the Trustee can enter into contracts with one or more individuals, firms, associations and/or corporations, in such form as he in his sole and absolute discretion shall determine, including, but not limited to, contracts for the furnishing of investment advisory services and contracts for opening discretionary accounts granting to such individuals, firms, associations and/or corporations the authority to purchase, sell and otherwise deal in securities and to exercise all of the powers granted to him hereunder with respect to the investment of the assets of all or any portion of the Trust.

7.04 Payments to Participants and Beneficiaries

At the direction of the Administrator, Trustee shall make payments from the Trust Fund to Participants and Beneficiaries. The Trustee shall incur no liability regarding any such payment made at the direction of the Administrator.

7.05 Payment of Expenses

The Trust Fund may be charged with, and the Trustee may pay therefrom, unless paid directly by the Employer, (1) such reasonable compensation to the Trustee as may be agreed upon between the Employer and the Trustee, and (2) all other proper charges and payments, including all reasonable expenses of the Trust, and all taxes which may be levied or assessed upon the Trust Fund. However, no Trustee who is a full time Employee of the Employer shall be compensated for his services as a Trustee. Rather, he may be reimbursed for reasonable expenses incurred in the performance of his duties.

7.06 Investment Manager

The Trustee or the Employer may appoint an investment manager to manage all or any Part of the Trust Fund. In such case, the Trustee shall have no fiduciary liability for the acts or omissions of such investment manager and shall be under no obligation to invest or otherwise manage the portion of the Trust Fund which is subject to the management of such investment manager.

An investment manager is any fiduciary, other than a named fiduciary under ERISA, who: (1) has the power to manage, acquire, or dispose of any part of the Trust Fund, (2) is registered as an investment adviser under the Investment Advisers Act of 1940 or is employed by a bank (as defined in that Act) or any insurance company qualified to perform the services described in clause (1), and (3) has acknowledged in writing that he is a fiduciary with respect to the Plan.

If an investment manager is appointed by the Employer, written notice thereof shall be given to the Trustee, or to the Employer if the investment manager is appointed by the Trustee. A written acceptance of such appointment executed by the investment manager, including his acknowledgment of his status as a fiduciary of the Plan under Section 3(38) of ERISA, shall be attached to this Agreement.

7.07 Disclosure of Information to Plan Participants

a. Upon the written request of a Participant, but not more often than once every twelve months, the Trustee shall provide a Participant with a statement of his account, including the vested portion thereof, if any, and, as applicable, a statement of the earliest date on which his benefits under the Plan will become partially or fully vested.

b. Upon the written request of a Participant, the Trustee shall furnish to the Participant, for a reasonable charge, copies of any documents or reports required to be furnished by law including, but not limited to:

1. Plan descriptions filed with the Department of Labor and the latest updated summary thereof;
2. Latest Annual Report of the Plan required to be filed with the Department of Labor;
3. The Trust Agreement and all amendments thereto; and
4. Any terminal report filed in connection with the termination of the Plan.

The aforementioned documents and reports may be examined by a Participant, without charge, at the principal office of the Trustee.

7.08 Execution of Instruments

Any instrument to be executed by the Trustee, or Trustees if more than one, may be made, executed, acknowledged, and delivered by any one Trustee; and any person, firm, or corporation, including any insurance company, bank, mutual fund, and stock holder or dealer, may rely upon and shall be protected in relying upon the signature of any one Trustee, with the same force and effect as though all Trustees had signed.

7.09 Joint Management

If at any time there is more than one individual Trustee, all Trustees shall jointly manage and control the Trust Fund unless the responsibilities set forth under this Article VII are allocated among them in accordance with Section 7.10. If such allocation is made, any Trustee to whom such allocation has not been made shall not be liable, either individually or as a Trustee, for any loss resulting to the Plan which may arise from the acts or omissions of a Trustee to whom such responsibilities have been allocated. Every Trustee, however, is subject to the requirements of Section 405(a) of ERISA, which prohibits any Trustee from facilitating or concealing another fiduciary's breach of fiduciary responsibility.

7.10 Allocation of Responsibilities

The Employer may allocate the responsibility to control and manage the assets of the Trust Fund among the Trustees if there is more than one Trustee. Any such allocation shall be executed in writing, signed by the Employer and the Trustees, and shall be attached to this Agreement.

7.11 Delegation of Responsibilities

The Trustees may delegate responsibilities, other than to control and manage the assets of the Trust Fund, to persons who are not designated as Trustees and are not named fiduciaries within the meaning of Section 402 of ERISA. The Trustees shall not be liable for the acts or omissions of such persons provided that the Trustees have not violated the provisions of Section 7.12 in making any such delegation.

7.12 Fiduciary Standards

Each Trustee shall discharge his duties with respect to the Plan solely in the interest of the Participants and Beneficiaries:

a. For the exclusive purpose of (i) providing benefits to Participants and their Beneficiaries, and (ii) defraying reasonable expenses of administering the Plan;

b. With the care, skill, prudence and diligence under the circumstances then prevailing that a prudent person acting in a like capacity and familiar with such matters would use in the conduct of an enterprise of a like character and with like aims;

c. By diversifying the investments of the Plan so as to minimize the risk of large losses, unless under the circumstances it is clearly prudent not to do so; and

d. In accordance with the Plan insofar as the Plan is consistent with the provisions of ERISA.

The Trustees shall not cause the Plan or Trust to engage in any transaction if he knows or should know, that such transaction is a prohibited transaction described in Section 406(a) of ERISA, nor shall the Trustee deal or act in a manner prohibited by Section 405(a) of ERISA. No person may serve as a Trustee, fiduciary, custodian, counsel, agent, employee, or consultant of the Plan or Trust, if such service would violate the provisions of Section 411 of ERISA.

7.13 Accounting

The Trustee shall keep accurate and detailed accounts of all investments, receipts, disbursements and other transactions hereunder. All accounts, books and records relating to such transactions shall be open to inspection and audit at all reasonable times by any person.

Such accounting shall include a description of all securities and investments purchased and sold, with the cost and net proceeds or such purchase or sales, and shall show all cash, securities and other property held at the end of each Plan Year. The assets of the Trust Fund shall be valued as of the last business day of each such Plan Year at their fair market value.

7.14 Removal, Resignation, and Succession of Trustees

A Trustee may be removed by the Employer at any time. A Trustee may resign any time upon thirty days' written notice to the Employer unless such notice is waived by the Employer. Upon such removal or resignation of the Trustee, the Employer shall appoint a successor Trustee who shall have the same powers and duties as those conferred upon the Trustee herein. Upon such acceptance of appointment by the successor Trustee, the departing Trustee shall assign, transfer and pay over to such successor Trustee the funds and property then constituting the Trust. The departing Trustee is authorized, however, to reserve such reasonable sum of money, as would a prudent man acting under the same circumstances, for payment of fees and expenses in connection with the settlement of accounts or otherwise, and any balance of such reserve remaining after the payment of such fees and expenses shall be paid over to the successor Trustee.

The Administrator may, within sixty days after the removal or resignation of a Trustee, request that such Trustee file with the Employer and the Administrator a written account setting forth all investments, receipts and disbursements and other transactions effected by the Trustee during the twelve-month period ending with the date of such removal or resignation.

7.15 Acting and Remaining Trustees

Upon the removal, resignation, or death of any Trustee, the remaining Trustees shall have all the rights, powers, and duties of such former Trustee. If there is no remaining Trustee, the Company shall appoint a successor Trustee (or an Acting Trustee to serve until such time as a permanent Trustee is appointed).

ARTICLE VIII

Amendment and Termination

8.01 Amendment

a. This Agreement and the Plan and Trust embodied herein may be amended by the Employer at any time and in any manner which it deems advisable; provided, however, that no said amendment shall:

1. Provide for the use or diversion of the Trust assets for any purpose other than the exclusive benefit of the Participants and their Beneficiaries and for administrative expenses of the Plan and Trust;

2. Provide for reversion to the Employer, directly or indirectly, of any interest, ownership or control of the assets of the Trust or of any segregated account;

3. Increase the duties and liabilities of the Trustee without his written consent.

b. No amendment to the Plan shall be effective to the extent that it has the effect of decreasing a participant's Account Balance. For purposes of this paragraph, a plan amendment which has the effect of decreasing a participant's Account Balance or eliminating an optional form of benefit with respect to benefits attributable to service before the amendment shall be treated as reducing an Account Balance.

c. If the vesting schedule is amended, all Participants who have at least three Years-of-Service at the time such amendment is adopted shall be entitled to the greater of the nonforfeitable percentage that could be provided by either the preamendment schedule or the postamendment schedule at every point in time. Furthermore, no amendment to the plan shall have the effect of decreasing any Participant's nonforfeitable percentage determined without regard to such amendment as of the later of the date such amendment is adopted or the date it becomes effective.

d. Anything in this Section to the contrary notwithstanding, this Agreement may be amended retroactively by the Company in order to qualify the Plan and Trust as meeting the requirements of Section 401(a) or any other Section of the Code and any applicable requirements of the Department of Labor.

8.02 Voluntary Termination of Plan

The Employer shall have the power to terminate the Plan at any time by appropriate resolution, a certified copy of which shall be delivered to the Trustee. The Trustee shall thereupon notify all Participants of such termination and shall provide for the full vesting of Account Balances and distribution of the Trust assets in accordance with Sections 8.04 and 8.05.

8.03 Involuntary Termination of Plan

In the event that the Employer is legally dissolved or declared bankrupt, makes a general assignment for the benefit of creditors, or merges or consolidates with, or transfers its assets or liabilities to, any other company which does not assume the obligations of the Employer under this Agreement, the Plan shall be terminated and the Trust assets shall inure to the benefit of the Participants, who shall be 100% vested in their Account Balances at such time. The Trust assets shall be distributed in accordance with Sections 8.04 and 8.05.

8.04 Vesting Upon Termination

Upon the termination of the Plan and Trust in the situation described in Sections 8.02 and 8.03 or upon termination or partial termination in operation, or complete discontinuance of contributions to the Plan, each Participant shall be fully vested in, and be entitled to recover, as a minimum, his Account Balance under this Plan.

a. Termination of the Plan Only—upon a termination of the Plan or a complete discontinuance of contributions to the Plan pursuant to this Article, the Trust shall continue in existence and each Participant of the terminated Plan shall continue to share in the Trust earnings as though the Plan were still in effect; except that no further contributions thereto shall be made by the Employer. No benefits may be distributed by the Trustee except pursuant to the terms of the Plan or upon a subsequent termination of the Trust. The Administrator may direct the Trustee to apply the assets of the Trust to purchase nontransferable annuity contracts, either individually or on a group basis, on the lives of Participants and Beneficiaries of the terminated Plan, or to convert existing life insurance policies to such contracts in order to provide the benefits required by the Plan. The Administrator may direct the Trustee to hold such contracts in the Trust for the benefit of such Participants and Beneficiaries.

b. Termination of Plan and Trust—upon a termination of the Plan and Trust, each Participant shall have a nonforfeitable interest in his Account Balance and the Trustee shall distribute to each Participant and Beneficiary the benefits required under the Plan, or have annuity contracts purchased in order to provide such benefits.

Any termination of the Plan or Trust shall be by resolution of the Employer, a certified copy of which shall be filed with the Administrator, the Trustee, and the appropriate District Director of the Internal Revenue Service, and notification thereof shall be made to the Participants and Beneficiaries.

8.05 Distribution Upon Termination

In the event of termination of the Plan and Trust, or complete discontinuance of contributions to the Plan pursuant to this Article, the Trust shall remain in existence and all amounts vested hereunder shall be held and distributed to the Participants in the manner specified in Section 5.06. When all such amounts have been distributed, the Trust shall terminate and the Trustee shall be completely discharged upon rendering a full, complete and satisfactory account to the Employer.

8.06 Merger of the Plan

In the event of the merger or consolidation of this Plan with any other Plan, or any transfer of assets or liabilities of this Plan, each Participant in this Plan shall (if the Plan is terminated) receive a benefit, immediately after the merger, consolidation or transfer, which is equal to or greater than the benefit which he would have been entitled to receive immediately before the merger, consolidation or transfer (if the Plan had then terminated).

8.07 Successor in Business

Notwithstanding any other provisions with regard to termination of the Plan, any successor in business may continue this Plan and Trust.

ARTICLE IX

Provisions Relating to the Company

9.01 Right to Discontinuance

It is the expectation of the Employer that it will continue this Plan and Trust indefinitely and will contribute to the Plan and Trust such amounts as may be needed to provide the benefits set forth under this Agreement, but continuance of the Plan and Trust is not assumed as a contractual obligation of the Employer and the right is reserved by the Employer at any time to reduce, suspend or discontinue its contributions hereunder. However, a permanent discontinuance of contributions will be deemed to be a termination of the Plan.

9.02 Employment Rights

This Agreement shall not be construed as giving any Employee, or any other person, any right, legal or equitable, against the Employer, the Trust, or any fiduciary, or against the principal or income of the Trust, except as provided by law or as specifically provided for in this Agreement. All Employees shall remain subject to discharge from employment to the same extent as if this Agreement had never been executed.

ARTICLE X

Claims Procedure

10.01 Claims by Participant

Upon the filing of a claim for Plan benefits by a Participant, a Participant's authorized representative or the Beneficiary of a Participant (hereinafter referred to as a "Claimant"), the provisions of this Article with respect to claims procedures shall apply, and the Claimant shall have no further right except as provided for herein. For the purposes of this Article, a claim shall mean "a request for a Plan benefit by a Claimant," and a claim shall be deemed "filed" when a written communication is made by the Claimant which is reasonably calculated to bring the claim to the attention of the Employer, the Administrator or Trustee.

10.02 Notification to Claimant of Decision

If a claim is filed by a claimant and it is wholly or partially denied, the Administrator shall furnish to the Claimant, within sixty days after receipt of the claim, written notice of its decision in accordance with the provisions of Section 10.03.

10.03 Content of Notice

The Administrator shall provide to every Claimant who is denied a claim for benefits written notice setting forth, in a manner calculated to be understood by the Claimant, the following information:

a. The specific reason or reasons for the denial;
b. Specific reference to pertinent Plan provisions on which the denial is based;
c. A description of any additional material or information necessary for the Claimant to perfect the claim and an explanation of why such material or information is necessary; and
d. An explanation of the Plan's claim review procedures.

10.04 Review Procedure

Within sixty days following the receipt by the Claimant of written notification of denial of a claim, the Claimant shall have the right to appeal the denial of his claim to the Administrator for a full and fair review. The right of a Claimant to appeal an adverse decision shall include the following:

a. The Claimant may request a review of the decision upon written application to the Trustee;
b. The Claimant may review pertinent documents;
c. The Claimant may submit issues and comments in writing.

10.05 Decision on Review

a. Unless special circumstances (such as the need to hold a hearing) require an extension of time for processing a request for review, the Administrator shall render a decision within 60 days after the receipt of such a request. In the event special circumstances exist which require any extension of time for processing a request for review, the Administrator shall render a decision not later than 120 days after receipt of such request. The Administrator shall have authority to hold a hearing with respect to any issue submitted for his review; provided, however, that he gives reasonable notice of the time, place and subject matter of the hearing to the Claimant, the Employer, and the Trustee.

b. The decision rendered by the Administrator shall be in writing and shall include specific reasons for the decision written in a manner calculated to be understood by the Claimant, and specific references to the pertinent Plan provisions on which the decision is based.

10.06 Notice

a. All claims and requests required to be given under this Article by a Claimant shall be mailed to the Administrator and/or the Trustee, at such addresses as they shall designate by written notice. All notices and decisions required to be given under this Article by the Administrator or Trustee shall be mailed to the Claimant at his last known address as it appears from the records maintained by the Administrator, or at such other address as the Claimant shall designate by written notice.

b. All such claims, notices, requests and decisions shall be deemed to have been duly given and made when deposited, registered mail prepared, in a depository regularly maintained by the United States Postal Service.

ARTICLE XI

Miscellaneous

11.01 Exclusive Benefit

This Plan has been established for the exclusive benefit of Participants and their Beneficiaries. Except as provided in Sections 4.03 and 11.09, in no event shall any part of the principal or income of the Trust be used for, or diverted to, any other purpose whatsoever, or be paid to, or revert to, the Employer.

11.02 Release of Liability

As a condition precedent to making a distribution to any Participant or to his legal representative or Beneficiary, such Participant, legal representative or Beneficiary may be required to execute a receipt therefor, and a release in such form as shall be determined by the Trustee.

11.03 Spendthrift Clause

The interest of a Participant in this Plan shall not be subject to assignment or transfer or otherwise alienable, either by a voluntary or involuntary act of such Participant or any operation of law, nor be subject to attachment, execution, garnishment, sequestration or other seizure under any legal, equitable or other process.

Notwithstanding the above, the voluntary and revocable assignment of not more than ten percent of any benefit payment made by any Participant receiving benefits under the Plan shall not be considered as an alienation or assignment under this Section.

In addition, the creation, assignment or recognition of a right to any benefit payable to an Alternate Payee under a Qualified Domestic Relations Order shall not be considered as an alienation or assignment of a benefit under this Section.

11.04 Construction

This Agreement shall be administered, construed, and enforced according to the laws of the State of New State. Federal law shall govern in any instance in which State law is preempted.

11.05 Interpretation

In all matters concerning the interpretation of this Agreement and the operation of the Plan and Trust, the decision made by the Trustee shall be final and conclusive upon all parties. All such decisions shall apply uniformly to all Participants in like situations.

11.06 Meanings

Whenever used in this Agreement, unless the context indicates otherwise, the singular shall include the plural and the plural shall include the singular; the male gender shall include the female.

11.07 Severability

If any provision of this Agreement is held invalid or unenforceable, such invalidity or unenforceability shall not affect any other provision, and the Agreement shall be construed and enforced as if such provision had not been included.

11.08 Headings

The headings and sub-headings in this Agreement are inserted for the convenience of reference only and are not to be considered in the construction of the provisions hereof.

11.09 Qualification

With respect to a newly adopted plan (i.e., not a restatement), in the event that this Agreement and the Plan and Trust embodied herein are not initially approved and qualified by the Internal Revenue Service as meeting the requirements of Section 401 and related Sections of the Code, or any applicable requirements of the Department of Labor, then and in such an event, the Employer may recover contributions made pursuant hereto prior to the initial determination as to qualification. Prior to such initial determination, no Participant or Beneficiary of a Participant shall have any Vested Right.

11.10 Delegation of Authority by the Employer

Whenever the Employer is permitted or required by this Agreement to do or perform any act or matter or thing, it may be done and performed by any qualified individual duly authorized by the Employer (which, in the case of a corporation, shall be the Board of Directors).

11.11 Litigation Involving the Trust Fund

In any action or proceeding involving the Trust or any property constituting part or all thereof, or the administration thereof, the Employer, the Administrator and the Trustee shall be the only necessary parties and no Employees or former Employees of the Employer or their Beneficiaries or other person having or claiming to have any interest in the Trust or under the Plan shall be entitled to notice of, or to participate in, the proceedings, unless required by law.

Any final judgement which is not appealed or appealable that may be entered in any such action or proceedings, shall be conclusive and binding on the parties hereunder, and all persons having or claiming to have any interest in the Trust or under the Plan.

11.12 Inclusion of Employers

Any corporation, partnership, proprietorship, or other business entity may become an adopting Employer if, with the approval of the Company, it agrees to adopt the Plan and files with the Employer such written instruments evidencing such adoption as may be required by the Employer.

11.13 Inclusion of Employees of Adopting Employer

Any Employee of a business entity which adopts the Plan in the manner described under Section 11.12 shall become a Participant of the Plan according to the provisions of Article III.

11.14 Transfers of Employees Between Adopting Employers

A transfer of employment by an Employee from one adopting Employer to another adopting Employer shall not be deemed a termination of employment or of participation. Such an Employee's Years-of-Service and Years-of-Participation with all adopting Employers under this Plan shall be aggregated, and simultaneous employment with two or more adopting Employers shall be treated as one period for determining such Years-of-Service and Years-of-Participation. A Participant's benefits resulting from contributions by two or more adopting Employers shall be treated as contributions from a single entity for purpose of computing the benefits of such Participant pursuant to the provisions of the Plan.

11.15 Accounting

The Trustee and the Administrator shall maintain separate records for each adopting Employer under the Plan. The benefits of each Participant shall be determined on the basis of the contributions made to the Plan on behalf of such Participant by such one or more business entities as may be the Employer of such Participant at such time as contributions are made.

11.16 Missing Participant

If a benefit is forfeited because the Participant or Beneficiary cannot be found, such benefit will be reinstated if a claim is made by the Participant or Beneficiary.

ARTICLE XII

Policies

12.01 Ownership

The Trustee shall be the sole owner of any Policies purchased in accordance with Section 7.02 and shall reserve in each Policy the right to select and change the Beneficiary and to exercise all options and other privileges available under the Policy, which rights and privileges shall be exercised in accordance with the terms of this Agreement. The Trust shall be named as Beneficiary in each Policy, and any proceeds arising from the death of the insured shall be paid in accordance with the terms of this Plan.

12.02 Uniformity

All Policies shall be in such form and shall be purchased from such legal reserves life insurance companies as the Trustee shall determine, provided that all Policies shall be as nearly uniform as possible in regard to basic options, cash policy values, and other material features, except that Policies may be especially rated because of a Participant's physical condition.

12.03 Dividends

If any Policy purchased under the terms of the Plan and Trust is a participating one, the Trustee shall have the right to select any dividend option provided that it is not in conflict with any terms of this Agreement. Any dividends payable when there is no premium due shall be used to increase the proceeds of the Policy.

12.04 Lapse

Each Policy shall provide that in the event of lapse for nonpayment of premiums, the cash value shall be used to provide reduced paid-up insurance and retirement benefits.

12.05 Cancellation

Each policy may be cancelled by the Trustee immediately upon the Insured's termination of employment prior to his death, and the proceeds from such cancellation shall be credited to the Insured Account Balance.

ARTICLE XIII

Provisions Relating to Insurer

13.01 Responsibility

a. No Insurer shall be deemed a party to this Agreement, be responsible for the validity thereof, nor be responsible to see that any action of the Trustee is authorized by the terms of this Agreement.

b. No Insurer shall have any obligations to determine whether a person for whom the Trustee applies for a Policy is, in fact, eligible for participation under this Agreement, nor be obligated to determine any fact, the determination of which is necessary for the proper issuance of any Policy, and any Insurer shall be fully protected in relying upon the advice and direction of the Trustee.

13.02 Liability

Any change made or action taken by any Insurer upon written direction of the Trustee shall fully discharge such Insurer from all liability with respect thereto, and no Insurer shall be obligated to see to the distribution or further application of any monies paid by it to the Trustee or paid in accordance with the written direction of the Trustee.

13.03 Coverage

Except as may be otherwise provided in any binding receipt issued by an Insurer, there shall be no coverage and no death benefit payable under any policy to be purchased from any Insurer until such contract shall have been issued and the premiums therefor shall have been paid.

ARTICLE XIV

Rollovers

14.01 Rollover Contributions

A Participant shall be allowed to contribute amounts received in certain distributions from qualified retirement plans which constitute "rollover" distributions described in Sections 402(a)(5), 403(a)(4), and 408(d)(3) of the Code. Contributions may also be effected through direct plan-to-plan transfers.

In order to contribute any amount to this Trust under the provisions of this Section, the Participant shall represent in writing:

1. That the amounts to be rolled over or transferred constitute:
   a. The entire amount (excluding employee contributions) of a qualified total distribution (as defined in Code Section 402(e)(2)(E)(i)); or
   b. The entire amount (excluding employee contributions) distributed from an Individual Retirement Account (or received from the redemption of an Individual Retirement Annuity) and that no portion of such amount is attributable to any source other than the entire amount of a previous qualified total distribution (as defined in Code Section 402(e)(2)(E)(i)); or
   c. The entire amount of the proceeds from the sale of property received in a qualified total distribution as defined in Code Section 402(e)(2)(E)(i)), together with all the unsold property received in such distribution, less the amount of employee contributions; and
2. In the case of a rollover, that the Participant is acting within the time period prescribed under the Code during which such amounts may be recontributed to a qualified plan without the Participant incurring liability for federal income taxes on the receipt of such amounts.

The Trustee shall have the right to reject any rollover contribution that includes property that he deems unsuitable to hold under this Plan.

14.02 Segregation; Investment

If a rollover contribution is made, a separate account shall be maintained under this Plan representing the assets attributable to such contribution. The Employer shall, with the consent of the Participant, either administer such account separately, allocating to such account only the earnings and losses of the assets held in such account, or direct the Trustee to invest the assets attributable to such account as an additional account of the Participant hereunder, without separate investments, and with earnings and losses allocated in accordance with Article VI of this Plan.

14.03 Death Benefit from Rollover Account

In addition to the Death Benefit payable under Section 5.04 of this Agreement, but subject to the limitations of the Code, all account balances, proceeds of insurance contracts and investments attributable to a Rollover Account under this Article shall also be payable to the Beneficiary so named according to Section 3.02.

ARTICLE XV

Loans to Participants

15.01 Proscription Against Participant Loans

Effective on the Effective Date of this Restatement, no loans shall be made from the Trust to Participants or Beneficiaries under this Plan.

Any outstanding loans existing on the Effective Date of this Restatement shall be governed by the terms of the Loan Agreement and the provisions of this Plan immediately before the Effective Date of this Restatement, except that no such loan shall be renewed, extended, or modified in any way after the Effective Date of this Restatement; and with respect to any loans granted, renewed, extended, or modified in any way on or after August 18, 1985, and prior to the Effective Date of this Restatement, a Participant must obtain the consent of his or her spouse, if any, to the use of any portion of the Account Balance as security for the loan. Spousal consent shall be obtained no earlier than the beginning of the 90-day period that ends on the date on which the loan is to be so secured. The consent must be in writing, must acknowledge the effect of the loan, and must be witnessed by a plan representative or notary public. Such consent shall thereafter be binding with respect to the consenting spouse or any subsequent spouse with respect to that loan. A new consent shall be required if the Account Balance is used for renegotiation, extension, renewal, or other revision of the loan.

ARTICLE XVI

Top Heavy Plan Requirements and Administration

16.01 Notwithstanding the prior provisions of this Plan and Trust, for any Top Heavy Plan Year the following provisions will apply:

16.02 Definitions

a. *Aggregate Account* means, with respect to each Participant, the value of all accounts maintained on behalf of a Participant, whether attributable to Employer or Employee contributions.

b. *Compensation*—has the same meaning as the term is defined in Article I.

c. *Key Employee* means any Employee or former Employee (and his Beneficiaries) who, at any time during the Plan Year or any of the preceding four (4) Plan Years, is:

1. An officer of the Employer (as that term is defined within the meaning of the regulations under Code Section 416) having annual compensation greater than 50 percent of the amount in effect under Code Section 415(b) for any such Plan Year.

2. One of the ten Employees owning (or considered as owning within the meaning of Code Section 318) the largest interests in all Employers required to be aggregated under Code Sections 414(b),(c), and (m) or (o). However, an Employee will not be considered a top ten owner for a Plan Year if the Employee earns less than $30,000. (or such amount adjusted in accordance with Code Section 415(c)(1)(A) as in effect for the calendar year in which the Determination Date falls). If two Employees have the same interest in the Employer, the Employee having greater annual compensation from the Employer shall be treated as having a larger interest.

3. A "Five Percent Owner" of the Employer. "Five Percent Owner" means any person who owns (or is considered as owning within the meaning of Code Section 318) more than five percent of the outstanding stock of the Employer or stock possessing more than five percent of the total combined voting power of all stock of the Employer or, in the case of an unincorporated business, any person who owns more than five percent of the capital or profits interest in the Employer. In determining percentage ownership hereunder, Employers that would otherwise be aggregated under Code Sections 414(b), (c), and (m) shall be treated as separate Employers.

4. A "One Percent Owner" of the Employer having annual compensation from the Employer of more than $150,000. "One Percent Owner" means any person who owns (or is considered as owning within the meaning of Code Section 318) more than one percent of the outstanding stock of the Employer or stock possessing more than one percent of the total combined voting power of all stock of the Employer or, in the case of an unincorporated business, any person who owns more than one percent of the capital or profits interest in the Employer.

5. In determining percentage ownership hereunder, Employers that would otherwise be aggregated under Code Sections 414(b), (c), (m), and (o) shall be treated as separate Employers. However, in determining whether an individual has Compensation of more than $150,000., Compensation from each Employer required to be aggregated under Code Sections 414(b), (c), and (m) shall be taken into account. In addition, inherited benefits will retain the character of the benefits of the Employee who performed the services for the Employer.

d. *Non-Key Employee* means any Employee who is not a Key Employee.

e. *Super Top Heavy Plan* means that, as of the Determination Date, the sum of the present value of Accrued Benefits and the Aggregate Accounts of Key

Employees under this Plan and any plan of an Aggregation Group exceeds ninety percent (90%) of the present value of Accrued Benefits and the Aggregate Accounts of all Participants under this Plan and any Plan of an Aggregation Group.

f. *Top Heavy Plan* means that, as of the Determination Date, the sum of the present value of Accrued Benefits and the Aggregate Accounts of Key Employees under this Plan and any plan of an Aggregation Group exceeds sixty percent of the present value of Accrued Benefits and the Aggregate Accounts of all Participants under this Plan and any plan of an Aggregation Group.

g. *Top Heavy Plan Year* means that the Plan is a Top Heavy Plan for the period in question.

h. *Valuation Date* is defined in Article I.

16.03 Determination of Top Heavy Status

a. This Plan shall be a Top Heavy Plan for any Plan Year in which, as of the Determination Date, the sum of the Aggregate Accounts of Key Employees and the Present Value of Accrued Benefits of Key Employees under this Plan and any Plan of an Aggregation Group exceeds sixty percent of the sum of the Aggregate Accounts and the Present Value of Accrued Benefits of all Participants under this Plan and any Plan of an Aggregation Group.

Effective with the first day of the first Plan Year beginning after December 31, 1986, the accrued benefit of a participant other than a Key Employee shall be determined under (a) the method, if any, that uniformly applies for accrual purposes under all defined benefit plans maintained by the employer, or (b) if there is no such method, as if such benefit accrued not more rapidly than the slowest accrual rate permitted under the fractional rule of section 411(b)(1)(c) of the Code.

If any Participant is a Non-Key Employee for any Plan Year, but was a Key Employee for any prior Plan Year, such Participant's Account Balance shall not be taken into account for purposes of determining whether this Plan is a Top Heavy Plan (or whether any Aggregation Group which includes this Plan is a Top Heavy Group).

If any former Participant has not performed any services for any Employer maintaining the Plan at any time during the five-year period ending on the Determination Date, any Account Balance for such former Participant (and the account of such former Participant) shall not be taken into account. If, however, after the five-year period the former Participant performs services for the Employer, the Participant's total Account Balance shall again be taken into account.

b. This Plan shall be a Super Top Heavy Plan for any Plan Year in which, as of the Determination Date, the sum of the Present Value of Accrued Benefits and the Aggregate Accounts of Key Employees under this Plan and any Plan of an Aggregation Group exceeds ninety percent of the sum of the Present Value of Accrued Benefits and the Aggregate Accounts of all Participants under this Plan and any Plan of an Aggregation Group.

c. *Aggregate Account*—a Participant's Aggregate Account as of the Determination Date is the sum of:

1. His Participant's Account Balance as of the most recent valuation occurring within a twelve-month period ending on the Determination Date;

2. An adjustment for any contributions due as of the Determination Date. Such adjustment shall be the amount of any contributions actually made after the Valuation Date but before the Determination Date, except for the first Plan Year when such adjustment shall also reflect the amount of any contributions made after the Determination Date that are allocated as of a date in that first Plan Year;

3. Any Plan distributions made within the Plan Year that includes the Determination Date or within the four preceding Plan Years. However, in the case of distribu-

tions made after the Valuation Date and prior to the Determination Date, such distributions are not included as distributions for Top Heavy purposes to the extent that such distributions are already included in the Participant's Aggregate Account as of the Valuation Date. Notwithstanding anything herein to the contrary, all distributions will be counted;

4. Any Employee contributions, whether voluntary or mandatory. However, amounts attributable to qualified deductible Employee contributions shall not be considered to be a part of the Participant's Aggregate Account;

5. With respect to unrelated rollovers and plan-to-plan transfers (ones which are both initiated by the Employee and made from a plan maintained by one Employer to a plan maintained by another Employer), if this plan provides for rollovers or plan-to-plan transfers, it shall always consider such rollover or plan-to-plan transfer as a distribution for the purposes of this Section. If this Plan and Trust is the plan accepting such rollovers or plan-to-plan transfers, it shall not consider such rollovers or plan-to-plan transfers accepted after December 31, 1983 as part of the Participant's Aggregate Account. However, rollovers or plan-to-plan transfers accepted prior to January 1, 1984 shall be considered as part of the Participant's Aggregate Account;

6. With respect to related rollovers and plan-to-plan transfers (ones either not initiated by the Employee or made to a plan maintained by the same Employer), if this Plan and Trust provides the rollover or plan-to-plan transfer, it shall not be counted as a distribution for purposes of this Section. If this Plan and Trust is the plan accepting such rollover or plan-to-plan transfer, it shall consider such rollover or plan-to-plan transfer as part of the Participant's Aggregate Account, irrespective of the date on which such rollover or plan-to-plan transfer is accepted.

d. *Aggregation Group* means either a Required Aggregation Group or a Permissive Aggregation Group as hereinafter determined.

1. *Required Aggregation Group*—in determining a Required Aggregation Group hereunder, each plan of the Employer in which a Key Employee is a Participant, and each other plan of the Employer which enables any plan in which a Key Employee participates to meet the requirements of Code Sections 401(a)(4) or 410, will be required to be aggregated. For purposes of this Section, each Plan of the Employer shall include Keogh Plans and any terminated Plan that covered a Key Employee and was maintained during the five-year period ending on the Determination Date. Such group shall be known as a Required Aggregation Group.

In the case of a Required Aggregation Group, each plan in the group will be considered a Top Heavy Plan if the Required Aggregation Group is a Top Heavy Group. No plan in the Required Aggregation Group will be considered a Top Heavy Plan if the Required Aggregation Group is not a Top Heavy Group.

2. *Permissive Aggregation Group*—The Employer may also include any other plan not required to be included in the Required Aggregation Group, provided the resulting group, taken as a whole, would continue to satisfy the provisions of Code Sections 401(a)(4) or 410. Such group shall be known as a Permissive Aggregation Group.

In the case of a Permissive Aggregation Group, only a plan that is part of the Required Aggregation Group will be considered a Top Heavy Plan if the Permissive Aggregation Group is a Top Heavy Group. No plan in the Permissive Aggregation Group will be considered a Top Heavy Plan if the Permissive Aggregation Group is not a Top Heavy Group.

3. Only those Plans of the Employer in which the Determination Dates fall within the same calendar year shall be aggregated in order to determine whether such Plans are Top Heavy Plans.

e. *Determination Date* means (1) the last day of the preceding Plan Year, or (2) in the case of the first Plan Year, the last day of such Plan Year.

f. *Present Value of Accrued Benefit*—in the case of a defined benefit plan, a Participant's Present Value of Accrued Benefits shall be determined under the provisions of the applicable defined benefit plan.

g. *Top Heavy Group* means an Aggregation Group in which, as of the Determination Date, the sum of:

1. The Present Value of Accrued Benefits of Key Employees under all Defined Benefit Plans included in the group, and

2. The Aggregate Accounts of Key Employees under all defined contribution plans included in the group, exceeds sixty percent (60%) of the corresponding sum determined for all Participants.

16.04 Top Heavy Requirements

a. 1. Vesting Requirements

Years-of-Service	*The Nonforfeitable Percentage is:*
Less than 2	0%
2	20%
3	40%
4	60%
5	80%
6 or more	100%

If the vesting schedule under the Plan and Trust shall shift in or out of the above schedule for any Plan Year because of the Plan's Top Heavy Status, such shift will be treated as an Amendment to the Plan and the provisions in Section 8.01 (c) of the Plan shall apply.

a. 2. For purposes of this section, a Year-of-Service during which the Employer did not maintain the Plan or a predecessor plan shall not be credited as a Year-of-Service.

b. Employer Contribution—the Administrator may separately account for that portion of each Participant's Account attributable to Top Heavy Plan Years and Non-Top Heavy Plan Years.

c. Minimum Allocations Required for Top Heavy Plan Years—For any Top Heavy Plan Year, the sum of the Employer's contributions and forfeitures allocated to the Participant's Account of each Non-Key Employee shall be equal to at least three percent of such Non-Key Employee's Compensation. However, should the sum of the Employer's contributions and forfeitures allocated to the Participant's Account of each Key Employee for such Top Heavy Plan Year be less than three percent of each Key Employee's Compensation, the sum of the Employer's contributions and forfeitures allocated to the Participant's Account of each Non-Key Employee shall be equal to the largest percentage allocated to the Participant's Account of each Key Employee. In determining the highest rate of contribution applicable to any Key Employee, amounts that Key Employees elect to defer under a qualified cash or deferred arrangement maintained by the Employer shall be taken into account.

d. Extra Minimum Allocation Permitted for Top Heavy Plans other than Super Top Heavy Plans—if a Key Employee is a Participant in both a defined contribution plan and a defined benefit plan that are both part of a Top Heavy Group (but neither of such plans is a Super Top Heavy Plan), the Defined Contribution Fraction and the Defined Benefit Fraction set forth in regulations under Code Section 415, which are hereby incorporated by this reference, shall remain unchanged, provided the

Participant's Account of each Non-Key Employee who is a Participant receives an extra allocation (in addition to the minimum allocation set forth above) equal to not less than one percent of such Non-Key Employee's Compensation; otherwise, the Fractions must be adjusted pursuant to Section 16.05.

e. For purposes of the minimum allocations set forth above, the percentage allocated to the Participant's Account of any Key Employee shall be equal to the ratio of the sum of the Employer's contribution and forfeitures allocated on behalf of such Key Employee divided by the Compensation for such Key Employee.

f. For any Top Heavy Plan Year, the minimum allocations set forth above shall be allocated to the Participant's Account of all Non-Key Employees who are Participants and who are employed by the Employer on the last day of the Plan Year, including Non-Key Employees who (1) failed to complete a Year-of-Service, (2) declined to make mandatory contributions (if required) to the Plan, and (3) are excluded from participation or who failed to receive a contribution merely because the Employee's Compensation was less than a stated amount.

g. Notwithstanding anything in this Section to the contrary, a Key Employee shall be treated as a Non-Key Employee for purposes of receiving the minimum contributions provided by this Section.

h. Notwithstanding anything herein to the contrary, in any Plan Year in which a Non-Key Employee is a Participant in both this Plan and a defined benefit pension plan included in a Top Heavy Aggregation Group, the Employer shall not be required to provide a Non-Key Employee with both the full separate minimum defined benefit plan benefit and the full separate Defined Contribution Plan allocations. Instead, the Employer can satisfy the minimum benefits requirement of Section 416(c) by providing any one of the following safe harbor rules of Regulation 1.416-1(M-10):

1. The defined benefit minimum is provided;
2. The defined benefit minimum is offset by the benefits provided under the defined contribution plan in a floor offset approach;
3. The defined contribution plan provides aggregate benefits (under a comparability of plans analysis) at least equal to those in the defined benefit plan; or
4. A minimum contribution or allocation of contributions and forfeitures equal to five percent of compensation is provided under the defined contribution plan for each year the Plan is Top Heavy. The five percent figure shall be increased to seven and one-half percent if the plan is one described in Section 16.03(d).

i. A Year-of-Service with the Employer shall not be taken into account under this paragraph if:

1. The Plan was not a Top Heavy Plan for any Plan Year ending during such Year-of-Service; or
2. Such Year-of-Service was completed in a Plan Year beginning before January 1, 1984.

16.05 Factor to Determine Denominators

a. For any Top Heavy Plan Year, 1.0 shall be substituted for 1.25 in computing the Fractions set forth in regulations under Code Section 415, which are hereby incorporated by this reference, unless the extra minimum allocation is being made pursuant to Section 16.04(d), and, if applicable, 16.04(h)(4). However, for any Plan Year in which this Plan is a Super Top Heavy Plan, 1.0 shall be substituted for 1.25 in any event.

b. Special Rule for Defined Contribution Fraction—at the election of the Administrator, in determining the Defined Contribution Plan fraction for any Plan Year ending after December 31, 1982, the amount taken into account for the denominator for each Participant for all Plan Years ending before January 1, 1983 shall be an amount equal to the product of (a) the amount of the denominator (as in effect for the Plan Year ending in 1982) for Plan Years ending in 1982, multiplied by (b) the "transition fraction."

For purposes of the preceding paragraph, the term "transition fraction" shall mean a fraction (a) the numerator of which is the lesser of (1) $51,875. or (2) 1.4 multiplied by twenty-five percent (25%) of the Participant's compensation for the Plan Year ending in 1981, and (b) the denominator of which is the lesser of (1) $41,500. or (2) twenty-five percent of the Participant's compensation for the Plan Year ending in 1981.

Notwithstanding the foregoing, for any Top Heavy Plan Year, $41,500. shall be substituted for $51,875. in determining the "transition fraction."

IN WITNESS WHEREOF, the Sponsor, by its Duly Authorized Officers and with its Corporate Seal affixed, and the Trustees have caused these presents to be signed on this 15th day of December, 1990.

____
President

CORPORATE SEAL:

____
President, Trustee

____
Secretary, Trustee

____
Trustee, Trustee

ATTEST: ______________________
Secretary

7:2 Workers' Compensation Forms

Each state in the United States has enacted Workers' Compensation laws. These laws generally provide that employees who are injured on the job are entitled to compensation for any medical expenses and for wages lost due to the injury. In return, employees are not permitted to sue their employers for injuries sustained on the job.

This statutory scheme is premised on a system of workers' compensation insurance to which employers must subscribe. The following are examples of workers' compensation forms, used by employers and insurance companies in Pennsylvania, which give an idea of the statutory requirements for compensation, for physical examinations of injured employees, and for termination of benefits.

7:2.1 Generic Worker's Compensation Claim Form

WORKERS' COMPENSATION CLAIM FORM

Policy Number	Policy Period	Agent's Name	LARS Loc. Code

C-2 (5-78)

STATE OF NEW YORK
WORKERS' COMPENSATION BOARD

EMPLOYER'S REPORT OF INJURY

Send this notice directly to Chairman, Workers' Compensation Board at address shown on reverse side within ten (10) days after accident occurs. Copy also should be sent to your insurance carrier.

PLEASE PRINT OR TYPE — INCLUDE ZIP CODE IN ALL ADDRESSES — EMPLOYEE'S SS# MUST BE ENTERED BELOW

WCB CASE NO.	CARRIER CASE NO.	CODE NO.	DATE OF ACCIDENT	EMPLOYEE'S S.S. NO.

(ENTER CASE NUMBERS, IF KNOWN, IN ABOVE SPACES)

	(a) NAME	(b) MAIL ADDRESS	(c) OSHA CASE OR FILE NO.
1. EMPLOYER			
(d) LOCATION (if different from mail address)			(e) E.R. NO.
2. INSURANCE CARRIER			
3. INJURED PERSON	(First Name) (Middle Initial) (Last Name)	(Home Address Give Number and Street, City, State, Zip Code and Apt. No.)	

EMPLOYER

4. Nature of business: (State principal products manufactured or sold or services rendered) ________
5. Address where accident occurred *(Include county)* ________

ACCIDENT

6. Date of accident: ____ 19__, Day of Week ____ Hour of Day____ A.M.____ P.M.
   If occupational illness, date of initial diagnosis: ____ 19____
7. (a) Date disability began: ____ 19__, Hour of Day____ A.M.____ P.M.
   (b) Was injured paid in full for this day? ____
8. Name of Department (where regularly employed) and foreman ________
9. When did you or foreman first know of injury? ________
10. Names and addresses of witnesses: ________

INJURED PERSON

11. (a) Marital status: ____ (b) Sex ____
12. Age: ____ 13. Did you have on file employment certificate or permit? ____
14. Occupation: (a) Job title for which employed: ____
    (b) Occupation when injured: ____
15. (a) How long employed by you? ____ (b) Piece or time worker? ____
    (c) Hours per day: ____ (d) Days per week: ____
16. Earnings in your employ: (a) Rate per: Hour $____ Day $____Week $____ Month $____
    (b) Total earnings paid during year prior to date of accident: (include bonuses paid, value of board, lodging, etc.) $____ Average per week: $____
    (c) Bonuses or premiums paid and included in item 16(b) above: $____ (d) Estimated value of board, lodging, or other advantages in addition to wages: (included in item 16(b) above) $____
    (e) Calendar weeks in past 52 in same kind of work as at time of injury: ____

NATURE OF INJURY OR OCCUPATIONAL DISEASE

17. State nature of injury and part or parts of body affected: (as "Injury to Chest," etc.) ____
18. Did you provide medical care? ____ If so, when? ____
19. Name and address of doctor: ____
20. Name and address of hospital: ____
21. Probable length of disability: ____
22. (a) Has employee returned to work? ____ (b) If so, give date: ____
    (c) At what occupation? ____ (d) At what weekly wage? $____

NOTE: Form C-11 must be filed each time there is any change in the employment status as reported in item 22 above.

FATAL CASES

23. Has injured died? ____ (a) If so, give date of death: ____
    (b) Name and address of nearest relative: ____

CAUSE OF ACCIDENT OR OCCUPATIONAL DISEASE

24. (a) What was employee doing when accident occurred? (Describe briefly as "loading truck," "operating press," "shoveling dirt," "painting with spray gun," "walking downstairs," etc.) ____
    (b) Where did accident occur? (Specify whether on the employer's premises, and indicate if in street, factory yard, on loading platform, in factory, etc.) ____
25. How was accident or occupational disease sustained? (Describe fully, stating whether injured person slipped, fell, was struck, etc., and what factors led up to or contributed to accident. Use additional sheets, if necessary.) ____
26. (a) What specific machine, tool, appliance, gas, liquid, or other substance or object was most closely connected with this accident or occupational disease? ____
    (b) If mechanical apparatus or vehicle, what part of it? (State if gears, pulley, motor, etc.) ____
27. Were mechanical guards or other safeguards (such as goggles) provided? ____ (a) Were they in use at time of accident? ____ (b) Was machine, tool, or object defective? ____ If so, in what way? ____

DATE OF THIS REPORT: ____

	Enter "X" in this box if accident was reported on Form C-2.1
	Enter "X" in this box if accident was previously reported on Form C-2.5

FIRM NAME: ____
SIGNED BY: ____ Official Title
TEL NO. ____

THE WORKERS' COMPENSATION BOARD EMPLOYS AND SERVES THE HANDICAPPED WITHOUT DISCRIMINATION.

C-2 C-2 C-2 C-2 C-2

Form LC-3274-11 Printed in U.S.A.

WORKERS' COMPENSATION CLAIM FORM page 2

INSTRUCTIONS TO EMPLOYERS

Reports should be sent directly to the district offices at these addresses:

ALBANY 12241 — 1949 North Broadway. For all accidents in following counties: Albany, Clinton, Columbia, Dutchess, Essex, Franklin, Fulton, Greene, Hamilton, Montgomery, Orange, Putnam, Rensselaer, Saratoga, Schenectady, Schoharie, Ulster, Warren, Washington.
BINGHAMTON 13901 — State Office Building, Hawley Street. For all accidents in following counties: Broome, Chemung, Chenango, Cortland, Delaware, Otsego, Schuyler, Steuben, Sullivan, Tioga, Tompkins.
BUFFALO 14203 — State Office Building, 125 Main Street. For all accidents in following counties: Cattaraugus, Chautauqua, Erie, Niagara.
HEMPSTEAD 11550 — 175 Fulton Avenue. For all accidents in following counties: Nassau, Suffolk.
NEW YORK CITY 10047 — Two World Trade Center. For all accidents in following counties: Bronx, Kings, New York, Queens, Richmond, Rockland, Westchester.
ROCHESTER 14614 — 155 Main Street West. For all accidents in following counties: Allegany, Genesee, Livingston, Monroe, Ontario, Orleans, Seneca, Wayne, Wyoming, Yates.
SYRACUSE 13202 — State Office Building, East Washington Street. For all accidents in following counties: Cayuga, Herkimer, Jefferson, Lewis, Madison, Oneida, Onondaga, Oswego, St. Lawrence.

WORKERS' COMPENSATION LAW

Sec. 13 Treatment and care of injured employees.

(a) "The employer shall promptly provide for an injured employee such medical, surgical, optometric or other attendance or treatment, nurse and hospital service, medicine, optometric services, crutches, eye-glasses, false teeth, artificial eyes and apparatus for such period as the nature of the injury or the process of recovery may require.****"

Sec. 51 Posting of notice regarding compensation.

"Every employer who has complied with section fifty of this chapter shall post and maintain in a conspicuous place or places in and about his place or places of business typewritten or printed notices in form prescribed by the chairman, stating the fact that he has complied with all the rules and regulations of the chairman and the board and that he has secured the payment of compensation to his employees and their dependents in accordance with the provisions of this chapter, but failure to post such notice as herein provided shall not in any way affect the exclusiveness of the remedy provided for by section eleven of this chapter.****"

Sec. 52 Effect of Failure to secure compensation.

"Failure to secure the payment of compensation shall constitute a misdemeanor, punishable by a fine of not more than five hundred dollars or imprisonment for not more than one year, or both. Where the employer is a corporation, the president, under this section.****" secretary and treasurer thereof shall be liable for failure to secure the payment of compensation

Sec. 110 Record and report of injuries by employers.

"Every employer shall keep a record of all injuries, fatal or otherwise, received by his employees in the course of their employment. Within ten days after the occurrence of an accident resulting in personal injury, which shall cause a loss of time from regular duties beyond the working day or shift on which the accident occurred, or which shall require medical treatment beyond ordinary first aid or more than two treatments by a physician or person rendering first aid, a report thereof shall be made in writing by the employer to the chairman of the workers' compensation board upon blanks to be procured from the chairman for that purpose. Such report shall state the name and nature of the business of the employer, the location of his establishment or place of work, the name, address and occupation of the injured employee, the time, nature and cause of the injury and such other information as may be required by the chairman. An employer shall furnish a report of any other accident resulting in an injury received by an employee in the course of his employment or an occupational disease incurred by an employee in the course of his employment whenever directed by the chairman. With the approval of the chairman an employer may report upon a single report form, in such detail as may be required by the chairman, all injuries to his employees within any calendar month which have caused either no loss of time or in which the employees have returned to their regular employment at their regular wages after not more than three days if there is no evidence of further disability and there is no indication for further treatment. Every such employer shall submit to the chairman his application upon a form approved by the chairman, and shall set forth such information as shall be required as to the facilities maintained by him for the care and treatment of employees, shall set forth the manner of keeping records of all injuries, and shall agree promptly to submit full and complete information as to any such case that shall require further treatment or that may be requested by the chairman. An employer who refuses or neglects to make a report as required by this section shall be guilty of a misdemeanor, punishable by a fine of not more than five hundred dollars."

C-2 (5-78) Reverse
Form LC-3274-11

7:2.2 Petition for Termination, Suspension or Modification of Compensation

LIBC-40 (2-78)

COMMONWEALTH OF PENNSYLVANIA
DEPARTMENT OF LABOR AND INDUSTRY
BUREAU OF WORKERS' COMPENSATION
3607 Derry Street
Harrisburg, Pa. 17111

PETITION FOR TERMINATION, SUSPENSION, OR MODIFICATION OF COMPENSATION
SECTION 413

(Type or Print Clearly)

EMPLOYE ____________________ EMPLOYE'S SOCIAL SECURITY NUMBER ____________________

CLAIMANT IF OTHER THAN EMPLOYE ____________________

ADDRESS ____________________ DATE OF ORIGINAL INJURY ____________________

CITY OR TOWN ______ STATE ______ ZIP ______

VS.

DEFENDANT EMPLOYER ____________________ INSURANCE CARRIER ____________________

ADDRESS ____________________ ADDRESS ____________________

CITY OR TOWN ______ STATE ______ ZIP ______ CITY OR TOWN ______ STATE ______ ZIP ______

TO YOUR HONORABLE REFEREE:

____________________, employer in the above case, hereby petitions that compensation payable thereunder be ☐ terminated, ☐ suspended, or ☐ modified as of ____________________, 19__, on the grounds that the (disability) (status) of ____________________ entitled to compensation under ☐ Notice of Compensation Payable, ☐ Agreement, or ☐ Award has changed as follows: ____________________

____

____

____

____

____

____

____

☐ A supersedeas is (requested) (allowable) for the following reasons: ____________________

____

EMPLOYER OR INSURER ____________________

by ____________________

SUBSCRIBED AND SWORN TO BEFORE ME, THIS ______ DAY OF ____________________, 19__

AT ____________________

My Commission expires on the ______ day of ____________________, 19____

THIS AFFIDAVIT MAY BE SWORN TO BEFORE A COMPENSATION REFEREE OR ANY OTHER PERSON AUTHORIZED TO ADMINISTER AN OATH.

PLEASE ENTER MY APPEARANCE FOR PETITIONER:

ATTORNEY ____________________

ADDRESS ____________________ ZIP ______

NOTICE: Petition should be completed in original and five copies, either typed or printed, and mailed or delivered to th Department at the address in the upper left corner. Affidavit need only be made on the original petition.

7:2.3 Fatal Claim Petition for Compensation by Dependents of Deceased Employees

LIBC-363 (Rev. 1-78)
Commonwealth of Pennsylvania
Department of Labor and Industry

Bureau of Workers' Compensation
3607 Derry Street
Harrisburg, Pa. 17111

FATAL CLAIM PETITION FOR
COMPENSATION BY DEPENDENTS
OF DECEASED EMPLOYES

Decedent............................

Decedent's S. S. No....................

Petitioner...........................

..............................19.......

Street Number........................

....
Insurance Carrier

....
City & State Zip Code

....
Address Zip Code

Defendant............................

....
Address Zip Code

TO THE BUREAU OF WORKERS' COMPENSATION, COMMONWEALTH OF PENNSYLVANIA

The petitioner respectfully alleges that:

(1) ....died on.................................19.......
(Name of deceased employe) (Date of death)

(2) a - Name and address of employer...

b - Business of employer..

(3) The accident occurred on..
(State month, day, year and hour)

(4) The accident occurred while decedent was employed..............................

....
(Give full details as to type of employment and/or place where accident occurred and what employe was doing at the time)

(5) The nature and cause of the accident were...

....

(6) The cause of death was..............................as given by...............
....

(7) The decedent received aid from the following doctors and/or hospitals:

....
(Give names and addresses. If none, so state)

(8) Expenses of the last sickness and burial amounted to ....

Amount paid to employer...

(9) The weekly wages of deceased at the time of accident were........................

7:2.4 Petition for Finding of Violation of Workmen's Compensation Act

LIBC-686 REV 3-87

COMMONWEALTH OF PENNSYLVANIA
DEPARTMENT OF LABOR AND INDUSTRY
BUREAU OF WORKERS' COMPENSATION
3607 DERRY STREET
HARRISBURG, PA 17111

PETITION FOR FINDING OF VIOLATION OF THE TERMS OF THE WORKMEN'S COMPENSATION ACT AND/OR REGULATIONS AND/OR ASSESSMENT OF PENALTIES

TYPE OR PRINT CLEARLY

CLAIMANT	DEFENDANT EMPLOYER
ADDRESS	ADDRESS
CITY OR TOWN STATE ZIP CODE	CITY OR TOWN STATE ZIP CODE
SOCIAL SECURITY NUMBER OF CLAIMANT	INSURANCE CARRIER
______, 19___ DATE OF ACCIDENT	ADDRESS
CLAIMANT'S REPRESENTATIVE, IF APPLICABLE	CITY OR TOWN STATE ZIP CODE

TO THE BUREAU OF WORKERS' COMPENSATION, COMMONWEALTH OF PENNSYLVANIA:

1. The Claimant, ______________, or his/her Representative, ______________, believes that the Respondent, (Insurer/Self-Insurer) ______________ has violated the terms of the Workmen's Compensation Act and/or Regulations in the processing or payment of compensation to the Claimant(s) in that: (Specify, in detail, the nature of the alleged violation(s) and the Section of the Law/Regulation which applies. Attach an additional sheet, if necessary.)

2. The Claimant requests that the Respondent be required to Show Cause, or that this Petition be otherwise assigned for hearing, as to why the Respondent should not be found to have violated the terms of the Workmen's Compensation Act and/or Regulations promulgated thereunder.

7:2.5 Notice of Compensation Payable

COMMONWEALTH OF PENNSYLVANIA
DEPARTMENT OF LABOR AND INDUSTRY
BUREAU OF OCCUPATIONAL INJURY
AND DISEASE COMPENSATION
HARRISBURG, PA. 17111

NOTICE
OF
COMPENSATION
PAYABLE

______ SOCIAL SECURITY NUMBER

______ EMPLOYER/INSURER CLAIM NUMBER

______ DATE OF THIS NOTICE

This Notice is to be sent to injured employee with the first payment of compensation and a copy filed with the Department of Labor and Industry.

Injured Employee ______

Address ______

Employer ______

Address ______

Nature of Injury ______

Check if injury is:
(1) Permanent loss under 306 (c) ☐
(2) Eye injury ☐
(3) Radiation injury ☐

Compensation payable as follows:

1. Weekly disability rate $ ______

   Check applicable: ☐ Maximum allowable

   ☐ Below maximum based on average weekly wage of $ ______ *

   *A completed wage statement in accordance with Section 309 must be attached to this Notice if rate below maximum.

2. Payments begin on ______ for injury which occurred on ______ (Compensation is not payable for first 7 days of disability unless disability exceeds 13 days.)

3. Payments will hereafter be made: ☐ weekly ☐ Biweekly ☐ Other (Specify) ______ until employee returns to work without loss of income or disability otherwise ceases or changes in effect; HOWEVER, any termination or modification of these payments must be by agreement or final receipt, order of Departmental referee or Workmen's Compensation Board, or as otherwise provided in rules and regulations of the Department, or as limited under Section 306 (c) for amputation or other specific loss thereunder.

4. If injury involves loss under Section 306 (c) and employee has returned to work, complete the following information:

   (a) Compensation is payable for ______ weeks for loss of ______

   (b) Employee returned to work without loss of income on ______

   (c) Healing period payable for ______ weeks (Up to (b) above and subject to 7-day waiting period)

   (d) Total (a) and (c), payable ______ weeks

5. Remarks ______

______

NOTICE TO EMPLOYEE: If any questions arise involving these payments, contact representative named at bottom of this Notice. If you cannot resolve any problem with employer representative, you may call the Bureau toll free at 800-482-2383

☐ LIBERTY MUTUAL INS. CO. (BUREAU CODE # 025)
☐ LIBERTY MUTUAL FIRE INS. CO. (BUREAU CODE # 257)
☐ LIBERTY INSURANCE CORP. (BUREAU CODE #2138)

(TYPE ONLY): Employer/Insurer ______

Representative ______

Phone Number ______

OIDC-495 (8/72) 37-CSF-2 R-3

7:2.6 Supplemental Agreement for Compensation for Disability or Permanent Injury

LIBC-337 (2-78)

COMMONWEALTH OF PENNSYLVANIA
DEPARTMENT OF LABOR AND INDUSTRY

SUPPLEMENTAL AGREEMENT FOR COMPENSATION FOR DISABILITY OR PERMANENT INJURY

BUREAU OF WORKERS' COMPENSATION
1171 SOUTH CAMERON STREET
HARRISBURG, PA 17104-2501

Every question must be answered either with appropriate statement or figures, or the word "NONE".

SOCIAL SECURITY NO. ______________________

INJURY DATE ______________________

Date ______________________ EMPLOYER-INSURER NO. ______________________

Whereas, the undersigned employer and employee are parties to a compensation agreement or award of the above number and it is now hereby agreed between the parties hereto that the status of the disability of the said employee changed on ______________________ as follows: ______________________

It is further agreed that on and after .... compensation shall be payable to the said employee at the rate of $..................... per week for .... weeks; or, if the future period of disability is uncertain, then to continue at said rate until terminated by a further supplemental agreement, order of the Workers' Compensation Board or Referee, or by final receipt.

Further matters agreed upon ______________________

Note:—Weekly wages must be computed in accordance with Section 309 of the Act.

______________________ (Witness for employee)

______________________ (Witness's Address)

______________________ (Witness for employer)

______________________ (Witness's Address)

______________________ (Signature of employee)

______________________ (Employer)

______________________ (Employer's Address)

☐ **LIBERTY MUTUAL INS. CO. (BUREAU CODE #025)**
☐ **LIBERTY MUTUAL FIRE INS. CO. (BUREAU CODE #257)**
☐ **LIBERTY INSURANCE CORP. (BUREAU CODE #2138)**

______________________ (Address)

______________________ (Claimant)

______________________ (Street) (City)

______________________ (County) (State)

Insurer's office to which correspondence regardin this agreement is to be sent:

____

____

____

37-CSF-6 R3

7:2.7 Agreement to Stop Weekly Compensation Payments

LIBC-340 REV 6-88
COMMONWEALTH OF PENNSYLVANIA
DEPARTMENT OF LABOR AND INDUSTRY
BUREAU OF WORKERS' COMPENSATION
HARRISBURG, PA 17111

AGREEMENT TO STOP WEEKLY WORKERS' COMPENSATION PAYMENTS

(FINAL RECEIPT)

(TYPE OR PRINT CLEARLY)

EMPLOYE ______________________ SOCIAL SECURITY NUMBER ______________________

EMPLOYER ______________________ DATE OF INJURY OR DISEASE ______________________

INSURER ______________ BUREAU CODE ______________ CO. CODE ______________ INSURER CLAIM NUMBER ______________

NOTICE TO EMPLOYES:

Signing this form means your weekly workers' compensation payments will stop. You may file a petition to reopen your claim within three years of the date to which payments were made.

The signing of this form will not affect your right to receive payment for reasonable and necessary medical bills related to your injury or disease under the Workmen's Compensation Act. If you have any questions regarding this form, speak with your representative or call the Pennsylvania Bureau of Workers' Compensation Information Hotline using the toll-free Number 1-800-482-2383.

SIGN THIS FORM IF:

- Beginning and ending dates and total amount paid shown below are correct; AND
- You are fully recovered from your injury or disease.

DO NOT SIGN THIS FORM IF:

- You are not fully recovered from your work injury or disease; OR
- You have returned to work but are earning less because you are unable to do your former job due to your work related injury; OR
- Your employer or the insurance company is withholding your last workers' compensation check unless you sign this form.

Received of (INSURER) ______________________ by Check No. __________ the sum of $ ______________ as final payment of compensation due me under the Pennsylvania Workmen's Compensation Act for the injury or disease incurred by me in the above case. Total amount of compensation received by me, including the final payment shown above, is $ ______________ in temporary or total disability benefits for wage loss covering a period of ______________________ weeks from the date my disability began on ______________ until I was able to return to work on ______________ without loss of earning power due to the injury or disease incurred by me. Medical and/or healing arts bills have been paid in the amount of $ __________.

____
EMPLOYE'S SIGNATURE DATE

____
ADDRESS

The employer/insurance company hereby agrees that no representations have been made to claimant other than those contained in this agreement and that this complies with 34 Pa. Code 121.17(a).

____
EMPLOYER/INSURANCE COMPANY SIGNATURE

37-CSF-7 R6

7:2.8 Statement of Wages

COMMONWEALTH OF PENNSYLVANIA
DEPARTMENT OF LABOR AND INDUSTRY
BUREAU OF WORKERS' COMPENSATION
HARRISBURG, PENNSYLVANIA 17111

STATEMENT
OF
WAGES

____
EMPLOYE SOCIAL SECURITY NUMBER

____
EMPLOYER/INSURER CLAIM NUMBER

EMPLOYE ______________________

ADDRESS ______________________

EMPLOYER ______________________

ADDRESS ______________________

DATE OF INJURY ______________________

THE FOLLOWING WAGE INFORMATION MUST BE COMPLETED IN ACCORDANCE WITH SECTION 309 OF THE PENNSYLVANIA WORKMEN'S COMPENSATION ACT AND ATTACHED TO NOTICE OF COMPENSATION PAYABLE OR AGREEMENT IN THE EVENT INJURED EMPLOYE OR DEPENDENT WILL RECEIVE LESS THAN THE MAXIMUM COMPENSATION RATE ALLOWABLE.

1. If wages fixed by:

(a) week .... $__________

(b) Month $__________ times 12 divided by 52 = $__________

(c) Year $__________ divided by 52 = $__________

2. If wages fixed by day, hour, or output, including overtime and bonus:

	FROM	TO	WAGES	BOARD* LODGING*	GRATUITIES**	TOTAL	DAYS WORKED
1st Period	______	______	$______	$______	$______	$______	______
2nd Period	______	______	$______	$______	$______	$______	______
3rd Period	______	______	$______	$______	$______	$______	______
4th Period	______	______	$______	$______	$______	$______	______

* include at actual value of board and/or lodging

** include if employe receives at least 1/3 of wages in tips or gratuities

Computation:

(a) Highest period

$__________ divided by 13 weeks = $__________

(b) Last two completed quarters

$__________ total wages divided by total days times 5 = $__________

(c) If employment less than one full period

$__________ total wages divided by __________ total days worked times __________ total number of work days in period divided by 13 = $__________

3. If occupation exclusively seasonal:

$__________ total wages from all occupations during 12 calendar months preceding injury divided by 50 = $__________

4. Wages under Section 309(f): $__________

REMARKS ______________________

____

BASED ON ABOVE INFORMATION, THE HIGHEST AVERAGE WEEKLY WAGE FOR INJURED EMPLOYE IS $__________

☐ LIBERTY MUTUAL INS. CO. (BUREAU CODE #025)
☐ LIBERTY MUTUAL FIRE INS. CO. (BUREAU CODE #257)
☐ LIBERTY INSURANCE CORP. (BUREAU CODE #2138)

COMPENSATION PAYABLE: $__________ PER WEEK

____
EMPLOYER/INSURER NAME

LIBC-494 (8/72) 37-CSF-5 R1

7:2.9 Short-term Disability Claim Form

SHORT-TERM DISABILITY CLAIM FORM

NOTICE AND PROOF OF CLAIM FOR DISABILITY BENEFITS DB-450(12-81)

CLAIMANT: Read The Following Instructions Carefully

1. USE THIS FORM ONLY IF YOU BECOME SICK OR DISABLED **WHILE EMPLOYED** OR IF YOU BECOME SICK OR DISABLED **WITHIN FOUR (4) WEEKS AFTER TERMINATION OF EMPLOYMENT.** USE **GREEN** CLAIM FORM **DB-300** IF YOU **BECOME** SICK OR DISABLED AFTER HAVING BEEN **UNEMPLOYED MORE THAN FOUR (4) WEEKS.**
2. YOU MUST COMPLETE ALL ITEMS OF PART A-THE **"CLAIMANT'S STATEMENT".** BE ACCURATE. CHECK ALL DATES.
3. BE SURE TO DATE AND SIGN YOUR CLAIM (SEE ITEM 12.). IF YOU CANNOT SIGN THIS CLAIM FORM, YOUR REPRESENTATIVE MAY SIGN IN YOUR BEHALF. IN THAT EVENT, THE REPRESENTATIVE'S RELATIONSHIP TO YOU AND HIS ADDRESS SHOULD BE NOTED UNDER HIS SIGNATURE.
4. **DO NOT MAIL THIS CLAIM UNLESS YOUR DOCTOR COMPLETES AND SIGNS PART B- THE "DOCTOR'S STATEMENT".**
5. YOUR COMPLETED CLAIM SHOULD BE MAILED **WITHIN TWENTY (20) DAYS AFTER YOU BECOME SICK OR DISABLED TO YOUR LAST EMPLOYER OR HIS INSURANCE COMPANY.**

PART A- CLAIMANT'S STATEMENT (Please Print or Type) ANSWER ALL QUESTIONS

1. My Name is ______ (First, Middle, Last)
2. My Social Security Number is: ☐☐☐ ☐☐ ☐☐☐☐
3. Address ______ (Number, Street, City or Town, State, Zip Code, Apt. No.)

   Tel. No. ______
4. My Age is ______
5. Married (Check One) ☐ Yes ☐ No
6. My disability is (if injury, also state how, when and where it occurred) ______
7. I became disabled on ______ (Mo. Day Year)

   a. I worked on that day............ ☐ Yes ☐ No

   b. I have since worked for wages or profit ☐ Yes ☐ No If "Yes", give dates ______
8. Give name of last employer. If more than one employer during last eight (8) weeks, name all employers.

Employer's			Dates of Employment		Average Weekly Wages (Include Bonuses, Tips, Commissions, Reasonable Value of Board, Rent etc.)
Business Name	Business Address	Telephone No.	From Mo. Day Yr.	Through Mo. Day Yr.	

9. My job is or was ______ (Occupation) ______ (Name of Union and Local No., If member)
10. For the period of disability covered by this claim

    a. Are you receiving wages, salary or separation pay: .... ☐ Yes ☐ No

    b. Are you receiving or claiming:

    (1) Worker's Compensation for work-connected disability .... ☐ Yes ☐ No

    (2) Damages for personal injury............ ☐ Yes ☐ No

    (3) Unemployment Insurance Benefits............ ☐ Yes ☐ No

    (4) Disability Benefits under the Federal Social Security Act............ ☐ Yes ☐ No

    If "yes" is checked in any of the items a, b(1), b(2), b(3), or b(4), fill in the following:

    I have ☐ Received or ☐ Claimed from ______ for the period ______ (Date) to ______ (Date)
11. I have received disability benefits for another period or periods of disability within the 52 weeks immediately before my present disability began .... ☐ Yes ☐ No

    If Yes, fill in the following: I have been paid by ______ From ______ To ______
12. I have read the instructions above. I hereby claim Disability Benefits and certify that for the period covered by this claim I was disabled; and that the foregoing statements, including any accompanying statements, are to the best of my knowledge true and complete.

SIGN HERE

Claim signed on ______ (Date) ______ (Claimant's Signature)

If signed by other than claimant, print below: name, address, and relationship of representative.

______ (Name and Address) ______ (Relationship)

IF YOU HAVE ANY QUESTIONS ABOUT CLAIMING DISABILITY BENEFITS, CONTACT THE NEAREST OFFICE OF THE NEW YORK STATE WORKERS' COMPENSATION BOARD, OR WRITE TO: WORKERS' COMPENSATION BOARD, DISABILITY BENEFITS BUREAU, 100 BROADWAY-MENANDS, ALBANY, N.Y. 12241.	SI SE LE OCURREN ALGUNAS PREGUNTAS RESPECTO A RECLAMAR BENEFICIOS POR INCAPACIDAD, COMUNIQUESE CON SU OFICINA MAS CERCANA DE LA JUNTA DE COMPENSACION OBRERA DE NUEVA YORK, O ESCRIBA A: WORKERS' COMPENSATION BOARD, DISABILITY BENEFITS BUREAU, 100 BROADWAY-MENANDS, ALBANY, N.Y. 12241.

DOCTOR MUST COMPLETE PART B ON REVERSE SIDE

ANY PERSON WHO KNOWINGLY AND WITH INTENT TO DEFRAUD ANY INSURANCE COMPANY FILES A STATEMENT OF CLAIM CONTAINING ANY MATERIALLY FALSE INFORMATION, OR CONCEALS FOR THE PURPOSE OF MISLEADING, INFORMATION CONCERNING ANY FACT MATERIAL THERETO, COMMITS A FRAUDULENT INSURANCE ACT, WHICH IS A CRIME.

SHORT-TERM DISABILITY CLAIM FORM page 2

NOTICE AND PROOF OF CLAIM FOR DISABILITY BENEFITS

IMPORTANT: USE THIS FORM ONLY WHEN THE CLAIMANT BECOMES SICK OR DISABLED **WHILE EMPLOYED OR** BECOMES SICK AND DISABLED **WITHIN FOUR (4) WEEKS AFTER TERMINATION OF EMPLOYMENT.** OTHERWISE USE GREEN CLAIM FORM DB-300.

PART B- DOCTOR'S STATEMENT (Please Print or Type)

The doctor's statement must be filled in completely. For item 7-d, give approximate date. Make some estimate. Delay in the payment of Disability Benefits may be prevented. If disability is caused by or arising in connection with pregnancy, enter estimated delivery date under "Remarks".

1. Claimant's Name ____________ (First / Middle / Last) 2. Age ______ 3. ☐ Male ☐ Female
4. Diagnosis/Analysis: ____________
   a. Claimant's Symptoms: ____________
   b. Objective Findings: ____________
5. Claimant Hospitalized? From ______ To ______
6. Operation Indicated? a. Type ______ b. Date ______
7. Enter Dates for the Following:

	Mo.	Day	Year
a. Date of your first treatment for this disability			
b. Date of your most recent treatment for this disability			
c. Date Claimant was unable to work because of this disability			
d. Date Claimant will be able to perform usual work			

(Even if considerable question exists, estimate date. Avoid use of terms such as unknown or undetermined.)

8. In your opinion, is this disability the result of injury arising out of and in the course of employment or occupational disease? ☐ Yes ☐ No

   If yes, has Form C-4, C-4C or C-4P been filed with the Board? ☐ Yes ☐ No

   Remarks (Attach additional sheet, if necessary): ____________

9. I affirm that I am a ______ (Physician, Podiatrist, Chiropractor, Dentist) Licensed in the State of ______ License No. ______

   Doctor's Signature ______ Date ______
   Doctor's Name (Please Print) ______ Tel No. ______
   Office Address ______ (Number / Street / City or Town / State / Zip Code)

EMPLOYER'S NOTICE OF GROUP ACCIDENT AND HEALTH CLAIM

1. Name of Employer		2. Policy Symbol & Number
3. Address		
4. Name of Employee		5. Effective Date of Employee's Coverage
6. Date of Employment	7. Date Laid Off	8. Date Employment Terminated
9. Average Weekly Wages for eight weeks preceeding Disability $	10. Number or days worked each week - Please check: M T W T F S S	
11. Do facts warrant consideration as Workers' Compensation Claim?		12. Occupation
13. Do you deduct from this Employee's wages contributions toward the cost of this coverage? Yes No	14. Is the Employee claiming or receiving wages, salary, separation pay, unemployment insurance Workers' Compensation benefits or other benefits for the period covered by this Disability? Yes No	
15. If salary, do you wish to be reimbursed? Yes No	16. Date Employee last worked	
17. Date Disability began	18. Has Employee returned to work?	19. If so, Date

20. Dated ______ 19 ___ Signature For Employer ______ Phone No. ______

TITLE ______

GB-4M24a Ptd. in U S A DB-450(12-81)

7:3 Health Insurance Forms and Other Flexible Benefits

With the rising cost of medical care, employer-provided health insurance has become a crucial employee benefit. Components of health coverage can range from basic hospitalization to comprehensive coverage. The forms that follow provide examples of standard hospitalization and health insurance enrollment forms. In addition to basic hospitalization, most employers also provide other benefits such as vision and dental care, life insurance and flexible benefits programs. The remainder of this section provides examples of enrollment and claims forms that pertain to these benefits.

7:3.1 Hospital Plan Enrollment Form

This form is an example of an application that is used to enroll employees and their dependents in a basic hospitalization plan. Frequently, surgical benefits and major medical coverage are added to the basic hospitalization plan. They are "wrapped around" the basic hospital coverage to provide more complete medical protection.

Surgical coverage pays surgeons' fees for any operation performed. Major medical coverage covers the remainder of health benefits costs that are not covered by either the basic or surgical benefits plans. Major medical coverage is "diagnostic," that is, the coverage takes effect and payment is made only after an illness or disease is diagnosed and treated.

APPLICATION FOR ENROLLMENT IN HOSPITAL PLAN

Empire
Blue Cross Blue Shield

622 Third Avenue
New York, N.Y. 10017

Hospital Application
(Submit only through your Group)

(HEREAFTER REFERRED TO AS THE PLAN)

Instructions:
1. Print all information in ink.
2. Complete all 15 items.
3. Submit only through your group.

GROUP ADMINISTRATOR COMPLETES

Group Number	Sub. Div.	Group Name
Group Address (No. & Street, City, State, Zip Code)		

APPLICANT COMPLETES

1. Social Security Number

2. Last Name	First Name	Continue Middle Name Here	3. Date of Birth Mo. Day Yr.

4. ☐ Male ☐ Female ☐ Single ☐ Married ☐ Widowed ☐ Divorced ☐ Legally Separated	5. Date Employed Mo. Day Yr.	6. Date of Marriage Mo. Day Yr.	7. First Name of Spouse	8. Spouse's Birthdate Mo. Day Yr.

9. Applicant's Occupation	10. Street Address (No. and Street)

City	State	Zip Code

11. If you presently have hospital or medical insurance with another insurance company please answer the following:	Type of Policy ☐ Ind. ☐ Family ☐ Group ☐ Non-Group	Policy Holder's Name	Name of Insurance Company

12. List below name(s) of unmarried children under 19 years (or who became 19 in this calendar year)

First Name List in order of age (oldest first)	Relationship Son	Relationship Dgtr.	Date of Birth Mo.	Date of Birth Day	Date of Birth Year

13. If you or your spouse is now a subscriber of this or any Blue Cross or Blue Shield Plan please insert all information below. In addition, if you wish to have that contract cancelled and membership transferred to the contract being applied for please indicate by checking the appropriate box. ☐ Yes ☐ No

Certificate Number		Suffix	

Plan Name

14. **120 Day Hospital Service Contract**

Please Check appropriate box for Individual or Family Coverage

Important: To cover spouse and/or dependent children apply for a Family Contract.

Type of Contract	Suffix	Monthly Charges
Individual	K10	☐ **$ 49.60**
Family	W10	☐ **$112.95**

Your contract contains a limitation on benefits for conditions, symptoms and diseases which were present prior to the effective date of your coverage.

Refer to your contract for a full explanation of your benefits.

I hereby apply for the Hospital Service Contract of the type checked. If this application is for a family contract, the names of my spouse and unmarried children under 19 years of age are listed, and I make this application on their behalf as well as my own. I understand that for the purposes of this application, a child shall be considered under 19 until December 31 of the year in which he attains the age 19 years. If application is accepted, benefits under certificate issued will be available from the effective dates shown. Unless my employer pays all the charges for said contract, I agree to pay the charges thereon in advance, and I direct my employer, as Remitting Agent, to deduct such charges from my wages or salary and to remit them to the Plan until further notice. If I am now a subscriber under an existing contract identical to the one applied for herein, I agree that such existing contract shall continue and this application shall not apply thereto, but that the effective date of such existing contract shall be deemed changed, except for computing waiting periods, to the effective date of the contract to be issued pursuant to this application. All information furnished hereon is true and complete and shall be deemed representations made to induce issuance of the contract applied for.

15. Signature	Date signed:	Effective Date Mo. Day Yr.	OKEdit ☐	Suffix	T.C.	Certificate Number

(Last five columns: FOR OFFICE USE ONLY)

LGL0093 2 Reprinted with permission of Empire Blue Cross and Blue Shield, New York, N.Y. (4-88)

7:3.2 Comprehensive Hospitalization Coverage Application

Hospital coverage does not have to be separated from the rest of the group health insurance program. All health coverage may be combined with one carrier. This type of coverage, called comprehensive coverage, is usually diagnostic in approach.

This form is an example of a form that may be used to enroll employees in a comprehensive group health insurance program. This same form can also be used to wrap surgical and major medical coverage around a basic hospitalization plan provided by a different carrier. The shaded areas at the top are to be completed by the employer, and the white areas must be completed by the employee.

If used correctly, the form serves two purposes. First, it is a communication device that asks employees to verify the type of coverage (single or dependent) they want to receive. It alerts them of their enrollment in the program and that there also may be a payroll deduction for the coverage.

The form's second purpose is demonstrated in the question that item 10 raises: "Does your spouse have group health coverage through another employer, union, etc.?" Once this question has been answered, the form becomes the employer's permanent record of whether the employee's spouse has group health insurance under another program. Then, when a claim is submitted, every effort should be made to coordinate payment on the claim.

This comprehensive coverage form attempts to be all-inclusive by providing space for dependent and optional benefits (e.g., optical and/or dental) to be filled in (item 11). Right below (item 12), there is also space allocated for the listing of a beneficiary for accidental death and dismemberment insurance, which takes effect when an employee is injured on a company business trip. As with Form 7:3.1, one copy of this form should be submitted to the carrier and the other kept in the personnel department as a permanent record.

HEALTH INSURANCE APPLICATION

COMPREHENSIVE HEALTH INSURANCE APPLICATION

Please type or print. Press firmly.

Employer—*Complete all shaded areas at the top of the card.* **Employee**—*Complete all unshaded areas.*

Name of employer		Group number		Account number
Date of full-time employment *(month, day, year)*	Date of eligibility *(month, day, year)*			Annual salary
1. Employee's name *(last, first, middle initial)*		Certificate number	2. Employee's job title	
3. Date of birth *(month, day, year)*	4. ☐ Male ☐ Female	5. ☐ Single ☐ Married ☐ Widowed ☐ Divorced		
6. Do you want dependent coverage? ☐ Yes ☐ No *(If "yes," complete sections 8, 9, 10, and 17.)*			7. Social Security number	

Fill in only if your plan has dependent benefits:

8. Number of eligible dependents *(including spouse)*	9. Birthday of spouse *(month, day, year)*	10. Does your spouse have group health coverage through another employer, union, etc.? ☐ Yes ☐ No

Fill in only if your plan has optional benefits:

11. Indicate benefits desired: ☐ None ☐ All ☐ All, except following:

Fill in only if your plan has group life or AD&D benefits:

12. Beneficiary's name *(last, first, middle initial)*	14. Relationship to you
13. Beneficiary's address *(street, city, state, zip)*	

Unless otherwise provided herein, if two or more beneficiaries are named, the proceeds shall be paid in equal shares to the named beneficiaries if surviving the insured, or to the survivor or survivors. If no beneficiary survives, payment shall be made in accordance with the terms of the policy. Subject to revocation by me by written notice to my employer, I request the coverage provided from time to time by my employer's group plan(s) and authorize the required deduction (if any) from my wages.

X__________________________ X__________________________

15. Date signed

16. Employee's signature

For insurance company/administrator use only

Effective date	Salary/Wage	Coverages—Class and/or amount							
		Life	AD&D	LTD	A&S	Dental	Health		

Note: Attach a copy of all beneficiary changes to this card.

17. Fill in only for dependent coverage:

Dependent's name *(last, first, middle initial)*	Date of birth	Relationship

7:3.3 Coverage Waiver Form

If eligible employees refuse to participate in a health care plan, a permanent record should be made, regardless of whether they decide at a later date to accept coverage. Not having such written documentation of an employee's waiver of coverage is risky. The employee (or his or her family) may, at another time, claim otherwise. This form is an example of a form that might be used for this purpose.

WAIVER OF COVERAGE

MEDICAL/DENTAL/VISION COVERAGE WAIVER/DROP FORM

I, ______________________, an employee of ______________________,
Employee Subsidiary
elect to:

_____ Decline coverage under the company's medical/dental/vision plan with ______________________ Insurance Company.

_____ Drop all coverage under the company's medical/dental/vision plan with ______________________ Insurance Company.

______________________ Employee Signature ______________________ Date

______________________ Witness ______________________ Date

7:3.4 Life Insurance Application

Group life insurance coverage is usually offered to employees as part of the insurance package obtained from the insurance carrier. More often than not, there is no cost for the basic coverage. Frequently, there is an option for the employee to obtain additional coverage, which sometimes extends to the employee's spouse and/or other dependents. Form 7:3.4 is an example of a form used for obtaining additional life insurance coverage for the employee, the employee's spouse, and/or their children.

Employers should ask employees to periodically review the names of their beneficiaries, ensuring that the named beneficiaries are, in fact, still correct.

APPLICATION FOR LIFE INSURANCE

APPLICATION FOR VOLUNTARY TERM LIFE INSURANCE

Please complete the entire application

Amount of Coverage Desired ($25,000 increments): $ ______	Amount of Children's Coverage: ☐ $5,000 ☐ $7,500 ☐ $10,000 *Beneficiary for Children's coverage is the applicant

Full Name (Last, First, Middle):	Sex M☐ F☐

Address (Street, City, State, Zip Code):

Birthdate:	Place of Birth:	Height:	Weight:

Beneficiary (Last, First, Middle):	Relationship:	Address (Street, City, State, Zip Code):

Unless otherwise stated, this beneficiary designation is revocable and beneficiaries designated to share proceeds shall share equally and with the right of survivorship.

1. Have you consulted a physician or received any medical care, advice or treatment (including prescribed medications you have taken) for any condition or illness during the past 12 months? ☐ Yes ☐ No
2. Have you received medical or surgical care or advice during the past five years? ☐ Yes ☐ No
3. Have you ever had or been told you had nervous or lung disorders, heart disease or murmur, high blood pressure, rheumatic fever, ulcers, cancer, diabetes, arthritis, kidney disease, albumin or sugar in urine, tuberculosis, severe injury or disease? ☐ Yes ☐ No
4. Name/address of regular physician ______
5. Have you ever had life or health insurance declined, postponed, rated, cancelled, or renewal refused? ☐ Yes ☐ No

   (If "Yes," Please Give Details.) ______
6. Will any of the insurance proposed in this application replace any life insurance or annuities now in force? ☐ Yes ☐ No

   (If "Yes," Please Give Details.) ______

If you answered "Yes" to Questions 1, 2, and/or 3, Please Give Full Details Below . . . (If you need more space, attach a separate sheet signed and dated.)

Nature of illness or injury and type of treatment	Date of treatment	Physician's name and address *(Include your medical or clinic I.D. number if any.)*

AGREEMENT

I represent to the best of my knowledge and belief that the answers on this application are complete, true, and provided to obtain insurance. I understand and agree that no coverage shall take effect as a result of this application unless this application is approved by [insurance company]; I further agree that my coverage shall begin on the "Effective Date" to be assigned by [insurance company], provided I am actively at work.

Date Signed	Signature of Applicant

PLEASE READ AND SIGN AUTHORIZATION ON BACK OF APPLICATION

PAYROLL DEDUCTION AUTHORIZATION—EMPLOYEE COVERAGE

Subject to revocation by me in writing, I hereby authorize ______ (Name of Employer) to deduct from my wages the premium for the above coverage, and to remit such premiums to [insurance company].

DATE SIGNED __/__/__ SIGNATURE OF EMPLOYEE ______

APPLICATION FOR VOLUNTARY TERM LIFE INSURANCE

page 2

Please Read Below, Date, and Sign

AUTHORIZATION AND ACKNOWLEDGMENT

For underwriting purposes, I give my permission to:

Any physician or other medical practitioner, hospital, clinic, other medical or medically related facility, insurance or reinsurance company, or employer to give Life Insurance Company (LIC) ALL INFORMATION on my behalf (except as limited below), including findings on medical care, psychiatric or psychological care or examination, or surgery as they apply to me or any of my children who are to be insured.

LIMITATIONS, if any:

I understand all or part of this information may be sent to the insurance carrier. It may also be made available to any reinsurer, employee, or contractor who processes transactions that concern my insurance I may have applied for or have with LIC.

I know that my medical records, including any alcohol or drug abuse information, may be protected by federal regulations—42CFR Part 2. I give my permission to LIC to get any and all such information for the purposes described in this form. I specifically consent to the redisclosure of such information as set forth in this form. I may revoke this authorization as it applies to any information protected by this federal regulation at any time, but not to the extent action has been taken in reliance on it.

I understand that my additional written consent will be required before any information described above is given, sold, transferred, or in any way, relayed to another party not previously specified (unless otherwise provided by law). My additional consent must be provided on a form that states the new use of the information or why another party needs it.

I know that I have a right to get a copy of this form. A photocopy of this form will be as valid as the original. This form will be valid for 30 months from the date shown below or for 2 years from the date the policy is issued, whichever is earlier.

I acknowledge that I have been given LIC's Insurance Information Practices Notice and Notice Regarding the plan.

____________________ x____________________________

Date Signature of Proposed Insured

7:3.5 Flexible Benefits Enrollment Form

Flexibility in benefits programs is a radical concept that shifts more of the benefits selection responsibility from the employer to the employee. This approach was invented by consultants who recognized the opportunity that Internal Revenue Code Section 125 provided for getting pretaxed dollar contributions for insurance costs (including premiums).

The consultants' idea was a simple one: Employees should make decisions regarding their benefits to ensure that they are selecting only those benefits (including health care, child care, and insurance benefits) that are relevant and suitable for their particular needs. Additionally, if employees have a choice in determining where their premium dollars are spent and they follow certain requirements, then the dollars paid for their specific benefits can be deducted from wages before taxes are taken out. Recently, the tax protection was reduced to include only those dollars set aside and spent during the year, but the tax benefit otherwise remains in effect.

In addition to the tax benefit, employers stand to gain much more by using the flexible benefits approach. Flexible benefits enable employers to spend money on only those benefits that their employees select. Employees, in turn, must be more aware of benefits than ever before because they have to make the decision regarding their coverages.

Besides shifting some costs of health care benefits to employees, flexible benefits set a new tone as well. For instance, employees would never want to take away any benefit once it is offered, unless the removed benefit—and this must be conveyed to employees—is being replaced with a new and improved benefit. Flexible benefits help solve this problem.

An organization must be large to even consider administering a flexible benefits plan. If there is insufficient participation, the insurance carrier may withdraw from the proposal. Also important to consider is the question of comprehensive expense. An organization must determine how much extra effort will be required if a flexible plan is introduced.

This is an example of an enrollment form that may be used for a flexible benefits program. It is simple to use and can be easily revised by those organizations whose plans differ in the options that they offer.

The flexible benefits enrollment form alerts employees of the price they will be charged for the premiums. The form also subtly warns employees that premium costs will come out of their wages. The option letter column refers to the specific program selected.

FLEXIBLE BENEFITS ENROLLMENT FORM

Flexible Benefits Plan Enrollment Form

Name:
Location:
Social Security Number:

Plan Year:
April 1, 19____
March 31, 19____

			Option Letter	*Price Tag (Pre-Tax)*
Medical Plan	☐ Single	☐ Family	☐	$
Dental Plan	☐ Single	☐ Family	☐	$
Life Insurance			☐	$
Employee AD&D			☐	$
Dependent AD&D			☐	$
Health Care Spending Account				$
Dependent Care Spending Account				$
Vacation			☐	$
Long-Term Disability			☐	$
	▶ Your Pre-Tax Total			$
	▶ Your Allowance			$
	▶ If your Pre-Tax Total is *greater* than your Allowance, write the difference here			$
	▶ If your Pre-Tax Total is *less* than your Allowance, write the difference here			$
Long-Term Disability	After-Tax $		☐	
Dependent Life Insurance	After-Tax $		☐	

SIGNATURE ____________________ DATE ____________________

BUSINESS PHONE ____________________

7:3.6 Claims Forms

Claim forms are usually prepared by insurance companies and are used to activate the insurance. (The employee gets reimbursed from the insurance company.) There are benefits managers who are of the opinion that the claim forms should never be seen by the human resources department after they are completed.

Other benefits managers are of the opposite opinion. They argue that if claims are not reviewed before they are sent to the insurance carrier, the employer loses all control of the claims process. However, maximum care must be taken to ensure that the confidentiality of claims is maintained at all times. This means that each employee's claims should be filed separately, away from the rest of the employee's personnel data file. Three sample claim forms are provided at the end of this chapter:

- Conventional group health first-time insurance claim (Form 7:3.6A);
- Flexible benefits claim (Form 7:3.6B); and
- Dental insurance claim (Form 7:3.6C).

7:3.6A Conventional Group Health First-time Insurance Claim

HEALTH INSURANCE CLAIM FORM

CONVENTIONAL GROUP HEALTH FIRST-TIME INSURANCE CLAIM

Employee Instructions

EMPLOYEE: Read and Detach This Page Before Completing Part 1

When to File a First Notice of Claim Form

1. A new claim is being submitted for a different family member.
2. A new claim is being submitted for a completely different illness or injury.

How to File a Claim

1. Complete the applicable items on pages 2 and 3.
2. Promptly mail page 2, with any itemized bills, to the insurance company at the above address.
3. Ask your doctor to complete and mail page 3 directly to the insurance company.
4. If you receive additional bills in connection with this claim after you have mailed page 2 of this form, do not complete another form. Identify the bills by adding your employer's name and employee Social Security number. Mail them to the insurance company.

Important:

All medical bills that you send to the insurance company must show the name of your employer and employee Social Security number. You may write your employer's name anywhere on the face of the bill. Also, all bills must show name of patient, date of service, and charge.

In addition, all bills for items listed below must show:

Prescription: Rx number. Note—Cash register receipts or cancelled checks are not accepted as bills.
Doctors: Type of treatment and diagnosis.
Registered Nurses: Time spent.
Anesthesia: Anesthesia time.
X-Ray & Laboratory: Type of work done.

CONVENTIONAL GROUP HEALTH FIRST-TIME INSURANCE CLAIM

page 2

PART 1: Complete for all claims.

EMPLOYEE NAME *(Last and First)*	EMPLOYEE DATE OF BIRTH MONTH / DAY / YEAR	EMPLOYEE SOCIAL SECURITY NO. — —	PATIENT NAME

EMPLOYEE ADDRESS Number Street *City* *State* *Zip Code*	EMPLOYEE TELEPHONE NUMBER AREA CODE / NUMBER

IS EMPLOYEE ☐ MARRIED ☐ SEPARATED ☐ SINGLE ☐ DIVORCED ☐ WIDOWED	*(If divorced and claim is for dependent child, please furnish other parent's name, address, employer and employer's address)*

DO YOU HAVE MORE THAN ONE EMPLOYER? *(If Yes, give name and address of other employer)* ☐ YES ☐ NO	EMPLOYER TELEPHONE NUMBER AREA CODE / NUMBER

IF YOU ARE ELIGIBLE FOR BENEFITS FROM ANY OTHER GROUP HEALTH INSURANCE (INCLUDING MEDICARE) PLEASE GIVE NAME AND ADDRESS OF OTHER INSURANCE OR EMPLOYER.

IS PATIENT ☐ EMPLOYEE ☐ CHILD ☐ SPOUSE ☐ OTHER	IS PATIENT ☐ MALE ☐ FEMALE	PATIENT'S DATE OF BIRTH MONTH / DAY / YEAR; PATIENT'S SOCIAL SECURITY NO. — —	IS PATIENT ELIGIBLE FOR MEDICARE BENEFITS? ☐ YES ☐ NO *If Yes, enter date of eligibility* ______

NATURE OF ILLNESS OR INJURY	OCCUPATIONAL ILLNESS OR INJURY ☐ YES ☐ NO	IF CLAIM IS DUE TO ACCIDENT STATE WHEN, WHERE AND HOW ACCIDENT OCCURRED

PART 2: Complete if you are married or separated.

NAME OF SPOUSE	SPOUSE'S DATE OF BIRTH MONTH / DAY / YEAR	SPOUSE'S SOCIAL SECURITY NUMBER — —	IS YOUR SPOUSE EMPLOYED? ☐ YES *(Give name/location of employer)* ☐ *NO* *(Give name/location of last employer and date last worked)*

EMPLOYER'S PHONE NO. AREA CODE / NUMBER	NAME OF SPOUSE'S GROUP HEALTH BENEFIT CARRIER (OTHER THAN THIS PLAN)	CERTIFICATE OR POLICY NUMBER

PART 3: Complete if for a dependent other than your spouse.

NAME OF DEPENDENT	DEPENDENT DATE OF BIRTH	IF CLAIM IS FOR DEPENDENT CHILD AGE 19 OR OVER, INDICATE ☐ STUDENT ☐ HANDICAPPED *GIVE NAME AND LOCATION OF SCHOOL* ______ ☐ PART TIME ☐ FULL TIME

IS DEPENDENT EMPLOYED? *(If Yes, give name and address of employer)* ☐ YES ☐ NO	EMPLOYER'S PHONE NO. AREA CODE / NUMBER
NAME OF DEPENDENT'S OTHER BENEFIT CARRIER	CERTIFICATE OR POLICY NUMBER

PART 4: Complete for all claims.

I hereby certify that the above statements are complete and accurate to the best of my knowledge. I also agree to reimburse [insurance company] to the extent of any overpayment which is in excess of the amounts payable under the benefit plan with [insurance company].

ANY PERSON WHO KNOWINGLY AND WITH INTENT TO INJURE, DEFRAUD, OR DECEIVE ANY INSURANCE COMPANY, FILES A STATEMENT OF CLAIM CONTAINING ANY FALSE, INCOMPLETE OR MISLEADING INFORMATION MAY BE GUILTY OF A CRIMINAL ACT PUNISHABLE UNDER LAW.

EMPLOYEE SIGNATURE ______________________ DATE ______________

EMPLOYEE PLEASE SIGN ON PAGE 3 ALSO

PART 5: FOR INTERNAL USE ONLY.

BENEFITS IN FORCE ☐ YES ☐ NO	ACCOUNT	DATE BENEFITS BECAME EFFECTIVE EMP MO. / DAY / YEAR; DEP. MO. / DAY / YEAR	DATE BENEFITS TERMINATED EMP MO. / DAY / YEAR; DEP. MO. / DAY / YEAR

SIGNATURE OF EMPLOYEE CERTIFYING BENEFITS	DATE

PAGE 2

CONVENTIONAL GROUP HEALTH FIRST-TIME INSURANCE CLAIM

page 3

EMPLOYEE NAME *(Last and First)*	EMPLOYEE DATE OF BIRTH MONTH / DAY / YEAR	EMPLOYEE SOCIAL SECURITY NO. — —	PATIENT NAME

EMPLOYEE ADDRESS *Number* *Street*	*City*	*State*	*Zip Code*	EMPLOYEE TELEPHONE NUMBER AREA CODE / NUMBER

TO BE COMPLETED BY EMPLOYEE

AUTHORIZATION TO PAY BENEFITS TO PHYSICIAN: I hereby authorize payment directly to the undersigned Physician of the Surgical and/or Medical Benefits, if any, otherwise payable to me for the services described below but not to exceed the reasonable and customary charge for those services.	SIGNED (EMPLOYEE) DATE
AUTHORIZATION TO RELEASE INFORMATION: I hereby authorize the undersigned Physician to release any information acquired in the course of my examination or treatment.	SIGNED (PATIENT, OR PARENT IF MINOR) DATE

PART 6: TO BE COMPLETED BY ATTENDING PHYSICIAN

14. DATE OF:	*ILLNESS (FIRST SYMPTOM) OR INJURY (ACCIDENT) OR PREGNANCY (LMP)*	15. DATE FIRST CONSULTED YOU FOR THIS CONDITION	16. HAS PATIENT EVER HAD SAME OR SIMILAR SYMPTOMS? ☐ YES ☐ NO
17. DATE PATIENT ABLE TO RETURN TO WORK	18. DATE OF TOTAL DISABILITY FROM	THROUGH	DATE OF PARTIAL DISABILITY FROM / THROUGH
19. NAME OF REFERRING PHYSICIAN			20. FOR SERVICES RELATED TO HOSPITALIZATION GIVE HOSPITALIZATION DATES ADMITTED / DISCHARGED
21. NAME & ADDRESS OF FACILITY WHERE SERVICES RENDERED *(If other than home or office)*			22. WAS LABORATORY WORK PERFORMED OUTSIDE YOUR OFFICE? ☐ YES ☐ NO CHARGES:

23. DIAGNOSIS OR NATURE OF ILLNESS OR INJURY. RELATE DIAGNOSIS TO PROCEDURE IN COLUMN D BY REFERENCE TO NUMBERS 1, 2, 3, ETC. OR DX CODE

1.

2.

3.

4.

24. A DATE OF SERVICE	B* PLACE OF SERVICE	C PROCEDURE CODE (IDENTIFY:)	FULLY DESCRIBE PROCEDURES, MEDICAL SERVICES OR SUPPLIES FURNISHED FOR EACH DATE GIVEN *(Explain Unusual Services or Circumstances)*	D DIAGNOSIS CODE	E CHARGES	F

25. SIGNATURE OF PHYSICIAN OR SUPPLIER	26.	27. TOTAL CHARGE	28. AMOUNT PAID	29. BALANCE DUE
SIGNED *DATE*	30. YOUR SOCIAL SECURITY NO — —	31. PHYSICIAN'S OR SUPPLIER'S NAME, ADDRESS, ZIP CODE & TELEPHONE NO.		
32. YOUR PATIENT'S ACCOUNT NO.	33. YOUR EMPLOYER I.D. NO.	I.D. NO.		

*PLACE OF SERVICE CODES

1—(IH)— Inpatient Hospital	*4—(H)— Patient's Home*	*7—(NH)— Nursing Home*	*0—(OL)— Other Locations*
2—(OH)— Outpatient Hospital	*5— Day Care Facility (PSY)*	*8—(SNF)— Skilled Nursing Facility*	*A—(IL)— Independent Laboratory*
3—(O)— Doctor's Office	*6— Night Care Facility (PSY)*	*9— Ambulance*	*B— Other Medical/Surgical Facility*

APPROVED BY AMA COUNCIL ON MEDICAL SERVICE 6-74

ANY PERSON WHO KNOWINGLY AND WITH INTENT TO INJURE, DEFRAUD, OR DECEIVE ANY INSURANCE COMPANY, FILES A STATEMENT OF CLAIM CONTAINING ANY FALSE, INCOMPLETE OR MISLEADING INFORMATION MAY BE GUILTY OF A CRIMINAL ACT PUNISHABLE UNDER LAW.

7:3.6B Flexible Benefits Claim Form

STATEMENT OF CLAIM FOR FLEXIBLE HEALTH PLAN

PART 1—EMPLOYEE/RETIREE COMPLETES

1. NAME (FIRST, LAST) EMPLOYEE/RETIREE	2. SEX ☐ M ☐ F	3. SOCIAL SECURITY NUMBER-EMPLOYEE/RETIREE	4. TELEPHONE NUMBER HOME ( ) OFFICE ( )
5. PATIENT'S NAME (FIRST, LAST)	6. SEX ☐ M ☐ F	7. PATIENT'S DATE OF BIRTH MO. DAY YR.	8. PATIENT'S OCCUPATION

9. ADDRESS OF EMPLOYEE/RETIREE

NUMBER STREET CITY STATE ZIP CODE

10. IS PATIENT A FULL TIME STUDENT? ☐ YES ☐ NO	11. IS PATIENT MEDICARE ELIGIBLE? ☐ YES ☐ NO	12. RELATIONSHIP OF PATIENT TO EMPLOYEE/RETIREE 1. ☐ SELF 2. ☐ SPOUSE 3. ☐ CHILD ☐ OTHER	13. WAS THIS AN ☐ ACCIDENT ☐ SUDDEN ILLNESS?

INDICATE NATURE OF ACCIDENT/INJURIES SUSTAINED. IF SUDDEN OR SERIOUS ILLNESS GIVE DIAGNOSIS/ACUTE SYMPTOMS.	14. DATE OF ACCIDENT/ILLNESS MO. DAY YR.

15. TIME OF ACCIDENT/ ILLNESS ☐ AM ☐ PM	16. IS ILLNESS OR INJURY CONNECTED WITH YOUR EMPLOYMENT? ☐ YES ☐ NO	17. IS THE PATIENT, SPOUSE, OR DEPENDENT ALSO EMPLOYED OR HAVE OTHER HEALTH INSURANCE COVERAGE? ☐ YES ☐ NO IF YES, PLEASE FILL OUT THE INFORMATION IN BOXES 17A, B AND C.

17A. NAME OF EMPLOYER, UNION OR OTHER GROUP	17B. NAME AND ADDRESS OF OTHER HEALTH INSURANCE CARRIER	17C. OTHER INSURANCE I.D. NUMBER

18. INJURY RELATED TO MOTOR VEHICLE ACCIDENT? ☐ YES ☐ NO	19. I CERTIFY THAT THE ABOVE STATEMENTS ARE CORRECT AND HEREBY AUTHORIZE ANY DOCTOR OR ORGANIZATION TO PROVIDE PERTINENT RECORDS TO INSURANCE COMPANY	SUBSCRIBER'S SIGNATURE

I DIRECT MEDICAL PAYMENT TO ☐ MYSELF ☐ MY PROVIDER	DO YOU WANT THIS CLAIM TO BE PROCESSED THROUGH YOUR FLEXIBLE SPENDING ACCOUNT? ☐ YES ☐ NO

20. PLACE OF SERVICE 1. ☐ INPATIENT HOSPITAL 2. PATIENT'S HOME 3. ☐ PHYSICIAN'S OFFICE AND LABORATORY 4. ☐ OUTPATIENT HOSPITAL 5. ☐ OTHER (SPECIFY)	HOSPITAL NAME AND ADDRESS

21. TIME OF TREATMENT FOR ACCIDENT/ILLNESS ☐ A.M. ☐ P.M.	22. DATE ADMITTED/ TREATED MO. DAY YR.	23. DATE DISCHARGED MO. DAY YR.	24. WAS SURGERY PERFORMED ☐ YES ☐ NO	IF YES, BY WHOM

TYPE OF SURGERY	25. DATE OF SURGERY MO. DAY YR.

PART II—PROVIDER OF SERVICES COMPLETES

26. DIAGNOSIS	27. NAME OF REFERRING DOCTOR (IF ANY)	28. REFER ☐ YES ☐ NO

DESCRIPTION OF SERVICE	PL	TY	PROCEDURE	CD	MOD 1 MOD 2	DX
1.						
2.						
3.						
4.						

EXAMINER I.D.	FEE PAID	STUDENT	EMPLOY	OTHER COVERAGE

DATE OF SERVICE FROM	FEE CHARGED	DATE OF SERVICE TO	UNITS	RCP	MED. ALLOW	CC	PROVIDER NO.	INIT.
1. MO. DAY YR.		MO. DAY YR.						
2. MO. DAY YR.		MO. DAY YR.						
3. MO. DAY YR.		MO. DAY YR.						
4. MO. DAY YR.		MO. DAY YR.						

MED B	ESTATE OF	TOTAL CHARGES	MED ASSIGNED ☐ YES ☐ NO		MED. DEDUCTIBLE	MED PAID		GROUP NUMBER

PROVIDER'S NAME	**MY FEE** ☐ HAS ☐ HAS NOT **BEEN PAID TO ME**
ADDRESS	
CITY, STATE AND ZIP CODE	PROVIDER'S SIGNATURE / DATE SIGNED
TELEPHONE NO. ( ) AREA CODE / PROVIDER'S IRS OR TAX I.D. NO. / PROVIDER CODE / INIT.	I CERTIFY THAT I PERSONALLY RENDERED AND/OR AUTHORIZED THE ABOVE SERVICES / RECEIPT DATE

STATEMENT OF CLAIM FOR FLEXIBLE HEALTH PLAN page 2

PLEASE READ THIS ENTIRE SECTION BEFORE BEGINNING TO FILL OUT YOUR CLAIM FORM

- THIS ALL PURPOSE CLAIM FORM MAY BE USED FOR THE SUBMISSION OF ALL EXPENSES COVERED UNDER [COMPANY] FLEXIBLE HEALTH PLAN.
- **Use a separate claim form** for each person for whom a claim is to be filed.
- **Fill out the form completely and accurately;** all the requested information is essential for fast and accurate processing of your claim(s).
- **Your identification number** is the number on your [insurance company] card. Always use the **employee's or retiree's** identification number on the claim form.

HOW TO FILL OUT YOUR CLAIM FORM

- Always complete all items in Part I of the form, sign and date the claim form, and give it to your doctor or other provider of services who will complete Part II.
- An original itemized bill may be submitted in lieu of completion of Part II. The itemized bill must show name of patient, charges, type and date of services rendered and diagnosis.
- For prescription drugs, you must include the original drug bill. The drug bill must show name of patient, date of purchase, prescription number, separate charge for each prescription and name of prescribing doctor. If your drug bills are incomplete, you may use a Licensed Pharmacist's Statement, signed by the dispensing pharmacist. You may obtain this form by calling the toll-free number.

FLEXIBLE SPENDING ACCOUNT. If the employee has elected to participate in the Flexible Spending Account, this claim may be automatically processed after health plan reimbursement. If you want this claim to be submitted for FSA reimbursement, check the appropriate box on the front of the claim form.

IMPORTANT NOTE REGARDING HOSPITAL CLAIMS:

- IN MOST SITUATIONS THE HOSPITAL WILL BILL [INSURANCE COMPANY] DIRECTLY. IN THESE SITUATIONS YOU ARE NOT REQUIRED TO COMPLETE THIS CLAIM FORM. IF YOU RECEIVE A HOSPITAL BILL FOR COVERED SERVICES, COMPLETE PART I OF THIS FORM, ATTACH THE ITEMIZED HOSPITAL BILL AND SUBMIT BOTH TO THE ADDRESS INDICATED ON THIS CLAIM FORM.

BE SURE TO COMPLETE BOXES 14, 15 AND 16 WHEN YOU ARE BEING BILLED FOR OUTPATIENT SERVICES.

CLAIM FILING INSTRUCTIONS FOR EMPLOYEE/RETIREE OVER AGE 65

If you are eligible for MEDICARE, there are specific claim filing instructions for each coverage option. Please follow the appropriate instructions.

MEDICARE ELIGIBLE PARTICIPANTS

1. BASIC SUPPLEMENTAL TO MEDICARE
   - First, file your claim with Medicare.
   - After you have received your Explanation of Medicare Benefits, send a copy attached to your completed claim form to the address indicated below.
2. SUPPLEMENTAL MAJOR MEDICAL
   - First, file your claim with Medicare.
   - After you have received your Explanation of Medicare Benefits, send a copy and an itemized bill which fully describes the services rendered attached to your completed claim form to the address indicated below.

ACTIVE EMPLOYEES

If you are an active employee of [company] and have elected your Group's coverage, attach the bill to the completed claim form and submit them to the address indicated below. After you have received the Explanation of Benefits from [insurance company] send a copy of the EOB and bill with the claim form to Medicare. These same filing instructions will apply if your covered spouse is age 65 through 69.

"Any person who knowingly and with intent to defraud any insurance company or other person files a statement of claim containing any materially false information, or conceals for the purpose of misleading, information concerning any factual material thereto, commits a fraudulent insurance act, which is a crime."

7:3.6C Dental Claim Form

DENTAL CLAIM FORM

Shaded Area is for Plan Use Only

1. Identification Number: WSU
2. Group Number or Enrollment Code: WSU080
3. Patient's Name (First, Middle Initial, Last)
4. Patient's Date of Birth Mo. Day Year / /
5. Patient's Sex Female ( ) Male ( )
6. Patient's Relationship to Subscriber: Self ( ) Spouse ( ) Child ( ) Other ( ) Explain:
7. Subscriber's Name (First, Middle Initial, Last)
8. Daytime Telephone Number (Include Area Code)

Subscriber's Address (Street and Apt. or Box Number) ☐ Check If New Address | City | State | Zip Code

9. Is the patient covered under other Dental Insurance? No ☐ Yes ☐

If yes, other insurance name:

Name of Policy Holder | Policy or ID Number

If the subscriber is married, is the spouse employed? If yes, give the name of the spouse's employer No ☐ Yes ☐

OFFICE USE ONLY: POI, SOPL

10. Was patient's condition due to:
- Work related accident? No ☐ Yes ☐
- An auto accident? No ☐ Yes ☐
- Other accidental injury? No ☐ Yes ☐

If yes, give the date of accident: Mo. Day Year / /

If an accident, was another party at fault? No ☐ Yes ☐

If yes, please attach a statement with details as to when, where, and the manner in which the injury occurred.

(To be completed by Dentist. See instructions on reverse.)

FACIAL / LINGUAL / RIGHT / LEFT / PERMANENT / PRIMARY / FACIAL

13. MISSING TEETH: Identify missing teeth on chart with X. Indicate, by tooth number, the date each tooth was lost or extracted, if known:

TOOTH	DATE	TOOTH	DATE

11. I certify that the above information is correct and apply for benefits under my dental coverage with Blue Cross and Blue Shield of the National Capital Area. I authorize any dentist or physician in possession of information concerning the patient to furnish such information to Blue Cross and Blue Shield of the National Capital Area upon request.

Signature of Subscriber or Spouse — Date

14. ORTHODONTIA: Is orthodontic treatment included in the services listed below? No ☐ Yes ☐

If yes, is this initial treatment? No ☐ Yes ☐

Date appliance was placed:

Expected completion date of orthodontic treatment:

Total charge for active treatment

12. ASSIGNMENT OF BENEFITS: (Please see the reverse side of this form for further information) No ☐ Yes ☐

If "yes" block above is marked, I authorize Blue Cross and Blue Shield of the National Capital Area to pay benefits directly to the provider of the services listed below.

Signature of Subscriber or Spouse — Date

The Plan may, at its discretion, accept or deny an assignment of benefits.

15. CROWNS, BRIDGES AND DENTURES: Do services include the replacement of a crown, bridge or denture? No ☐ Yes ☐ Mo. Day Year

If yes, indicate date of original placement or restoration and original teeth involved: / /

Reason for replacement: Original Damaged ☐ Lost or Stolen ☐ Other: (explain)

RPL ☐ SPI ☐

16. **Description of Services** (See instructions on reverse.)

Date of Service M	D	Y	A.D.A. Procedure Code	Detailed Description of Services	Tooth No. or Letter	Surfaces	No. of Times Perf.	Place			Charge	Other Ins. Cons.	Other Ins. Paid	A D I	Remark, Notes
											.				
											.				
											.				
											.				
											.				
											.				
											.				
											.				
											.				
											.				

OFFICE USE ONLY: P = RC =

18. TOTAL CHARGE .

19. Are x-rays enclosed? No ☐ Yes ☐

17.

☐ PREDETERMINATION OF BENEFITS

The treatment listed is necessary in my professional judgement and I request Predetermination of Benefits. Note: Dentist's Tax ID Number or Social Security Number is required.

☐ WORK COMPLETED—PAYMENT REQUESTED

I certify that the above services have been performed by me or under my personal supervision and are necessary in my professional judgement. Charges shown are my usual charges.

Dentist's Signature

20.

Dentist's Name — Tax ID No. or SSN

Address

City — State — Zip Code

Reviewed By: PAY ☐ PID ☐

DENTAL CLAIM FORM

page 2

DENTAL CLAIM FORM — GENERAL INFORMATION

Use this claim form to submit a claim for services which are covered under the Dental Program. To avoid delay in having your claim processed, please complete a separate claim form for each patient, and be sure that all information is complete and correct. Items 1 through 12 of this form must be completed by the subscriber or spouse, and items 13 through 20 are to be completed by the dentist.

When the claim form has been completed and signed, please mail it to:

INSTRUCTIONS FOR COMPLETING PATIENT AND SUBSCRIBER INFORMATION

Items 1 - 11: Complete all items as indicated on the front of the form.

Item 9: Please check yes or no in item 9, and provide the spouse's employment information, if subscriber is married.

If payment has been received from another insurance company, please attach a copy of their Explanation of Benefits.

Item 12: **ASSIGNMENT OF BENEFITS** - Benefits for services provided by participating and contracting dentists are made payable directly to the dentist, whether or not benefits are assigned. Benefits for services provided by non-participating and non-contracting dentists located within our service area are made payable directly to the subscriber, regardless of any assignment of benefits. However, if the non-participating dentist is located outside our service area and you would like benefits due you for this claim sent directly to the dentist, complete item 12 on the reverse side of this form. Also be sure the dentist's Tax ID Number or Social Security Number is included in item 20 with the dentist's name and address.

INSTRUCTIONS FOR COMPLETING DENTIST INFORMATION

Item 13: **MISSING TEETH** - Each claim for services involving missing or extracted teeth must include the information requested in item 13.

Item 14: **ORTHODONTIA** - Claims for orthodontic services must include the information requested in item 14. It is not necessary for the orthodontic treatment to be completed before submitting the claim.

Item 15: **CROWNS, BRIDGES AND DENTURES** - Please complete this information on any claim for a crown, bridge or denture.

Item 16: **ADA PROCEDURE CODES** - American Dental Association codes.

TOOTH NO. OR LETTER - Refer to tooth chart on front of this claim form.

SURFACES - Use the following codes to identify tooth surfaces:

B = Buccal or facial, D = Distal
M = Mesial, I = Incisal, L = Lingual, O = Occlusal

PLACE - Please check the appropriate column on the claim form to indicate the place of service:

Off = Office, IN = Inpatient Hospital OP = Outpatient Hospital

CHARGE - Indicate charge for services listed on each line.

Item 17: **PREDETERMINATION OF BENEFITS** - If no dates of service are indicated on the claim, we will provide an estimate of the benefits available for the services listed. The estimates are based on the information we have at the time the claim is reviewed. Estimates will be subject to eligibility, deductibles, and Plan maximums. Therefore, they may be affected by other payments made between the time the estimate is given and the services are rendered. Actual payments will be made in the order that the claims are received.

If you are requesting a Predetermination of Benefits, mark the Predetermination of Benefits block under item 17. In addition, the dentist's name, address, and Tax ID Number or Social Security Number must be clearly written in item 20 of this claim form.

Item 19: **X-RAYS** - Post-operative x-rays are required for review of claims for endodontic services, and pre-operative x-rays are required for review of claims for crowns and the placement of bridges. We may also occasionally request x-rays for certain other procedures. All x-rays will be returned to the dentist after the claim has been reviewed.

7:4 Model Vacation Policies

One of the most common employee fringe benefits which employers provide is paid vacation time. Employers are not required to provide any vacation time, but many provide anywhere from one to four weeks of employment, depending on an employee's length of service.

Keep in mind that paid vacation time is not considered "hours worked" for purposes of overtime requirements. Therefore, an employee who has eight hours vacation during one week and works 39 hours in that week is not entitled to overtime pay, because the actual "hours worked" equal only 39.

Every employer needs a vacation policy to deal with the basic questions, such as:

- Who is entitled to paid vacation, and how much?
- How is vacation time accumulated?
- How are vacations requested?
- When must vacations be taken?
- Can accrued time be lost?

In addition, possible discrimination problems may occur when religious holidays are not provided, there are wage differentials between men and women performing the same kinds of work, or age is considered in the formula (see Appendix A).

This is one of the areas in which policy and procedure are so intertwined that they are presented together in the samples below. Needless to say, vacation policies and procedures, once set, should be included in the employee handbook.

7:4.1 Sample Policy 1

It is this company's policy to grant vacations with pay to provide qualifying employees with periods for rest and recreation in recognition of services performed.

Vacation Allowance

1. *Weekly payroll employees*. The vacation allowance for eligible employees for each vacation year is based on length of service and vacation group according to the following schedule:

Completed Years of Service	*Vacation Allowance*		
	Group I	*Group II*	*Group III*
1–4	2 weeks	3 weeks	4 weeks
5–9	3 weeks	3 weeks	4 weeks
10 or more	4 weeks	4 weeks	4 weeks

The vacation allowance for employees whose vacation allowances prior to the effective date of this policy differed from the applicable allowance in the schedule above will be based on this schedule or the previous allowance, whichever is greater.

The weekly vacation allowance is the normally scheduled workweek.

2. *Biweekly payroll employees*. The vacation allowance for eligible employees for each vacation year is 22 workdays.
3. Employees are not eligible for paid vacations during the first year of employment.

Eligibility Provisions: General

1. Vacation benefits under this plan apply to all permanent full-time and part-time employees normally scheduled to work at least 20 hours per week. Part-time employees normally scheduled to work less than 20 hours per week and temporary employees are not eligible for paid vacation benefits.
2. The vacation year is defined as the 12-month period commencing with the employee's first employment anniversary date and each subsequent employment anniversary date thereafter.

Eligibility Provisions: Position Change or Status Change

1. An employee promoted, demoted, or transferred to a position having a different vacation allowance will begin accruing vacation allowance on the basis of the vacation allowance for the new position.
2. A part-time employee changed to full-time status, or vice versa, will begin or cease accruing vacation allowance on the basis of the new status.

Eligibility Provisions: Holidays, Leaves of Absence, Illness Occurring During Vacation

1. If a designated holiday is observed during an employee's vacation period, the employee will be eligible for additional time off with pay equal to the holiday time off for which the employee is eligible.
2. An employee's vacation allowance for a vacation year will be reduced by one-twelfth for each full month of unpaid leave of absence during the previous year. An employee's vacation allowance for a vacation year will not be reduced by any unpaid leave of absence of less than one month nor by any paid leave of absence. An employee entering active military service or commencing a leave of absence of six months will receive vacation pay for unused earned vacation allowance and accrued vacation allowance since the employee's most recent anniversary date.
3. An employee will not receive additional vacation time off because of illness or disability occurring while on vacation.

Vacation Pay

1. Weekly vacation pay for full-time weekly payroll employees will be computed by multiplying the employee's current straight-time hourly rate exclusive of shift premiums by the number of hours of vacation allowance taken.
2. Weekly vacation pay for eligible part-time employees will be computed by multiplying the employee's current straight-time hourly rate exclusive of shift premiums by the average number of hours paid per week during the previous vacation year.
4. An employee will be paid vacation pay on the last scheduled working day before a vacation period, provided the vacation pay information is reported to the payroll office for the week preceding that in which the vacation will be taken.

Vacation Scheduling

1. Department heads will schedule vacations, giving due consideration to staffing requirements, employees' length of service, and employee preferences, in the order listed. Employees are notified of the scheduled starting dates of vacations not less than 60 days in advance, except when individual employee circumstances preclude such notice.
2. A vacation may be scheduled at any time during the employee's vacation year and may be taken over the vacation year end, provided it commences in the vacation year in which due.
3. Vacations should normally be taken in units of at least one week. However, if the department head approves, an employee may take one week of his or her vacation allowance in several days.
4. Whenever possible, employees should take their total vacations. Pay in lieu of vacation will not be granted unless absolutely necessary to meet staffing requirements and only upon approval of human resources. In no case will pay be granted in lieu of the first week of a vacation for a given year.

Eligibility Provisions: Terminating Employees

1. In all cases, a terminating employee will receive pay in lieu of any unused vacation allowance earned as of the employee's most recent employment anniversary date. Accrued vacation allowance is computed on the basis of one-twelfth of the employee's annual vacation allowance for each full month of employment between the employee's most recent employment anniversary date and the date of termination.
2. Additionally, a terminating employee will receive pay in lieu of vacation allowance accrued during the current vacation year, provided the termination was due to one of the following reasons: resignation with notice; release of the employee, including termination of grant; retirement; or death of the employee.
3. A terminating employee will not receive pay in lieu of vacation allowance accrued during the current vacation year in the event the employee is resigning or retiring with insufficient notice or without notice or is being discharged.

Vacation Allowance Accrual Schedule

	Basic Vacation Allowance		
*Months of Employment**	*Two Weeks (Hours)*	*Three Weeks (Hours)*	*Four Weeks (Hours)*
1	6¾	10	13½
2	13¼	20	26½
3	20	30	40
4	26¾	40	53½
5	33½	50	67
6	40	60	80
7	46¾	70	93½
8	53½	80	107
9	60	90	120
10	66¾	100	133½
11	73¼	110	146½
12	80	120	160

*Full months of employment since the employee's most recent employment anniversary date.

For part-time employees:

$$\frac{\text{Average hours}}{40} \times \text{hours indicated above} = \text{Vacation allowance}$$

For example, assume average hours = 20; the employee has worked for six months of the current year, and if a full-time employee would be entitled to two weeks a year (or 40 hours for six months). Therefore:

$$\frac{20}{40} \times 40 = 20 \text{ hours vacation allowance}$$

7:4.2 Sample Policy 2

Length of Continuous Service (as of the first of the month employed)	*Paid Vacation Earned per Month*
Under 3 years	1 day
3 years to 5 years	1¼ days
5 years to 10 years	1½ days
More than 10 years	1¾ days

- Employees may accrue vacation days up to a maximum of 21 days.
- Department heads must give prior approval to all vacations (30 days' notice requested).
- Management reserves the right to schedule a vacation shutdown during a summer period (July or August) not to exceed 10 consecutive working days. Employees without enough accrued vacation time will have time off without pay. If it will exercise this prerogative, management will inform employees of its intent by March 1.
- Human resources will be notified prior to any vacation.
- Except in emergencies, vacations may not be taken unless sufficient time has been accrued.
- Vacations may be taken in full-day units only.
- Employees will be paid for accrued vacation time only upon termination of employment.
- For purposes of vacation, continuous service will be from the date of full-time employment (figured back to the first of that month). Short-term disability or sickness for which the employee is paid will not be considered an interruption. Accrual will not continue during a long-term disability or any leave of absence (including, but not limited to, maternity, military, and so forth).
- Human resources will keep records of all vacation time earned and taken. In the event of a dispute, its decision is final.
- Vacation is accrued on the first of a given month for that calendar month.

7:3.3 Sample Policy 3—Production Environment

General Rules

1. The company will usually close its entire plant for two weeks, sometime during the summer, for an annual vacation.
2. The time of the closing will be announced on or before January 31 of each year.
3. All employees, with the exception of a small skeleton crew required to handle correspondence, make emergency shipments from stock, and do maintenance work that can be handled better when the plant is closed, will be expected to take their vacations at that time.
4. Insofar as it is possible to do so, this skeleton crew will be made up of people who wish to work and who are not entitled to the full two weeks of vacation with pay.
5. Vacations, if any, due to members of the skeleton crew will be scheduled at other convenient times.
6. Management may grant other vacations, provided they do not interfere with the operation of the company, under rules covering leaves of absence.
7. The company intends that every employee will take the vacation to which he or she is entitled, but if, for any reason, an employee forgoes his or her vacation at the company's request, he or she will be given vacation pay in addition to regular pay for time actually worked. Unused vacations may not be carried over and taken in a later year.

Eligibility

1. Each year, employees are eligible for vacation according to the following continuous service requirements:
   - Less than six months by July 1—None
   - Six months by July 1—One week
   - One year by July 1—Two weeks
   - Ten years by anniversary date—Three weeks
   - Eighteen years by anniversary date—Four weeks
   - Twenty-five years by anniversary date—Five weeks
2. Vacation pay of hourly employees will be the greater of:
   - 40-hour base pay (in effect on July 1 of the current calendar year) for each week of eligibility; or
   - 2 percent of the previous calendar year W-2 earnings times each week of eligibility.
3. Except in unusual cases, employees will receive their vacation pay at the time the vacation is taken.
4. Employees who terminate for any reason will receive their accrued vacation pay at termination, calculated in accordance with the above and their seniority on the date of termination.

5. Salaried personnel will be entitled to vacations as indicated in the preceding paragraphs, but will be paid in accordance with the salary in effect at the time the vacation is taken.

7:4.4 Sample Policy 4—Earning of Annual and Sick Leave

Earning of Annual and Sick Leave

1. Annual and sick leave will be earned by each full-time employee and each part-time employee who has a regular tour of duty, except that no employee will earn annual or sick leave while serving under emergency appointment.
2. The earning of such leave will be based on the equivalent of years of full-time service and will be creditable at the end of each calendar month or at the end of each regular pay period in accordance with the following schedule:
    - Less than 3 years of service, at the rate of .0461 hours of annual leave and .0461 hours of sick leave for each hour of regular duty;
    - At least 3 years but less than 5 years of service, at the rate of .0576 hours of annual leave and .0576 hours of sick leave for each hour of regular duty;
    - At least 5 years but less than 10 years of service, at the rate of .0692 hours of annual leave and .0692 hours of sick leave for each hour of regular duty;
    - At least 10 years but less than 15 years of service, at the rate of .0807 hours of annual leave and .0807 hours of sick leave for each hour of regular duty; and
    - 15 or more years of service, at the rate of .0923 hours of annual leave and .0923 hours of sick leave for each hour of regular duty.
3. Notwithstanding the above, no employee will be credited with annual or sick leave for any overtime hour; for any hour of leave without pay; while he or she is on leave with or without pay, until such time as he or she returns to active duty, except when inability to return to duty is caused by illness or incapacity; or for any hour of a holiday or other nonwork day that occurs while he or she is on leave without pay.

Use of Annual Leave

1. The employee must apply for annual leave and may use it only when the appointing authority or his or her designated representative approves.
2. Annual leave will not be charged for nonwork days (for example, holidays).
3. The minimum charge to annual leave records will not be less than one-half hour.
4. The immediate supervisor may recommend, and the department head may approve, annual leave requests for a maximum period of up to 120 hours, workload permitting.
5. The appointing authority must approve annual leave requests for periods in excess of 120 hours.

Enforced Annual Leave

1. The company may require an employee to take annual leave whenever, in its administrative judgment, such action would be in the best interest of the employee.

2. No employee will be required to reduce his or her accrued annual leave to less than 30 working days or the equivalent thereof in hours, except that an employee may be required to take any part or all of his or her accrued leave before being granted leave without pay.

Payment of Annual Leave Upon Separation

Each employee will, upon separation, be paid the value of his or her accrued leave in a lump sum, disregarding any final fraction of an hour. The payment for such leave will be computed as follows:

- When an employee is paid wages on an hourly basis, multiply his or her regular hourly rate by the number of hours of accrued annual leave.
- When an employee is paid on other than an hourly basis, determine his or her hourly rate by converting the number of hours worked per week.

7:4.5 Vacation Tracking Sheet

Vacation is probably the most universally offered time off benefit. In addition to the attendance sheets kept by the payroll department (discussed in Chapter 5), a vacation accrual form is used to help keep each employee's vacation time records accurate. This form is a sample vacation accrual form.

VACATION TRACKING SHEET

VACATION ACCRUAL FORM

NAME ______________________ EMPLOYEE NO. ______________________

EMPLOYED ______________________ REV. ANNIV. DATE ______________________

ENTITLEMENT: Weeks as of Jan. 1st __________ OTHER ______________________

DATE	EXPLANATION	WEEK	DAY	DAYS ENTITLED	DAYS TAKEN	DAYS DUE
	REGULAR VACATION:					

Personal Days: (1) ______________________ (2) ______________________

Comp. Days ______________________

7:4.6 Request for Leave of Absence

Organizations that allow employees to take leaves of absence, with or without pay, should have employees fill out a leave of absence request form. The form states in writing the terms of the leave of absence agreement. It serves as a permanent record of the leave of absence request and its approvals.

REQUEST FOR LEAVE

REQUEST FOR LEAVE OF ABSENCE

Name: __________ __________ Department: __________ __________ Date: __________

To: Human Resources Dept.

I hereby request a leave of absence ______ with pay ______ without pay,

from __________ (Date) to __________ (Date), for a total of ________ working days,

for the following reasons:

____ Maternity Leave	____ Marriage Leave
____ Medical Leave	____ Education Leave
____ Military Leave	____ Adoption Leave
____ Jury Duty	____ Personal Leave
____ Death in Family	____ Other

I make this request for a leave of absence with the full understanding that my current job may be eliminated during the term of my leave of absence, or that the vacancy created by my absence may be filled by another employee. I further understand that should my current job be eliminated, or filled by another, I may be considered for other positions within the company that would be comparable to my former position. In the event that no such comparable position is, or becomes, available during the one-month period following the termination of my leave of absence, my status will be changed to that of a terminated employee.

______________ Date ______________________ Signature

All requests for paid or unpaid leaves of absence must be accompanied by the appropriate documentation (doctor's certification, military orders, subpoena).

____

____

Please refer to the employee handbook for requirements for each type of leave of absence.

Department Approval: ______________________ Manager ____________ Date

Human Resources Department Approval: ______________________ Manager/Officer ____________ Date

Management Approval (if necessary): ______________________ ____________ Date

Chapter 8

Executive Compensation

The performance of a company's executives can relate directly to the company's profit margin. Employers, therefore, have developed methods of compensation by which executives' earnings are correlated to the company's earnings, often by some form of ownership interest. This chapter examines the various components of a chief executive deferred compensation arrangement. It includes the following: (1) Employment Guarantee, (2) Incentive Stock Option Agreement, (3) Phantom Stock Agreement, (4) Phantom Stock Agreement Letter of Intent, (5) Trust Agreement and (6) Golden Parachute Agreement.

8:1 Employment Agreement Deferred Compensation Package

Note that the foregoing documents were drafted in conjunction with the Chief Officer Employment Agreement that appears at 1:1.5 and may be used with it to create a comprehensive compensation package. Note, however, that these documents should be reviewed by competent legal counsel to ensure that they reflect the various state and federal laws in effect at the time of their use.

8:1.1 Sample Guarantee

In order to induce executives into accepting a position, the employer's stockholders often execute base salary and bonus payment guarantees. The following represents an example of such a guarantee.

GUARANTEE

In order to induce [NAME OF EMPLOYEE] (the "Executive") to enter into the Employment Agreement dated _____, 19___ (the "Employment Agreement"), between the Executive and [NAME OF CORPORATION], a [STATE OF INCORPORATION] corporation (the "Company"), the undersigned stockholders of the Company hereby irrevocably guarantee to the Executive and his estate and heirs the payment of the Base Salary and Bonus (each of the foregoing as defined in the Employment Agreement) in accordance with the terms of the Employment Agreement.

This Guarantee is a guarantee of collectibility and is conditioned and contingent upon an attempt to collect from the Company. The Executive may proceed against the undersigned only after making a good faith demand for payment against the Company and thereafter upon delivery by the Executive to each of the undersigned of a demand for payment of the Base Salary or Bonus to the extent the obligations of the Company under the Employment Agreement with respect to the payment thereof remain unsatisfied. The liability of the undersigned hereunder shall continue in full force and effect until the Company's obligations to pay the Base Salary and the Bonus in accordance with the terms of the Employment Agreement are fully satisfied and discharged; *provided, however*, that the liability of the undersigned hereunder with respect to the payment of the Bonus shall terminate in the event that the Executive shall elect to defer receipt thereof in accordance with Section 5(c) of the Employment Agreement upon the Company's deposit of the Bonus with the trustee under the Trust Agreement to be entered into between the Company and such trustee pursuant to said Section.

The undersigned shall be entitled to all rights of subrogation to the claims of the Executive against the Company to the extent of any payments made by the undersigned to the Executive under this Guarantee.

Any reference to the undersigned, the Company or the Executive shall be deemed to include their respective successors, permitted assigns, heirs and legal representatives, and all covenants and agreements of the undersigned contained herein (other than those contained in the following paragraph) shall inure to the benefit of the permitted assigns and heirs and legal representatives of the Executive. Neither the Executive nor any of the undersigned shall assign or delegate their respective rights and obligations hereunder without the prior written consent of the Executive, in the event of such assignment or delegation by any of the undersigned, or each of the undersigned, in the event of such assignment or delegation by the Executive.

This Guarantee shall be governed by and construed in accordance with the laws of the State of _________ applicable to agreements made and performed therein.

IN WITNESS WHEREOF, this Guarantee has been executed this _____ day of _________, 19____.

____

[NAME OF EMPLOYER]

Agreed To And Accepted As Of
The Date First Above Written:

____

[NAME OF EMPLOYEE]

8:1.2 Sample Bonus Payment Deferral Notice

Executives often wish to defer payment of the bonus portion of their executive compensation package. Upon such deferral, the bonus amount is invested for the executive who is paid these amounts upon a certain specified date or event. However, the executive must usually elect the deferral and formally notify his or her employer of such election. The form that follows provides one example of such a deferral notice.

8:1.3 Sample Incentive Stock Option Agreement

An incentive stock option is a right granted by the issuing corporation to an employee to purchase shares of the corporation's capital stock at a fixed price for a specified period of time. Such a stock based plan is used to provide executives with incentives to work harder to ensure the financial success of a corporation. The following document is an example of the type of agreement required when providing such deferred compensation to executives.

INCENTIVE STOCK OPTION AGREEMENT, dated as of ______, 19____, between [NAME OF EMPLOYER], a [STATE OF INCORPORATION] corporation (the "Company"), and [NAME OF EMPLOYEE] (the "Optionee").

Pursuant to the 19____ Stock Option Plan of the Company (the "19____ Plan"), the Company, acting through the Compensation and Stock Option Committee (the "Committee") of the Board of Directors of the Company (the "Board"), granted to the Optionee, effective as of ______, 19____, an option to purchase up to an aggregate of [   ] shares (the "Shares") of Common Stock, $______ par value (the "Common Stock"), of the Company at the price of $______ per Share (the "Option Price"), such option to be for the term and upon the terms and conditions contained in the 19____ Plan and this Agreement.

NOW, THEREFORE, in consideration of the premises and mutual covenants and obligations hereinafter set forth, the parties hereto hereby agree as follows:

1. *Option; Option Price.* Pursuant to said action of the Committee, the Company has granted to the Optionee the option (the "Option") to purchase, upon and subject to the terms and conditions of this Agreement and the 19____ Plan (which are incorporated by reference herein and which in all cases shall control in the event of any conflict with the terms, definitions and provisions of this Agreement), the Shares at the Option Price per Share. The Option is intended to qualify for Federal income tax purposes as an "incentive stock option" within the meaning of Section 422 of the Internal Revenue Code of 1986, as amended (the "Code").
2. *Term.* The term (the "Option Term") of the Options commences on ______, 19____ and expires on ______, 19____ unless such Option shall theretofore have been terminated in accordance with the terms hereof or the provisions of the 19____ Plan.
3. *Time of Exercise.*
   (a) Unless accelerated at the discretion of the Committee or as otherwise provided herein, the Option shall become exercisable as to [   ] Shares on ______, 19____, as to an additional [   ] Shares on ______, 19____, as to an additional [   ] Shares on ______, 19____, as to an additional [   ] Shares on ______, 19____, and as to an additional [   ] Shares on ______, 19____, and the Option shall remain exercisable as to all of such Shares until the expiration of the Option Term, subject to earlier termination as provided in paragraphs

(b) and (c) of this Section 3 or as provided in the 19____ Plan; *provided, however*, that, unless waived by the Board, the Option shall in no event be exercisable during the 180-day period immediately following the effective date of the Registration Statement on Form S-1 filed by the Company under the Securities Act of 1933 for the initial public offering of the Common Stock. Subject to the provisions of Sections 4 and 7, Shares as to which the Option becomes exercisable pursuant to the foregoing provisions may be purchased at any time thereafter prior to the expiration or termination of the Option.

(b) If the Optionee shall cease to be an employee of the Company or any of its subsidiaries as a result of a Termination for Cause or a Voluntary Termination (each of the foregoing as defined in the Employment Agreement), the Option and any exercise rights which may have become vested pursuant to Section 3(a) shall terminate concurrently with such cessation.

(c) If the Optionee shall cease to be an employee of the Company or any of its subsidiaries as a result of a Termination Without Cause (as defined in the Employment Agreement), the Option shall thereafter be exercisable only to the extent to which the Option shall have become vested pursuant to Section 3(a) as of the date of such cessation, and such vested exercise rights shall in any event terminate upon the earlier of (A) the expiration of the Option Term and (B) three months after the date of such cessation.

(d) If the Optionee shall cease to be an employee of the Company or any of its subsidiaries as a result of his death or disability (as defined in the Employment Agreement), or if the Optionee shall die during the three-month period referred to in Section 3(c), the Option shall thereafter be exercisable by the Optionee, or such person as shall have acquired by will or by the laws of descent and distribution the right to exercise the Option, only to the extent to which the Option shall have become vested pursuant to Section 3(a) as of the date of such cessation, and such vested exercise rights shall in any event terminate upon the earlier of (i) the expiration of the Option Term and (ii) one year after the date of such cessation.

4. *Procedure for Exercise*.

(a) The Option may be exercised, in whole or in part (but for the purchase of whole Shares only), by delivery of a written notice (the "Notice") from the Optionee to the Secretary of the Company, which Notice shall:

(i) state that the Optionee elects to exercise the Option;

(ii) state the number of Shares with respect to which the Optionee is exercising the Option (the "Optioned Shares");

(iii) include any representations of the Optionee required under Section 7(b) hereof;

(iv) state the method of payment for the Optioned Shares pursuant to Section 4(b);

(v) in the event that the Option shall be exercised by any person other than the Optionee pursuant to Sections 3(c) and 3(d), include appropriate proof of the right of such person to exercise the Option; and

(vi) state the date upon which the Optionee desires to consummate the purchase of the Optioned Shares (which date must be prior to the termination of such Option).

(b) Payment of the Option Price for the Optioned Shares shall be made in cash or by personal or certified check payable to the order of the Company.

(c) Upon receipt of such Notice and payment, the Company shall as promptly as practicable deliver or cause to be delivered a certificate or certificates representing the Shares with respect to which the Option is so exercised. The certificate or certificates for such Shares shall be registered in the name of the person or persons so exercising the Option (or, if the Option is exercised by the Optionee and if the Optionee shall so request in the Notice, such certificate or certificates shall be registered in the name of the Optionee and his or her spouse, jointly, with right of survivorship) and (as provided above) shall be delivered to or upon the written order of the person or persons exercising the Option.

(d) In the event the Option shall be exercised by any person or persons after the death or legal disability of the Optionee, such Notice shall be accompanied by appropriate proof of the right of such person or persons to exercise the Option. All Shares purchased upon the exercise of the Option as provided herein shall be fully paid and nonassessable.

5. *No Rights as a Stockholder*. The Optionee shall not have any privileges of a stockholder with respect to any Optioned Shares until the date of the issuance of a stock certificate evidencing such Shares pursuant to his exercise of the Option.

6. *Adjustments.*

(a) Subject to Section 6(b), if, at any time while the Option is outstanding, the Common Stock is changed by reason of a stock split, reverse stock split, stock dividend or recapitalization, or converted into or exchanged for other securities as a result of a merger, consolidation or reorganization, the Committee shall make appropriate adjustments in the number and class of shares of stock subject to the Option and the Option Price of the Option in accordance with Section 9.a of the 19____ Plan. Each such adjustment shall be subject to the provisions of the 19____ Plan (or any similar or successor provision of the 19____ Plan which may be hereafter adopted).

(b) In the event of the dissolution or liquidation of the Company, or reorganization, merger or consolidation in which the Company is not the surviving corporation, or a sale of all or substantially all of the assets of the Company to another person or entity, the provisions of the 19____ Plan (or any similar or successor provisions of the 19____ Plan which may be hereafter adopted) shall apply.

7. *Additional Provisions Related to Exercise.*

(a) The Option shall be exercisable only on such date or dates and during such period and for such number of Shares as are set forth in this Agreement.

(b) To exercise the Option, the Optionee shall follow the procedures set forth in Section 4. Upon and as a condition to the exercise of the Option at a time when there is not in effect a registration statement under the Securities Act of 1933 relating to the Shares issuable upon exercise of the Option, the Optionee hereby represents and warrants, and by virtue of such exercise shall be deemed to represent and warrant, to the Company that the Optioned Shares are being acquired for investment and not with a view to the distribution thereof, and the Optionee shall provide the Company with such other representations and warranties as may be required by the Committee in order to ensure compliance with applicable Federal and state securities, blue sky and other laws or otherwise. No Shares shall be purchased upon the exercise of the Option unless and until the Company and/or the Optionee shall have complied with all applicable Federal or state registration, listing and/or qualification requirements and all other requirements of law or of any regulatory agencies having jurisdiction.

(c) The Option shall not be affected by any change of duties or position of the Optionee (including transfer to or from a subsidiary), so long as the Optionee continues to be an employee of the Company or one of its subsidiaries. Neither the Option nor any provision of this Agreement or the 19____ Plan shall confer upon the Optionee any right to continue in the employ of the Company or any of its subsidiaries or interfere in any way with the right of the Company or its subsidiaries or the stockholders of the Company, as the case may be, to terminate the Optionee's employment or to increase or decrease the Optionee's compensation at any time.

8. *Restriction on Transfer of Option.* The Option may not be transferred, pledged, assigned, hypothecated or otherwise disposed of in any way by the Optionee, except by will or by the laws of descent and distribution, and may be exercised during the lifetime of the Optionee only by the Optionee. If the Optionee dies, the Option shall thereafter be exercisable, during the period specified in Section 3(d), by his executors or administrators to the full extent to which the Option was exercisable by the Optionee at the time of his death. In the event of the legal disability of the Optionee, the Option shall thereafter be exercisable by the Optionee's legal representative. The Option shall not be subject to execution, attachment or similar process. Any attempted assignment, transfer, pledge, hypothecation or other disposition of the Option contrary to the provisions hereof, and the levy of any execution, attachment or similar process upon the Option, shall be null and void and without effect.

9 *Restriction on Transfer of Optioned Shares.*

(a) Until the earlier of (i) ______, 19____ or (ii) the consummation of an initial public offering of the Common Stock of the Company under the Securities Act of 1933 (the "Securities Act"), the Optionee shall not sell, transfer or otherwise dispose of any Optioned Shares. If the Corporation shall at any time register for sale to the public shares of Common Stock under the Securities Act, the Executive shall not sell, transfer or otherwise dispose of any Optioned Shares (other than Optioned Shares included in such registration) without the prior written consent of the Company for such period as may be requested by the underwriters and approved by the Board.

(b) For purposes of this Section 9, Optioned Shares shall include any shares of capital stock of the Company the Optionee may receive as a dividend or other distribution on, or in exchange for, the Optionee's Optioned Shares.

10. *Limitation on ISO Treatment.* To the extent that the aggregate fair market value (as determined in accordance with the 19____ Plan on the date of grant) of stock with respect to which incentive stock options are exercisable for the first time by the Optionee during any calendar year (under all stock option plans of the Company and its parent, if any, and its subsidiaries) exceeds

$100,000, such options shall be deemed to be non-qualified stock options rather than incentive stock options.

11. *Disqualifying Dispositions.* As provided in Section 15 of the Plan, if Optioned Shares are disposed of within two years following the date of this Agreement or one year following the transfer of such Optioned Shares to the Optionee (a "Disqualifying Disposition"), the Optionee shall, immediately prior to such Disqualifying Disposition, notify the Company in writing of the date and terms of such disposition and provide such other information regarding such disposition as the Company may reasonably require. For purposes of this Paragraph, the term "disposition" shall have the meaning assigned to such term by Section 425(c) of the Internal Revenue Code.

12. *Restrictive Legend.* In order to reflect the restrictions on disposition of Optioned Shares, all stock certificates representing the Optioned Shares issued shall, if required by the Committee, have affixed thereto a legend substantially in the following form:

    "THE SHARES REPRESENTED BY THIS CERTIFICATE HAVE NOT BEEN REGISTERED UNDER THE SECURITIES ACT OF 1933. THE SHARES HAVE BEEN ACQUIRED FOR INVESTMENT AND MAY NOT BE PLEDGED, HYPOTHECATED, SOLD OR TRANSFERRED IN THE ABSENCE OF AN EFFECTIVE REGISTRATION STATEMENT FOR THE SHARES UNDER THE SECURITIES ACT OF 1933 OR AN OPINION OF COUNSEL TO THE COMPANY THAT SUCH REGISTRATION IS NOT REQUIRED UNDER SAID ACT. IN ADDITION, THE TRANSFER OF SUCH SHARES IS SUBJECT TO THE TERMS AND CONDITIONS OF AN OPTION AGREEMENT BETWEEN THE HOLDER THEREOF AND [NAME OF EMPLOYER]."

13. *Notices.* All notices, claims, certificates, requests, demands and other communications hereunder shall be in writing and shall be deemed to have been duly given, delivered and received if personally delivered or if sent by nationally-recognized overnight courier, by telecopy, or by registered or certified mail, return receipt requested and postage prepaid, addressed as follows:

    (a) if to Company, to:

        [NAME OF EMPLOYER]
        [ADDRESS]

    (b) if to the Optionee, at his last address appearing in the records of the Company;

    or to such other address as the party to whom notice is to be given may have furnished to the other parties in writing in accordance herewith. Any such notice or communication shall be deemed to have been delivered and received (i) in the case of personal delivery, on the date of such delivery, (ii) in the case of nationally-recognized overnight courier, on the next business day after the date when sent, (iii) in the case of telecopy transmission, when received, and (iv) in the case of mailing, on the fifth business day following the day on which the piece of mail containing such communication is posted.

14. *No Waiver*. No waiver of any breach or condition of this Agreement shall be deemed to be a waiver of any other or subsequent breach or condition, whether of like or different nature.
15. *Optionee's Undertaking*. The Optionee hereby agrees to take whatever additional actions and execute whatever additional documents the Company may in its judgment deem necessary or advisable in order to carry out or affect one or more of the obligations or restrictions imposed on the Optionee pursuant to the express provisions of this Agreement.
16. *Modification of Rights*. The rights of the Optionee are subject to modification and termination in certain events as provided in this Agreement and the 19___ Plan. Without limiting the generality of the foregoing, the Committee may, at its discretion and with the consent of the Optionee, establish a new Option Price for the Option so as to increase or decrease the Option Price.
17. *Withholding of Taxes*. The obligation of the Company to deliver Shares upon the exercise of the Option shall be subject to applicable federal, state and local tax withholding requirements.
18. *No Obligation to Exercise Option*. The granting of the Option shall impose no obligation upon the Optionee to exercise such Option.
19. *Governing Law*. This Agreement shall be governed by, and cons rue in accordance with, the laws of the State of _____ applicable to contracts wholly performed therein.
20. *Counterparts*. This Agreement may be executed in any number of counterparts, each of which shall be deemed to be an original, but all of which together shall constitute one and the same instrument.
21. *Entire Agreement*. This Agreement and the 19___ Plan (and any other writings referred to herein) constitute the entire agreement between the parties with respect to the subject matter hereof and thereof, merging any and all prior agreements.

IN WITNESS WHEREOF, the parties hereto have executed this Option Agreement as of the date first written above.

[NAME OF EMPLOYER]

By: ____________________________
Name:
Title:

____
[NAME OF OPTIONEE]

8:1.4 Sample Phantom Stock Agreement and Letter of Intent

Phantom stock is a right to a bonus based on the performance of "phantom" (rather than real) shares of a corporation's common stock over a period of time. The bonus is typically an amount equal to the difference between the fair market value of the shares of common stock at the date of grant and the fair market value of the stock at a later specified date. The following document is an example of a phantom stock agreement that can be used to provide an executive with an incentive to work harder to ensure the financial success of the corporation. A letter of intent outlining additional inducements for employment as they relate to the phantom stock agreement appears at 8:1.4A.

PHANTOM STOCK AGREEMENT dated _____, 19___, between [NAME OF EMPLOYER], a [STATE OF INCORPORATION] (the "Company"), and [NAME OF EMPLOYEE] (the "Executive").

Concurrently with the execution and delivery of this Agreement, the Company and the Executive are entering into an employment agreement (the "Employment Agreement") pursuant to which the Company is employing the Executive, and the Executive is accepting such employment, as the Chairman of the Board of Directors and Chief Executive Officer of the Company on the terms and conditions contained therein.

To further induce the Executive to enter into the Employment Agreement and use his best efforts to further the growth and success of the Company, the Company desires to grant to the Executive the right to receive upon the occurrence of a Realization Event (as hereinafter defined) (i) future payments of cash based upon the value of the Company's Series B Convertible Preferred Stock, $_____ par value (the "Series B Stock"), and Series C Preferred Stock, $_____ par value (the "Series C Stock"; and the Series B Stock and Series C Stock, collectively, the "Preferred Stock"), or (ii) shares of Preferred Stock, on the terms and conditions hereinafter set forth.

NOW, THEREFORE, in consideration of the premises and mutual covenants and obligations set forth herein, the parties hereto hereby agree as follows:

1. *Series B Stock.* Unless otherwise noted, all references in this Agreement to the Series B Stock (either alone or together with the Series C Stock as the Preferred Stock) shall be deemed to include the shares of Common Stock, $_____ par value (the "Common Stock"), of the Company into which shares of Series B Stock may be converted. In the event shares of Series B Stock shall have been converted into shares of Common Stock, any calculation required to be made pursuant to this Agreement based on shares of Series B Stock shall be made without taking into consideration the fact that such shares of Series B Stock had been converted.
2. *Certain Definitions.* As used in this Agreement, the following terms shall have the following respective meanings:
   (a) "Net Proceeds" shall mean the aggregate amount of cash received by holders of Preferred Stock (collectively, the "Holders") upon the Transfer

of shares of Preferred Stock in connection with the consummation of a Realization Event, less the aggregate amount of all costs, fees and expenses paid or otherwise incurred by them (including reasonable attorney's and other professional fees) in connection therewith.

(b) "Phantom Stock Units" shall mean, collectively, the Series B Phantom Stock Units and the Series C Phantom Stock Units.

(c) "Realization Event" shall mean (i) the Transfer by any Holders of in excess of 50% of the aggregate number of shares of Preferred Stock held by all Holders prior to such Realization Event, in either case whether by (A) the direct Transfer of shares of Preferred Stock to any other person or entity (other than to Holders' respective affiliates or pursuant to a distribution by them to any of their respective partners or stockholders), (B) the redemption or repurchase of shares of Preferred Stock by the Company, (C) the merger or consolidation of the Company with or into another corporation or entity in connection with which the Holders receive cash or other property of any corporation or entity upon such merger or consolidation, and (D) the voluntary or involuntary liquidation, dissolution or winding-up of the Corporation which results in a distribution of cash or other property on or with respect to the then outstanding shares of Preferred Stock.

(d) "Series B Phantom Stock Unit" and "Series C Phantom Stock Unit" shall mean, respectively, a unit of measurement of the value of a share of Series B Stock or Series C Stock, with none of the attendant rights of a holder of Preferred Stock, including the right to vote such shares of Preferred Stock.

(e) "Series B Realization Percentage" shall mean, with respect to a Realization Event involving the Transfer of shares of Series B Stock, the fraction, expressed as a percentage, (i) the numerator of which is the number of shares of Series B Preferred Stock Transferred by the Holders upon the consummation of such Realization Event and (ii) the denominator of which is the total number of shares of Series B Preferred Stock held by the Holders on the date hereof, reduced by the number of shares of Series B Preferred Stock Transferred by the Holders after the date hereof and prior to such Realization Event.

(f) "Series C Realization Percentage" shall mean, with respect to a Realization Event involving the Transfer of shares of Series C Stock, the fraction, expressed as a percentage, (i) the numerator of which is the number of shares of Series C Preferred Stock Transferred by the Holders upon the consummation of such Realization Event and (ii) the denominator of which is the total number of shares of Series C Preferred Stock held by the Holders on the date hereof, reduced by the number of shares of Series C Preferred Stock Transferred by the Holders after the date hereof and prior to such Realization Event.

(g) "Transfer" shall mean (i) when used as a verb, the act of selling, transferring, assigning or otherwise disposing of any shares of Preferred Stock for value and (ii) when used as a noun, the sale, transfer, assignment or other disposition of any shares of Preferred Stock for value.

3. *Grant of Phantom Stock Units*. The Company hereby grants to the Executive an aggregate of [ ] Phantom Stock Units, consisting of [ ] Series B Phantom Stock Units and [ ] Series C Phantom Stock Units. The Company shall maintain on its books an account (the "Account") of the

number of Phantom Stock Units held by the Executive, which Account shall be adjusted from time to time pursuant to Section 4(c) to reflect payments of cash or issuances of Preferred Stock to the Executive with respect to such Phantom Stock Units pursuant to Section 4.

4. *Payment for Phantom Stock Units.*

(a) In the event that a Realization Event will result in the receipt of only cash by the Holders upon the consummation thereof, the Company shall pay to the Executive upon or as soon as practicable following the consummation of such Realization Event an amount in cash equal to the sum of (i) the product obtained by multiplying (A) the per share amount of the Net Proceeds received with respect to the Series B Stock Transferred in connection with such Realization Event by (B) the aggregate number of Series B Phantom Stock Units held by the Executive at the time of the consummation of such Realization Event, by (C) the Series B Realization Percentage with respect to such Realization Event,(ii) the product obtained by multiplying (A) the per share amount of the Net Proceeds received with respect to the Series C Stock Transferred in connection with such Realization Event by (B) the aggregate number of Series C Phantom Stock Units held by the Executive at the time of the consummation of such Realization Event, by (C) the Series C Realization Percentage with respect to such Realization Event. Payments of cash due from the Company pursuant to this Section 4(a) shall be made by check to the order of the Executive.

(b) In the event that a Realization Event will result in the receipt of property other than cash by the Holders upon the consummation thereof, the Company shall issue to the Executive immediately prior to or upon the consummation of such Realization Event (i) that number of shares of Series B Stock equal to the product obtained by multiplying the aggregate number of Series B Phantom Stock Units held by the Executive prior to such Realization Event by the Series B Realization Percentage with respect to such Realization Event and (ii) that number of shares of Series C Stock equal to the product obtained by multiplying the aggregate number of Series C Phantom Stock Units held by the Executive prior to such Realization Event by the Series C Realization Percentage with respect to such Realization Event. Upon the issuance of such shares, the Executive shall be entitled to participate in such Realization Event with respect to all such shares of Preferred Stock issued to him pursuant to this Section 4(b) in connection therewith on the same terms as the Holders, as the case may be.

(c) Upon the payment of amounts pursuant to Section 4(a) or the issuance of shares of Preferred Stock pursuant to Section 4(b) in connection with a Realization Event, the Company shall reduce (i) the number of Series B Phantom Stock Units credited to the Executive's Account by an amount equal to the product obtained by multiplying the aggregate number of Series B Phantom Stock Units held by the Executive prior to such Realization Event by the Series B Realization Percentage applicable to such Realization Event and (ii) the number of Series C Phantom Stock Units credited to the Executive's Account by an amount equal to the product obtained by multiplying the aggregate number of Series C Phantom Stock Units held by the Executive prior to such Realization Event by the Series C Realization Percentage applicable to such Realization Event.

5. *Exchange of Preferred Stock for Phantom Stock Units*. In the event that at any time on or after the fifth anniversary of the date hereof there remain in the Account any Series B Phantom Stock Units or Series C Phantom Stock Units, the Company may, at its sole option, at any time or from time to time on or after such fifth anniversary issue to the Executive in exchange for all or any portion of (a) such remaining Series B Phantom Stock Units an equal number of shares of Series B Preferred Stock and (b) such remaining Series C Phantom Stock Units, an equal number of shares of Series C Stock, in each case by delivering to the Executive a certificate or certificates registered in the name of the Executive representing such shares of Preferred Stock. Upon the delivery of such certificate or certificates, the Account shall be adjusted to reflect the cancellation of the Phantom Stock Units exchanged for such shares of Preferred Stock.

6. *Dividends and Distributions*. In the event the Company shall pay a dividend on or make a distribution with respect to outstanding shares of Series B Stock or Series C Stock, whether in cash or other property, the Company shall pay to the Executive cash or such other property in an amount equal to the product obtained by multiplying the per share amount of such dividend or distribution by the number of Series B Phantom Stock Units (in the event of a dividend on or distribution with respect to the Series B Stock) or Series C Phantom Stock Units (in the event of a dividend on or distribution with respect to the Series C Stock) in the Executive's Account on the record date established for such dividend or distribution.

7. *Miscellaneous*.

   (a) All notices and other communications hereunder shall be in writing and shall be deemed to have been duly given, delivered and received if personally delivered or if sent by nationally-recognized overnight courier, by telecopy, or by registered or certified mail, return receipt requested and postage prepaid, addressed as follows:

      (i) if to the Executive, at his last address appearing in the records of the Company; and

      (ii) if to the Company, to:

         [NAME OF EMPLOYER]
         [ADDRESS];

   or to such other address as the party to whom notice is to be given may have furnished to the other parties in writing in accordance herewith. Any such notice or communication shall be deemed to have been delivered and received (i) in the case of personal delivery, on the date of such delivery, (ii) in the case of nationally-recognized overnight courier, on the next business day after the date when sent, (iii) in the case of telecopy transmission, when received, and (iv) in the case of mailing, on the fifth business day following the day on which such communication is posted.

   (b) This Agreement will be governed by, and construed and enforced in accordance with, the laws of the State of ______ applicable to agreements made and performed therein.

   (c) This Agreement (together with the other writings referred to herein) contains the entire agreement between the parties with respect to the subject matter hereof and supersedes all prior agreements or understandings between the parties with respect thereto.

(d) The section headings contained in this Agreement are for reference purposes only and shall not affect in any way the meaning or interpretation of this Agreement.

(e) This Agreement and the respective rights of the parties hereunder shall not be assigned or transferred in any way by any party without the consent of the other party hereto; *provided, however*, that the Company may delegate its obligation to make any cash payment hereunder to any of its subsidiaries or affiliates; and *provided further, however,* that the provisions hereof shall inure to the benefit of, and be binding upon, the respective heirs, legal representatives, successors and assigns of the parties including, with respect to the Company, successors by merger, consolidation, transfer of all or substantially all of the assets of the Company or otherwise.

(f) Nothing contained in this Agreement shall confer upon the Executive any right to continue in the employ of, as a director of or as an independent consultant to the Company or any of its subsidiaries or affiliates, or interfere in any way with the right of the Company or its subsidiaries or affiliates or the stockholders of the Company to terminate the Executive's employment, directorship or consultancy or to increase or decrease the Executive's compensation at any time.

(g) This Agreement shall terminate upon the termination of the Executive's employment under the Employment Agreement as a result of a Termination for Cause or a Voluntary Termination, and upon such termination the Executive shall have no further right to receive any payments hereunder (whether in cash or other property).

(h) In the event of the issuance to the Executive of any shares of Preferred Stock pursuant to this Agreement, the Executive agrees to provide the Company, as a condition to such issuance, with such representations and warranties as may be required by the Company in order to ensure compliance with applicable Federal and state securities, blue sky and other laws or otherwise. The Executive agrees to take whatever additional actions and execute whatever additional documents the Company may in its judgment deem necessary or advisable in order to carry out or effect the terms and provisions of this Agreement.

IN WITNESS WHEREOF, the parties have duly executed this Phantom Stock Agreement as of the date first above written.

[NAME OF EMPLOYER]

By: ______________________________
Name:
Title:

8:1.4A Sample Letter of Intent and Employment Inducement

LETTER OF INTENT

[DATE]

[NAME OF EMPLOYEE]

Dear [NAME OF EMPLOYEE]:

Reference is made to (i) the Employment Agreement dated as of the date hereof (the "Employment Agreement") between [NAME OF EMPLOYER] a [STATE OF INCORPORATION] corporation (the "Corporation"), and you and (ii) the Phantom Stock Agreement dated the date hereof (the "Phantom Stock Agreement") between the Corporation and you. Capitalized terms used and not otherwise defined herein shall have the respective meanings ascribed to them in the Employment Agreement or the Phantom Stock Agreement, as the case may be.

In order to induce you to enter into the Employment Agreement and the Phantom Stock Agreement, each of the undersigned stockholders of the Corporation hereby agrees with you as follows:

1. *Cooperation Regarding Alternative Employment.* In the event of the termination of your employment with the Corporation under the Employment Agreement pursuant to a Termination Without Cause, each of the undersigned shall use their respective reasonable best efforts to assist you in finding alternative employment that is reasonably acceptable to you.

2. *Right of Cosale.* In the event of a proposed Realization Event in connection with which you shall be entitled to receive from the Company shares of Preferred Stock and to participate in such proposed Realization Event, each of the undersigned agrees that as a condition to their Transfer of shares of Preferred Stock upon the consummation of such Realization Event, they will cause the transferor of such shares to purchase from you, simultaneously therewith and upon the same terms thereof, all of the shares of Preferred Stock issuable to you under the Phantom Stock Agreement in connection with such Realization Event.

Form continued on next page

Please acknowledge your agreement with and acceptance of the foregoing by signing the enclosed copy of this letter in the space provided below and delivering it to the Corporation on behalf of the undersigned.

Very truly yours,

[ ]

____

Agreed And Accepted
As Of The Date First
Written Above:

____
[NAME OF EMPLOYEE]

Stockholders to be determined.
Stockholders to be determined.

8:1.5 Sample Trust Agreement

Employers often establish various types of escrow accounts or trusts to enable them to fulfill their promises to an employee. The two basic types of trusts that may be used by the employer are rabbi trusts and secular trusts. The major difference between the two types of trusts are that the assets held in the rabbi trust are subject to the claims of the employer's creditors while the employee has a nonforfeitable right to the funds held in a secular trust, which are also protected from the employer and its creditors. The following document is an example of a rabbi trust that is used to fund an executive's deferred compensation arrangement.

TRUST AGREEMENT dated ______, 19___, between [NAME OF EMPLOYER], a [STATE OF INCORPORATION] corporation (the "Company"), and [NAME OF TRUSTEE] (the "Trustee").

On ______, 1990, the Company entered into an employment agreement (the "Employment Agreement") with [NAME OF EMPLOYEE] (the "Executive"), pursuant to which, among other things, the Company agreed to pay the Executive the amount of $______ (the "Bonus"), on the terms and conditions contained in the Employment Agreement.

Pursuant to Section 5(c) of the Employment Agreement, the Executive has elected to defer receipt of the Bonus. In connection therewith, the Company desires to set aside funds in order to provide for the payment of the Bonus to the Executive and to establish an irrevocable trust (the "Trust"), the assets of which will be subject to the claims of its creditors and which is designed to qualify as a "grantor trust" for Federal income tax purposes, and the Trustee is willing to serve as the trustee of the Trust, on the terms and conditions hereinafter set forth.

NOW, THEREFORE, in consideration of the premises and the mutual covenants and obligations hereinafter set forth, the parties hereto hereby agree as follows:

ARTICLE 1

General Duties of the Parties

Section 1.1. *General Duties of the Company*. The Company has paid the sum of $______ to the Trustee to be held in the Trust as specified in this Agreement. The Trust formed hereunder shall be referred to as "[NAME OF EMPLOYER/NAME OF EMPLOYEE] Trust." Such sum and the interest earned thereon and proceeds derived therefrom are hereinafter referred to as the "Trust Fund."

Section 1.2. *General Duties of Trustee*. The Trustee shall invest the Trust Fund in any or all of the following types of investments: United States Treasury bills, other short-term government and agency obligations, certificates of deposit, commercial paper, money-market mutual funds and other money market instruments, savings accounts and other deposits with a financial institution. The Company shall direct the Trustee in the manner in which the Trust Fund shall be invested.

Section 1.3. *Subject to Claims of Creditors*. The assets of the Trust shall at all times be subject to the claims of the Company's general creditors, whether currently existing or hereafter arising. If at any time the Company is unable to pay its debts as they mature or is subject to a pending proceeding as a debtor under the Bankruptcy Code, then the President or any Vice President of the Company shall notify the

Trustee of such fact and the Trustee shall hold the assets of the Trust in trust for the benefit of the general creditors of the Company and shall deliver any Trust assets to satisfy such claims as a court of competent jurisdiction may direct.

ARTICLE II
Administration of the Trust

Section 2.1. *Dealings with Trustee.*

(a) Persons dealing with the Trustee shall be under no obligation to see to the proper application of any money paid or property delivered to the Trustee or to inquire into the Trustee's authority as to any transaction.

(b) The Trustee shall be indemnified by the Company from and against any and all liability or expense, including all expenses reasonably incurred by the Trustee in its own defense if the Company fails to provide such defense, arising out of any investment or disbursement of any part of the Trust Fund made by the Trustee in accordance with this Agreement or any action or inaction with respect to the Trust. Subject to the foregoing, the Trustee shall not be indemnified against any liability or expense for any action or inaction taken or omitted by the Trustee which, under the circumstances, the Trustee knows constitutes a violation of law or a breach of its fiduciary duties.

Section 2.2. *Administrative Powers.* In addition to and not by way of limitation of any other powers conferred upon trustees by law or conferred upon the Trustee by the terms of this Agreement, the Trustee is authorized and empowered in its discretion:

(a) to make, execute, acknowledge, and deliver any and all instruments required in connection with any transaction it enters into pursuant to the provisions hereof;

(b) to do all acts, whether or not expressly authorized hereby, which it may deem necessary or proper for the protection of the property held hereunder;

(c) to employ, at the expense of the Company, agents, accountants and counsel, and to rely upon information and advice furnished by them;

(d) subject to Section 3.1 hereof, to file any and all tax returns with respect to the Trust, to pay any and all of such tax liabilities, and to satisfy any and all tax reporting and withholding requirements with respect to the Trust as may be prescribed from time to time by law; and

(e) in any case in which the Trustee is authorized or required pursuant to the provisions of this Agreement to make any payment or distribution in its absolute discretion in kind or in money or partly in kind and partly in money, to make such payment or distribution and, for the purposes of any such payment or distribution, the judgment of the Trustee concerning the propriety thereof and the relative values of any property involved therein, shall be conclusive and binding upon all persons who might then or thereafter have any claim or interest under this Agreement.

Section 2.3. *Settlement of Accounts of Trustee.*

(a) The Trustee shall keep full accounts of all investments, receipts and disbursements and other transactions hereunder. The Trustee's financial statements, books, accounts and records with respect to the Trust shall be open to inspection by the Company and the Executive and their respective representatives upon reasonable notice at all reasonable times during business hours of the Trustee.

(b) The Trustee shall render to the Company monthly statements of its receipts and disbursements as Trustee hereunder. If within ten days after receipt of the account or any amended account the Company has not signed and returned a counterpart to the Trustee, nor filed with the Trustee notice of any objection to any act or transaction of the Trustee, the account or amended account shall become an account stated as between the Trustee and the Company. If the Company is satisfied with the account or the account becomes adjusted to its satisfaction, the Company shall in writing filed with the Trustee signify its approval of the account, and it shall become an account stated as between the Trustee and the Company.

(c) When an account becomes an account stated, such account shall be finally settled, and the Trustee shall be completely discharged and released, as if such account had been settled and allowed by a judgment or decree of a court of competent jurisdiction in an action or proceeding in which the Trustee, the Company, the Executive and all persons having or claiming to have any interest in the Trust Fund were parties.

(d) The Trustee, the Company and the Executive shall have the right to apply at any time to a court of competent jurisdiction for judicial settlement of any account of the Trustee not previously settled as hereinabove provided. In any such action or proceeding it shall be necessary to join as parties thereto only the Trustee, the Company and the Executive (although the Trustee may also join other parties as it deems appropriate), and any judgment or decree entered therein shall be conclusive.

Section 2.4. *Determination of Interests in the Trust Fund, Enforcement of Trust and Legal Proceedings.* The interests of all persons in the Trust Fund shall be determined in accordance with the terms of this Agreement. To protect the Trust Fund from any expense which might otherwise be incurred, it is imposed as a condition for the securing of any interest in the Trust Fund, and it is hereby agreed, that no other person may institute or maintain any action or proceeding against the Trustee or the Trust or join in any such action or proceeding unless such person shall have obtained (a) written authorization by the Company, (b) a judgment of a court of competent jurisdiction that, in refusing such authorization, the Company has acted fraudulently or in bad faith, or (c) the written consent of the Executive. Except as otherwise provided in Section 2.3 and in this Section 2.4, in any action or proceeding affecting the Trust the only necessary parties shall be the Company, the Executive and the Trustee, and no other person shall be entitled to any notice or process.

ARTICLE III

Taxes, Compensation of Trustee and Expenses of Administration

Section 3.1. *Taxes.* All taxes arising from any Trust Fund distribution which are required to be withheld and deposited with or for the benefit of the applicable taxing authority, including, but not limited to, United States federal income tax, all applicable state and city income taxes, FICA taxes and state disability insurance taxes (hereinafter collectively referred to as "withholding taxes") shall be computed and paid or deposited by the Trustee solely out of the Trust Fund. The Trustee shall prepare and file all tax returns required with respect to the Trust Fund, including, but not limited to, IRS Form 1041 and all information returns (such as Forms W-2 or 1099-MISC). Any taxes on the Trust Fund or the income thereof or which the

Trustee is required to pay with respect to the interest of any person therein shall be paid by the Trustee from the Trust Fund.

Section 3.2. *Expenses and Compensation.* The Trustee shall be paid a fair and just compensation as agreed between the Company and the Trustee for its reasonable expenses of management and administration of the Trust, including reasonable compensation of counsel and any agents engaged by the Trustee to assist it in such management and administration. All expenses of managing and administering the Trust, including, without limitation, the compensation of the Trustee, accounting and legal fees and expenses, and any other expenses related to the administration of the Trust, shall be payable to the Trustee from the Trust Fund.

ARTICLE IV

For Protection of Trustee

Section 4.1. *Evidence of Action by Company.* The Trustee may rely upon any certificate, notice or direction purporting to have been signed on behalf of the Company which the Trustee believes to have been signed by the Company or the person or persons authorized to act for the Company. The Trustee may rely upon any certificate, notice or direction of the Company which the Trustee believes to have been signed by a duly authorized officer or agent of the Company.

Section 4.2. *Advice of Counsel.* The Trustee may consult with any legal counsel, including counsel to the Company, with respect to the construction of this Agreement, its duties hereunder, or any act which it proposes to take or omit, and shall not be liable for any action taken or omitted in good faith pursuant to such advice.

Section 4.3. *Fiduciary Responsibility.*

(a) The Trustee shall carry out its duties hereunder and shall use the care, skill, prudence and diligence under the circumstances then prevailing that a prudent person acting in a like capacity and familiar with such matters should use in the conduct of an enterprise of like character and with like aims; *provided, however*, that the Trustee shall not be liable for any loss sustained by the Trust Fund by reason of the purchase, retention, sale or exchange of any investment in good faith or in accordance with the provisions of this Agreement.

(b) The Trustee's duties and obligations shall be limited to those expressly imposed upon it by this Agreement, notwithstanding any reference to the Employment Agreement.

Section 4.4. *Title to Assets.* The assets of the Trust shall remain solely those of the Company, and the Executive shall have no right, title or interest in the Trust assets. The Trust is not intended to serve as security for the payment of amounts owed to the Executive under the Employment Agreement if the Company or its successor is insolvent. Neither the Company nor the Trustee shall create a security interest in the assets of the Trust in favor of the Executive or any creditor of the Company.

ARTICLE V

Resignation and Removal of Trustee

Section 5.1. *Resignation of Trustee.* The Trustee may resign at any time by filing with the Company its written resignation. Such resignation shall take effect 60 days from the date of such filing or upon appointment of a successor pursuant to Section 5.3, whichever shall first occur.

Section 5.2. *Removal of Trustee.* The Company may remove the Trustee at any time by delivering to the Trustee a written notice of its removal and an appointment of a successor pursuant to Section 5.3. Such removal shall not take effect prior to 30 days from such delivery unless the Trustee agrees to an earlier effective date.

Section 5.3. *Appointment of Successor Trustee.* The appointment of a successor to the Trustee shall take effect upon delivery to the Trustee of (a) an instrument in writing appointing such successor executed by the Company and (b) an acceptance in writing executed by such successor, both acknowledged in the same form as this Agreement. All of the provisions set forth herein with respect to the Trustee shall relate to each successor with the same force and effect as if such successor had been originally named as a Trustee hereunder. If a successor is not appointed within 60 days after the Trustee gives notice of its resignation pursuant to Section 5.1, the Trustee or the Company may apply to any court of competent jurisdiction for appointment of a successor.

Section 5.4. *Transfer of Fund to Successor.* Upon the resignation or removal of the Trustee and the appointment of a successor, and after the final account of the Trust has been settled as provided in Article II, the Trustee shall transfer and deliver the Trust Fund to such successor.

ARTICLE VI

Payment and Termination of Trust; No Revocation

Section 6.1. *Payment and Termination.* The Trustee shall pay the Trust Fund to the Executive at such time or times and in the manner provided in the Deferral Notice and as otherwise provided in this Agreement. If the Executive is deceased at any time when payments from the Trust Fund are to be made to him, such payments shall be made to the Executive's beneficiaries or estate. The Trust shall terminate upon the payment of all of the Trust Fund in accordance with this Section 6.1.

Section 6.2. *No Revocation.* This Agreement may not be revoked in whole or in part.

ARTICLE VII

Miscellaneous

Section 7.1. *Laws of State of_________* to Govern. This Agreement and the Trust created hereby shall be construed and regulated by the laws of the State of _________, except as otherwise provided by Federal law.

Section 7.2. *Titles and Headings Not to Control.* The titles of Articles and headings of Sections in this Agreement are placed herein for convenience of reference only and, in case of conflict, the text of this Agreement, rather than such titles or headings, shall control.

Section 7.3. *Interpretation of the Trust Agreement.* The Trust hereby created has been established to pay the obligations of the Company, is subject to the rights of the general creditors of the Company and is intended to be (a) classified as a grantor trust as defined in Section 671 *et seq.* of the Internal Revenue Code of 1986, as amended, and (b) classified as a component of a "plan which is unfunded and is maintained by an employer primarily for the purpose of providing deferred compensation for a select group of management or highly-compensated employees" under Sections 201(2), 301(a)(3), and 401(a)(1) of the Employee Retirement Income Security Act of 1974, as amended. Accordingly, all provisions of this Agreement shall be interpreted in a manner that satisfies the requirements that must be met in order that the Trust be so classified.

Section 7.4. *Notices.* All notices, claims, certificates, requests, demands and other communications hereunder shall be in writing and shall be deemed to have been duly given, delivered and received if personally delivered or if sent by nationally-recognized overnight courier, by telecopy, or by registered or certified mail, return receipt requested and postage prepaid, addressed as follows:

(a) if to the Trustee, to:

[NAME OF TRUSTEE]
[ADDRESS] and

(b) if to the Company, to:

[NAME OF EMPLOYER]
[ADDRESS]

or to such other address as the party to whom notice is to be given may have furnished to the other party in writing in accordance herewith. Any such notice or communication shall be deemed to have been received (i) in the case of personal delivery, on the date of such delivery, (ii) in the case of nationally-recognized overnight courier, on the next business day after the date when sent, (iii) in the case of telecopy transmission, when received, and (iv) in the case of mailing, on the fifth business day following that on which the piece of mail containing such communication is posted.

Section 7.5. *Entire Agreement; Amendments.* This Agreement (together with the other writings referred to herein) contains the entire agreement between the parties with respect to the subject matter hereof and supersedes all prior agreements or understandings between the parties with respect thereto. This Agreement may be amended only by an agreement in writing signed by the parties.

IN WITNESS WHEREOF, the parties have caused this Agreement to be executed as of the date first above written.

[NAME OF EMPLOYER]

By ______________________________
Name:
Title:

[NAME OF TRUSTEE]

By ______________________________
Name:
Title:

8:2 Golden Parachutes and Golden Handcuffs

Generally, "golden parachutes" are termination agreements that protect key employees from the effects of a corporate takeover. Typically, golden parachutes are "triggered" by a change in control or ownership of the corporation. They provide key employees who are terminated or who, under certain circumstances, resign as a result of a takeover with either continued compensation for a specified period following the key employees' departure or with a lump-sum payment.

This section provides an example of a typical golden parachute agreement that can be used to protect such key employees.

THIS AGREEMENT is between [NAME OF EMPLOYER], a [STATE OF INCORPORATION] corporation (hereinafter the "Company"), and [NAME OF EMPLOYEE] (hereinafter the "Employee"), dated as of the _____ day of _____, 19____.

WITNESSETH:

WHEREAS, the Company considers it essential to the best interests of the Company and its shareholders that its key personnel be encouraged to remain with the Company and to continue to devote full attention to the Company's business as the [PARENT CORPORATION] proceeds to sell the Company. In this connection, the Company recognizes that during such a disposition and period of uncertainty, questions and concerns of employees may result in the departure or distraction of key personnel to the detriment of the Company and its shareholders. The Board of Directors of the Company (the "Board") has determined that appropriate steps should be taken to reinforce and encourage the continued attention and dedication of key employees of the Company to their assigned duties without distraction in the face of circumstances arising from the disposition or change in control of the Company;

WHEREAS, the Employee is a key Employee of the Company;

WHEREAS, the Company believes the Employee has made valuable contributions to the productivity and profitability of the Company;

WHEREAS, should the Company receive any proposal from a third person concerning a possible business combination with, or acquisition of equity securities of, the Company, the Board believes it imperative that the Company and the Board be able to rely upon the Employee to continue in his or her position, and that the Company be able to receive and rely upon the Employee's advice, if so requested, as to the best interests of the Company and its shareholders without concern that the Employee might be distracted by the personal uncertainties and risks created by such a proposal; and

WHEREAS, should the Company receive any such proposals, in addition to the Employee's regular duties, the Employee may be called upon to assist in the assessment of such proposals, advise management and the Board as to whether such proposals would be in the best interests of the Company and its shareholders, and to take such other actions as the Board might determine to be appropriate;

NOW, THEREFORE, to assure the Company that it will have the continued undivided attention and services of the Employee and the availability of the Employee's advice and counsel during the disposition of the Company, and to induce the Employee to remain in the employ of the Company, and for other good and valuable consideration, the Company and the Employee agree as follows:

1. *Change in Control.* For purposes of this Agreement, a Change in Control of the Company shall be deemed to have occurred if (a) any "person" (as such term is used in Sections 13(d) and 14(d) of the Securities Exchange Act of 1934, as amended (the "Exchange Act")) becomes the "beneficial owner" (as defined in Rule 13d-3 under the Exchange Act), directly or indirectly, of securities of the Company representing 51% or more of the combined voting power of the Company's then outstanding securities; or (b) the shareholders of the Company approve an agreement for the sale or disposition by the Company of all or substantially all the Company's assets.
2. *Termination Following Change in Control.*
   (a) If any of the events described in Section 1 hereof constituting a Change in Control of the Company shall have occurred and if at the date thereof the Employee is employed on a full time basis by the Company, the Employee shall be entitled to the benefits set forth in Section 4 upon any termination of the Employee's employment by the Company within eighteen (18) months following a Change in Control for any reason except the following:
      (i) Termination by reason of the Employee's death, provided the Employee has not previously given a "Notice of Termination" pursuant to Section 3;
      (ii) Termination by reason of retirement in accordance with and under the Company's Retirement Plan (or any plan in substitution thereof); or
      (iii) Termination for "cause." For purposes of this Agreement, "cause" shall mean the willful and continued failure of the Employee to substantially perform his or her duties or action by the Employee involving willful misfeasance or gross negligence related to his or her employment or the commission of any felony; provided that, termination for cause based on the Employee's willful and continued failure to substantially perform his or her duties shall not be effective unless the Employee shall have received written notice from the Company of such failure and demand for substantial performance 30 days prior to such termination and the Employee has failed after receipt of such notice to resume the diligent performance of his or her duties.

   A termination of the Employee's employment by the Company shall not have occurred, for purposes of this Section 3(a), where the Employee continues in employment with the purchaser of 51% or more of the securities representing the combined voting power of the outstanding securities of the Company or all or substantially all of the Company's assets.

   (b) The Company shall also provide the Employee with the benefits set forth in Section 4 upon any termination of employment with the Company by the Employee for good reason within eighteen (18) months after a Change in Control; provided that the Employee shall have been employed on a full-time basis by the Company at the time of such Change in Control. For purposes of this Agreement, "good reason" shall mean the occurrence of any one of the following events without the Employee's consent:
      (i) The assignment of the Employee to any duties substantially inconsistent with his or her position, duties, responsibilities or status with the Company immediately prior to the Change in Control or a

substantial reduction of the duties or responsibilities, as compared with the duties or responsibilities immediately prior to the Change in Control;

(ii) A reduction by the Company in the amount of the Employee's base salary and bonus opportunity or other employee perquisites as compared to what was paid immediately prior to the Change in Control;

(iii) The relocation of the Employee's principal office to a location more than thirty-five (35) miles from the location of such office immediately prior to the Change in Control;

(iv) Any failure of the Company to obtain the assumption of the obligation to perform this Agreement by any successor as contemplated in Section 7; or

(v) Any breach by the Company of any of the provisions of this Agreement or any failure by the Company to carry out any of its obligations hereunder.

3. *Notice of Termination.* Any termination of the Employee's employment with the Company by the Company as contemplated by Subsection 2(a) or by the Employee as contemplated by Subsection 2(b) shall be communicated by written "Notice of Termination" to the other party hereto. Any "Notice of Termination" shall indicate the effective date of termination which shall not be more than 30 days after the date the Notice of Termination is delivered (the "Termination Date"), the specific provision in this Agreement relied upon, and will set forth in reasonable detail the facts and circumstances claimed to provide a basis for such termination.

4. *Termination Benefits.* Subject to the conditions set forth in Sections 2 and 7(b), the following payments (subject to any applicable payroll or other taxes required to be withheld) shall be paid to the Employee:

(a) *Compensation.* The greater of the Employee's effective annual base salary and bonus at the Termination Date or the Employee's effective annual base salary and bonus immediately prior to the Change in Control; and

(b) *Health Insurance Benefits.* The equivalent cash value, at standard independent insurance premium rates, of purchasing, as of the Termination Date, benefits for the Employee on an individual basis which are equal to the Employee's participation (including dependent coverage) in the health insurance plan, calculated as if such benefits were continued during the one (1) year period following the Termination Date; payable in a lump sum as soon as practicable following the Termination Date, but in no event later than fifteen (15) days thereafter.

5. *Payment of Certain Costs.* If a dispute arises regarding a termination of the Employee or the interpretation or enforcement of this Agreement, subsequent to a Change in Control, all of the legal fees and expenses incurred by the Employee in successfully contesting any such termination or obtaining or successfully enforcing any right or benefit provided for in this Agreement or in otherwise successfully pursuing his or her claim will be paid by the Company, to the extent permitted by law. The Company further agrees to pay pre-judgment interest on any money judgment obtained by the Employee calculated at the prime interest rate in effect from time to time from the date that payment to the Employee should have been made under this Agreement.

6. *Continuing Obligations.* The Employee hereby agrees that all documents, records, techniques, business secrets and other information which have come into the Employee's possession from time to time during his or her employment by the Company, shall be deemed to be confidential and proprietary to the Company and the Employee further agrees to retain in confidence any confidential information known to him or her concerning the Company and its subsidiaries and their respective businesses so long as such information is not publicly disclosed.
7. *Successors.*
   (a) The Company shall require any successor (whether direct or indirect, by purchase, merger, consolidation or otherwise) to all or substantially all of the business and/or assets of the Company, by Agreement in form and substance satisfactory to the Employee, to expressly assume and agree to perform this Agreement in the same manner and to the same extent that the Company would be required to perform it if no such succession had taken place. Failure of the Company to obtain such agreement prior to the effectiveness of any such succession shall be a breach of this Agreement and shall entitle the Employee to compensation from the Company in the same amount and on the same terms as the Employee would be entitled hereunder if the Employee were to terminate employment for Good Reason following a Change in Control, except that for purposes of implementing the foregoing, the date on which any such succession becomes effective shall be deemed the Termination Date. For purposes of this Agreement, "Company" shall mean the Company as hereinbefore defined and any successor to its business and/or assets as aforesaid which assumes and agrees to perform this Agreement or which otherwise becomes bound by all the terms and provisions of this Agreement by operation of law.
   (b) This Agreement shall inure to the benefit of and be enforceable by the Employee's personal or legal representatives, executors, administrators, successors, heirs, distributees, devises and legatees. If the Employee should die while any amounts are payable to him or her hereunder, all such amounts, unless otherwise pro-aided herein, shall be paid in accordance with the terms of this Agreement to the Employee's devisee, legatee or other designee or, if there be no such designee, to the Employee's estate.
8. *Notices.* For the purposes of this Agreement, notices and all other communications provided for herein shall be in writing and shall be deemed to have been duly given when delivered personally or by telecopier or mailed by United States registered or certified mail, return receipt requested, postage prepaid, addressed as follows:

   (a) If to the Employee: [NAME]
   [ADDRESS]
   (b) If to the Company: [NAME]
   [ADDRESS]

   or to such other address as either party may have furnished to the other in writing in accordance herewith, except that notices of change of address shall be effective only upon receipt.

9. *Governing Law.* The validity, interpretation, construction and performance of this Agreement shall be governed by the laws of the State of _________.
10. *Miscellaneous.* No provisions of this Agreement may be modified, waived or discharged unless such waiver, modification or discharge is agreed to in writing and signed by the Employee and the Company. No waiver by either party hereto at any time of any breach by the other party hereto of, or compliance with, any condition or provision of this Agreement to be performed by such other party shall be deemed a waiver of similar or dissimilar provisions or conditions at the same or any prior or subsequent time. No agreements or representatives, oral or otherwise, express or implied, with respect to the subject matter hereof have been made by either party which are not set forth expressly in this Agreement.
11. *Severability.* The invalidity or unenforceability of any provisions of this Agreement shall not affect the validity or enforceability of any other provisions of this Agreement, which shall remain in full force and effect.
12. *Non-assignability.* This Agreement is personal in nature and neither of the parties hereto shall, without the consent of the other, assign or transfer this Agreement or any rights or obligations hereunder, except as provided in Section 11. Without limiting the foregoing, the Employee's right to receive payments hereunder shall not be assignable or transferable, whether by pledge, creation of a security interest or otherwise, other than a transfer by the Employee's will or trust or by the laws of descent or distribution or by order of a court of competent jurisdiction, and in the event of any attempted assignment or transfer contrary to this paragraph, the Company shall have no liability to pay any amount so attempted to be assigned or transferred.
13. *Term of Agreement.* This Agreement shall commence on the date hereof and shall continue in effect through ______, 19____ unless otherwise extended by written notice by the Company; provided, however, if a Change in Control of the Company shall have occurred during the original or extended term of this Agreement, this Agreement shall continue in effect for a period of twelve (12) months beyond the month in which such Change in Control occurred.
14. *Arbitration.* Any dispute or controversy arising under or in connection with this Agreement shall be settled exclusively by arbitration in accordance with the rules of the American Arbitration Association then in effect. Judgment may be entered on the arbitrator's award in any court having jurisdiction.

IN WITNESS WHEREOF, the parties have caused this Agreement to be executed and delivered as of the day and year first above set forth, thereby mutually and voluntarily agreeing that this Agreement supersedes and replaces any prior similar agreements for such termination benefits.

[NAME OF EMPLOYER]

By ______________________________
President

____
[NAME OF EMPLOYEE]

Chapter 9

Job Safety

An employee's right to a healthful workplace is ensured primarily under the Occupational Safety and Health Act (OSHA). As advances are made in science and technology, OSHA's reach is extended to limit workers' exposure to new hazards and to require employers to comply with more stringent regulations regarding a safe work environment. This chapter presents the forms and notices required by OSHA, provides an example of a hazard communications policy that employers can adapt and examines the various issues that relate to drug and alcohol abuse such as employment screening and employee testing.

9:1 Occupational Safety and Health Act Forms

The following sections contain examples of information postings for employees as well as the report forms that are required by OSHA for reporting job related injuries and illnesses. Note that the forms at section 9:1.2 must be kept by the employer for a period of five years.

9:1.1 Sample Notice Postings and OSHA Injury and Illness Reporting Forms

The two posters at 9:1.1A are examples of OSHA approved notice postings. The first outlines the basic employer/employee responsibilities provided in OSHA. The second covers the rights of employees that transport goods or otherwise are required to operate motor vehicles. Sections 9:1.1B and 9:1.1C cover employee safety rules and accident report form.

9:1.1A Employee Information Postings

JOB SAFETY & HEALTH PROTECTION

The Occupational Safety and Health Act of 1970 provides job safety and health protection for workers by promoting safe and healthful working conditions throughout the Nation. Provisions of the Act include the following:

Employers

All employers must furnish to employees employment and a place of employment free from recognized hazards that are causing or are likely to cause death or serious harm to employees. Employers must comply with occupational safety and health standards issued under the Act.

Employees

Employees must comply with all occupational safety and health standards, rules, regulations and orders issued under the Act that apply to their own actions and conduct on the job.

The Occupational Safety and Health Administration (OSHA) of the U.S. Department of Labor has the primary responsibility for administering the Act. OSHA issues occupational safety and health standards, and its Compliance Safety and Health Officers conduct jobsite inspections to help ensure compliance with the Act.

Inspection

The Act requires that a representative of the employer and a representative authorized by the employees be given an opportunity to accompany the OSHA inspector for the purpose of aiding the inspection.

Where there is no authorized employee representative, the OSHA Compliance Officer must consult with a reasonable number of employees concerning safety and health conditions in the workplace.

Complaint

Employees or their representatives have the right to file a complaint with the nearest OSHA office requesting an inspection if they believe unsafe or unhealthful conditions exist in their workplace. OSHA will withhold, on request, names of employees complaining.

The Act provides that employees may not be discharged or discriminated against in any way for filing safety and health complaints or for otherwise exercising their rights under the Act.

Employees who believe they have been discriminated against may file a complaint with their nearest OSHA office within 30 days of the alleged discriminatory action.

Citation

If upon inspection OSHA believes an employer has violated the Act, a citation alleging such violations will be issued to the employer. Each citation will specify a time period within which the alleged violation must be corrected.

The OSHA citation must be prominently displayed at or near the place of alleged violation for three days, or until it is corrected, whichever is later, to warn employees of dangers that may exist there.

Proposed Penalty

The Act provides for mandatory penalties against employers of up to $1,000 for each serious violation and for optional penalties of up to $1,000 for each nonserious violation. Penalties of up to $1,000 per day may be proposed for failure to correct violations within the proposed time period. Also, any employer who willfully or repeatedly violates the Act may be assessed penalties of up to $10,000 for each such violation.

There are also provisions for criminal penalties. Any willful violation resulting in death of an employee, upon conviction, is punishable by a fine of up to $250,000 (or $500,000 if the employer is a corporation), or by imprisonment for up to six months, or both. A second conviction of an employer doubles the possible term of imprisonment.

Voluntary Activity

While providing penalties for violations, the Act also encourages efforts by labor and management, before an OSHA inspection, to reduce workplace hazards voluntarily and to develop and improve safety and health programs in all workplaces and industries. OSHA's Voluntary Protection Programs recognize outstanding efforts of this nature.

OSHA has published Safety and Health Program Management Guidelines to assist employers in establishing or perfecting programs to prevent or control employee exposure to workplace hazards. There are many public and private organizations that can provide information and assistance in this effort, if requested. Also, your local OSHA office can provide considerable help and advice on solving safety and health problems or can refer you to other sources for help such as training.

Consultation

Free assistance in identifying and correcting hazards and in improving safety and health management is available to employers, without citation or penalty, through OSHA-supported programs in each State. These programs are usually administered by the State Labor or Health department or a State university.

Posting Instructions

Employers in States operating OSHA approved State Plans should obtain and post the State's equivalent poster.

Under provisions of Title 29, Code of Federal Regulations, Part 1903.2(a)(1) employers must post this notice (or facsimile) in a conspicuous place where notices to employees are customarily posted.

More Information

Additional information and copies of the Act, specific OSHA safety and health standards, and other applicable regulations may be obtained from your employer or from the nearest OSHA Regional Office in the following locations:

Atlanta, GA	(404) 347-3573
Boston, MA	(617) 565-7164
Chicago, IL	(312) 353-2220
Dallas, TX	(214) 767-4731
Denver, CO	(303) 844-3061
Kansas City, MO	(816) 426-5861
New York City, NY	(212) 337-2378
Philadelphia, PA	(215) 596-1201
San Francisco, CA	(415) 744-6670
Seattle, WA	(206) 442-5930

Elizabeth Dole

Elizabeth Dole, Secretary of Labor

Washington, DC
1990 (Reprinted)
OSHA 2203

U.S. Department of Labor

Occupational Safety and Health Administration

Attention

Drivers

Did You Know That. . .

You can act to protect yourself and the public from unsafe working conditions. For example, you can:

- refuse to operate a commercial motor vehicle that fails to meet Federal safety requirements.
- refuse to violate a DOT regulation.
- report violations of vehicle safety requirements.
- refuse to drive under conditions that you reasonably believe might cause serious injury to yourself or the public.

Did You Know That. . .

It is illegal for your employer to discriminate* against you in any way solely because you take any of these actions. For example, your employer may not:

- fire or demote you.
- assign you to an undesirable job or shift.
- take away your seniority.
- take away earned sick leave or vacation time.
- blacklist or threaten you.

Did You Know That. . .

If you believe you have been discriminated against you should complain to any OSHA office as soon as possible, then OSHA will investigate and may be able to restore your job and status if your complaint is substantiated.

More Information

You can obtain more information about these safety and health rights from the nearest OSHA Regional Office in the following locations:

Atlanta	(404) 347-3573
Boston	(617) 565-7164
Chicago	(312) 353-2220
Dallas	(214) 767-4731
Denver	(303) 844-3061
Kansas City	(816) 426-5861
New York	(212) 337-2378
Philadelphia	(215) 596-1201
San Francisco	(415) 995-5672
Seattle	(206) 442-5930

**Interstate truckers and bus drivers: To obtain protection against discrimination, you must first seek from your employer, and be unable to obtain, correction of the alleged violation.*

Washington, D.C.
1989
OSHA 3113

Elizabeth Dole, Secretary of Labor

U.S. Department of Labor
Occupational Safety and Health Administration

9:1.1B Model Safety Rules

Below is an example of the type of safety rules that employers should establish in order to meet the requirements of OSHA.

Safety Rules

1. Everything in and about the plant shall be kept clean and in good order. Each employee will be held responsible for the condition of the plant and the equipment under his or her control.
2. Running, shouting, throwing objects and "horseplay" are strictly forbidden.
3. Keep yourself in physical condition to do a day's work.
4. Wear clothes suited to the job - gloves, if needed. Use goggles and other protective equipment provided.
5. Listen to the Supervisor's instructions and have them clearly in mind before starting work.
6. If you don't know how to do the job safely, ask your supervisor.
7. Always use all safeguards provided.
8. Keep material out of walkways, particularly boards with nails in them.
9. Warn employees working above or below you.
10. When working with another employee, be sure he or she knows what you are going to do before you drop a load or do anything which might injure him or her. Good team work promotes safety.
11. Have both hands free for going up or down ladders. See that ladders are firmly placed before using them. See that all rungs are securely nailed.
12. Report unsafe conditions to your Supervisor.
13. Get help for lifting heavy objects. Learn to lift the correct way.
14. Report all injuries promptly. Get immediate First Aid.
15. Keep your mind on your job. Alertness prevents accidents.
16. Never try to oil, clean or adjust machinery while it is in use.
17. Never throw anything from a height until you are sure no one is below.
18. Do not look at welders or cutters while they work. You might ruin your eyes.
19. Do not wear ragged sleeves, loose coats, flowing ties or loose jumpers while working around machinery.
20. Do not use improper or broken tools; they are dangerous.
21. Do not ride loads being lifted by cranes.
22. Do not get under loads which are being carried by cranes.
23. Do not hoist a load until it is securely made and balanced.
24. Never start machinery, operate valves, or change electric switches until you know by personal investigation that it is safe.
25. Do not fix electrical equipment of any kind, unless your work requires it.
26. Never turn compressed air on anyone or on yourself; it is extremely dangerous.

27. If an employee's full rim glasses are broken or damaged as a result of a witnessed on-the-job accident, not involving horseplay, replacement of the broken parts will be paid for by the Company. Lenses will not be paid for if the prescription is changed.
28. The wearing of shorts will be authorized whenever not in conflict with safety requirements.
29. The Company will reimburse an employee for the purchase of safety shoes in the amount of $10.00 per pair limited to two (2) pairs per year.

9:1.1C Employer Accident Report Form

ACCIDENT REPORT FORM

TO: Personnel Department

FROM:

SUBJECT: Accident Report DATE ____________________

Name of Employee ____ S.S.# ________________________

Home Address ____

Department ____ Position ________________________

Nature of injury and part(s) of body affected (e.g., sprained middle finger of left hand)

____

____

Was medical care provided? ____

If yes, give name and address of physician or hospital ______________________________________

____

If no, state why ____

____

Date and time of accident ____

Where did it happen? ____

____

What was employee doing when the accident occurred? ______________________________________

____

____

When was supervisor notified? ____

Date disability began, if any ____

What do you recommend be done to prevent a reoccurrence of this accident and accidents due to same cause or causes? ____

____

____
Officer-in-Charge

9:1.2 OSHA Injury and Illness Reporting Forms

As noted in Questions 524-565 and 528.1S-565, OSHA sets out standards and procedures designed to ensure job safety. This section provides the basic forms required by OSHA when reporting and tracking occupational injuries and illnesses. Note that the employer is required to keep these forms on site for 5 years from the date of the incident.

9:1.2A Supplementary Record of Occupational Injuries and Illnesses

Bureau of Labor Statistics
Supplementary Record of
Occupational Injuries and Illnesses

U.S. Department of Labor

This form is required by Public Law 91-596 and must be kept in the establishment for *5 years.* Failure to maintain can result in the issuance of citations and assessment of penalties.	Case or File No.	Form Approved O.M.B. No. 1220-0029

Employer

1. Name

2. Mail address *(No. and street, city or town, State, and zip code)*

3. Location, if different from mail address

Injured or Ill Employee

4. Name *(First, middle, and last)* — Social Security No.

5. Home address *(No. and street, city or town, State, and zip code)*

6. Age — 7. Sex: *(Check one)* Male ☐ Female ☐

8. Occupation *(Enter regular job title, not the specific activity he was performing at time of injury.)*

9. Department *(Enter name of department or division in which the injured person is regularly employed, even though he may have been temporarily working in another department at the time of injury.)*

The Accident or Exposure to Occupational Illness

If accident or exposure occurred on employer's premises, give address of plant or establishment in which it occurred. Do not indicate department or division within the plant or establishment. If accident occurred outside employer's premises at an identifiable address, give that address. If it occurred on a public highway or at any other place which cannot be identified by number and street, please provide place references locating the place of injury as accurately as possible.

10. Place of accident or exposure *(No. and street, city or town, State, and zip code)*

11. Was place of accident or exposure on employer's premises? Yes ☐ No ☐

12. What was the employee doing when injured? *(Be specific. If he was using tools or equipment or handling material, name them and tell what he was doing with them.)*

13. How did the accident occur? *(Describe fully the events which resulted in the injury or occupational illness. Tell what happened and how it happened. Name any objects or substances involved and tell how they were involved. Give full details on all factors which led or contributed to the accident. Use separate sheet for additional space.)*

Occupational Injury or Occupational Illness

14. Describe the injury or illness in detail and indicate the part of body affected. *(E.g., amputation of right index finger at second joint; fracture of ribs; lead poisoning; dermatitis of left hand, etc.)*

15. Name the object or substance which directly injured the employee. *(For example, the machine or thing he struck against or which struck him; the vapor or poison he inhaled or swallowed; the chemical or radiation which irriatated his skin; or in cases of strains, hernias, etc., the thing he was lifting, pulling, etc.)*

16. Date of injury or initial diagnosis of occupational illness — 17. Did employee die? *(Check one)* Yes ☐ No ☐

Other

18. Name and address of physician

19. If hospitalized, name and address of hospital

Date of report — Prepared by — Official position

OSHA No. 101 (Feb. 1981)

9:1.2B Illness and Injury Log

Form 6.02-A
OSHA LOG OF ILLNESSES AND INJURIES

OSHA No. 200

Bureau of Labor Statistics
Log and Summary of Occupational
Injuries and Illnesses

NOTE: **This form is required by Public Law 91-596 and must be kept in the establishment for *5 years*. Failure to maintain and post can result in the issuance of citations and assessment of penalties.** *(See posting requirements on the other side of form.)*	**RECORDABLE CASES:** You are required to record information about every occupational **death**; every nonfatal occupational **illness**; and those nonfatal occupational **injuries** which involve one or more of the following: loss of consciousness, restriction of work or motion, transfer to another job, or medical treatment (other than first aid). *(See definitions on the other side of form.)*

Case or File Number Enter a nonduplicating number which will facilitate comparisons with supplementary records. (A)	Date of Injury or Onset of Illness Enter Mo./day. (B)	Employee's Name Enter first name or initial, middle initial, last name. (C)	Occupation Enter regular job title, not activity employee was performing when injured or at onset of illness. In the absence of a formal title, enter a brief description of the employee's duties. (D)	Department Enter department in which the employee is regularly employed or a description of normal workplace to which employee is assigned, even though temporarily working in another department at the time of injury or illness. (E)	Description of Injury or Illness Enter a brief description of the injury or illness and indicate the part or parts of body affected. Typical entries for this column might be: Amputation of 1st joint right forefinger; Strain of lower back; Contact dermatitis on both hands; Electrocution--body. (F)
					PREVIOUS PAGE TOTALS →
					TOTALS (Instructions on other side of form.) →

OSHA No. 200

U.S. Department of Labor

For Calendar Year 19 ____ Page ___ of ___

Company Name

Establishment Name

Establishment Address

Form Approved O.M.B. No. 1220-0029

Extent of and Outcome of INJURY						Type, Extent of, and Outcome of ILLNESS												
Fatalities	Nonfatal Injuries					Type of Illness							Fatalities	Nonfatal Illnesses				
Injury Related	Injuries With Lost Workdays				Injuries Without Lost Workdays	CHECK Only One Column for Each Illness *(See other side of form for terminations or permanent transfers.)*							Illness Related	Illnesses With Lost Workdays				Illnesses Without Lost Workdays
Enter DATE of death. Mo./day/yr.	Enter a CHECK if injury involves days away from work, or days of restricted work activity, or both.	Enter a CHECK if injury involves days away from work.	Enter number of DAYS *away from work.*	Enter number of DAYS of *restricted work activity.*	Enter a CHECK if no entry was made in columns 1 or 2 but the injury is recordable as defined above.	Occupational skin diseases or disorders	Dust diseases of the lungs	Respiratory conditions due to toxic agents	Poisoning (systemic effects of toxic materials)	Disorders due to physical agents	Disorders associated with repeated trauma	All other occupational illnesses	Enter DATE of death. Mo./day/yr.	Enter a CHECK if illness involves days away from work, or days of restricted work activity, or both.	Enter a CHECK if illness involves days away from work.	Enter number of DAYS *away from work.*	Enter number of DAYS of *restricted work activity.*	Enter a CHECK if no entry was made in columns 8 or 9.
(1)	(2)	(3)	(4)	(5)	(6)	(7) (a)	(b)	(c)	(d)	(e)	(f)	(g)	(8)	(9)	(10)	(11)	(12)	(13)

Certification of Annual Summary Totals By ____________ Title ____________ Date ____________

OSHA No. 200

POST ONLY THIS PORTION OF THE LAST PAGE NO LATER THAN FEBRUARY 1.

9:2 Hazard Commmunications Policies

As noted in Questions 566-578 and 567.1S-578.17S, OSHA also provides for various right-to-know requirements that govern the manufacture, importing, distribution, and handling of hazardous products such as chemicals. The policy at 9:2.1 provides an example of a program for dealing with hazardous chemicals.

9:2.1 Sample Hazard Communications Program

Hazard Communications Program

The purpose of this hazard communications program is to ensure that the hazards of all chemicals used by [NAME OF EMPLOYER] (hereinafter referred to as the "Company") are evaluated and that necessary information concerning such hazards is transmitted to affected employees within our company.

This hazard communications program provides information to the Company's employees about the hazardous chemicals to which they are exposed by means of labels and other forms of warning material, safety data sheets and information and training.

In order to ensure that the information required is available, a material safety data sheet will be provided to any employee asking for the composition of any chemical used at his job site. The material safety data sheet must be completed by the customer and/or vendor obtained by the Company and should contain all the information regarding the chemicals used at our job locations, and, should be similar to OSHA Form 20, as defined by the U.S. Department of Labor. In order to ensure that the employees know about the chemicals they are handling, it will be mandatory that every chemical purchased by the Company should contain the appropriate material safety data sheet (MSDS) and the labeling required by law.

Training Program

The Company will provide all employees in contact with any hazardous chemical a periodic regular training program containing the following:

1. Methods and observations that detect the presence or release of hazardous chemicals in the work area;
2. Monitoring conducted by the employer, continual monitoring devices, visual appearance or odor of chemicals;
3. A session providing the opportunity for employee questions and answers pertaining to the chemicals being used by the Company; and
4. The measures that the employees can take to protect themselves from these hazards, including procedures the employer has implemented to protect the employees from exposure to hazardous chemicals, such as appropriate work practices, emergencies and personal protective equipment to be used.

New employees and employees of outside contractors will be instructed on the above four points, as appropriate, before commencing work on the premises.

Special attention will be paid to employees for whom English is a second language, to ensure they understand the content of their training.

Supervisors will be alert for, and advise employees of any special hazards that may be involved in nonroutine tasks that may occur from time to time.

Policy

It is the policy of the Company to have a written and uniform policy establishing a Hazardous Chemicals Communications program concerning the use of Hazardous Chemicals by its employees.

Objective

The purpose of this policy is to inform employees of the hazards they are exposed to with the use of chemicals on the job site, by the use of a Hazardous Communications Program, labels and other forms of warning, material safety data sheets and information and training.

Procedure

The Purchasing Department will require "Material Safety Data Sheets" on all new purchased chemicals regardless where the chemical is purchased or where it will be used in any Company location. "Material Safety Data Sheets" must be furnished to the location(s) using the chemical and remain on file, and accessible to all employees.

1. "Material Safety Data Sheets" must be kept on file by each location using hazardous chemicals and must be updated when required.
2. Information as to the location and availability of the "Material Safety Data Sheets" file shall be posted in case of accidental exposure to an employee of a hazardous chemical. "Material Safety Data Sheets" contain important safety information for emergency and first-aid procedures.
3. The Company will provide personal protective equipment suggested by or outlined in "Material Safety Data Sheet" of the hazardous chemicals used by or in close proximity to its employees.

Responsibility

Superintendents and first-line supervisors are responsible for:

1. Maintaining "Material Safety Data Sheet" Files and updating when necessary.
2. Issuing proper personal protective equipment as may be required by "Material Safety Data Sheet" and requiring employees to sign personal equipment receipts and returning signed forms for proper distributions.
3. Instructing employee(s) in proper use and maintenance of personal protective equipment.
4. Instructing employee(s) in the proper and safe use of chemicals used at their respective Company locations.

Training And Employee Information

1. The Company will provide employees with information and training on hazardous chemicals in their work area.
2. The [ ] Department will be responsible for the training of employees in hazard communications.

3. Information and training shall meet the U.S. Department of Labor, OSHA standards.

Records

1. Maintenance of proper records will be kept by the job clerk and the superintendent.
2. All medical tests will be kept for the length of the respective employee's employment plus five (5) years.

Discipline

Any employee who fails to wear personal safety protective equipment when it is required will be subject to disciplinary action in accordance with Safety Rules, General Plant and Work Rules.

APPROVED BY:

____

9:2.2 Material Safety Data Sheet

The following form can be used to implement a hazard communications program in order to comply with OSHA's Hazard Communication Standard.

Material Safety Data Sheet
May be used to comply with
OSHA's Hazard Communication Standard,
29 CFR 1910.1200. Standard must be
consulted for specific requirements.

U.S. Department of Labor
Occupational Safety and Health Administration
(Non-Mandatory Form)
Form Approved
OMB No. 1218-0072

IDENTITY *(As Used on Label and List)*	*Note: Blank spaces are not permitted. If any item is not applicable, or no information is available, the space must be marked to indicate that.*

Section I

Manufacturer's Name	Emergency Telephone Number
Address *(Number, Street, City, State, and ZIP Code)*	Telephone Number for Information
	Date Prepared
	Signature of Preparer *(optional)*

Section II — Hazardous Ingredients/Identity Information

Hazardous Components (Specific Chemical Identity; Common Name(s))	OSHA PEL	ACGIH TLV	Other Limits Recommended	% *(optional)*

Section III — Physical/Chemical Characteristics

Boiling Point		Specific Gravity (H_2O = 1)	
Vapor Pressure (mm Hg.)		Melting Point	
Vapor Density (AIR = 1)		Evaporation Rate (Butyl Acetate = 1)	
Solubility in Water			
Appearance and Odor			

Section IV — Fire and Explosion Hazard Data

Flash Point (Method Used)	Flammable Limits	LEL	UEL
Extinguishing Media			
Special Fire Fighting Procedures			
Unusual Fire and Explosion Hazards			

(Reproduce locally) OSHA 174, Sept. 1985

9:3 Drugs and Alcohol

Employers are generally very concerned about the use of drugs and alcohol in the workplace not only because of safety considerations, but also because of the overall societal interest in combatting drug and alcohol abuse. As a result, many employers have instituted policies regarding the use of drugs and alcohol on the premises and policies regarding drug testing. In fact, the U.S. Department of Transportation has promulgated regulations which require employers engaged in interstate trucking to test employees for drug and alcohol consumption. Additionally, many employers are offering employee assistance programs to educate their employees about the dangers of drug and alcohol abuse.

There are a number of methods by which employers can test employees for drug use. First, employers can test applicants for employment for drug use, and many employers are already doing this. Second, employers can test employees for whom there is reasonable suspicion of drug or alcohol use. Third, employers can institute a system whereby they periodically test different segments of the employee population. For example, every other month an employer can test employees with even number social security numbers. This periodic testing gives employees some notice of a drug and alcohol test, but also allows employers to periodically and systematically test their employees. Finally, employers may institute a random drug testing policy whereby employees are chosen on an entirely random basis and are tested at random times for evidence of drug or alcohol use. There are many restrictions on an employer's ability to test employees randomly, including constitutional concerns and concerns for employee privacy. The United States Supreme Court has allowed random testing in job categories where public safety is a dominant factor, but employers should be extremely careful if they are interested in random testing. Legal advice and assistance is of paramount importance in this area.

This section provides some samples of Drug and Alcohol Policy Statements and Testing Policies.

9:3.1 Sample Drug and Alcohol Abuse Policy

Statement Of Policy On Drug And Alcohol Abuse

In order to ensure a safe and efficient drug and alcohol free workplace, and ensure compliance with Federal regulations, the following company policy has been adopted and will be observed by all employees.

Use Prohibited

No employee will use a Schedule I drug of the Schedule of Controlled Substances of the Drug Enforcement Agency or an amphetamine, narcotic or any other habit-forming drug *except where permitted* by the Federal Motor Carrier Safety Regulations.

The Schedule I drugs include: opiates, opium derivatives, marijuana, hallucinogenic substances, depressants, and stimulants. Except as indicted above, this means that the employee shall not consume any of these controlled substances while off duty or on duty. Any violation of this policy will result in discharge.

Impairment Prohibited

No employee will report for work or will work impaired by any drug or controlled substance or alcohol. Impaired means under the influence of a substance such that the employee's motor senses (*i.e.*, sight, hearing, balance, reaction, reflex) or judgment either are or may be presumed affected. An employee may use a substance administered by or under the instructions of a physician who has advised the employee that the substance will not affect the employee's ability to safely perform his duties. For any controlled substance that is lawfully prescribed, *i.e.*, which is administered under the instructions of a physician, the employee will notify his supervisor prior to the start of his shift. Any violation of this policy will result in discharge.

Possession Prohibited

No employee at any work site will possess any quantity of any unlawful controlled substance or alcohol. For any controlled substance that is lawfully prescribed, *i.e.*, which is administered under the instructions of a physician, the employee will notify his supervisor prior to the start of his shift. "Work site" means any motor vehicle, office, building, yard or other property operated by the company, or any other location at which the employee is to perform work. "Possess" means to have either in or on the employee's person, personal effects, motor vehicle or areas substantially entrusted to the control of the employee. Any violation of this policy will result in discharge.

Drivers Substance Screening

For purposes of ensuring compliance with the Federal Motor Carrier Safety Regulations and the company policy, both current drivers and new applicants for positions as drivers will be subject to drug screening under the circumstances described below. Substance screening means testing of urine to determine use or impairment.

Applicants

Prior to assuming a position, every applicant will be subject to substance screening incident to a pre-employment physical. Refusal to submit to such a screening will make it impossible to medically qualify the applicant, and the applicant cannot be hired.

Employees

The substance screening of drivers will be in accordance with the circumstances described below.

Reasonable Cause Testing

When there is reasonable evidence to suspect a driver has reported to work or is working impaired, the driver may be subject to substance screening. Refusals to submit to such screening will be considered insubordination and the driver will automatically be discharged.

Biennial Testing

Drivers will be required to submit to controlled substance testing at least once every two years during the medical examination required by the Federal Motor Carrier Safety Regulations.

Employee Substance Screening

Reasonable Cause Testing

When there is reasonable evidence to suspect an employee has reported to work or is working under the influence, the employee may be subject to substance screening. Refusals to submit to such screening will be considered insubordination and the employee will automatically be discharged.

Test Results

The test results will be reviewed to determine whether there is any indication of controlled substance abuse. All test results are confidential. The company's Medical Review Officer (a qualified medical doctor) will be the sole custodian of individual test results. The Medical Review Officer will only advise the company as to whether the test results were negative or positive. Test results will not be released to any other person or company without the written authorization of the tested individual. Test results will not be released unless in accordance with Federal law or a valid governmental request.

An Employee Assistance Program will be available to help employees solve drug and alcohol problems by providing educational information concerning the effects and consequences of drug and alcohol use on their personal health, safety and work environment.

9:3.2 Sample Substance Abuse Testing Policy

Testing Policy

Drugs And Controlled Substances

[Employer's name] has a significant business interest in ensuring the efficiency and productivity of its employees, and an obligation to ensure the health and safety of its employees on the job. To this end, [the employer] has established the following rules and regulations regarding the use, sale, or possession of illegal drugs or controlled substances on the job. These rules and regulations are mandatory and express conditions of employment.

In furtherance of its goal to ensure a drug-free workplace, the company has established the following drug-testing procedures for its employees and applications for employment.

The company may require blood and/or urine samples in the following situations:

1. As a precondition of employment, all applicants for employment are required to submit blood and/or urine samples that will be used for drug testing.
2. At the sole discretion of the company, a current employee may be required to submit blood and/or urine samples for purposes of drug testing if the employee is involved in an accident at the workplace or on duty that indicates the possible illegal use of drugs or controlled substances.
3. When the company has reasonable cause to believe that an employee is using, selling, or in possession of drugs at the workplace, or is present on company premises under the influence of drugs, the company reserves the right, in its sole discretion, to require that such employee submit blood and/or urine samples for the purpose of drug testing. Reasonable cause to believe that an employee is using, selling, or in possession of drugs at the workplace or is present on company premises under the influence of drugs may include, but is not limited to, excessive absenteeism, declining productivity, excessive tardiness, and/or other suspect behavior that is deemed by individuals trained in such detection to indicate the use, sale, or possession of illegal drugs.

If an employee is required to submit to drug testing under these rules, the employee's refusal to submit to drug testing is grounds for immediate discharge.

9:3.3 Sample Substance Abuse Testing Consent Form

SUBSTANCE ABUSE SCREENING CONSENT FORM

I, ______________________________, understand and agree that the test I am about to
(Name)
receive includes a:

☐ Blood test for substance abuse.

☐ Urine test for substance abuse.

I understand that if I decline to sign this consent and thereby decline to take the test, the Human Resources Department will be notified.

The results, after appropriate medical review, will be reported to the Human Resources Department. Legally prescribed medication taken under the direction of a physician will not be reported as positive.

I have taken the following drugs or substances within the last 5 days:

	Indicate Name and Amount
☐ Sleeping pills	______________________
☐ Diet pills	______________________
☐ Pain relief pills	______________________
☐ Cold tablets	______________________
☐ Anti-malarial drugs	______________________
☐ Any other medication or substance	______________________

I hereby consent ☐

Refuse to consent ☐

to the test(s) for substance abuse. Further, I release the individual(s) who are responsible for conducting the examination and/or test(s) from any liability or future claims.

Signed: ______________________

Date: ______________________

Witness: ______________________

9:3.4 Government Contractors and the Requirements of the Drug-Free Workplace Act of 1988

The Drug-Free Workplace Act of 1988 requires most federal government contractors, as well as recipients of federal grants, to take specific steps to ensure a drug-free workplace. The law requires employers to prepare and distribute an anti-drug policy statement prohibiting any drug related activities in the workplace. The following is a sample statement and policy which can be adapted to your specific organization.

Drug-Free Workplace Program

1.0 Purpose

The purpose of this program is to establish a drug-free workplace to promote and sustain employee health and safety and the security of the workplace.

2.0 Application

This program applies to all Company employees.

3.0 Policy

3.1 Illegal Drug Prohibition

The Company strictly prohibits the manufacture, distribution, sale, possession, or use of illegal or illegally obtained drugs in the workplace.

3.2 Under The Influence Prohibition

Employees must report to work in a condition fit for duty. The Company prohibits job performance while under the influence of illegal drugs. Employees using prescribed drugs which have potential for adversely affecting job performance shall notify their manager before reporting to work.

4.0 Definitions

4.1 Illegal Drugs

Any controlled substances included in Schedule I and II as defined by Section 802(6) of Title 21 of the United States Code, the possession of which is unlawful under Chapter 13 of that Title. Illegal drugs do not include use of controlled substances pursuant to a valid prescription or other uses authorized by law.

4.2 Medications

Medication prescribed by an employee's physician and used in accordance with the prescription, or medications purchased over-the-counter and used in accordance with the labeled directions.

4.3 Other Substances

Stimulants, sedatives, inhalants, alcohol, etc., which are not controlled substances, but may be improperly or abusively used.

4.4 Under The Influence Of Drugs

An employee will be considered under the influence of drugs when management has information about an employee's conduct that would cause a reasonable person to believe the employee is demonstrating signs of impairment due to illegal drugs or has used illegal drugs on company property.

5.0 Responsibilities

5.1 Executive Charged With Implementations

Has responsibility for implementing, interpreting, and monitoring compliance with this policy.

5.2 Managers

Shall maintain a safe and efficient work environment, guarding against all types of accidents and preserving high standards of job performance. They will attempt to assist employees in early assessment and treatment of drug abuse problems.

Shall refer employees to the Human Resources Department where an employee is suspected of being under the influence of drugs or is found to be in the possession of illegal drugs or drug-related paraphernalia.

5.3 Employees

Shall, as a condition of employment, abide by the terms of this policy. Employees who use illegal drugs have the primary responsibility to seek help through the Human Resources Department or through treatment services or drug abuse.

Employees must report to their Managers, within five calendar days, any conviction under a criminal drug statute for violations occurring in the workplace.

5.4 Human Resources Department

Shall establish a disciplinary policy which covers violations of the Company's Drug-Free Workplace Policy. This disciplinary policy will be communicated to all employees.

To the extent legally possible, the Human Resources staff should protect the confidentiality of employee communication concerning illegal drug use and alcohol abuse. Exceptions include disclosure requirements mandated by law or regulation and the extreme case of danger to self and/or others, and the failure to maintain an agreed upon rehabilitation program.

6.0 Guidelines

The Company prohibits the manufacture, distribution, sale, possession, use or abuse of illegal or illegally obtained drugs in the workplace. The Company discourages drug abuse by employees under any conditions on the basis that it is detrimental to health and safety. In this regard, employee's attention is called to the Company's Statement of Policy on a drug-free workplace. The Company will take appropriate and reasonable measures in accordance with applicable law and this policy to eliminate workplace risks caused by drug abuse. These measures may include disciplinary steps up to and including termination of employment and notification of law enforcement agencies for possible criminal prosecution.

The Company's drug-free workplace policy is a two-part program: education and treatment.

6.1 Education

As part of the Company's efforts to encourage employees to become or remain drug-free, information and training will be provided on an ongoing basis regarding the effects of drug abuse and addictive disease.

Managerial personnel will be trained to identify the behavioral and physiological signs of employee drug abuse.

6.2 Treatment

The Company offers a Treatment Program which provides referral and treatment to employees with drug abuse problems with the goal of rehabilitating them for continued productive employment.

Drug counseling and referral programs are available through the Human Resources Department. Employees who voluntarily refer themselves to the Human Resources Department for assessment of need, evaluation, referral and continuing treatment will be provided drug counseling and referred to appropriate assistance programs for treatment.

The Company encourages employees to seek help voluntarily with drug abuse problems before their work performance, health, and safety and that of others are adversely affected. While participation is confidential, the program can neither absolve nor protect the employees from the consequences of continued substandard work performance or policy infractions. Refusal to cooperate with a drug abuse treatment plan may constitute grounds for termination.

6.3 Confidentiality

To the extent permitted under the law, information contained in employee records regarding participation in treatment programs shall be limited to those persons having a need to know. Rehabilitation is the primary objective of this drug abuse treatment program.

7.0 Procedures

7.1 Drug-Free Workplace Agreement

All employees are required to sign the Drug-Free Workplace Agreement (Attachment 1) agreeing to abide by this policy and the Statement of Policy (Attachment 2).

7.2 Drugs

Possessing, consuming, purchasing, or selling illegal drugs or being under the influence of illegal drugs in the workplace is in violation of this policy and will result in disciplinary action.

7.3 Assistance Programs

The Company provides health benefits through which employees have access to professional services to aid them with drug problems. In addition, the Company is committed to providing drug abuse education programs for all employees. All employees who suspect that they have a drug problem are encouraged to use the resources of this health benefit before the problem affects their employment status. Participation is voluntary and confidential but will not shield an employee from discipline, up to and including termination of employment, should an employee be involved in an incident under drug-related circumstances.

7.4 Medications

The influence of properly used medications on the employee's behavior and performance shall be considered a medical problem, and management's actions shall be in accordance with procedures for dealing with employees who have medical problems. Abusive use of medication by an employee in the workplace shall be considered a violation of this policy and may result in disciplinary action up to and including termination of employment.

7.5 Other Substances

Improper or abusive use of otherwise legal substances in the workplace such as stimulants, sedatives, alcohol, etc. by an employee shall be considered a violation of this policy and will result in disciplinary action.

7.6 Search

All U.S. Government property may be subject to search at any time. Personal property may be subject to reasonable lawful search with or without notice when justified by circumstances or workplace conditions. In general, the Company intends that any search undertaken for drugs not be casual, routine, or random, but only where sufficient corroborating evidence exists which would lead a reasonable person to believe that this policy is being violated.

Suspected illegal drugs and drug-related paraphernalia will be confiscated and turned over to the appropriate law enforcement authority for testing and/or further action.

7.7 Criminal Drug Offense Convictions

1. Employees are required to notify their Managers of any criminal drug statute conviction they may have, occurring in the workplace, within five (5) calendar days, after the conviction. Failure to comply may result in disciplinary action up to and including termination of employment.
2. Managers shall notify the [Executive charged with implementation] of an employee drug offense conviction within one (1) working day after learning of the conviction.
3. The Executive shall notify, if applicable, the Contracting Officer of procuring federal government agency in writing of an employee conviction, within ten (10) calendar days, after the Company learns of the conviction. The notice shall include the position title of the employee.
4. Assuming notification under 7.7 (3) has occurred, the Executive shall notify the Contracting Officer, within thirty (30) calendar days of the notice above, of the sanctions on remedial measures imposed on any employee convicted of drug abuse violations occurring in the workplace.

8.0 Contract Clause

Department of Defense Contracts require the clause at 48 C.F.R. 252.223-7500 be included in all contracts which require access to classified information, the contracting officer determines inclusion if necessary for reasons of national security, or to protect the health or safety of those using the products or services under the contract. The contract clause mandates that a program of testing for illegal drugs for employees in sensitive positions be established.

9.0 Point Of Contact

[EXECUTIVE CHARGED WITH IMPLEMENTATION]

10.0 Attachment

Attachment 1 - Drug-Free Workplace Agreement
Attachment 2 - Statement of Policy

11.0 References

None

Attachment 1:

Drug-Free Workplace Agreement

I have read and I agree to abide by the Company's Drug-Free Workplace Policy and Program concerning the prohibition of unlawful manufacture, distribution, dispensation, possession, or use of a controlled substance in the workplace. I understand that violations of these prohibitions may result in disciplinary action against me, up to and including termination of employment.

I acknowledge receipt of a copy of the Company's "Drug-Free Workplace Policy Statement" and its "Drug-Free Workplace Program." I agree to notify the Company in writing if I am convicted of a criminal drug offense occurring in the workplace no later than five (5) calendar days.

____________________ ____________________

Signature Printed Name

____

Date

Attachment 2:

Drug-Free Workplace Statement Of Policy

My Fellow Employees:

The illegal use of drugs has impacted every element of our society, either directly or indirectly, in many profound ways. From our children who are solicited in their schools or playgrounds or wounded in drug-war crossfires to our elder citizens who are mugged or assaulted by drug addicts; all are affected. While not as dramatic, drugs have had an adverse impact on the workplace as well. A recent study conducted by North Carolina's Research Triangle Institute estimated that the annual cost to employers for employee drug abuse is $60 billion. The Department of Defense has issued regulations aimed at combating drug abuse in the workplace. Here are some of their findings:

> The use of illegal drugs, on or off duty, is inconsistent with law-abiding behavior expected of all citizens. Employees who use illegal drugs, on or off duty, tend to be less productive, less reliable, and prone to greater absenteeism resulting in the potential for increased cost, delay, and risk to the government contract.
>
> The use of illegal drugs, on or off duty, by employees can impair the ability of those employees to perform tasks that are critical to proper contract performance and can also result in the potential for accidents on duty and for failures that can pose a serious threat to national security, health, and safety.
>
> The use of illegal drugs, on or off duty, by employees in certain positions can result in less than the complete reliability, stability, and good judgment that are consistent with access to sensitive information. Use of illegal drugs also creates the possibility of coercion, influence, and irresponsible action under pressure that may pose a serious risk to national security, and health and safety.

I endorse and agree with these conclusions and find them applicable to all work performed at the Company. For that reason, it shall be the stated policy of the Company to prohibit the unlawful manufacture, distribution, dispensing, possession, or use of a controlled substance in the workplace.

Violations of this policy will be dealt with expeditiously in accordance with the Company's established procedures. Each case will be individually examined and can result in sanctions, including termination or remedial action such as referral for treatment.

As a further condition of employment, you must advise your supervisor of any criminal drug statute conviction for a violation occurring in the workplace no later than five (5) calendar days of such conviction. If you need further information on this or any other aspect of the drug-free workplace program, contact the Office of Human Resources.

____

President

Chapter 10

Employment Termination

In our changing economy, the workplace has become a less secure environment. As business transitions occur in order to remain competitive, job positions are eliminated or distinctively changed. Employers, who recognize these changes are often beyond an employee's control, continue their business responsibility by assisting the employee financially following termination.

This chapter outlines involuntary and voluntary terminations including severance pay options, releases and waivers and sample resignation and termination policies that include manager and human resources responsibilities.

10:1 Sample Severance Policy

This section presents an example of a severance policy that is designed to provide compensation to minimize the economic hardship that results when an employee is involuntarily terminated. As noted in the introduction to the sample policy, the personnel manager is responsible for administering the provisions of such policies although when adapting the sample policy provisions to an employer's particular situation, the chief executive and financial officers will provide substantial guidance on the terms of the policy actually implemented.

Severance Allowance Policy

The Company will attempt to pay a severance allowance to all regular employees who are *involuntarily* terminated for reasons beyond their control in accordance with the procedures outlined below.

The purpose of severance allowance is to minimize the economic hardship resulting from termination by providing income to an individual during the transition from one job to another.

The [   ] is responsible for administering this policy and approving any exceptions to it. The Company reserves the right to change, amend or discontinue this plan at any time in its sole discretion.

Procedures

I. Eligibility

A. The Company will pay severance allowance to all permanent employees who are involuntarily terminated as the result of a *reduction in force* or *performance problems which are beyond the employees' ability to control.* (Termination for performance problems which are beyond the control of the employee include situations where a selection error has been made, where the individual is genuinely trying to improve but simply cannot come up to job standards, or where personal or family constraints are adversely impacting on performance.)

B. Severance allowance *will not be paid* if an employee is terminated for any of the following reasons:

1. Voluntary resignation
2. Cause
3. Excessive absence
4. Excessive lateness
5. Unsatisfactory performance clearly within the employee's ability to correct
6. Retirement
7. Death

C. Temporary employees *are not eligible* for severance.

D. An employee will *not* receive severance pay if, concurrent with or immediately subsequent to their termination, any of the following events occur: (a) another job has been offered by the Company and refused by the employee; (b) another job has been offered by the Company and accepted by the employee; (c) another job has been offered by any affiliated, subsidiary, or successor company (including any company that purchases business assets from the Company) and either accepted or refused by the employee; or (d) the employee retires under any retirement plan of the Company. Additionally, if anyone of the foregoing events occurs during the period of severance pay eligibility, severance pay eligibility will cease upon the occurrence of that event, and if the severance pay was paid in a lump sum, the employee will be required to repay any pro rata portion of the lump sum which would have been paid subsequent to the occurrence of that event.

E. Managers of terminating employees must obtain the approval of their immediate superior and the [Personnel/Human Resources Department] *before* notifying employees that they are eligible for severance allowance.

II. Amount Of Severance Allowance

A. The amount of severance allowance will be based on the employee's *continuous* service at the time of termination in accordance with the following schedule:

Years of Continuous Service	*Weeks of Base Salary*
Less than 3	2
3 but less than 4	3
4 but less than 5	4
5 but less than 6	5
6 but less than 7	6
7 but less than 8	7
8 but less than 9	8
9 but less than 10	9
10 but less than 11	10
11 but less than 12	11
12 but less than 13	12
13 but less than 14	13
14 but less than 15	14
15 but less than 16	15
16 but less than 17	16
17 but less than 18	17
18 but less than 19	18
19 but less than 20	19
20 but less than 21	20
21 but less than 22	22
22 but less than 23	24
23 but less than 24	26
24 but less than 25	28
25 but less than 26	30
26 but less than 27	32
27 but less than 28	34
28 but less than 29	36
29 but less than 30	38
30 and over	40 (Maximum)

B. Continuous service is defined as all service with the Company *since* the most recent date of hire or rehire.

C. Severance allowance will be granted in addition to any vacation, personal days, and floating holidays.

III. Payment Of Severance Allowance

A. The terminating employee may elect to be paid severance allowance either in a lump sum or bi-weekly installments.

B. If severance is paid in bi-weekly installments, the terminated employee may continue to participate in the Company's Medical and Life Insurance plans while receiving severance allowance. The Payroll Department will deduct the terminated employee's share of the cost of these benefits from his or her bi-weekly severance allowance payment. (Additionally, all terminated employees will be accorded any rights to continuation of group medical insurance that are required by the Consolidated Omnibus Budget Reconciliation Act of 1985.)

C. Employees will not earn paid vacation or personal days while receiving severance allowance.

D. The employee's participation in the Company's Retirement, Savings, Long Term Disability, Business Travel and Accident Insurance plans will end on the employee's termination date; the terminated employee may *not* continue to participate in these plans while receiving severance allowance.

E. If the terminating employee obtains a new job outside the Company, the bi-weekly payments will stop and the unpaid amount will be disbursed in a lump sum.

F. The Payroll Department will withhold appropriate Federal, State and Local taxes from all severance allowance payments.

IV. Claim Procedure

A. When an employee terminates employment, a member of the [Personnel/Human Resources Department] will meet with the employee and accept an appropriate benefit application.

B. The [Personnel/Human Resources Department] shall either approve or deny the claim for a benefit, and shall designate the date of the employee's termination of service. Within 90 days thereafter, the [Personnel/Human Resources Department] shall advise the employee in writing (a) of its decision, or (b) of the special circumstances which require an extension of time of not more than 90 days in which it shall reach its decision.

C. In the event that any claim for benefits is wholly or partially denied, written notice of such denial shall be provided to the employee, setting forth, in a manner calculated to be understood by the employee, (a) the specific reason for the denial; (b) specific reference to the Employee Handbook provisions on which the denial is based; (c) a description of any additional material or information necessary for the employee to complete the claim and an explanation of why such material or information is necessary; and (d) an explanation of the claim review procedure.

D. The employee may appeal the denial of the claim to the Director of the [Personnel/Human Resources Department] for a full and fair review. A request for such review shall be made in writing to the Director within 60 days after receipt by the employee of written notification of the denial. If no written notice has been received within the 90 or 180 day period after a benefit claim has been filed, then the claim shall be considered denied and the 60 day period shall commence with the day after the end of the 90 or 180 day period. As part of this review procedure, the employee or a person he selects may review any documents related to his claim and may submit issues and comments in writing to the Director. The Director, in his sole discretion, may determine to hold a hearing if he considers such hearing to be necessary in order to provide a full and fair review of the claim denial. If such a hearing is held, the employee may appear in person or be represented by a person he selects.

E. Except as set out in Subparagraph F. below, the Director shall render his decision within 60 days after receipt of the request for review. The Director's decision shall be written in a manner calculated to be understood by the employee and shall include specific reference to the Policy provisions on which the decision is based as the specific reasons for the decision. Unless a civil action is instituted thereafter by the applicant, the Director's final determination with respect to any claim for benefits shall be binding and conclusive.

F. If special circumstances, such as the need to hold a hearing, require an extension of time for processing, a decision shall be rendered not later than 120 days after receipt of the request for review.

G. If as set out in Subparagraph F. above, the Director requires an extension of time because of special circumstances, written notice of the extension shall be furnished to the employee applicant prior to the beginning of the extension period of time.

10:2 Waivers and Releases

Some state and federal laws, especially in the area of employment discrimination, set out strict rules regarding releases. Consequently, unless these rules are followed, the release may not be effective. Competent counsel should be consulted in all cases.

10:2.1 General Releases

In return for the severance benefits granted to employees as a result of an involuntary termination of employment, the employer will require the departing employee to execute a waiver of release that insulates the employer from any future or existing liability that may arise out of the severed employment relationship. The three releases that follow at 10:2.1A through 10:2.1C range from a simple blanket release to more complicated releases that specifically address forfeiting rights to sue under various federal and state discrimination statutes (see 10:2.1B) including the right to sue under the ADEA.

10:2.1A Generic Release Form

General Release

KNOW ALL MEN BY THESE PRESENTS THAT [EMPLOYEE], doth hereby remise, release and forever discharge [EMPLOYER], its shareholders, directors, officers, and employees and their heirs, executors and administrators, of and from all, and all manner of, actions and causes of action, suits, debts, dues, accounts, bonds, covenants, contracts, agreements, judgments, claims and demands whatsoever in law or equity, especially which against the said [EMPLOYER], Inc., he ever had, now has, or which his heirs, executors, administrators, successors or assigns, or any of them, hereafter can, shall or may have, for, or by reason of any cause, matter or thing whatsoever, from the beginning of the world to the "termination date" defined in the Termination Agreement to which the within release is attached, especially those matters arising out of the Employment relationship between ____________ and ____________ during the period from August, 1972, through the termination date.

IN WITNESS WHEREOF, have hereunto set hand(s) and seal(s) the day of , 199 .

WITNESS:

______________________________ ______________________________(SEAL)

10:2.1B

Release of Rights Under Federal and State Discrimination Statutes

General Release And Agreement

NOTICE:

Various state and federal laws, including the Civil Rights Act of 1964 and the Age Discrimination in Employment Act, prohibit employment discrimination based on age, sex, race, color, national origin, religion, disability, or veteran status. These laws are enforced through the Equal Employment Opportunity Commission (EEOC), the Department of Labor and the [STATE ENFORCEMENT AGENCY].

If you sign this General Release and Agreement and accept the agreed-upon special severance allowance and other termination benefits [ALTERNATIVE: accept the employment termination program], you are giving up your right to file a complaint against [NAME OF EMPLOYER] with the aforementioned federal, state and local agencies or in local, state or federal courts for any reason that relates to your employment or termination therefrom up until the date of execution of this Agreement.

We encourage you to discuss the following release language with an attorney. In any event, you should thoroughly review and understand the effect of the release before acting on it. Therefore, please take this release home and consider it for twenty-one (21) days before you decide to sign it. [ALTERNATIVE (to be used whenever a waiver is requested in connection with an exit incentive or other employment termination program offered to a group or class of employees)]: Therefore, please take this release home and consider it for at least forty-five (45) days before you decide to sign it. Attached to this Agreement for your review during this forty-five day period is information regarding:

- The class, unit, or group of individuals covered by this employment termination program;
- The eligibility factors for the program;
- The time limits applicable to the program;
- The job titles and ages of all individuals eligible or selected for the program; and
- The ages of all individuals in the same job classification or organizational unit who are not eligible or selected for the unit.

General Release And Agreement

As consideration for the special severance allowance and other termination benefits offered to me by [NAME OF EMPLOYER] (hereinafter referred to as "Company") (attached as Exhibit A and incorporated herein), I release and discharge the Company, its directors, officers, agents, employees, subsidiaries and any and all affiliate companies, as well as any successor to the Company, from all claims, liabilities, demands and causes of action fixed or contingent, which I may have or claim to have against the Company arising from my employment or as a result of my termination from employment up to the date of execution of this Agreement, and do hereby covenant not to file a lawsuit to assert such claims. This includes but is not limited to claims arising pursuant to the Age Discrimination In Employment Act, or any other federal, state or municipal law or regulation relating to discrimination in employment or equal opportunity or any claims growing out of any legal restrictions on the Company's right to terminate its employees.

I agree that I will not at any time publicize, write about, divulge or discuss the existence of this General Release and Agreement, with any person or entity whatsoever, other than my attorneys in this matter.

[ALTERNATIVE (*to be used in releases under the ADEA*): I understand that this Agreement is revocable by me for a period of seven (7) days following execution hereof. This Agreement shall not become effective or enforceable until this seven-day revocation period has ended.]

I have carefully read and fully understand all the provisions of this Notice, General Release and Agreement which set forth the entire agreement between me and the Company, and I acknowledge that I have not relied upon any representation or statement, written or oral, not set forth in this document.

IN WITNESS WHEREOF, has hereunto set his/her hand and seal this day of , 199 .

____

10:2.2 Sample Accidental Injury Claim Release

Below is an example of the type of release that can be used by employers to obtain a release of any claims against it by injured employees. It is drafted to reflect the laws of the state of Pennsylvania and should be reviewed in light of the laws of the particular state in which the employer adapting it is located.

Release Of All Claims

I, ________________, residing at ____________________________, hereby release and forever discharge everyone who may be liable to me from all claims and liability of any kind in connection with or in any way arising out of my accident on or about _________, 19____. I also release and forever discharge [EMPLOYER], all of its current, former and future officers, employees, agents, shareholders, affiliates, successors and assigns, and all of their heirs, executors and administrators, from all claims and liability of any kind arising from any cause or conduct at any time before the signing of this release, whether or not such claims or liability have anything to do with my accident on that date.

I recognize that any harm I have suffered or may suffer in the future may not now be fully known and may be different or more serious than is now expected, but I nevertheless agree that this release applies to all injuries, damages and losses of any kind that are now unanticipated, unexpected or unknown, as well as all injuries, damages and losses, if any, which already have developed and are now known or anticipated.

I have not been coerced or pressured into signing this release and am doing so of my own free will, in exchange for good and valuable consideration. I am not relying upon any promise, statement or representation concerning the accident, the nature, extent or duration of any injuries, damages or losses, legal liability for any injuries, damages or losses, or concerning anything else, and I am relying solely on my own judgment and the written terms of this release.

I have carefully read and clearly understand the meaning of this release. I agree that it is to be interpreted under and governed by Pennsylvania law, and I intend to be legally bound by its terms.

Signed, Sealed and Delivered by:

________________________________ (SEAL)

Witnessed by:

Dated: ________________________ ________________________________

10:3 Model Resignation/Termination Policy and Supplemental Implementation Forms

Employers that wish to assume business responsibility for the changes in their workforce structure often continue to assist employees financially after they have been terminated. This usually is formally outlined in the company's resignation and termination policy. Such policies not only help ease the employees' financial burdens during the period until reemployment but also help ensure that the employer uniformly administers its resignation and termination procedures and does not inadvertently treat similarly situated employees in different ways. Below is an example of a model resignation and termination policy that is designed to provide fair and equitable treatment for terminated employees.

Resignation/Termination Policy

1. Policy

1.1 The Company recognizes that continuous employment cannot always be provided to salaried employees, that conditions may arise which necessitate the termination of employees, and that when it becomes necessary to reduce manpower levels, a reduction in force may need to be implemented. If a termination of employment, other than discharge for cause, has been initiated by the Company, there may be circumstances when, in the sole discretion of the Company, some measure of Compensation may be granted to the employee to assist the individual during the transition toward finding other employment.

2. Objective

2.1 It is the objective of this Policy to establish guidelines with regard to employee termination. The guidelines set forth herein are for reference purposes only and in no way bind the Company or create an obligation to pay benefits under this Policy. Payments under this Policy will be made at the sole discretion of the Company, which discretion may be exercised in a nonuniform manner.

3. Procedure

3.1 Definitions

3.1.1 Voluntary Resignation. A voluntary, permanent separation initiated by the employee.

3.1.2 Mutual Resignation. A resignation resulting from mutual agreement between the employee and his immediate supervisor.

3.1.3 Involuntary Termination. A termination initiated entirely by the supervisor or the Company. An employee shall not be deemed to have incurred a termination of employment in the event of a sale of any portion of the Company's business if the employee continues in employment with the successor company, unless otherwise specified.

3.1.4 Temporary Reduction in Force. A temporary suspension of the employee's position as a result of changes in business conditions.

3.1.5 Permanent Reduction in Force. A termination resulting from decrease in staff or a staff reorganization which results in the immediate elimination of the employee's position.

3.1.6 Discharge for Cause. A termination initiated entirely by the supervisor or the Company based upon a cause initiated by the employee that has been determined as not being in the best interests of the Company.

3.2 Notice of Termination

3.2.1 From the Employee. Individuals who terminate their employment are expected to give the Company a minimum of two weeks notice of their intention to resign. In some cases a longer period may be appropriate. A letter of resignation should be submitted to the immediate supervisor and a copy sent to the Director, Human Resources.

3.2.2 From the Company. The Company may give at least two weeks notice to an employee whose services are no longer required (cases of Discharge for Cause, excluded). Should the Company for any reason determine that the employee's continued presence at the work location is not advisable for the entire period of notice then, up to two weeks pay may, in the sole discretion of the Company, be offered in lieu of notice. It is the responsibility of the employee's immediate supervisor to give notice to the employee and to inform him of the appropriate severance arrangements.

3.3 Separation Pay Allowance

The Company, in its sole discretion, may grant separation pay allowance to individuals whose services are no longer required where the circumstances surrounding the termination make this appropriate. The Company has no obligation to grant a termination payment when it determines that such payment is not appropriate in a particular case. The following guidelines will be used, by the Company in determining eligibility for and amount of separation pay:

3.3.1 Eligibility Guidelines

a. Voluntary Resignation. No separation pay allowance.

b. Mutual Resignation. Separation pay will be mutually agreed upon between the resigning employee and his/her supervisor, ranging from 0 to the maximum of 20 weeks, subject to the approval of the Vice President for Human Resources. If no mutual agreement can be reached, or if such agreement is out of line with past practice, the Vice President of Human Resources will set the level.

c. Involuntary Termination. Separation pay allowances will vary by type of involuntary termination as discussed in paragraphs d, e, and f of this section. (No separations allowance is payable when a successor company rehires the terminated employee.)

d. Temporary Reduction in Force. If the employee is not recalled within 6 months of termination, separation pay may be allowed on the basis of the following criteria:

(1) employee's employment record with the company (including disciplinary, performance and attendance records)

(2) amount of notice given prior to layoff

(3) ability of company to pay separation allowance

(4) whether employee has accepted alternative employment

(5) likelihood of ultimate recall and timing thereof

e. Permanent Reduction in Force. The same criteria will be applied as under (d).

f. Discharge for Cause. No separation pay allowance.

3.3.2 Calculation of Separation Pay Allowance. It is recommended that supervisors calculate separation pay allowance on the basis of the weekly salary rate in effect on the employee's last day of work. In the case of an exempt employee, the individual's monthly or annual rate of pay should be converted to a weekly basis.

Service	*Weekly Separation Allowance*
One week severance allowance may be paid for each full year of service up to a maximum of twenty weeks of payments.	
Less than 1 year	0

3.3.3 Withholding Tax. All payments on the date of termination or thereafter are subject to City, State and Federal Withholding Tax.

3.3.4 Schedule of Payment

a. Temporary Reduction in Force. When a reduction in force is expected to be temporary in nature, (up to six months duration), the employee will be separated in accordance with the Company's termination procedure and will be able to take any and all earned, but unused vacation. If the employee is not recalled to work after six months following the date of initial lay-off, the employee may be eligible to receive Separation Pay Allowance in accordance with Sections 3.3 through 3.3.3. If the employee is subsequently rehired, any future vacation and/or severance payments will be calculated based upon the employee's most recent date of hire.

b. Permanent Reduction in Force. When a reduction in force is immediately considered permanent, the employee will be paid for all time worked since the last prior pay date, and, in the sole discretion of the Company, may be paid Separation Pay allowance in accordance with Sections 3.3 through 3.3.3. The employee will be separated in accordance with the Company's termination procedure, Sections 3.4, and will be paid for any earned but unused vacation.

3.3.5 Termination of Employee Benefits

a. Voluntary Termination. All employee benefits will be terminated as of the end of the employee's last working day with the exception of Group Life Insurance which will terminate 31 days after the last day worked. The employee who wishes to convert his Group Life Insurance benefits to an individual policy will be appropriately advised during the exit interview or by the Human Resources Department, upon request.

b. Temporary Reduction in Force. Disability and Business Travel coverage will stop on the employee's last day of work. Group Life; Accidental Death and Dismemberment; Basic Medical; Major Medical; and Dental insurance will continue during the period of temporary lay-off, but not longer than six months from the last day of active employment. An employee on temporary lay-off will be placed on an approved leave of absence for purposes of continued Pension Plan eligibility. Savings Plan contributions will be suspended during the period of temporary lay-off. If the employee is participating in an IU Employee Stock Purchase Plan, contributions to the Plan may be allowed during the period of temporary lay-off. Accrual of any form of incentive compensation will be suspended during the temporary lay-off. Accrued vacation entitlement for the next succeeding calendar year will be pro-rated for the number of months actually worked in the current calendar year.

c. Permanent Termination. Disability and business travel coverage will stop on the employee's last day of work. Life and accidental death and dismemberment coverage will stop 31 days after the employee's last day worked. If, in the Company's sole discretion, Separation Pay Allowance is granted to the employee, medical and dental plan coverage will continue, at no cost to the employee, for the period of time covered by Separation Pay. If no Separation Pay is granted, medical and dental coverage stop on the employee's last day worked. All other benefits stop on the employee's last day worked.

d. Discharge for Cause. Should an employee be discharged for cause, no benefits or salary will be paid beyond termination notice date.

3.3.6 Other Employment. When an employee obtains other employment during temporary lay-off or during the period of separation pay allowance, all salary and benefit coverage will be discontinued. Employees should keep their supervisors and the Human Resources Department advised of their current employment status.

3.4 Responsibilities

3.4.1 Manager or Supervisor

a. Involuntary Termination, Mutual Resignation or Temporary or Permanent Reduction in Force.

(1) Identify employees to be recommended for termination and inform the Human Resources Department of all facts pertaining to the termination(s), so that the Form 576 and Termination Checklist can be initiated (Exhibit 1). The form 576 must be processed to arrive in Payroll at least three days prior to the effective date of termination.

(2) Personally inform each employee clearly communicating the reasons for the termination, and give the employee a notice letter (Exhibit II).

(3) Calculate (obtaining appropriate Human Resources review and approval) and communicate to the employee the termination arrangements which have been determinated (separation pay allowance, benefits continuance, and outplacement assistance that can be provided by the Human Resources Department).

(4) Inform Human Resources of any change in employment status of employees on separation pay allowance, or temporary lay-offs.

b. Voluntary Resignation.

(1) Notify the Director, Human Resources as soon as possible after receiving the employee's resignation.

3.4.2 Human Resources

a. Involuntary Termination, Mutual Resignation or Temporary or Permanent Reduction in Force.

(1) Review personnel records of employee recommended for severance and resolve any questionable cases.

(2) Process each employee Form 576 and initial Termination Checklist. The effective date of termination, regardless of whether or not a separation pay allowance is continued, is to be designated as the last day worked. This date is significant as it will relate to the cancellation of employee benefits coverage and other earned compensation, e.g., unused vacation and pay in lieu of notice. The status form will also indicate eligibility for rehire, if applicable.

(3) Forward Termination Checklist to Accounting and Purchasing Departments. They will check employee's records for any outstanding loans and/or travel advances, credit cards and purchases charged to the employee. If there are no outstanding advances, the Checklist will be initialed and returned to the Human Resources Department.

(4) Exit Interview. On the employee's last day of work, he will be interviewed by a member of the Human Resources Staff. At the time of the exit interview, the employee will return any Company property in his possession. This will normally include his building pass, keys, credit cards, administrative manual, organizational charts, and any other items that have been issued to him.

(5) Provide employment reference information to prospective employers.

b. Voluntary Resignation.

(1) All of the above, except (4)

3.4.3 Reinstatement Eligibility. Employees terminated as a result of a temporary or permanent reduction in force are normally eligible for reemployment when opportunities commensurate with their background or education and experience become available.

4. Responsibility

4.1 It is the responsibility of each Manager and/or Supervisor to ensure compliance with this Policy, (which includes making initial recommendations as to separation allowances when appropriate).

4.2 It is the responsibility of the Personnel Administration, to ensure the continuity of this Policy, (which includes monitoring and reviewing of separation allowances to ensure continuity and consistency).

10:3.1 Supplemental Implementation Forms

The following forms are designed to help smoothly administer the process of terminating employees when a business is forced to restructure its workforce. The forms that are provided include a sample employee notification and a checklist of the necessary actions employers should take when completing an exit or termination interview.

10:3.1A Sample Employee Notification

NOTE: Personnel Administration must be notified of all terminations prior to communicating this information to the employee. This letter should be given to each employee personally by his immediate supervisor after the latter has verbally informed the employee of the contents. Where appropriate, the letter can be made more personalized provided essential elements of policy are reproduced as stated in the form letter.

It has become necessary to implement a reduction in force at International Mill Service.

As a result, I regret to inform you that it will be necessary to terminate your employment with IMS effective (insert last date worked). On that date, you will receive any additional compensation due you plus any amounts due in lieu of notice. In order to aid you during this transition period you will receive a separation pay allowance calculated on a weekly basis and payable semi-monthly for _____ weeks. This payment will continue until _________ or until you secure employment prior to this date. Your final paycheck will include payment for any earned but unused vacation.

Group Life Insurance coverage will continue 31 days after the last day worked.

I very much regret the necessity of this action and sincerely hope you will be successful in finding suitable employment in the near future.

Sincerely,

Immediate Supervisor

10:3.1B Resignation-Termination Checklist

Name of Employee____________________________________ Date____________
Last First Initial

Department____________ Title _____ Supervisor ______________________

Date of Termination _______________ Last Working Date ________________

Pay-Through Date ________________ Comments ______________________

____

Personnel Actions

______________________________ ______________________________
Date Initials Assistant Controller-Domestic

______ Clearance from Accounting Department
______ Clearance from Purchasing Department
______ Form 576
______ Exit Interview
______ Personnel Folder Refiled
______ Cancellation of ESPP

Items Explained To Employee

______ Final Paycheck Procedure
______ Conversion of Insurance Plans
______ Pension Date and Initials __________________

Materials Received From Employee

______ Building Pass
______ Keys
______ Air Travel Card
______ Gasoline Travel Card
______ All Credit Cards

Completed by: ____

Index

A

B

C

D

E

G

H

I

J

L

M